SASOL

BIRDS

OF SOUTHERN AFRICA

IAN SINCLAIR

PHIL HOCKEY AND WARWICK TARBOTON

ILLUSTRATED BY

PETER HAYMAN AND NORMAN ARLOTT

STRUIK

Struik Publishers
Cornelis Struik House
80 McKenzie Street
Cape Town 8001

Reg. no. 63/00203/07

First published in 1993

Text based on Ian Sinclair's
Field Guide to the Birds of Southern Africa (Struik 1987)

The plates were illustrated by Peter Hayman, with the exception
of those on pages 263-271, 295-333, 341-371, 389-411 which were
illustrated by Norman Arlott, and those on pages 381-387 which
were illustrated by Simon Barlow.

Project co-ordinator: Eve Gracie
Editorial assistant: Brenda Brickman
Proof-reader: Tessa Kennedy

Concept design by Neville Poulter
Designed by Tamsyn Ivey
Habitat map by Pam Eloff
Silhouettes by Dave Snook
Paste-up: Clarence Clarke
DTP conversion by Struik DTP

Reproduction by Unifoto (Pty) Ltd, Cape Town
Printed and bound by Tien Wah Press (Pte) Ltd, Singapore

ISBN 1 86825 196 9 (softcover)
ISBN 1 86825 299 X (hardcover)

SPONSOR'S FOREWORD

The variety and numbers of birds are often cited as a barometer of the state of health of the environment. We subscribe to this hypothesis and believe that an awareness of and concern for our avifauna will eventually lead to active conservation of birds and our natural surroundings.

The goal of the user-friendly Sasol *Birds of Southern Africa* is to encourage birders and potential birders in South Africa to become better acquainted with the birds they see around them.

We hope that this guide will assist birders in identifying birds in the diversity of habitat with which our subcontinent is blessed. An environment on which we to some measure depend for our quality of life, but on which wild birds are totally dependent for their very existence.

Paul du P. Kruger
Managing Director, Sasol Limited

Sasol and the environment

'Protecting the environment is an obligation, not a choice.'

Sasol believes the quality of the air, water and soil should be protected for the continued benefit of all ecosystems. In this way, the needs of the present and future generations will be met, enabling them to live in an environment of acceptable quality.

Sasol's management is committed to act responsibly towards the environment and to consider the effects of Sasol's operations on the environment when making decisions.

ACKNOWLEDGEMENTS

ARTIST'S ACKNOWLEDGEMENTS

I would like to acknowledge the help of the following people and institutions for their assistance in the compilation of this book.

The staff of the British Museum (Natural History) at Tring, and in particular Peter Colston, Michael Walters, Jo Bailey, Mark Adams and Mrs F.E. Warr, for allowing reference to their skin, spirit and skeleton collection; Dr Alan Kemp, the curator of the ornithology department, Transvaal Museum in Pretoria, for invaluable data and the loan of slides of captured birds of prey, for the skins sent to the UK and spirit specimens at Cape Town; Joris Komen, curator of birds, State Museum of Namibia, for the loan of eagles in spirit to the British Museum and to me at the FitzPatrick Institute of African Ornithology, University of Cape Town; Dr Clem Fisher, Liverpool Museum, for access to skins; the Library of BirdLife International (I.C.B.P), Cambridge, for the loan of *Bokmakierie*; the South African Museum, Cape Town for study skins; David Allan of the FitzPatrick Institute for providing dead bustards for measurement and for his advice; Rob Hume of the Royal Society for the Protection of Birds for checking a bookful of queries while on a visit to Kenya. Sally Michael and George Reynolds kindly provided accommodation and comfort during my many visits to the British Museum.

Peter Hayman
Suffolk, April 1993

PUBLISHER'S ACKNOWLEGEMENTS

Enormous thanks are due to both the artists, Peter Hayman and Norman Arlott, for their painstaking attention to detail in illustrating the species that appear in this book. That they did not allow their artistic standards to fall, even when they were under considerable pressure of deadline, is self-evident in the pages that follow.

For their support and assistance in the compilation of the book, the Publishers would also like to thank the following individuals and institutions: Sasol Limited for their generous sponsorship; the Transvaal Museum, and in particular Dr Alan Kemp and Tamar Cassidy; the Director and staff of the Percy FitzPatrick Institute of African Ornithology, University of Cape Town; and the South African Museum, Cape Town.

The authors, Ian Sinclair, Phil Hockey and Warwick Tarboton, tolerated the endless checking of facts and demands on their time with grace and good humour and their forbearance is appreciated almost as much as their knowledge and skill.

The consultants' contributions added considerably to the wealth of information presented in the book and thanks are thus due to Dave Allan, Richard Brooke, Adrian Craig, Richard Dean, Morné du Plessis, Tony Harris, John Isom, Dave Johnson, Joris Komen, Terry Oatley, Barry Rose, and Peter Ryan.

A book of this nature is essentially a team effort, with a major role being played by the 'back room boys' who provide the support and persistence necessary to bring the project to fruition. For their help in the production of the book we owe a debt of gratitude to Simon Barlow, Tamsyn Ivey, Tessa Kennedy, Brenda Brickman, Clarence Clarke and Aletta van der Westhuizen.

CONTENTS

INTRODUCTION

Southern Africa's birds in perspective

Southern Africa is defined as Africa south of a line between the Kunene and Zambezi rivers, encompassing Namibia, Botswana, Zimbabwe, South Africa, Lesotho, Swaziland and southern and central Mozambique, as well as oceanic waters within 200 nautical miles of the coast. The region covers a land area of approximately 3,5 million square kilometres, slightly less than three per cent of the world's land area. Bird diversity within the region is high – the bird list for the Kruger National Park alone is two-thirds as long as the list for the whole of Australia. More bird species breed in southern Africa than in the whole of the United States and Canada combined, and the total list of more than 900 species exceeds 10 per cent of the world's total. Of these, 133 species are endemic or have ranges extending only slightly outside the region (near-endemic).

The reason for the high diversity of birds in southern Africa is, to a large extent, geographical. The climate ranges from cool-temperate in the south-west to hot and tropical in the north. In addition to the latitude gradient, there is a gradient of increasing rainfall from west (winter rainfall) to east (summer rainfall). The combination of these gradients, coupled with a range of altitudes from sea level to 3 500 metres, has produced a variety of habitats unrivalled in any other region of the African continent.

Ornithologically, southern Africa is one of the better known areas of Africa, although very few surveys have been conducted recently in Mozambique. The distributions of most species are fairly well known, and the ongoing 'Southern African Bird Atlas Project', scheduled for publication in 1995, will greatly refine and enhance this knowledge, as well as providing a quantitative basis on which to assess the relative abundance of species. Knowledge of the biology of many species has improved greatly in recent years. An upsurge in public interest in birds has also improved the quality of bird identification in the region, and the production of this book is a testimony to that interest and a tribute to the knowledge gained in recent years.

Aims of the book

This book is intended primarily as a field guide with the principal aim of assisting birdwatchers to identify birds in the field. It makes no pretence to being a handbook or biological treatise. It is devoted to identification features of the different species, sexes and ages of southern African birds, as well as calls and habitat preferences. There are several groups of birds which have many representatives in southern Africa and present 'classic' identification problems. Examples include raptors, waders, terns, larks, cisticolas and pipits. Emphasis is given in the text and plates to the separation of potentially confusing species and to those identification features or the combination of features which are diagnostic of a particular species.

Another principal aim of the book is to illustrate as many different plumages of each species as is possible within the confines of a field guide. Special attention is paid to plumage variations as they relate to age, sex and season, and, where features visible in flight are characteristic or diagnostic, these have been illustrated. This express aim has resulted in the most comprehensive set of illustrations of southern African birds ever produced in one volume.

Bird classification and nomenclature

An entirely new classification of the world's birds was proposed in 1990, based on genetic research undertaken over the past 15 years (Sibley & Ahlquist 1990, Sibley

& Monroe, 1990). Genetic research has shed light on several 'old' taxonomic problems, and the techniques have become increasingly refined. It is possible, perhaps likely, that a new classification of birds will be accepted worldwide in the near future. However, we have chosen to adopt the classification currently used by the Southern African Ornithological Society (Clancey 1980, Maclean 1984, with updates by the SAOS List Committee) for two main reasons. Firstly, the new genetically based classification has not yet received worldwide acceptance; secondly, the changes proposed to the existing classification are so great that, at present, a field guide adopting the new scheme would be confusing in its ordering of species, which would differ substantially from any other field guide currently in use in Africa. Where we have deviated from the standard species ordering, this has been done to facilitate identification, where similar-looking species occur in different genera or families.

With few exceptions, the common English names used in this book are the same as those in *Robert's Birds of Southern Africa* (Maclean 1984), and are the names currently used by the SAOS. In two types of situation, the common names used to identify species differ from those of Maclean (1984). The first situation involves 'splits', whereby a bird's status has been changed from one species to two. This has happened in five instances: the old species' name is given in parentheses below, followed by the two new names. (Black Korhaan) = Northern Black Korhaan, Southern Black Korhaan; (Knysna Lourie) = Knysna Lourie, Livingstone's Lourie; (Burchell's Coucal) = Burchell's Coucal, Whitebrowed Coucal; (Bleating Warbler) = Greybacked Bleating Warbler, Greenbacked Bleating Warbler; (Spotted Prinia) = Spotted Prinia, Drakensberg Prinia.

The second situation involves species whose current common name in use in southern Africa is ambiguous in that a different species (or in some cases, genus) with the same common name occurs elsewhere. In order to minimize the changes to these names, we have added only a geographical descriptor: 'African', 'Southern' or 'Eastern'. The species concerned are listed below, with the new descriptor in parentheses. (Eastern) White Pelican, (Southern) Bald Ibis, (Southern) Crowned Crane, (African) Green Pigeon, (African) Scops Owl, (Southern) Anteating Chat, (Eastern) Bearded Robin, (African) Whitethroated Robin, (African) Moustached Warbler, (African) Barred Warbler, (Southern) Masked Weaver and (Southern) Brownthroated Weaver. In addition, we have changed the generic name of Namaqua Prinia from *Prinia* to *Phragmacia*; a change soon to be ratified by the SAOS List Committee. The motive underlying all the above changes is that the field guide should be as comprehensive and unambiguous as possible.

Bird habitats

A habitat is the particular environment in which an organism lives. Each species has its own unique set of environmental requirements: some birds live at sea, but come ashore to nest, others live in the air, only settling at nest sites, some are entirely terrestrial and have even lost the power of flight, some live in grasslands, others in forests – the variability in where birds live is almost unlimited. Of the 900-odd species of birds occurring in southern Africa the majority are land birds that depend on terrestrial ecosystems (about 690 species), while the species dependent on aquatic ecosystems can be divided into those that live in the oceans (pelagic species, numbering about 50) and those that don't (about 160 species).

Starting with land birds, which are by far the most diverse bird group in south-

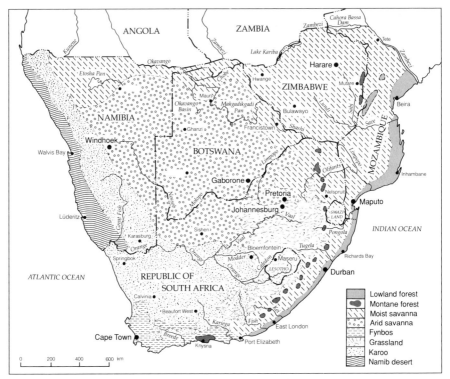

HABITAT MAP OF SOUTHERN AFRICA

ern Africa, a glance at the individual species' maps in this field guide will show that the same distribution patterns are frequently repeated – some bird species, for example, are confined to the eastern interior of the subcontinent, while others are restricted to the west. Many such distributions coincide with the position of the major biotic regions, or biomes. There are eight such regions in southern Africa and these provide a useful basis for looking at the places where land birds live. Where biomes occur and what the floral characteristics of each are, is dictated by the climate and especially by three climatic variables – minimum winter temperature, the amount of summer rain, and whether the rain falls in summer or winter. The biomes of southern Africa are forest, savanna, fynbos, grassland, nama-Karoo (summer rainfall Karoo), succulent Karoo (winter rainfall Karoo), and Namib desert. Few Karoo-dwelling bird species are confined to only the nama-Karoo or the succulent-Karoo and for our purpose these two biomes are treated as one.

Southern Africa's aquatic systems can be subjected to subdivision at a finer resolution. The five wetland categories usually recognized are the marine environment, estuaries, rivers, lakes and marshes. From a waterbird perspective, however, the most appropriate breakdown of aquatic types would be lagoons, estuaries, lakes and pans (all open water or open shoreline habitats and one unit), rivers, marshlands, sea shore and oceans. The habitat map shows the boundaries of the main terrestrial regions in southern Africa; at this scale the locations of most inland aquatic systems in southern Africa are too small to feature.

Forests

The forest biome covers a tiny proportion of southern Africa and occurs as a series of scattered islands of varying size stretched along the eastern side of the subcontinent where the rainfall is highest. Forests are formed by a variety of evergreen tree species which create a closed canopy, deeply shading the interior of the forest. Two distinct types of forest occur in southern Africa and many forest-living birds are found in either one or the other, but not in both. The first is the forest found at higher altitudes, termed Afro-montane (or simply montane) forest. It extends as discontinuous islands from almost sea-level in the southern Cape through Natal and the eastern Transvaal into eastern Zimbabwe, and northwards through Africa to Ethiopia, at higher altitudes closer to the equator. The second forest type, lowland forest, is confined to low-lying areas along the eastern coastal plain. It has a distinctly different floral community and contains many bird species not found in the montane forests; it is also usually richer in bird species than montane forests. Lowland forests occur as fragmented remnants extending from the eastern Cape northwards to Tanzania. Lowland forests also penetrate eastwards into the savanna as narrow ribbons along the larger rivers and these are referred to as riparian forest.

Savanna

The term 'savanna' embraces a range of wooded country from the tall, broadleafed miombo woodland of Zimbabwe and northern Mozambique, to the arid thornveld of the Kalahari. Its essential feature is deciduous trees with an understorey of grass, irrespective of the spacing between the trees or the type of trees. The term 'bushveld' is widely used in South Africa in reference to this biome type. Usually the term 'woodland' is used if the trees form a closed canopy, and 'parkland' if the trees are scattered. There are two distinct subdivisions in this biome: arid savanna and moist savanna, and many bird species are confined to one or other of these. Arid savanna is centred in the western half of the savanna region and is usually dominated by *Acacia* species, and often called 'thornveld'; the trees are often widely spaced and scrubby. By contrast, moist savanna forms the eastern and northern parts of the savanna region where the rainfall is higher and it is dominated by broadleafed tree species. Generally the woodland or savanna is labelled according to the dominant tree species found in it. In the north-east where *Brachystegia* species dominate, it is referred to as brachystegia woodland or miombo. The mopane, *Colophospermum mopane*, is another widespread species that often grows in almost monospecific stands and these areas are referred to as mopane woodland.

Fynbos

Floristically the fynbos biome, which is confined to the southern Cape, is an extremely rich biome in which an enormous variety of *Protea*, *Erica*, *Restio* and other species are found. These form shrublands of various types depending on the topography and underlying soil type: mountain fynbos, coastal fynbos, renosterbos and strandveld are examples. Despite its high plant diversity, the fynbos biome is poor in birds, both in numbers of species and individuals. It does, however support several interesting endemics.

Grassland

The grassland biome is confined to South Africa and centres on the high-lying interior plateau known as the 'highveld'. It is a treeless region, varying greatly in topography from flat plains to rugged mountainous areas and can vary from short grasslands on turf soils to tall grasslands elsewhere. The grasslands have been extensively modified by agriculture and most arable areas are cultivated for crop production: only rocky, mountainous or high-lying cold areas have escaped such changes. The highest altitudes in southern Africa are reached in this biome in the Maluti mountains (above 3 000 m) where an alpine grassland community is found. Several of southern Africa's endemic bird species occur in this biome.

Karoo

The two Karoo biomes cover a large part of the south-western interior of the subcontinent where the annual rainfall is less than 250 mm. The succulent Karoo is located near the west coast in the winter rainfall area and the nama-Karoo in the area of summer rainfall. Both are semi-desert shrublands with extensive areas of rocky outcrop and limited grass cover. There is little permanent surface water to be found in the Karoo, except for that in man-made dams. The Karoo is not rich in birdlife but it is of special interest in that it supports a high proportion of southern Africa's endemic bird species.

Namib Desert

This desert, lying mainly in Namibia, runs north-south along the western seaboard of southern Africa. It is a region of extremely low rainfall (less than 50 mm per annum) and consists of gravel plains, sand dunes, or rugged, rocky hills and mountains. The vegetation is sparse, although it transforms briefly after the infrequent rains. Birdlife is likewise sparse but several of the species present are endemic to the biome.

Lagoons, estuaries, dams, lakes, and pans

These water bodies differ in their origin and ecological functioning but they are all essentially bodies of open water with bare shorelines, and they all tend to support similar communities of waterbirds.

Estuaries are shallow, open-water bays formed where rivers meet the sea and they connect to the sea through a narrow mouth. There are many estuaries along the southern and eastern coast of which the largest is Lake St Lucia. Extensive mudflats are often found on them which provide feeding areas for an array of waterbirds, especially waders. Lagoons, which are simply partly enclosed, protected arms of the sea, also provide mudflats of this nature. Apart from the coastal lakes which have developed from estuaries, there are virtually no natural lakes in southern Africa. There are, however, a great many (more than half a million) man-made dams on the subcontinent which resemble lakes and offer open water that is attractive to a variety of waterbirds. Pans are natural depressions which fill with water after periods of heavy rain. When filled, many of the pans support spectacular numbers of waterbirds.

Rivers

Southern Africa is poorly endowed with large perennial rivers: many of its rivers cease flowing during the dry season, and some flow at even less frequent intervals. Two of the region's largest rivers, the Zambezi and Kavango, are of interest in that they provide habitat for river specialists such as the African Skimmer, Rock Pratincole, Pel's Fishing Owl and Whitebacked Night Heron.

Marshlands

Vleis, sponges, bogs, swamps, floodplains and marshes are all wetlands dominated by emergent aquatic vegetation. Each of these terms has a particular connotation, for example a bog is supported on a substratum of peat and a sponge is located at the headwaters of a river. The emergent vegetation may vary from site to site: some are dominated by reedbeds of *Typha* or *Phragmites*, others by sedges or grass. The essential feature of marshlands is that they are wet underfoot and they provide dense cover in the form of reeds, sedge or grass. The Okavango Delta supports the most extensive area of marshland in southern Africa but many other smaller areas occur in Caprivi, Mozambique and Zululand.

Seashore

The interface between the ocean and the continent is a narrow strip of either sandy beach or rocky outcrop that is subject to tidal action. The number of species found here is limited, but in some cases their numbers are spectacular. A few species endemic to the subcontinent are confined to this area.

Ocean

A diverse and distinctive community of birds live in the open sea, mainly species of albatross, petrels and shearwaters. Most do not come within sight of the coast except during severe storms. Some species occur in both the warm (Indian) and cold (Atlantic) oceans, while others are confined to one or the other; some are summer visitors and others winter visitors to southern African waters.

Additional aids to birding

The support and information available for birding in most of southern Africa is as good or better that that available elsewhere on the continent. In addition to field guides, handbooks and locality guides which cover the entire region, there are several national or local guides, as well as an excellent network of local bird clubs and societies.

Many bird species are best identified or located on the basis of call, and there are several excellent cassette tapes available. The most recent and comprehensive of these is Guy Gibbon's (1991) 'Southern African Bird Sounds', published by Southern African Birding, P.O. Box 24106, Hillary 4024. This collection includes calls of 880 southern African species.

The names and addresses of the region's bird clubs are listed below, and a list of other useful reference works is provided on page 412.

Bird societies and clubs

Societies and clubs play an important role in communication and co-ordination between birders. Most also hold regular meetings and outings, and many produce their own newsletter. Bird clubs in South Africa and Namibia, with the exception of the Diaz Cross Bird Club, are affiliated to the Southern African Ornithological Society (SAOS).

Southern African Ornithological Society, P.O. Box 84394, Greenside 2034.
The Wildlife Society of Southern Africa, P.O. Box 44189, Linden 2104.

Zimbabwe
Ornithological Association of Zimbabwe, P.O. Box 8382, Causeway, Zimbabwe.
Botswana
Botswana Bird Club, P.O. Box 71, Gaborone, Botswana.
Namibia
Namibian Bird Club, P.O. Box 67, Windhoek, Namibia.
Cape
Cape Bird Club, P.O. Box 5022, Cape Town 8000.
Eastern Cape Wild Bird Society, P.O. Box 27454, Greenacres 6057.
Diaz Cross Bird Club, 39 African St, Grahamstown 6140.
Orange Free State
Goldfields Bird Club, P.O. Box 580, Virginia 9430.
Orange Free State Ornithological Society, P.O. Box 6614, Bloemfontein 9300.
Natal
Natal Bird Club, P.O. Box 1218, Durban 4000.
Natal Midlands Bird Club, P.O. Box 2772, Pietermaritzburg 3200.
Transvaal
Lowveld Bird Club, P.O. Box 4113, Nelspruit 1200.
North-eastern Bird Club, P.O. Box 6007, Pietersburg Noord 0750.
Northern Transvaal Ornithological Society, P.O. Box 4158, Pretoria 0001.
Rand Barbets Bird Club, 2 Flint Rd, Parkwood 2193.
Sandton Bird Club, P.O. Box 650890, Benmore 2010.
Vaal Reefs Bird Club, P.O. Box 5129, Vaal Reefs 2621.
Wesvaal Bird Club, P.O. Box 2413, Potchefstroom 2520.
Witwatersrand Bird Club, P.O. Box 72091, Parkview 2122.

Specialist Interest Groups
Vulture Study Group, P.O. Box 72334, Parkview 2122.
African Raptor Information Centre, P.O. Box 4035, Halfway House 1685.
Southern African Crane Foundation, P.O. Box 2310, Durban 4000.
African Seabird Group, P.O. Box 341113, Rhodes Gift 7707.

Abbreviations used in this book
m = male
f = female
ad. = adult
sub-ad. = sub-adult
imm. = immature
juv. = juvenile
br. = breeding
non-br. = non-breeding
cm = centimetre
H = height
O = vagrant record (in maps)

FAMILY INTRODUCTIONS

flight, they stay very close to the surface of the water. During prolonged bad weather and in times of short food supply, they may venture close inshore. Small, loose colonies breed on remote oceanic islands in both hemispheres. Six species occur in the region.

Tropicbirds Family Phaethontidae 50
Mainly white, medium-sized seabirds identifiable by the combination of bill and tail streamer colour, and by the amount of black in the wings. Sexes are alike. Immatures are heavily streaked and barred, and lack the long tail streamers of adults. Tropicbirds plunge-dive to obtain their food, mainly flying fish. They breed under bushes, in holes in trees, or in clefts of cliffs on tropical islands. Three species occur as vagrants in the region.

Pelicans Family Pelecanidae 54
Large, heavily-built birds with grey, black and white plumage. The exceptionally long bill has a distensible pouch which is used as a scoop for catching fish and not, as popularly believed, to store food. Identifiable by the contrast of black and white on their wings and the bill base structure. Found in both salt- and fresh-water localities. Although ponderous in flight, pelicans are dynamic gliders. Very ungainly on land. They breed colonially either in trees or on the ground. Two species occur in the region.

Gannets and boobies Family Sulidae 50
Large white, or white and brown seabirds with cigar-shaped bodies and hefty, pointed bills. Inshore or open ocean feeders, they plummet from considerable heights into the ocean to pursue fish; the Redfooted Booby also pursues flying fish in the air. Colonial breeders on islands and cliffs. Four species occur in the region; the Gape Gannet is an endemic breeder, the others are vagrants.

Cormorants Family Phalacrocoracidae 52
Duck-like black, or black and white birds with long necks and tails. Cormorants forage on inland and in marine coastal waters, diving below the surface to catch fish with their long, hooked bills. Commonly seen with wings outstretched, which helps to dry the wings and keep the bird warm. Colonial breeders on rocky islands, cliffs and in trees. Five species occur in the region, three of which are endemic.

Darters Family Anhingidae 52
Medium-sized birds with very thin, long necks and elongated tails. Using their dagger-shaped bills, they spear fish under water, much like herons do from the surface. When swimming, the body is held submerged and, with only the slender neck and head visible, a Darter resembles a swimming snake, hence the name 'snakebird'. Colonial breeders in trees. The young are covered in white, fluffy down. One species occurs in the region.

Frigatebirds Family Fregatidae 54
Large, very long-winged and fork-tailed seabirds. Adapted to an aerial way of life, they rarely perch and never swim or walk. In the course of their superb soaring flight high over the ocean, they descend swiftly to harass boobies and terns, forcing them to disgorge their last meal, which the frigatebirds then

retrieve. They also prey chiefly on flying fish and squid. Colonial breeders on remote tropical islands. Two species are vagrant to the region.

Herons, egrets and bitterns Family Ardeidae 56
A family of variably-sized birds with long legs, long necks and powerful, dagger-like beaks. Most species are aquatic, preying on fish, frogs and aquatic insects, securing their prey by wading slowly in shallow water and lunging at prey when encountered. The white-plumaged species in the family are generally referred to as egrets. Bitterns are the most secretive, being cryptically marked and skulking by nature. Nineteen species occur in the region.

Hamerkop Family Scopidae 69
A strange-looking, medium-sized brown bird with a dorso-ventrally compressed bill and shaggy, elongated nape feathers. It is neither a stork nor a heron, but shows characters of both. Builds an enormous domed nest of mud, sticks and grass in a tree. A monotypic family, endemic to Africa and Madagascar.

Storks Family Ciconiidae 64
Large birds with long necks and legs, relatively short tails, and broad wings. Most species have striking black and white plumage. The Openbilled Stork has a gap between its mandibles which enables it to manoeuvre the bivalves on which it feeds. Storks nest singly or semi-colonially in trees or on cliffs. Eight species occur in the region.

Ibises and spoonbills Family Threskiornithidae 68, 70
Medium-sized birds with elongated, decurved or flattened bills, long legs and variable plumage coloration. They feed by probing in shallow water, mud or grass. Spoonbills feed by moving their bills from side-to-side in water, sifting out aquatic animals. Five species occur in the region, one of which is endemic.

Flamingoes Family Phoenicopteridae 68
Extraordinarily long-legged, long-necked, pink-coloured aquatic birds with short, heavy and decurved bills. Feed by partly submerging and inverting bill in water and filtering out micro-organisms and algae through fine sieves in the bill. Gregarious, sometimes in huge numbers. Highly nomadic. Two species occur in the region.

Ducks and geese Family Anatidae 72
Aquatic birds that occupy a range of freshwater habitats and spend most of their time swimming on open water. Variable in social habits (some gregarious, others solitary), feeding behaviour (some diving for food, others surface feeding or grazing), breeding behaviour (some on the ground, or over water, others in trees). Flight is fast and direct with the neck held outstretched. Records of escaped exotic wildfowl are regular. Twenty species occur in the region, two of which are endemic.

Secretarybird Family Sagittariidae 150
Very large, long-legged and long-necked bird of prey with a hooked bill, bare face and drooping crest. Prey ranges from large insects to reptiles and rodents: all prey is caught on the ground. A monotypic family, endemic to Africa.

Accipitridae

This diverse assemblage includes most of the birds of prey, the groups of which are listed below.

Vultures 82
Large birds with long, very broad wings designed for soaring. The heads of most are unfeathered to varying degrees. These scavengers gather round carcasses, fighting and jostling as they rip apart the hide with powerful, hooked bills. Eight species occur in the region, one of which is endemic.

Eagles 88
Medium to large birds of prey with long, broad wings and feathered legs, which distinguish them from Snake Eagles and Buzzards. They are noted for their soaring flight and their hunting prowess. Thirteen species occur in the region.

Buzzards 100
Although similar to eagles in shape, buzzards are generally smaller and have unfeathered legs. Plumages are very variable, making identification complex. Buzzards prey on insects, lizards, and small birds and mammals. Mostly tree nesters, they frequent well-wooded areas and open plains. Six species occur in the region, one of which is endemic.

Goshawks and sparrowhawks 108, 112
Small to medium-sized birds with rounded wings and long tails. Most have yellow or red eyes and some have very long toes designed for gripping their prey, which comprises mainly birds and small mammals. They hunt by a dash-and-seize technique. Twelve species occur in the region, one of which is endemic.

Harriers 104
Medium-sized birds with long, narrow wings and tails. They are distinctive in flight as they glide low over the ground, head down, with wings held in a shallow 'V'. In such flight, they suddenly stall, flopping to the ground to grasp their prey, which includes frogs and small rodents. Mostly seen over marshes and open fields. Five species occur in the region, one of which is endemic.

Osprey Family Pandionidae 88
Resembles medium-sized eagle with pale underparts and dark back. Preys exclusively on fish caught by plunge-diving in rivers, lakes, estuaries and shallow coastal waters. Feet are specially adapted for catching fish, having spiny soles and a reversible outer toe. Breeds singly, usually in large trees. A monotypic family with an almost worldwide distribution.

Falcons and kestrels Family Falconidae.....................................116
Small to medium-sized birds; they are swift, agile fliers on long, pointed wings. Some species are dynamic aerial hunters, stooping at great speeds to strike at their prey in mid-air. Mostly diurnal, some crepuscular. The female is often much larger than the male. Sixteen species occur in the region.

Francolins and quail Family Phasianidae 132
Ground-living gamebirds, mostly cryptically coloured, with far-carrying charac-

teristic call-notes. Variable in social habits (some living in flocks, others in pairs), behaviour (some sedentary, others nomadic or migratory), roosting habits (some sleep in trees, others on the ground) and sexual dimorphism (some monomorphic, others highly dimorphic). Nest built on the ground, well hidden. One member of this family (Chukar Partridge), introduced to southern Africa, survives ferally on Robben Island in Table Bay. Sixteen species occur in the region, five of which are endemic.

Guineafowl Family Numididae 138
Distinctively plumaged (black and white spotted) ground-living gamebirds with prominent casques or feather tufts on the crown. Sexes alike. Gregarious, sometimes in large flocks. Two species occur in the region.

Buttonquail Family Turnicidae 140
Small, ground-living quail-like birds. Cryptically marked, with reversed sexual dimorphism and reversed parental roles when breeding. Nomadic, found in open habitats. Two species occur in the region.

Rails, crakes, flufftails, gallinules, moorhens and coots
Family Rallidae 142
Small to medium-sized, ground-dwelling birds with long legs and toes. The very short tail is often held erect and flicked up and down. Good swimmers, they generally inhabit marshes and, notwithstanding their furtive behaviour, can frequently be seen clambering through reeds. Many species undertake long-distance migrations at night. Nineteen species occur in the region.

Cranes Family Gruidae 150
Very large, long-legged birds with relatively short bills. They inhabit wetlands and open grasslands and, when not breeding, aggregate in large flocks. All have complex dancing displays and some are extremely vocal. They fly with the neck outstretched. Three species occur in the region, one of which is endemic.

Finfoots Family Heliornithidae 142
Superficially resemble cormorants, with a heavy, pointed (not hooked) bill. Toes lobed, not webbed. Sexually dimorphic. Shy and retiring, found in pairs along wooded rivers. One species occurs in Africa.

Bustards Family Otididae 152
Medium to very large terrestrial birds, with long, sometimes very slender necks, and long legs. Variable in colour but usually cryptically mottled buff, brown and black above. They walk slowly, with the neck being swung back and forth. Reluctant to take to flight, the birds tend to crouch or run when alarmed. In some species males perform elaborate courtship displays, either puffing out throats or performing aerial flights. Some species have a lek-mating system. Eleven species occur in the region, six of which are endemic.

Sheathbills Family Chionididae 198
Chicken-like, white marine birds of uncertain taxonomic affinities which breed at remote sub-Antarctic islands and on the Antarctic Peninsula. They forage mainly by scavenging. One species occurs in the region as a vagrant.

Jacanas Family Jacanidae 144
A distinctive family of aquatic birds with extraordinarily long toes and toenails which enable them to walk on floating vegetation. Often gregarious in suitable habitat, when noisy and conspicuous. Most species are polyandrous breeders and males undertake all parental care. Two species occur in the region.

Painted snipes Family Rostratulidae 174
Medium-sized waders with long bills, rounded wings and short tails. Frequent marshes and the fringes of reedbeds, usually in pairs or small groups. Probe for food in soft mud. They have reversed sexual dimorphism and are polyandrous, all parental care being by the male. One species occurs in the region.

Oystercatchers Family Haematopodidae 158
Large waders with characteristic long, straight, orange-red bills and pinkish legs. Plumage black or black and white. Forage mainly on open shorelines and in estuaries. All species have highly ritualized and vocal displays. Two species occur in the region, one is endemic, the other a vagrant.

Plovers Family Charadriidae 160
Medium-sized to small waders with characteristically short bills and long legs. Inhabit a range of habitats from open coasts and marshes to deserts, grassland, savannas and inland waterbodies. Many species form flocks outside the breeding season. Nineteen species occur in the region.

Snipes, godwits, sandpipers, stints, curlews, phalaropes
Family Scolopacidae 168
A highly diverse family, ranging in size from large curlews to small stints. All species which occur in southern Africa, except the Ethiopian Snipe, breed in the northern hemisphere and migrate to southern Africa in summer. Marine and freshwater invertebrates are the principal food of all species. Most species occur on the open coast and at coastal estuaries and lagoons, although some are regular at inland waterbodies. Grey Phalarope occurs almost exclusively at sea. Thirty-five species occur in the region, many of them as vagrants.

Avocets and stilts Family Recurvirostridae 158
Medium-sized waders with very long legs and long, thin bills, either straight (stilts) or upcurved (avocets). Found mainly at estuaries and inland waterbodies, including hypersaline pans. They prey predominantly on aquatic invertebrates and typically breed at ephemeral waterbodies. Two species occur in the region.

Crab Plover Family Dromadidae 158
A large black and white wader with a characteristic heavy, black bill and very long, bluish-grey legs. Largely endemic to coasts of the tropical Indian Ocean; usually in flocks. Feeds on crabs, marine molluscs and worms. Breeds colonially in burrows abutting sandy beaches. A monotypic family.

Dikkops Family Burhinidae 196
Large, cryptically-coloured waders with large heads. Their large yellow eyes are indicative of their nocturnal habits. At night their mournful cries and whistles can be heard over great distances. Two species occur in the region.

Coursers and pratincoles Family Glareolidae 184, 196
Coursers are waders which generally inhabit the drier regions. Their long legs enable them to run swiftly and their cryptic back coloration blends well with their sandy or stony environment. In flight they show boldly patterned wings. Pratincoles are short-legged birds with long, pointed wings and black and white forked tails. When in flight they resemble huge swallows. Both groups have large eyes, indicative of their nocturnal and crepuscular habits. Insectivorous, they catch their prey in flight or on the ground. Eight species occur in the region, one of which is endemic.

Skuas, gulls and terns Family Laridae 198
Small to large waterbirds which frequent inland and coastal regions. Predominantly grey and white birds, with distinct immature plumages, gulls are usually identifiable by their wing and head patterns, and bill and leg coloration. Fork-tailed, terns are on average smaller than gulls and have a more buoyant, agile flight on long, pointed wings. When breeding, many terns display brightly coloured bills and black caps. Skuas are brown-coloured gull-like birds, that obtain much of their food by pirating from gulls and terns, chasing their victims in flight with great agility. Thirty-five species occur in the region, one of which is endemic as a breeding species. Many are vagrants to the region.

Skimmers Family Rynchopidae 220
Large, tern-like birds with fairly long, reddish bills. The bill is laterally compressed with an elongated lower mandible. They have a unique foraging behaviour, flying low over the water with the tip of the lower mandible inserted in the water to detect fish. Found mostly along large rivers, where they roost and breed colonially on sandbars. One species occurs in the region.

Sandgrouse Family Pteroclidae 212
Medium-sized, desert, semi-desert and dry savanna-dwelling birds with cryptically coloured plumage. They fly considerable distances daily to reach their water sources (each species preferring different drinking times), sometimes gathering in their thousands to drink. On the ground they look like very short-legged francolins but in flight they resemble swiftly flying doves. Four species occur in the region, two of which are endemic.

Pigeons and doves Family Columbidae 214
The term 'pigeon' normally refers to the larger species and 'dove' to the smaller members of this large family. Most have distinctive calls and many are identifiable by their tail patterns. All domestic pigeons are descendants of the Rock Dove of the northern hemisphere. Most species are granivorous but some eat fruit. In addition to the introduced Feral Pigeon, 14 species occur in the region.

Parrots and lovebirds Family Psittacidae 220
Small to medium-sized birds with vivid green, blue, brown and red coloration. The beak is short, stubby and deeply hooked, ideally adapted for cracking hard nuts and ripping open fruit. Flight is rapid and direct. Calls consist of shrieks and screams. Eight species occur in the region; one, the Roseringed Parakeet, is an aviary escapee which has established feral populations in suburban areas.

Louries Family Musophagidae 224
Medium-sized, long-tailed birds which, except for the drab Grey Lourie, display bright green, red and blue plumage. Mostly forest dwellers, they have loud, raucous calls and a distinctive bounding action as they leap from branch to branch through the canopy. Flight is laboured, with fast wing beats interspersed with long glides. Their diet consists mainly of fruit. Five species occur in the region, of which one is endemic.

Cuckoos Family Cuculidae 226
Variable in size, colour and appearance, all the cuckoos have zygodactylous feet and parasitic breeding habits. Some species are iridescently coloured, others are sombre coloured. In some the sexes are alike; others are highly dimorphic. Each species parasitizes either a single host species or a limited range of hosts. In some species eggs match the host's closely, in others they don't. Most are seasonal visitors to the region. Fourteen species occur in the region.

Coucals Family Centropodidae 232
Mainly rather large, long- and broad-tailed birds with strongly curved beaks which live in rank vegetation close to the ground. They utter liquid bubbling or hooting calls. Live solitarily or in pairs and most are sedentary. Unlike the closely related cuckoos, they build their own nests and raise their own young. Insectivorous; some species also prey on eggs and nestlings of other birds. Six species occur in the region, one of which is endemic.

Owls Families Tytonidae and Strigidae 234
Small to large nocturnal birds of prey. All have distinctive calls in the form of hoots, whistles or shrieks, and are most vocal just after dusk and before dawn. The Barn and Grass Owls (Tytonidae) differ from other owls (Strigidae) by their heart-shaped facial discs of pale, stiff feathers surrounding their small dark eyes. The plumage is soft and fluffy with brown, buff or grey colouring, often with heavy barring or streaking. Owls are silent fliers and their prey ranges from insects to mammals and birds and, in one species, fish. In general, owls are most easily located at night by their calls. Twelve species occur in the region.

Nightjars Family Caprimulgidae 238
Nocturnal, dove-sized birds with large heads and eyes, a wide gape for catching insects in flight, and very short, weak legs. Cryptically-coloured, they are difficult to locate during the day because they are superbly camouflaged as they rest in leaf litter and stony areas. Although it is not easy to distinguish between the species, a combination of the extent or absence of white in the wings and tails differentiates species in the field. As with owls, nightjars are best identified by their calls at night. Seven species occur in the region.

Swifts Family Apodidae 242
Their long, sickle-shaped wings make the flight of swifts rapid and effortless. They do not perch, but feed on insects caught while on the wing, and some species roost in flight at great heights. Their legs are very short and the toes point forward, an adaptation for clinging to their nesting places: rock faces, tree bark or palm fronds. Identification is based largely on size, rump pattern and tail shape. Thirteen species occur in the region.

Mousebirds Family Coliidae 246
Small, mouse-like, grey or brown birds with long, stiff tails, crests and bare faces. Gregarious, in flocks of up to 15 birds. Live in trees and feed on fruit and vegetable matter, climbing dexterously about the branches. Flocks sleep huddled together. Make rasping or whistling calls. Build open cup nests. Family endemic to Africa. Three species occur in the region, one of which is endemic.

Trogons Family Trogonidae 246
Brilliantly coloured forest-dwelling birds; females duller than males. Perch upright, hawking aerial insects like a flycatcher. Make a soft hooting call. Nest in holes in trees. One species occurs in the region.

Kingfishers Families Alcedinidae and Cerylidae 248
Very small to medium-sized birds, frequently dazzling blue and orange in colour, and with long, stout, pointed and often brightly-coloured bills. They frequent water and woodland habitats, feeding on fish, insects and reptiles. Fish-eating species often hover before plunge-diving to capture their prey, whereas insect- and reptile-eaters sit motionless on a perch before dashing after their prey with a fast, direct flight. Ten species occur in the region.

Bee-eaters Family Meropidae 252
A group of brightly coloured, slender birds that usually occur in flocks and have distinctive contact calls. They have long, slightly decurved bills, long, pointed wings and some species also have elongated central tail feathers. Insectivorous, they hawk their prey from the ground or exposed perches and are attracted to veld fires, where they glean insects flushed by the heat. Some are colonial breeders, nesting at the end of long tunnels excavated in sandy banks. Most are identified by their brilliant plumage colour combinations and tail projections. Nine species occur in the region.

Rollers Family Coraciidae 256
Stocky perching birds which derive their common name from their acrobatic, noisy display flights, during which they tumble through the air. Most species have a plumage combination of bright blues, greens, violets and browns. All nest in holes in trees. Although mostly insectivorous, they also eat reptiles and small rodents. Five species occur in the region.

Hoopoe, woodhoopoes and scimitarbills
Families Upupidae, Phoeniculidae and Rhinopomastidae 260
The four species in this group share little in common apart from their long, thin decurved bills. The Hoopoe is largely terrestrial, even nesting in holes in the ground, whereas woodhoopoes and scimitarbills are arboreal, gleaning insects from the bark of trees and nesting and roosting in tree cavities. Woodhoopoes are gregarious and co-operative breeders whereas the other two species are solitary or live in pairs. One species is endemic.

Hornbills Families Bucerotidae and Bucorvidae 258
Medium-sized to very large birds with long, heavy, decurved bills; some species have a casque on the upper mandible. Most are identifiable by bill and body coloration. While incubating the eggs, the female is sealed inside the nest cavity by

the male (Ground Hornbill excepted), and during this period she moults her flight feathers. Most hornbills are woodland inhabitants and their diet consists mainly of fruit and berries. However, an exception to this is the huge Ground Hornbill, which feeds on insects, reptiles and small rodents. Nine species occur in the region, one of which is endemic.

Barbets Family Capitonidae 264
Small birds with stout bodies and large heads and bills. They have an unusual toe arrangement in that two toes point forward and two back. All have distinctive calls, the tinker barbets having clinking call notes. Frugivorous and insectivorous forest- and bush-dwellers, they excavate nesting holes in dead trees. Nests are regularly parasitized by honeyguides. Ten species occur in the region, one of which is endemic.

Honeyguides Family Indicatoridae 262
Small, short-legged birds, honeyguides are usually drab in coloration and have short, stubby or pointed bills. Species identification is usually based on call, shape of bill, and habits. One species leads mammals, especially the honey badger and man, to beehives in the hope of sharing the spoils of a raided nest. They are unique in that they eat beeswax. Brood parasites, some lay their eggs in the nests of barbets and woodpeckers, others in nests of cisticolas and white-eyes. Six species occur in the region.

Woodpeckers and wrynecks Families Picidae and Jyngidae 268
Small to medium-sized birds with stout, pointed bills which are used to hammer and bore into wood to reach grubs and insects and to excavate nest holes. One species is terrestrial in rocky and mountainous habitats, the others arboreal. The tails are stiff and brace the birds as they cling to branches and move jerkily up tree trunks. Nine species occur in the region, two of which are endemic.

Broadbills Family Eurylaimidae 246
Rather nondescript, small, forest-dwelling birds that have the distinction of performing perform elaborate courtship displays in the breeding season. Solitary in occurrence and sedentary. Insectivorous, foraging like a flycatcher. One species occurs in the region.

Pittas Family Pittidae 246
Brightly coloured, forest-dwelling birds that forage on the ground but nest and display in trees. Males have distinctive calls and displays. Migratory or nomadic. One species occurs in the region.

Larks and finchlarks Family Alaudidae 272
Small, usually drab, terrestrial birds which resemble pipits but have shorter tails, stouter bills and dumpier bodies. Most species frequent open areas in the drier regions and are cryptically coloured to blend with their stony and sandy habitats. Those species that inhabit wood and bush areas are normally heavily streaked above and below. Identification is based on subtleties of plumage coloration, as well as bill shape and song. All build their nests on the ground. Twenty-five species occur in the region, 17 of which are endemic.

Swallows and martins Family Hirundinidae 282
Shorter- and less stiff-winged than swifts, they are frequently seen perched on telephone wires. Plumage colours range from glossy blues to reds and dull browns. All are aerial and insectivorous and have dorso-ventrally flattened bills with a wide gape. Some are colonial breeders, nesting in holes in riverbanks, or using mud pellets to build elaborate nests on man-made structures. Twenty-one species occur in the region, one of which is a breeding endemic.

Cuckooshrikes Family Campephagidae 288
Slow-moving, arboreal birds which superficially resemble cuckoos. Primarily insectivorous, they glean insects from the canopy in the evergreen forests they frequent and have soft calls. Sexual plumage differences are very slight except in the Black Cuckooshrike where the female is heavily barred green, yellow and brown. Three species occur in the region.

Drongos Family Dicruridae 288
Noisy, black insectivores. Bold and conspicuous, they are fearless when harassing large birds of prey, giving chase and diving at them in flight. They have stout, slightly hooked bills with prominent rictal bristles and they catch insects on the wing, darting, like flycatchers, from an exposed perch in wooded and open country habitats. Two species occur in the region.

Orioles Family Oriolidae 290
Resembling starlings in size and shape, these brightly coloured birds of forest and bushveld all have similar clear liquid calls. The males are a vivid yellow and are not easily located in their leafy surroundings. Females have drabber green and yellow plumages. They feed on a variety of fruits and insects and, occasionally, nectar. Four species occur in the region.

Crows and ravens Family Corvidae 292
Fairly large, black or black and white birds with strong bills. At close range, it can be seen that the black parts of the plumage are in fact glossy purple and green. They are found in a variety of habitats throughout the region and the Pied Crow has adapted successfully to cities. Four species occur in the region, with the House Crow, a recent arrival, having established itself in Natal and the south-western Cape.

Tits and penduline tits Families Paridae and Remizidae 294
Small, highly active arboreal birds with short, robust bills, some have black, white and grey plumages, others are yellow or grey. Usually in pairs or small groups of four to six, they are prominent and noisy members of mixed bird parties. The tits nest in holes whereas the penduline tits build an elaborate suspended felted nest. Eight species occur in the region, four of which are endemic.

Spotted Creeper Family Salpornithidae 294
Small, cryptically-marked, brown birds with long, decurved beaks. Forage by clambering about tree surfaces like woodpeckers, easily overlooked. Sedentary, confined to well-wooded habitats. Insectivorous. A monotypic family, endemic to Africa and India.

Babblers Family Timaliidae 296
Medium-sized black, white, brown and grey birds inhabiting reedbeds, woodland and forest fringes. Most are highly vocal and gregarious, feeding on fruit, insects and small reptiles. Some, perhaps all southern African species, are co-operative breeders. Five species occur in the region, one of which is endemic.

Bulbuls Family Pycnonotidae 298
Small to medium-sized brown, green and yellow birds with fairly short bills, hooked in some species. Occur in a wide range of habitats from desert fringes to montane forests. Found solitarily or in small groups, feeding on fruit and insects. Eleven species occur in the region, two of which are endemic.

Thrushes, chats, alethes, robins and rockjumpers
Family Turdidae 302
Small to medium-sized birds. Thrushes and alethes are generally found in well-wooded or forested habitats, as are some robins. Chats inhabit open areas from deserts to savannas, and rockjumpers are found in montane grassland and fynbos. Most species feed primarily on invertebrates, some include fruits and seeds in their diet. Forty-five species occur in the region, of which 16 are endemic.

Titbabblers, hyliotas, warblers, apalises, crombecs, eremomelas, Grassbird, Rockrunner, cisticolas and prinias
Family Sylviidae 318
A diverse group of mostly small birds, usually dully-coloured and lacking any marked sexual dimorphism. Tail length highly variable, ranging from very short (crombecs and eremomelas) to long (apalises, grassbird, prinias and some warblers and cisticolas). Bills mostly short and pointed. Cisticolas in particular can present major identification problems, and are best identified by call. Seventy-two species occur in the region, of which 14 are endemic.

Flycatchers and batises Family Muscicapidae 346
Generally small passerines of savanna, woodland and forest, typically with short, rounded wings and short, dorso-ventrally compressed bills. Plumage and tail length variable in the flycatchers. Flycatchers hunt from perches, taking insects either in the air or on the ground. Batises and Wattle-eyed Flycatchers are short-tailed, plumage a combination of black, white, grey and orange. These birds hunt by gleaning insects, mostly from leaves or bark, as well as in aerial pursuit. Nests are typically neat, cup-shaped structures, positioned on a branch or ledge. Twenty-two species occur in the region, of which five are endemic.

Wagtails, pipits and longclaws Family Motacillidae 350
Ground-living birds, the wagtails and pipits are long-tailed and have the habit of wagging their tails up and down while walking. Pipits are brown coloured and confusingly similar, being best identified by their call notes and choice of habitat. Longclaws have brightly coloured underparts and exceptionally long hind claws. All are insectivorous, most nest on the ground and live in grassland. Some seasonal visitors to the region from the northern hemisphere. Twenty-two species occur in the region, three of which are endemic and one of which is a breeding endemic.

Shrikes Family Laniidae 358
Small to medium-sized birds with medium to very long tails. Plumage of southern African species is predominantly grey, black and white. Bills are short, stout and hooked, and the feet are strong and sharp-clawed. Found in semi-desert, woodland and savanna; one species common in suburban gardens. Five species occur in the region.

Bush shrikes, boubous, tchagras, brubrus, puffbacks and White-tailed Shrike Family Malaconotidae 360
Small to medium-sized shrikes, most with heavy, hooked bills. Bush shrikes are brightly coloured, mostly yellow and orange below, and green and grey above. Boubous, with one exception, are predominantly black and white, whereas tchagras are more dully-coloured brown, black and grey. They inhabit a range of habitats from semi-desert to forest, many species favouring dense thickets and tangled vegetation. Most are highly vocal, with loud, ringing calls. Seventeen species occur in the region, six of which are endemic.

Helmetshrikes Family Prionopidae 364
Small to medium-sized birds with short, hooked bills and bristled foreheads. All southern African species are gregarious, occurring in groups, usually of 4-10 birds in woodland and savanna (three species) or forest (one species); all breed co-operatively. Four species occur in the region.

Starlings Family Sturnidae 366
Mostly medium-sized birds with strong, pointed bills. The *Lamprotornis* starlings are mostly iridescent blue and green in colour, others are variable. They eat insects and fruit and occur across the habitat spectrum. Some species are commensal with man and many species form flocks outside the breeding season. Two species are colonial breeders and at least one is a co-operative breeder. Fourteen species occur in the region; two are endemic and two introduced.

Oxpeckers Family Buphagidae 370
Medium-sized brown and buff-coloured birds with short, heavy, red or red-and-yellow bills which are laterally flattened. They are highly specialized feeders, spending much time perched on large wild and domestic animals from which they remove ectoparasites and loose skin with scissoring movements of the bill. This unusual feeding technique is aided by sharp, curved claws and stiff tail feathers for support. They are gregarious and breed co-operatively, favouring savanna and woodland. Two species occur in the region.

Sugarbirds and sunbirds Families Promeropidae and Nectariniidae 372
Most male sunbirds have brilliant plumage and are easily identifiable but the females are drabber and can be confusingly similar. The long, decurved bills are ideal for probing flowers for nectar but the birds also eat insects to supplement their diets. When probing flowers, they usually perch, rarely hovering. Their flight is fast and dashing. Sugarbirds are larger and longer-tailed than sunbirds with long, decurved bills, and are less brightly coloured. They are closely associated with proteas and are seasonal migrants. Twenty-three species occur in the region, seven of which are endemic.

White-eyes Family Zosteropidae 346
Small arboreal birds which have short, pointed bills, yellow, green and grey
plumage, and white rings around dark brown eyes. Gregarious, they behave like
tiny babblers, gathering in small parties and continually calling to keep contact.
They are insectivorous and frugivorous, occasionally also feeding on nectar.
Two species occur in the region, one of which is endemic.

Sparrows, weavers, bishops, queleas, widows and Cuckoo Finch
Family Ploceidae 380
Except for sparrows, the males of the species in this group are brightly coloured
(red, yellow, black) in summer, some with long tails, and drab in winter. Most
are polygamous, males weaving the nests, but females performing all parental
duties. Sparrows are mainly brown coloured; some exhibit sexual dimorphism
and all are monogamous. All are partly or wholly granivorous and live in grassland, marshy habitats or savanna. Thirty-five species occur in the region, four of
which are endemic and one introduced.

Pytilias, twinspots, crimsonwings, seedcrackers, firefinches, wax-bills and mannikins
Family Estrildidae 396
Small, mostly brightly-coloured birds, all sexually dimorphic. All have short,
conical bills, primarily adapted for eating seeds, but some species include insects
in their diet. Most forage on the ground or low in the vegetation, often in small
flocks. Twenty-eight species occur in the region, three of which are endemic.

Whydahs and widowfinches Family Viduidae 392
Small birds, with short conical bills adapted for seed-eating. Both groups exhibit
extreme sexual dimorphism during the breeding season. In whydahs, males are
black and buffy-yellow or black and white and have elaborate, elongated central
tail feathers. Male widowfinches are black, with variably-coloured bills and legs.
Females and non-breeding males of both groups are short-tailed with dull, mottled brown, black and buff plumages. Both whydahs and widowfinches are parasitic, with distributions matching those of their hosts. Seven, possibly eight
species occur in the region.

Canaries, siskins, finches and buntings Family Fringillidae 406
Small birds, they range from the brilliantly coloured to the drab and dowdy.
Most are seed- and insect-eaters and are terrestrial in habits, but use trees and
scrub for nesting. Highly prized by the cagebird industry for their fine, buzzy
songs. The more brightly-coloured canaries are sexually dimorphic. Twenty
species occur in the region, ten of which are endemic, and one introduced.

GLOSSARY

Accidental. A vagrant or stray species not normally found within the region.

Arboreal. Tree dwelling.

Colonial. Associating in close proximity, either while roosting, feeding or nesting.

Commensal. Living with or near another species, without being interdependent.

Crepuscular. Active at dawn and dusk.

Cryptic. Pertaining to camouflage coloration.

Diurnal. Active during daylight hours.

Eclipse plumage. Dull plumage attained by male ducks and sunbirds during a transitional moult, after the breeding season and before they acquire brighter plumage.

Endemic. A species whose breeding and non-breeding ranges are confined to a particular region.

Near-endemic. A species whose range is largely restricted to a region but extends slightly outside the region's borders. (In this book, this category includes mostly species whose ranges extend into the arid regions of south-western Angola.)

Breeding endemic. A species which breeds only in a particular region but undertakes movements or migrations during the non-breeding season such that a measurable proportion of the population leaves the region.

Feral. Species which have escaped from captivity and now live in the wild.

Flight feathers. The longest feathers on the wings and tail.

Flush. To put to flight.

Form. A colour variant within a species; variation may or may not be linked to subspecific status.

Fulvous. Reddish yellow or tawny.

Immature. A bird that has moulted from juvenile plumage but has not attained adult plumage. Can also include juvenile plumage.

Irruption. A rapid expansion of a species' normal range.

Juvenile. The first full-feathered plumage of a young bird.

Migrant. A species which undertakes (usually) long-distance flights between its breeding and non-breeding areas.

Mirrors. The white spots on the primaries of gulls.

Montane. Pertaining to mountains.

Nocturnal. Active at night.

Overwintering. A bird which remains in the subregion instead of migrating to its breeding grounds.

Palearctic. North Africa, Greenland, Europe, and Asia north of the Himalayas, southern China and South East Asia.

Pelagic. Ocean dwelling.

Race. A geographical population of a species; a subspecies.

Range. A bird's distribution.

Raptor. A bird of prey.

Resident. A species not prone to migration, remaining in the same area all year.

Rufous. Reddish brown.

Sub-adult. A bird intermediate in age and plumage between immature and adult.

Territory. The area a bird establishes and then defends from others.

Vagrant. Rare and accidental to the region.

ILLUSTRATED GLOSSARY

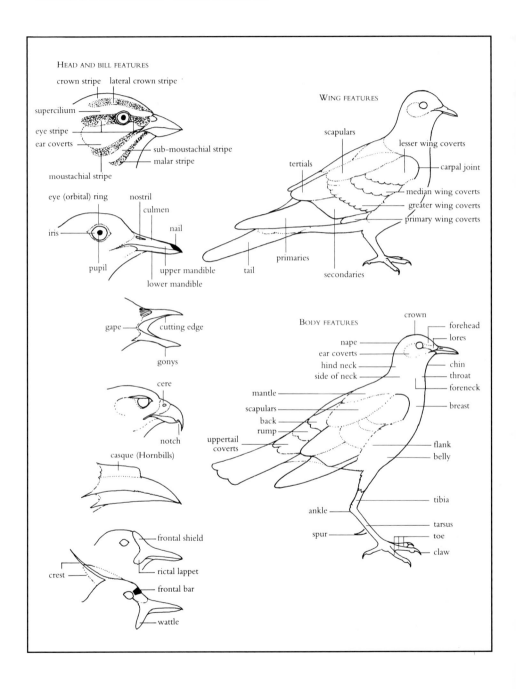

HEAD AND BILL FEATURES

crown stripe lateral crown stripe

supercilium

eye stripe

ear coverts

sub-moustachial stripe

malar stripe

moustachial stripe

eye (orbital) ring   nostril

culmen

nail

iris

pupil

upper mandible

lower mandible

gape   cutting edge

gonys

cere

notch

casque (Hornbills)

crest

frontal shield

rictal lappet

frontal bar

wattle

WING FEATURES

scapulars

lesser wing coverts

carpal joint

tertials

median wing coverts

greater wing coverts

primary wing coverts

tail

primaries

secondaries

BODY FEATURES

crown

forehead

lores

nape

ear coverts

hind neck

side of neck

chin

throat

foreneck

mantle

scapulars

back

rump

breast

uppertail coverts

flank

belly

tibia

ankle

spur

tarsus

toe

claw

30

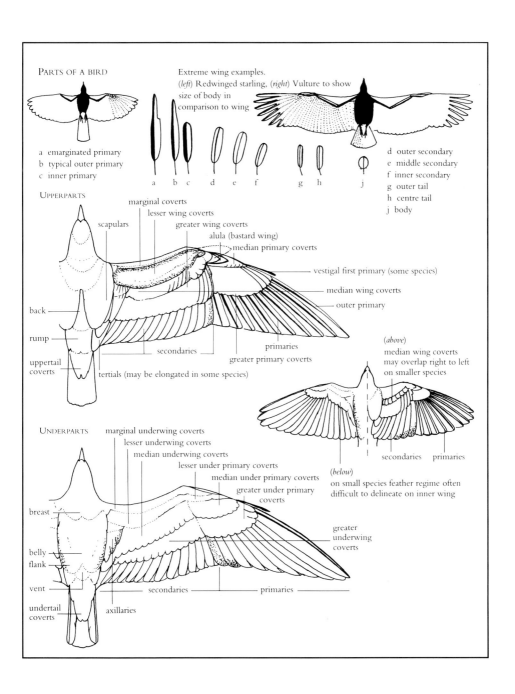

KING PENGUIN *Aptenodytes patagonicus* (2) 94 cm
The long pointed bill, large size and bright orange ear patches are distinctive.
SEXES alike but male larger. IMM. is a paler version of ad. HABITAT. Pelagic and ranges throughout southern oceans south of 40 °S. STATUS. Vagrant: two records from the southern Cape. CALL. Loud trumpeting during display. (Koningspikkewyn)

JACKASS PENGUIN *Spheniscus demersus* (3) 60 cm
The region's only resident penguin, it has a diagnostic black and white facial pattern.
Some birds show a double bar on the throat and chest – this is diagnostic of the Magellanic Penguin *S. magellanicus* which has not been positively recorded in the region. MALE has a heavier bill than female. JUV. is dark greyish blue with grey cheeks and lacks breast band. HABITAT. Occurs within 50 km of the shore and breeds on offshore islands. STATUS. Resident; endemic. Common but decreasing in numbers. CALL. Loud braying, especially at night. (Brilpikkewyn)

MACARONI PENGUIN *Eudyptes chrysolophus* (5) 70 cm
Distinguished from Rockhopper Penguin by stouter, more robust bill, larger body size, and orange-yellow eyebrows that meet on the forehead.
At sea differentiated from Rockhopper by pale pink patch on sides of gape and white spot on rump. SEXES alike. IMM. differs from imm. Rockhopper by yellow eyebrow starting above the eye. HABITAT. At sea and on sub-Antarctic islands. STATUS. Rare vagrant. Comes ashore when moulting. CALL. A loud trumpeting when in display. At sea a harsh 'aaark'. (Macaronipikkewyn)

ROCKHOPPER PENGUIN *Eudyptes chrysocome* (4) 61 cm
Has a short, stubby red bill and a pale yellow stripe extending from in front of the eye to the nape, where it ends in a golden shaggy crest. The eyebrow stripe does not meet on the forehead as it does in Macaroni Penguin.
SEXES alike. IMM. smaller than imm. Macaroni Penguin and distinguished by its conspicuous yellow eyebrow stripe starting well before the eye. HABITAT. Breeds on sub-Antarctic islands, and is pelagic south of 30 °S when not breeding. STATUS. Vagrant. CALL. Display call is a trumpeting 'wada, wada, wada'. (Geelkuifpikkewyn)

DABCHICK *Tachybaptus ruficollis* (8) 20 cm
When breeding, this very small, dark grebe has chestnut sides to the neck, and a diagnostic pale creamy spot at the base of the bill. In winter, distinguished from Black-necked Grebe by smaller size, dusky cheeks and throat.
SEXES alike. IMM. similar to non-breeding ad. but young bird may show black and white striping on cheeks. HABITAT. Virtually any open stretch of fresh water. STATUS. Common resident. CALL. Noisy; a distinctive whinnying trill. (Kleindobbertjie)

GREAT CRESTED GREBE *Podiceps cristatus* (6) 50 cm
Breeding ad. unmistakable, having a dark double crest and a rufous-edged ruff ringing the sides of head. Ruff of female is paler.
NON-BREEDING AD. has crest and ruff less pronounced. Body held low in water with neck very erect. In flight shows a pale wing bar. JUV. shows black and white striping on head. HABITAT. Large open stretches of fresh water. STATUS. Locally common resident. CALL. A barking 'rah-rah-rah' and various growls and snarls. (Kuifkopdobbertjie)

BLACKNECKED GREBE *Podiceps nigricollis* (7) 28 cm
Far smaller than Great Crested Grebe but larger than Dabchick.
SEXES alike. BREEDING AD. has black head and throat, and conspicuous golden ear tufts. NON-BREEDING AD. distinguished from Dabchick by larger size, white cheeks and throat and by distinctive head and bill shape. At close range the cherry red eye is obvious. IMM. resembles non-breeding ad. HABITAT. Open stretches of water, especially saline pans. STATUS. Resident, with local movements. CALL. Seldom heard: a mellow trill during display. (Swartnekdobbertjie)

KING PENGUIN
ad.

JACKASS PENGUIN

ad.

imm.

juv.

ad.

colour form
resembling
Magellanic
Penguin

JACKASS PENGUIN

moulting

MACARONI PENGUIN

ROCKHOPPER PENGUIN

imm.

ad.

imm.

ad.

br.

DABCHICK

ad. non-br.

ad. non-br.

ad. non-br.

br.

GREAT CRESTED GREBE

juv.

GREAT
CRESTED
GREBE

ad.

br.

ad. non-br.

BLACKNECKED GREBE

BLACKNECKED
GREBE

ad.
non-br.

WANDERING ALBATROSS *Diomedea exulans* (10) 125 cm
The white back distinguishes the ad. from all except Royal Albatross.
SEXES alike. IMM. in first plumage is dark with white face and underwings. With age plumage pales and progresses through various spotted and mottled stages. HABITAT. Southern oceans south of 30 °S. Breeds on sub-Antarctic islands. STATUS. Visits coastal waters chiefly in winter, ranging widely off the Cape and Natal coasts. CALL. Harsh, nasal 'waaaak'. (Grootmalmok)

ROYAL ALBATROSS *Diomedea epomophora* (9) 122 cm
Only distinguishable at close range from Wandering Albatross by black eyelids and black cutting edge to pinkish mandibles. The race sanfordi *is differentiated by having a thick black border to the underwings, from carpal joint to wing tip, and totally black upperwings.*
SEXES alike. IMM. resembles ad. and lacks the brown plumage of imm. Wandering Albatross. HABITAT. Southern oceans. STATUS. Vagrant. CALL. Not recorded in the region. (Koningmalmok)

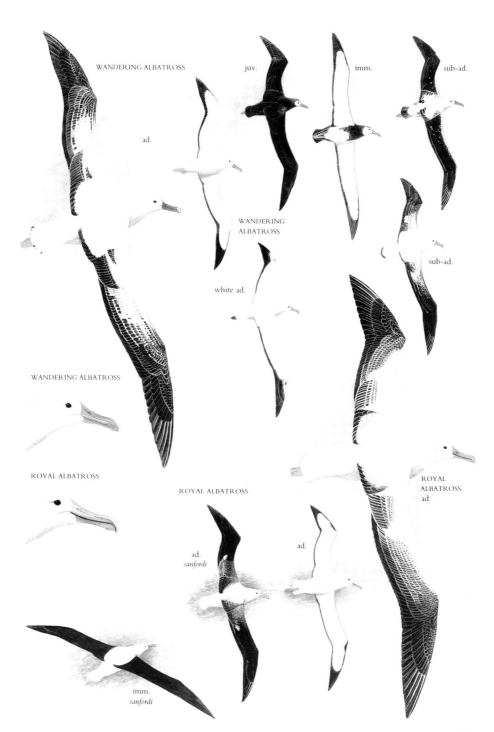

WANDERING ALBATROSS

ad.

juv.

imm.

sub-ad.

WANDERING
ALBATROSS

white ad.

sub-ad.

WANDERING ALBATROSS

ROYAL ALBATROSS

ROYAL ALBATROSS

ad.
sanfordi

ad.

ROYAL
ALBATROSS
ad.

imm.
sanfordi

SHY ALBATROSS *Diomedea cauta* (11) 98 cm
Largest of the 'dark-backed' albatrosses. The upperwing and mantle are paler than in other albatrosses. The underwing is white with a very narrow black border and shows a diagnostic black spot on the leading edge near the body.
SEXES alike. AD. has greyish cheeks with white crown; bill is pale olive with a yellow tip. IMM. has varying amounts of grey on head and neck and has smudges on sides of chest. The bill is greyish with a black tip; imm. Blackbrowed Albatross also has a grey bill with a black tip but is a smaller bird and has a dark (not white) underwing pattern. HABITAT. Southern oceans. STATUS. Common visitor to the coast. CALL. 'Waak', a loud, raucous call. (Bloubekmalmok)

BLACKBROWED ALBATROSS *Diomedea melanophris* (12) 90 cm
Ad. has a yellow bill with a reddish tip.
SEXES alike. IMM. has grey bill with black tip, and varying amounts of grey on head and sides of neck which sometimes join to form a collar. Underwing in first year plumage is all dark but lightens with age. Underwing of imm. Greyheaded Albatross is also dark but Greyheaded has an all-dark bill. Imm. Shy and Yellownosed Albatrosses have mostly white underwings with black borders. HABITAT. Southern oceans. STATUS. Visitor along the coast throughout the year but more abundant in winter. The most common albatross in Cape waters. CALL. Grunts and squawks when squabbling over food. (Swartrugmalmok)

YELLOWNOSED ALBATROSS *Diomedea chlororhynchos* (14) 80 cm
The smallest and most slender of the 'dark-backed' albatrosses.
AD. of Gough Island race has a grey wash on head and nape but differs from ad. Greyheaded Albatross in that the yellow on the bill is confined to the ridge of the upper mandible and the crown is white. SEXES alike. IMM. differs from all other imm. albatrosses by a combination of its all-black bill and white head. Underwing in ad. and imm. differs from Blackbrowed and Greyheaded Albatrosses by having narrower black borders. HABITAT. Southern oceans, breeding in summer on sub-Antarctic islands. STATUS. Fairly common in all coastal waters. Most abundant off the Natal coast. CALL. Loud bill clapping and a throaty 'weeeek'. (Geelneusmalmok)

GREYHEADED ALBATROSS *Diomedea chrysostoma* (13) 89 cm
Similar in size to Blackbrowed Albatross but differs by having a grey head and a black bill with a yellow ridge along the upper and lower mandibles.
SEXES alike. IMM. In the first year, the imm.'s head is darker grey than the ad.'s but cheeks may become almost white in the second and third years, attaining the pale grey head of the ad. in its fifth year. Imm. is best separated from imm. Blackbrowed by the all-dark (not black-tipped grey) bill. HABITAT. Southern oceans, breeding during summer on sub-Antarctic islands. STATUS. Rare north of 40 °S and a vagrant to the coast during winter. CALL. Grunts and squawks when fighting over food. (Gryskopmalmok)

LAYSAN ALBATROSS *Diomedea immutabilis* (905) 80 cm
The only small albatross in which the feet project beyond the tail tip in flight. Dark upperwing, except for white flash in primaries. Pale underwing has a dark leading and trailing edge and shows a variable amount of black streaking in the centre, especially towards the inner secondaries.
SEXES alike. IMM. resembles ad. HABITAT. North Pacific Ocean. STATUS. Very rare vagrant; one record off the southern Cape. CALL. Not recorded in the region. (Laysanse Malmok)

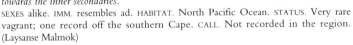

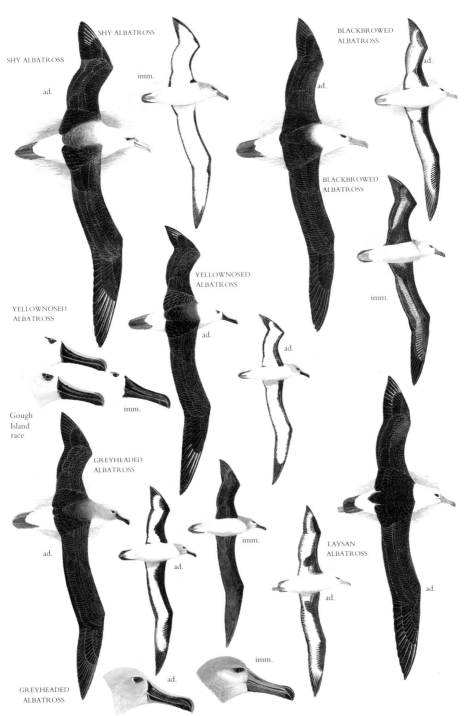

SHY ALBATROSS
ad.

SHY ALBATROSS
imm.

SHY ALBATROSS
ad.

BLACKBROWED
ALBATROSS
ad.

BLACKBROWED
ALBATROSS
ad.

BLACKBROWED
ALBATROSS
imm.

YELLOWNOSED
ALBATROSS

YELLOWNOSED
ALBATROSS
ad.

YELLOWNOSED
ALBATROSS
ad.

imm.

Gough
Island
race

GREYHEADED
ALBATROSS

ad.

ad.

imm.

LAYSAN
ALBATROSS
ad.

ad.

imm.

GREYHEADED
ALBATROSS

ad.

imm.

SOUTHERN GIANT PETREL *Macronectes giganteus* (17) 90 cm

This species has an all-white form which is unknown in Northern Giant Petrel, otherwise these two species are very similar and can only be identified with certainty at close range.
They are both large (the size of a small albatross), with heavy, pale-coloured bills (Southern Giant has a fleshy green bill with a darker green tip). Flight is less graceful than that of the albatrosses: a heavy-bodied, stiff-winged, clumsy flapping motion. SEXES alike. IMM. dark brown to black, becomes lighter with age; all-white form fledges white and remains so. HABITAT. Southern oceans. Scavenges around seal colonies off the Cape and Namibian coasts. STATUS. Common visitor to coastal waters. CALL. Harsh grunts when squabbling over food. (Reusenellie)

NORTHERN GIANT PETREL *Macronectes halli* (18) 90 cm

A flesh-coloured bill, tinged with green and with a reddish-brown tip, distinguishes this species from Southern Giant Petrel. The dark plumage is very variable in both species but tends more to grey in Northern Giant Petrel.
SEXES alike. IMM. uniform very dark brown, lightens with age. HABITAT. Southern oceans. Occurs more frequently than Southern Giant Petrel at seal colonies. STATUS. A common visitor, chiefly to the west coast. CALL. Similar to that of Southern Giant Petrel but slightly higher pitched. (Grootnellie)

LIGHTMANTLED SOOTY ALBATROSS *Phoebetria palpebrata* (16) 86 cm

Differs from Darkmantled Sooty Albatross by having an ashy-grey mantle which contrasts with darker head, wings and tail. The dark bill has a pale blue stripe on the lower mandible.
SEXES alike. IMM. is paler than imm. Darkmantled Sooty and the mottling on the back extends on to the lower back and rump. HABITAT. Southern oceans. A more southerly distribution than Darkmantled Sooty, rarely straying north of 45 °S. STATUS. Very rare vagrant. CALL. Silent at sea. (Swartkopmalmok)

DARKMANTLED SOOTY ALBATROSS *Phoebetria fusca* (15) 86 cm

An all-dark, very slender albatross with long narrow wings and an elongated, wedge-shaped tail which is usually held closed and appears pointed.
The back is uniformly dark, matching the upperwings. At close range the dark bill shows a cream to yellow stripe on the lower mandible and there is an incomplete white ring around the eye. SEXES alike. IMM. of both *Phoebetria* albatrosses are difficult to tell apart but this species has a conspicuous buff collar and mottling on the back. Might be mistaken for a giant petrel but that species has a short rounded tail, much shorter wings and a heavy-bodied appearance. HABITAT. Southern oceans, seldom north of 40 °S. STATUS. A rare winter vagrant. CALL. Silent at sea. (Bruinmalmok)

SOUTHERN
GIANT PETREL

ad.

NORTHERN
GIANT PETREL

ad.

NORTHERN
GIANT PETREL

imm.

SOUTHERN
GIANT PETREL

ad.

NORTHERN
GIANT PETREL

ad.

white
form

SOUTHERN
GIANT PETREL

LIGHTMANTLED
SOOTY ALBATROSS

ad.

ad.

DARKMANTLED
SOOTY ALBATROSS

ad.

imm.

imm.

ad.

ad.

DARKMANTLED
SOOTY ALBATROSS

LIGHTMANTLED
SOOTY ALBATROSS

WHITECHINNED PETREL *Procellaria aequinoctialis* (32) 54 cm
Differs from all other dark brown petrels by its large size and long, robust, pale greenish-horn bill with black saddle. The white chin varies in extent: it may encompass the whole throat and cheeks or may be absent. At long range resembles most other all-dark shearwaters and petrels but is darker brown in colour and the bill is always pale, sometimes showing as white. Race conspicillata *has more extensive white on sides of head, giving a spectacled appearance.*
SEXES alike. HABITAT. Southern oceans, breeding on sub-Antarctic islands. STATUS. A common visitor, exceptionally abundant over the trawling grounds of the western Cape where it competes aggressively with albatrosses for offal. CALL. Utters a screaming 'titititititi' when squabbling over food. (Bassiaan)

FLESHFOOTED SHEARWATER *Puffinus carneipes* (36) 49 cm
A dark brown shearwater with a dark-tipped, flesh-coloured bill and flesh-coloured legs and feet. Its larger size and dark underwing separate it from Sooty Shearwater, while its larger size, its bill and leg colour, and rounded tail distinguish it from Wedgetailed Shearwater. At long range, if the feet are visible they appear as a pale-coloured area on the vent.
SEXES alike. HABITAT. Coastal waters of the eastern Cape and Natal. STATUS. Present in small numbers throughout the year. CALL. Silent at sea. (Bruinpylstormvoël)

WEDGETAILED SHEARWATER *Puffinus pacificus* (41) 45 cm
Similar to Fleshfooted Shearwater in colour and size but lacks that species' flesh-coloured bill and feet. The tail is wedge-shaped but appears pointed in flight. Sooty Shearwater is larger, has a silvery underwing and lacks the pointed tail.
SEXES alike. HABITAT. Tropical and subtropical oceans. STATUS. Rare vagrant to Natal and the eastern Cape. CALL. Silent at sea. (Keilstertpylstormvoël)

SOOTY SHEARWATER *Puffinus griseus* (37) 46 cm
Differentiated from all other dark shearwaters by the silvery lining to the underwing. Wing beats are rapid, interspersed with short glides.
SEXES alike. HABITAT. Most abundant in Cape coastal waters where it forages on small shoaling fish. STATUS. Common throughout the year; most abundant in early spring. CALL. Silent at sea. (Malbaatjie)

GREATWINGED PETREL *Pterodroma macroptera* (23) 42 cm
A dark brown petrel which differs from similarly sized Sooty Shearwater by having a dark (not silvery) underwing and from the much larger Whitechinned Petrel by having a short black bill. In flight, the wings are held at a sharp angle at the wrist and the head appears heavy and downward pointing.
Flight action in strong winds is fast and dynamic: twisting, turning and wheeling in high arcs over the sea. SEXES alike. HABITAT. Southern oceans, breeding on sub-Antarctic islands. STATUS. Common visitor, chiefly in spring and summer. CALL. Silent at sea. A harsh, piercing 'keea-kee-kee-kee' is uttered over breeding grounds at night. (Langvlerkstormvoël)

KERGUELEN PETREL *Pterodroma brevirostris* (27) 34 cm
Very similar to Greatwinged Petrel in outline shape but is smaller and is greyish (not dark brown).
The head appears unusually large in this species and the sharp angle of the forehead shadows the face, imparting a hooded appearance in some lights. The dark underwings have pale areas on the leading edge and centre which reflect light and appear silvery. In a manner unusual for a petrel, this species flies very high over the ocean and sometimes hangs into the wind, much like a huge swift. SEXES alike. HABITAT. Southern oceans, breeding on sub-Antarctic islands in the summer. STATUS. Irregular winter vagrant, with most records being beached victims. CALL. Silent at sea. (Kerguelense Stormvoël)

WHITECHINNED
PETREL

FLESHFOOTED
SHEARWATER

WEDGETAILED
SHEARWATER

WHITECHINNED
PETREL

conspicillata

SOOTY
SHEARWATER

WEDGETAILED
SHEARWATER

SOOTY SHEARWATER

SOOTY
SHEARWATER

GREATWINGED
PETREL

KERGUELEN PETREL

GREATWINGED
PETREL

ANTARCTIC FULMAR *Fulmarus glacialoides* (19) 48 cm

A very pale grey, gull-sized petrel, with white underparts and white wing flashes at the base of the primaries. At close range the pink bill with its dark tip is diagnostic. Unlikely to be confused with any other petrel in the region.
SEXES alike. HABITAT. Southern oceans, breeding in the far south on Antarctic islands and mainland. STATUS. Uncommon winter visitor. Most frequently seen in western Cape trawling grounds where it scavenges offal. CALL. Utters a high-pitched cackle when squabbling over food. (Silwerstormvoël)

ANTARCTIC PETREL *Thalassoica antarctica* (20) 44 cm

Vaguely resembles Pintado Petrel but lacks the chequered back of that species and shows a conspicuous white stripe in each wing.
The head is dark and the white tail is narrowly tipped black. Underparts white. During the 24-hour sunlight of the Antarctic summer, the dark brown coloration bleaches to pale brown. SEXES alike. HABITAT. Antarctica, rarely north of the pack ice. STATUS. Very rare vagrant. CALL. Usually silent at sea and at the pack ice. (Antarktiese Stormvoël)

PINTADO PETREL *Daption capense* (21) 40 cm

A medium-sized black and white petrel with chequering on the back and two circular white patches on each upperwing.
The head is black and the tail white with a black tip. Throat is grizzled and the underparts are white. Underwing is white, narrowly bordered with black. SEXES alike. HABITAT. Southern oceans, breeding on islands in the Antarctic and sub-Antarctic. STATUS. Common winter visitor, being extremely abundant on the western Cape trawling grounds. CALL. When feeding, utters a high-pitched 'cheechee-cheechee'. (Seeduifstormvoël)

ATLANTIC PETREL *Pterodroma incerta* (26) 44 cm

Similar in size and shape to Whiteheaded Petrel, this is a dark brown bird with a conspicuous white lower breast and belly.
In worn plumage, the breast and throat can appear mottled brown but never pure white. The upperparts are a uniform dark chocolate brown with no suggestion of an open 'M' on the upperwings. SEXES alike. HABITAT. Southern Atlantic Ocean where it is an endemic breeder on the Tristan archipelago. STATUS. Extremely rare in the region with most records from the western Cape. One record from Natal. CALL. Silent at sea. (Bruinvlerkstormvoël)

WHITEHEADED PETREL *Pterodroma lessonii* (25) 46 cm

The white head has distinctive black lozenge-shaped patches around the eyes. Underparts white with contrasting dark grey underwings. Distinguished from the similarly patterned Grey Petrel (p. 46) by its white head and undertail. Upperwings greyish brown with a faint, darker, open 'M' pattern across the wings. An easily identified petrel with a fast, high-arcing flight action. Rarely attracted to ships.
SEXES alike. HABITAT. Southern oceans, not breeding near the region. Rarely ventures north of 40 °S. STATUS. Rare winter vagrant. CALL. Silent at sea. (Witkopstormvoël)

SOFTPLUMAGED PETREL *Pterodroma mollis* (24) 35 cm

Resembles Atlantic Petrel but is much smaller and has a white throat. Dark brown smudges on sides of breast form a complete breast band. The white underparts contrast with the dark underwings. Upperparts are dark with a faint, darker, open 'M' pattern across the upperwings. The rare dark form resembles Kerguelen Petrel (p. 40) but has broader, more rounded wings and is mottled on the belly. Does not have the same high-flying action as Kerguelen Petrel.
SEXES alike. HABITAT. Southern oceans, breeding on sub-Antarctic islands. STATUS. The most common 'gadfly' petrel on the Cape and Natal coasts, chiefly in winter and spring. CALL. Silent at sea. (Donsveerstormvoël)

ANTARCTIC FULMAR

ANTARCTIC PETREL

ATLANTIC PETREL

PINTADO PETREL

WHITEHEADED PETREL

SOFTPLUMAGED PETREL

dark form

SOFTPLUMAGED
PETREL

43

BLUE PETREL *Halobaena caerulea* (28) 30 cm
A small blue-grey petrel with white underparts and underwings. Diagnostic features are the black markings on the crown and nape, and the square-ended, white-tipped tail. The open 'M' pattern on the upperwings is less distinct than on the prions. This species flies faster and arcs higher over the waves than the prions.
SEXES alike. HABITAT. Southern oceans, seldom straying north of 40 °S. STATUS. Irregular winter vagrant, most records being beach-wrecked victims. CALL. Silent at sea. (Bloustormvoël)

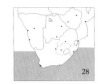

BROADBILLED PRION *Pachyptila vittata* (29) 30 cm
The largest of the prions, it is identifiable at sea only if seen at very close range when the broad, flattened bill is diagnostic. Other characters to look for are the unusually large head and broad grey smudges on the sides of the breast.
Taxonomic research has shown that this species includes Dove Prion *P.v. desolata* and Salvin's Prion *P.v. salvini*. SEXES alike. HABITAT. Southern oceans, breeding on the Tristan and Prince Edward islands. STATUS. The race *desolata*, which is smaller billed than the nominate *vittata*, is the most abundant prion along the coast in winter. Subject to 'wrecks', when thousands of corpses are washed ashore. CALL. Silent at sea. A loud, raspy dove-like cooing is given from the nest chamber. (Breëbekwalvisvoël)

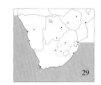

SLENDERBILLED PRION *Pachyptila belcheri* (30) 27 cm
Distinguished with difficulty from Broadbilled Prion but is generally much paler, especially around the head, and lacks the broad grey smudges on the sides of the breast. When seen at close quarters the very thin bill is diagnostic.
SEXES alike. HABITAT. Southern oceans, with a far more southerly distribution than other prions. STATUS. Rare winter vagrant. CALL. Silent at sea. (Dunbekwalvisvoël)

FAIRY PRION *Pachyptila turtur* (31) 24 cm
The smallest prion in the region and the one most easily identified. In coloration more blue, less grey than other prions with a very pale head and a diagnostic broad black tip to the tail. All other prions have narrow black tail bands.
SEXES alike. HABITAT. Southern oceans, breeding on the Prince Edward group of islands. STATUS. Rare winter vagrant. CALL. Silent at sea. (Swartstertwalvisvoël)

MATSUDAIRA'S STORM PETREL *Oceanodroma matsudairae* (918) 25 cm
In the region, this large, dark storm petrel could be mistaken only for Bulwer's Petrel. Matsudaira's Petrel is slightly smaller, and has a deeply forked tail, not the pointed tail of Bulwer's Petrel. Sometimes in flight shows a noticeable white crescentic flash at the base of the primaries.
SEXES alike. HABITAT. Open ocean. STATUS. Very rare vagrant to the east coast. CALL. Probably silent at sea. (Matsudairase Stormvoël)

BULWER'S PETREL *Bulweria bulwerii* (22) 27 cm
A small, prion-sized petrel which is uniformly dark brown and has a diagnostic long, wedge-shaped tail which is usually held closed and appears pointed. A pale grey-brown stripe runs across each upperwing on the edges of the secondary coverts. Flight is buoyant and graceful, with the bird swooping over wave tops, then dipping into the next trough.
SEXES alike. HABITAT. Open ocean, seldom close to shore. Breeds on islands in the North Atlantic. STATUS. Very rare vagrant. CALL. Silent at sea. (Bulwerse Stormvoël)

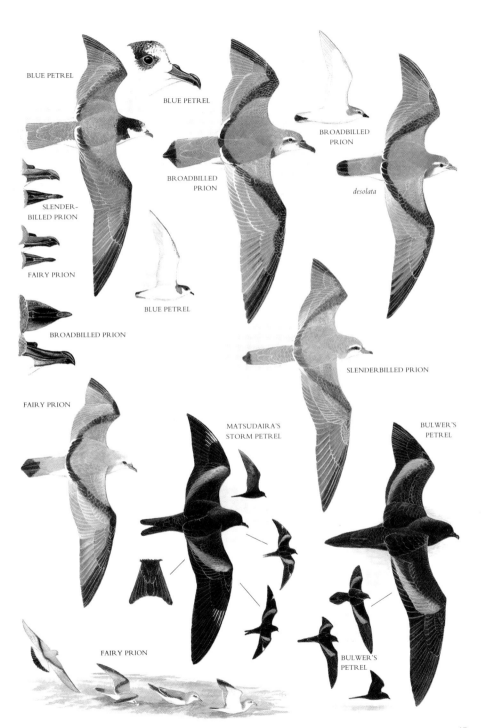

BLUE PETREL

BLUE PETREL

BROADBILLED
PRION

SLENDER-
BILLED PRION

BROADBILLED
PRION

desolata

FAIRY PRION

BLUE PETREL

BROADBILLED PRION

SLENDERBILLED PRION

FAIRY PRION

FAIRY PRION

MATSUDAIRA'S
STORM PETREL

BULWER'S
PETREL

FAIRY PRION

BULWER'S
PETREL

GREY PETREL *Procellaria cinerea* (33) 48 cm
This large brown and white petrel resembles Cory's Shearwater from which it is easily distinguished by having a dark underwing and tail.
The grey-brown of the head extends very low on the cheeks, leaving only a narrow white throat patch, with the result that at long range this species can appear dark headed. In flight, has shallow, stiff wing beats and a more direct flight action than other shearwaters, with less banking and shearing. SEXES alike. HABITAT. Southern oceans, breeding on the Tristan and Prince Edward groups of islands. STATUS. Rare winter vagrant. CALL. Silent at sea. (Pediunker)

CORY'S SHEARWATER *Calonectris diomedea* (34) 45 cm
The ashy brown upperparts and lack of a dark-capped effect or pale collar distinguish this large, heavy-bodied species from Great Shearwater. At close range shows a yellow bill, and individuals display varying amounts of white on the rump. Has a slower, more laboured flight than Great Shearwater and flies lower over the sea, not shearing and banking as much as other shearwaters.
SEXES alike. HABITAT. Open oceans in both the North and South Atlantic. Forages close inshore on small schooling fish. STATUS. Common summer visitor to the coast. CALL. Silent at sea. (Geelbekpylstormvoël)

GREAT SHEARWATER *Puffinus gravis* (35) 46 cm
Similar in size to Cory's Shearwater but distinguished by its distinctive dark cap, barred brown and buff back, dark smudge on lower belly and less marked white underwing. Flight action is more dynamic than Cory's Shearwater, flying higher over waves with more rapid wing beats.
SEXES alike. HABITAT. Open ocean, seldom close inshore, in North and South Atlantic. STATUS. Endemic breeder on Tristan archipelago. Common in Cape waters in early and late summer. CALL. Silent at sea. (Grootpylstormvoël)

MANX SHEARWATER *Puffinus puffinus* (38) 36 cm
After the Little and Audubon's, the smallest shearwater of the region. It is all black above and white below with white underwings.
Larger than Little Shearwater, it has a more extensive black cap which extends below the eye and a less fluttering flight. Flight action consists of long glides interspersed with a series of rapid wing beats. SEXES alike. HABITAT. Open seas in North and South Atlantic. Mainly coastal in the western Cape. STATUS. Uncommon visitor, chiefly in summer. CALL. Silent at sea. (Swartbekpylstormvoël)

AUDUBON'S SHEARWATER *Puffinus lherminieri* (40) 28 cm
In the field difficult to distinguish from Little Shearwater. In good light, this species' dark (not white) undertail coverts can be seen.
The sub-Antarctic race of Little Shearwater is dark grey above and can appear brownish: it is doubtful if this race and Audubon's Shearwater can be separated reliably in the field unless the undertail character were seen. SEXES alike. HABITAT. Tropical and subtropical oceans. STATUS. Rare vagrant to Natal, especially in late summer during cyclonic conditions. CALL. Silent at sea. (Swartkroonpylstormvoël)

LITTLE SHEARWATER *Puffinus assimilis* (39) 27 cm
This and Audubon's Shearwater are the smallest shearwaters of the region. Very similar to Manx Shearwater but distinguished by its smaller size, dumpier shape, shorter wings and its flight action of very rapid wing beats punctuated by short glides. At close range the black cap ending above the eye and giving the bird a white-faced appearance, can be seen (inset illustration). Sub-Antarctic race has dark face but is dark grey (not black).
SEXES alike. HABITAT. Open oceans in mixed flocks of Sooty Shearwaters and Cape Gannets. STATUS. Rare winter visitor to the south-western Cape coast. CALL. Silent at sea. (Kleinpylstormvoël)

GREY PETREL

CORY'S
SHEARWATER

GREY PETREL

CORY'S SHEARWATER

GREAT
SHEARWATER

GREAT
SHEARWATER

MANX
SHEARWATER

AUDUBON'S SHEARWATER

LITTLE SHEARWATER
tunneyi

47

WILSON'S STORM PETREL *Oceanites oceanicus* (44) 18 cm

Differs from all other storm petrels in wing shape and flight action. Larger than European Storm Petrel, with broader, more rounded and flattened wings and long spindly legs, usually held projecting beyond end of tail. Yellow webbing on feet cannot be seen when the bird is in flight. Flight is swallow-like and action is direct with frequent glides. Long legs dangle in water when feeding.
SEXES alike. HABITAT. Open oceans, breeding in Antarctica and on sub-Antarctic islands. STATUS. Abundant visitor along the coast throughout the year but chiefly during winter. CALL. Silent at sea. (Geelpootstormswael)

LEACH'S STORM PETREL *Oceanodroma leucorhoa* (43) 20 cm

Larger than European Storm Petrel. Best identified by long, narrow wings and distinctive flight action: it bounds low over the waves with quick jerky movements and sudden directional changes. When the bird spreads its tail, a clear fork can be seen.
SEXES alike. HABITAT. Open oceans in the North and South Atlantic. STATUS. Rare summer visitor to oceanic waters, mainly off the west coast. CALL. Silent in the region. (Swaelstertstormswael)

EUROPEAN STORM PETREL *Hydrobates pelagicus* (42) 15 cm

The smallest seabird in the region. It commonly occurs in large flocks and the black plumage, white rump and white flash on the underwing help identify it. The feet do not project beyond the end of the tail in flight, which is bat-like and direct. The bird sometimes hovers, pattering its feet over the water when feeding.
SEXES alike. HABITAT. Coastal waters of the North and South Atlantic. STATUS. Common summer visitor to Cape and Natal coastal waters. CALL. Silent in the region. (Swartpootstormswael)

BLACKBELLIED STORM PETREL *Fregetta tropica* (46) 20 cm

Larger than Wilson's Storm Petrel from which it differs by having white underwings and white belly with a broad black line down the centre. Distinguished from Whitebellied Storm Petrel by appearing much darker and by the black line down its belly; both species share similar flight characteristics, bounding over the waves and, when feeding, appearing to bounce off waves on their breasts.
SEXES alike. HABITAT. Southern oceans. STATUS. A fairly common passage migrant off the south-west Cape during spring and late summer. CALL. Silent at sea. (Swartstreepstormswael)

WHITEBELLIED STORM PETREL *Fregetta grallaria* (45) 20 cm
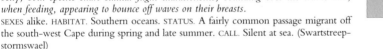
Very difficult to distinguish from Blackbellied Storm Petrel but always appears much paler, has the back feathers edged with grey and the totally white belly extending on to the vent and undertail coverts. Accompanies ships, where it is seen more often in the bow waves than in the wake.
SEXES alike. HABITAT. Southern oceans. STATUS. Rare vagrant to the Cape and Natal coasts. CALL. Silent at sea. (Witpensstormswael)

WILSON'S STORM PETREL

LEACH'S STORM PETREL

EUROPEAN STORM PETREL

BLACKBELLIED
STORM PETREL

WHITEBELLIED
STORM PETREL

49

REDTAILED TROPICBIRD *Phaethon rubricauda* (47) 50 cm
Ad. is almost pure white (tinged pink when breeding) with a stout red bill and two extremely long, wispy, red central tail feathers (not easily visible at long range).
SEXES alike. IMM. differs from imm. Whitetailed Tropicbird by being more barred on the back and by having more black on the wings. HABITAT. Tropical oceans and Indian Ocean islands. STATUS. A rare summer visitor to the eastern shores. CALL. Various grunts and cackles, and a deep 'kraak', resembling Caspian Tern. (Rooipylstert)

REDBILLED TROPICBIRD *Phaethon aethereus* (910) 46–50 cm
Ad. distinguished from ad. Redtailed Tropicbird by having a finely barred back which appears grey at a distance and long, white (not red) tail streamers.
SEXES alike. IMM. has heavily barred upperparts, and a broad black stripe through the eye to the nape. HABITAT. Oceanic islands and open sea. STATUS. Very rare vagrant. CALL. Largely silent at sea. (Rooibekpylstert)

WHITETAILED TROPICBIRD *Phaethon lepturus* (48) 44 cm
Ad. differs from ad. Redtailed Tropicbird by having two black patches on each wing and two elongated white central tail feathers which are conspicuous even at long range. The bill is orange-yellow in both ad. and imm.
SEXES alike. IMM. smaller than imm. Redtailed Tropicbird, which differs further by having solid black (not greyish) tips to the wings. HABITAT. Tropical oceans and islands. STATUS. Vagrant. CALL. Silent in the region. (Witpylstert)

BROWN BOOBY *Sula leucogaster* (52) 70 cm
Ad. is brown with a white lower breast and belly and a broad white stripe on the otherwise brown underwings extending from the body to the carpal region. Similar to imm. Cape Gannet, it has a long, cigar-shaped body outline, and a pointed bill and tail. The boundary between brown and white on the breast is clearly defined.
SEXES alike. IMM. is a paler version of ad. and has white belly flecked with brown. Lacks the white speckling of imm. Cape Gannet. HABITAT. Tropical oceans and islands. STATUS. Vagrant. CALL. Usually silent at sea. (Bruinmalgas)

REDFOOTED BOOBY *Sula dactylatra* (921) 81–92 cm
Brown morph confusable only with imm. Cape Gannet but is smaller and slimmer, has a much longer, pointed tail, and at close range shows vermilion feet and blue bill. White morph very similar to ad. Cape Gannet but has similar structural differences and has an all-white (not black) tail. In flight white morph shows a black carpal patch on the underwing, and vermilion feet.
SEXES alike. IMM. has greyish-yellow feet and a pinkish-blue bill. HABITAT. Tropical oceans. STATUS. Probably regular in tropical Mozambique and Namibian waters. CALL. Not recorded in the region. (Rooipootmalgas)

CAPE GANNET *Morus capensis* (53) 85 cm
Ad. is white with black flight feathers and a black, pointed tail. The bill is heavy, long, pointed and pale grey, while the nape and sides of neck are straw yellow.
SEXES alike. IMM. progresses through mottled brown and white stages when it could be confused with Brown Booby which is smaller and always shows a brown bib and white belly. HABITAT. Coastal. Breeds on islands off the Cape and Namibia. STATUS. Common resident; breeding endemic. CALL. When feeding in flocks at sea, the birds give a 'warrra-warrra-warrra' call. (Witmalgas)

AUSTRALIAN GANNET *Morus serrator* (54) 85 cm
Almost identical to Cape Gannet but has a higher pitched call, a darker blue eye and a gular stripe only one third the length of that of Cape Gannet.
SEXES alike. IMM. indistinguishable from imm. Cape Gannet except by gular stripe length. HABITAT. Coastal. STATUS. Vagrant. CALL. Similar to Cape Gannet but higher pitched. (Australiese Malgas)

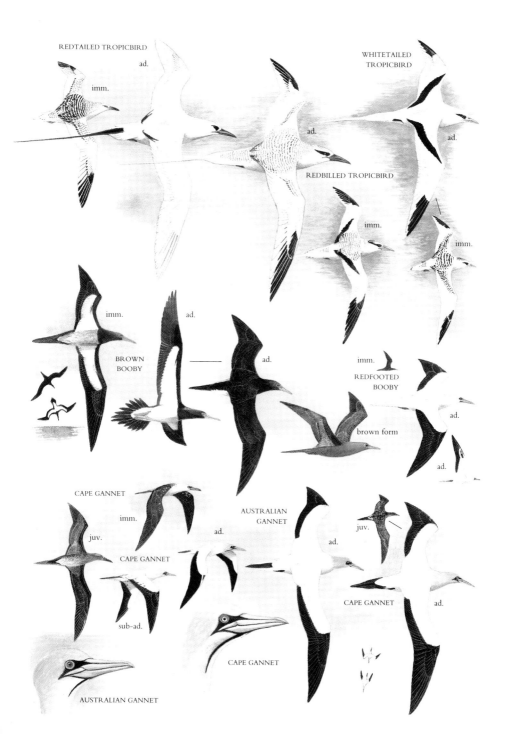

REDTAILED TROPICBIRD

ad.

imm.

WHITETAILED
TROPICBIRD

ad.

ad.

ad.

REDBILLED TROPICBIRD

imm.

imm.

imm.

ad.

BROWN
BOOBY

ad.

imm.

REDFOOTED
BOOBY

brown form

ad.

ad.

CAPE GANNET

imm.

juv.

AUSTRALIAN
GANNET

juv.

ad.

ad.

CAPE GANNET

sub-ad.

CAPE GANNET

CAPE GANNET

ad.

AUSTRALIAN GANNET

51

WHITEBREASTED CORMORANT *Phalacrocorax carbo* (55) 90 cm
The largest cormorant of the region. Ad. is glossy black with a white throat and breast, and a bright yellow patch at the base of the bill. During the breeding season has white flank patches.
SEXES alike. IMM. is dark brown with white underparts. HABITAT. Coastal and fresh waters. STATUS. Locally common resident. Roosts and breeds colonially. CALL. Silent except at breeding colonies when grunts and squeals are uttered. (Witborsduiker)

BANK CORMORANT *Phalacrocorax neglectus* (57) 76 cm
Larger and more robust than Cape Cormorant from which it differs by having dull black plumage and a thick woolly-textured neck, and by lacking the yellow facial skin. Eye and bill dark. In breeding plumage shows white flecks on head and a diagnostic white rump.
A small tuft of feathers on the forehead is erectile, giving the appearance of a small, rounded crest. SEXES alike. IMM. lacks white plumage flecks and has a dull-coloured eye. HABITAT. Coastal waters of the western Cape, and islands off the Namibian coast. STATUS. Resident; endemic. Common in small parties on offshore islands in Benguela current. CALL. Normally silent except at colonies. Call is a wheezy 'wheeee' given when bird alights near nest. (Bankduiker)

CAPE CORMORANT *Phalacrocorax capensis* (56) 65 cm
Intermediate in size between Bank and Crowned Cormorants. Ad. has glossy blue-black plumage with a bright yellow-orange patch at base of bill. The patch brightens during the breeding season.
SEXES alike. IMM. is dark brown with slightly paler underparts. HABITAT. A flock-feeding marine cormorant which enters harbours and estuaries. STATUS. Resident; breeding endemic. CALL. Silent except during the breeding season when various 'gaaaa' and 'geeee' noises are uttered. (Trekduiker)

REED CORMORANT *Phalacrocorax africanus* (58) 52 cm
A small black cormorant with pale spotting on back, and a long, unmarked tail. In breeding plumage ad. has a yellow-orange face patch and throat, and a small crest on forehead. A freshwater cormorant rarely seen at the coast.
SEXES alike. IMM. is dark brown above and white below. HABITAT. Freshwater dams, lakes and rivers. Roosts and breeds colonially. STATUS. Common resident. CALL. Silent except for cackling and hissing at breeding colonies. (Rietduiker)

CROWNED CORMORANT *Phalacrocorax coronatus* (59) 50 cm
Very like Reed Cormorant but differs by having an orange-red face and throat patch in breeding dress.
The erectile crest on the forehead is longer and more pronounced than that of Reed Cormorant, but the tail is shorter. SEXES alike. IMM. is dark brown above and differs from imm. Reed Cormorant by its shorter tail and brown (not white) underparts. HABITAT. Almost entirely marine, on islands off west coast and in estuaries and lagoons in the western Cape. STATUS. Locally common resident; endemic. CALL. Silent except for croaking sounds at breeding colonies. (Kuifkopduiker)

DARTER *Anhinga melanogaster* (60) 80 cm
The long egret-like neck, combined with slender head and elongated, pointed bill, should rule out confusion with cormorants.
BREEDING MALE shows rufous head and neck with long white stripe running from eye on to neck. FEMALE and NON-BREEDING MALE are pale brown on face and throat. When swimming, sometimes totally submerges body, leaving only its long neck and head showing, scything through the water with serpentine movements. IMM. shows buffy neck, more streaking on head and neck and lacks streaking on back. HABITAT. Freshwater dams, lakes and slow-moving streams; sometimes coastal lagoons and estuaries. STATUS. Common resident. CALL. A distinctive croaking. (Slanghalsvoël)

imm.

br.

ad.

WHITEBREASTED
CORMORANT

BANK CORMORANT

CAPE CORMORANT

CAPE
CORMORANT

imm.

CAPE
CORMORANT

CROWNED CORMORANT

ad.

ad.

REED
CORMORANT

imm.

DARTER

imm.

ad.

DARTER

CROWNED
CORMORANT
imm.

CROWNED
CORMORANT

REED CORMORANT

male br.

GREATER FRIGATEBIRD *Fregata minor* (61) 95 cm
A black bird with very long, pointed wings. The elongated forked tail appears pointed when held closed.
MALE is all-black with a red throat pouch and it lacks the white 'armpits' of male Lesser Frigatebird. FEMALE shows white breast and throat and a grey chin. IMM. has whitish or tawny head and white breast. HABITAT. Tropical seas and islands. STATUS. Rare vagrant recorded in late summer on east coast during or after cyclonic conditions. CALL. Silent at sea. (Fregatvoël)

LESSER FRIGATEBIRD *Fregata ariel* (922) 76 cm
Male readily identified by all-black plumage with diagnostic white 'armpits' extending from axillaries to sides of breast.
FEMALE distinguished from female Greater Frigatebird by black chin and throat, noticeable white collar and white on breast extending to 'armpits'. IMM. distinguished from imm. Greater Frigatebird, but has more extensive black on the belly and white on breast extends to white 'armpits'. Although smaller and more 'angular' than Greater Frigatebird, size-based identification requires direct comparison. HABITAT. Open ocean. STATUS. Vagrant to Mozambique waters; one record. CALL. Silent at sea. (Klein Fregatvoël)

EASTERN WHITE PELICAN *Pelecanus onocrotalus* (49) 180 cm
A very large white bird which assumes a pinkish flush in the breeding season. In flight, black primaries and secondaries contrast with white coverts. The orbital skin is pink, the bill pink and yellow and the pouch yellow.
SEXES alike. IMM. is dark brown and whitens progressively with age. HABITAT. Habitually fishes in groups on open freshwater lakes. Frequents estuaries in the western Cape, Namibia and Natal. Nests on the ground, usually on flat islands, in colonies. STATUS. Locally common resident. CALL. Usually silent; a deep 'mooo'-ing call at breeding colonies. (Witpelikaan)

PINKBACKED PELICAN *Pelecanus rufescens* (50) 140 cm
Considerably smaller than Eastern White Pelican, this species differs by being greyer with a pink back, and has an all-yellow bill pouch and orbital skin. In flight the primaries and secondaries do not contrast strongly with the coverts and appear more uniform.
Has a grey crest when breeding. SEXES alike. IMM. is dark brown at first and becomes greyer with age. Best distinguished from Eastern White Pelican by size. HABITAT. Coastal estuaries, less often on fresh water. Nests in colonies in trees. Feeds solitarily. STATUS. Resident from Zululand northwards, vagrant elsewhere. CALL. Usually silent; guttural calls uttered at breeding colonies. (Kleinpelikaan)

GREATER FRIGATEBIRD

male

female

imm.

LESSER FRIGATEBIRD

male

female

GREATER FRIGATEBIRD

imm.

EASTERN WHITE PELICAN

male br.

imm.

imm.

sub-ad.

br.

ad.

ad. non-br.

EASTERN WHITE PELICAN

ad. non-br.

PINKBACKED PELICAN

br.

ad.

PINKBACKED PELICAN

PINKBACKED PELICAN

imm.

imm.

ad.

GOLIATH HERON *Ardea goliath* (64) 140 cm
Its large size is diagnostic: it is the world's largest heron. In colour most closely resembles the smaller Purple Heron, but has an unstriped head and neck and dark legs.
SEXES alike. IMM. resembles ad. but is buffier below. HABITAT. Freshwater dams, lakes and sometimes estuaries. STATUS. Locally common resident in the north and east. Usually solitary or in pairs. CALL. A loud, low-pitched 'kwaaark'. (Reuse Reier)

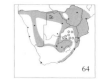

PURPLE HERON *Ardea purpurea* (65) 91 cm
Rufous head and neck and dark grey wings are distinctive; much smaller than Goliath Heron, and marked on the crown and neck with black stripes.
SEXES alike. IMM. lacks the grey nape and mantle of ad., is less streaked on the neck and has far less black on the crown. HABITAT. Aquatic, favouring sedges and reeds in freshwater and estuarine habitats: reluctant to feed in the open. STATUS. Common resident. CALL. Similar to Grey Heron's 'kraaark'. (Rooireier)

GREY HERON *Ardea cinerea* (62) 100 cm
A large, greyish heron distinguished from others by its white head and neck, and a black eye-stripe which ends on the nape in a wispy black plume. Bill yellow. In flight distinguished from Blackheaded Heron by uniform grey underwings.
SEXES alike. IMM. easily confused with imm. Blackheaded Heron but has light flanks and yellow upper legs (dark in Blackheaded Heron). HABITAT. Pans, dams, slow-flowing rivers, lagoons and estuaries. STATUS. Common resident. CALL. A harsh 'kraaunk' given in flight. (Bloureier)

BLACKHEADED HERON *Ardea melanocephala* (63) 96 cm
Slightly smaller than Grey Heron. The black-topped head and hind neck contrast with white throat. In flight the contrasting dark and pale underwing distinguishes it from Grey Heron which has a uniform grey underwing.
SEXES alike. IMM. has grey (not black) on head and neck. Distinguished from imm. Grey Heron by dark legs and thighs. HABITAT. More often seen stalking through open grasslands than around water. STATUS. Common resident. CALL. A loud 'aaaaark', and various hoarse cackles and bill clapping at nest. (Swartkopreier)

GOLIATH HERON
br.

ad.

GOLIATH HERON
imm.

PURPLE HERON
ad.

imm.

PURPLE HERON

imm.

GREY HERON

br.

GREY HERON   imm.

ad.   BLACKHEADED
HERON

imm.

ad.

YELLOWBILLED EGRET *Egretta intermedia* (68) 66 cm
Intermediate in size between Cattle and Great White Egrets. Separated from Great White Egret by noticeably shorter neck which is not held in such a pronounced 'S' shape, and by shorter bill. Gape does not extend behind the eye but ends just below it. Although not easily seen, yellowish upper legs are diagnostic.
Differs from Cattle Egret by larger size, longer bill and more slender appearance. When breeding attains long plumes on the back and chest, a red bill and upper legs. SEXES alike. IMM. like ad. HABITAT. Flooded veld and marshes and any damp grassy areas, but infrequently near open water. STATUS. Common resident. CALL. Typical heron-like 'waaaark'. (Geelbekwitreier)

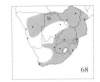

GREAT WHITE EGRET *Egretta alba* (66) 95 cm
The largest white heron of the region. Legs and feet black at all times.
Breeding bird has elaborate plumes, black bill and lime-green lores; in non-breeding plumage lacks plumes and bill is yellow. Differs from Yellowbilled Egret by its larger size, longer and heavier bill with gape extending behind the eye, and much longer, thinner neck, usually held kinked in an 'S' shape. Distinguished from Little Egret by much larger size and black (not yellow) toes. SEXES alike. IMM. like non-breeding ad. HABITAT. Freshwater dams, lakes, flooded meadows, and marine estuaries and lagoons. STATUS. Common resident. CALL. A low, heron-like 'waaaark'. (Grootwitreier)

LITTLE EGRET *Egretta garzetta* (67) 65 cm
The black legs and contrasting yellow toes distinguish this species from any other white heron in the region.
The bill is slender and always black. Feeds characteristically by dashing to and fro in shallow water in pursuit of prey. Usually forages alone: not gregarious except when breeding. (A rare black morph has been recorded elsewhere in the range.) SEXES alike. IMM. lacks the head plumes and aigrettes of ad. Toes are a duller yellow. HABITAT. Most freshwater situations and frequently along rocky coastlines and estuaries. STATUS. Common resident. CALL. A harsh 'waaark'. (Kleinwitreier)

CATTLE EGRET *Bubulcus ibis* (71) 54 cm
Breeding bird has red bill, and buff plumes on head, breast and mantle, but never becomes as dark as Squacco Heron. Bill is shorter and more robust than in other white herons and there is a noticeable shaggy bib and throat which gives this species a distinct jowl. The legs are never black, but vary from dark brown to yellowish green, and are red at the start of the breeding season.
SEXES alike. IMM. like non-breeding ad. HABITAT. Essentially non-aquatic; most often found in association with cattle or game. Highly gregarious. STATUS. Common resident. CALL. Typical heron-like 'aaaark' or 'pok-pok'. (Bosluisvoël)

SQUACCO HERON *Ardeola ralloides* (72) 42 cm
The smallest white heron of the region. At rest, looks more bittern-like but in flight shows all-white wings. Unlikely to be confused with Cattle Egret because of its very buffy appearance and its habits.
SEXES alike. IMM. browner on mantle and more streaked below than ad. HABITAT. Vegetated margins of freshwater lakes, pans and slow-moving rivers. Skulks in reedbeds and long grass, sitting motionless for long periods. STATUS. Common resident. CALL. Low-pitched, rattling 'kek-kek-kek'. (Ralreier)

MADAGASCAR SQUACCO HERON *Ardeola idae* (73) 47 cm
Breeding plumage is completely white. In non-breeding dress very difficult to distinguish from Squacco Heron but is slightly larger, has a noticeably heavier bill and much broader streaking on the throat and breast.
SEXES alike. IMM. like non-breeding ad. HABITAT. Similar to Squacco Heron but is found more often in open situations. STATUS. Vagrant to the region; only one record, from Zimbabwe. CALL. Usually silent. (Malgassiese Ralreier)

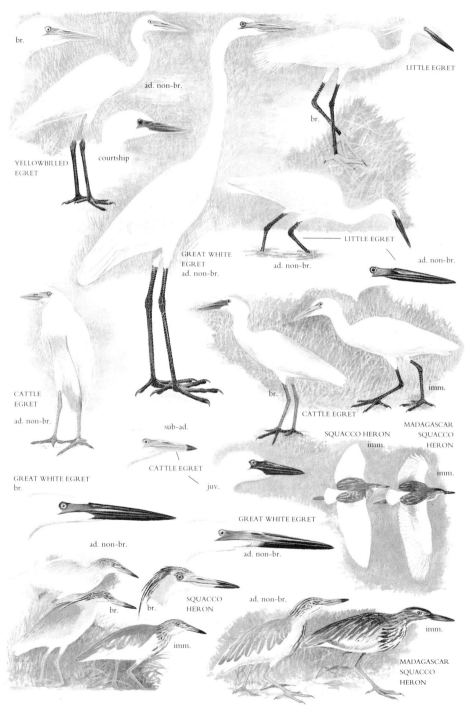

br.

ad. non-br.

LITTLE EGRET

br.

YELLOWBILLED
EGRET

courtship

LITTLE EGRET

GREAT WHITE
EGRET
ad. non-br.

ad. non-br.

ad. non-br.

CATTLE
EGRET

ad. non-br.

sub-ad.

br.

imm.

CATTLE EGRET

SQUACCO HERON
imm.

MADAGASCAR
SQUACCO
HERON

GREAT WHITE EGRET
br.

CATTLE EGRET

juv.

imm.

GREAT WHITE EGRET

ad. non-br.

ad. non-br.

ad. non-br.

br.

br.

SQUACCO
HERON

imm.

imm.

MADAGASCAR
SQUACCO
HERON

59

BLACK EGRET *Egretta ardesiaca* (69) 66 cm
A small, slate-black version of Little Egret (p. 58), with black legs and yellow toes. Lacks the rufous throat of Slaty Egret. Diagnostic feeding behaviour of forming an 'umbrella' over the head with wings held forward and outstretched. Has long nape and breast plumes.
SEXES alike. IMM. slightly paler than ad. and lacks long plumes. HABITAT. Freshwater lakes and dams, occasionally estuaries. STATUS. Resident with local movements. Rare to locally common. CALL. Seldom calls, a deep 'kraak'. (Swartreier)

SLATY EGRET *Egretta vinaceigula* (70) 60 cm
Very similar to Little Egret (p. 58) in shape and behaviour. In colour resembles Black Egret but differs by having greenish-yellow legs and feet, a rufous throat and by lacking the wing-canopy feeding action.
SEXES alike. IMM. like ad. HABITAT. Tropical wetlands. STATUS. Resident; uncommon and confined to upper reaches of Zambezi River and the Okavango swamps; vagrant to Zimbabwe and Transvaal. CALL. Unknown. (Rooikeelreier)

RUFOUSBELLIED HERON *Ardeola rufiventris* (75) 58 cm
A small heron with a sooty black head and breast, and rufous belly, wings and tail. In flight the bright yellow legs and feet contrast strongly with dark underparts.
FEMALE is duller than male. IMM. is dull brown, not rufous. HABITAT. Seasonal wetlands with sedges or grasses. Normally only seen when put to flight. STATUS. Uncommon summer visitor in the east but resident further north. CALL. Typical heron-like 'waaaaak'. (Rooipensreier)

WHITEBACKED NIGHT HERON *Gorsachius leuconotus* (77) 53 cm
The large dark head with conspicuous pale eye area, dark back and wings render this species unmistakable. The small white patch on the back is visible in flight and during display.
SEXES alike. IMM. distinguished from imm. Blackcrowned Night Heron (p. 62) by having a darker crown and an unmarked face, and from Bittern (p. 62) by lack of black moustachial stripes. HABITAT. Slow-moving streams and rivers overhung with thick tangles of reeds and trees. STATUS. Resident; an easily overlooked, uncommon species confined to the east and north. CALL. When disturbed gives a sharp 'kaaark'. (Witrugnagreier)

foraging

BLACK EGRET

SLATY EGRET

ad.

ad.

imm.

RUFOUSBELLIED HERON

ad.

imm.

imm.

WHITEBACKED NIGHT
HERON
ad.

imm.

imm.

ad.

imm.

BITTERN *Botaurus stellaris* (80) 64 cm
The largest bittern, it is more often heard than seen. The upperparts are streaked buff-brown and black with a dark crown and broad, conspicuous moustachial stripes. Underparts buff, heavily streaked dark brown. The black moustachial stripes and tawny (not grey) overall colour should eliminate confusion with imm. Blackcrowned Night Heron.
SEXES alike. IMM. like ad. HABITAT. Reed- and sedge beds and flooded grassland. STATUS. Rare resident. CALL. Deep, resonant booming, 3-5 syllables, reminiscent of grunting of distant lion. (Grootrietreier)

BLACKCROWNED NIGHT HERON *Nycticorax nycticorax* (76) 56 cm
The black crown, nape and back contrast greatly with grey wings and tail, and white underparts.
SEXES alike. IMM. superficially resembles Bittern but is pale grey (not tawny-coloured), and lacks black crown and moustachial stripes. HABITAT. Freshwater dams, streams and lagoons. During the day, flocks roost in reedbeds and trees, venturing out at dusk to feed. STATUS. Common resident. CALL. A characteristic harsh 'kwok' when flying to and from roosts. (Gewone Nagreier)

GREENBACKED HERON *Butorides striatus* (74) 40 cm
A small, dark grey heron with a black crown, dark green back and paler grey underparts. Legs and feet are bright orange-yellow. From behind could be confused with Dwarf Bittern. The black, wispy nape plume is not usually seen except when bird alights.
SEXES alike. IMM. is streaked brown and buff, and has orange legs. HABITAT. Frequents mangrove stands and coral reefs at low tide, and freshwater dams, lakes and sluggish rivers overhung with trees. STATUS. Fairly common resident. CALL. A characteristic 'baaek' sharp note when takes to flight. (Groenrugreier)

DWARF BITTERN *Ixobrychus sturmii* (79) 25 cm
Dark slaty-blue above, buff below overlaid with dark vertical stripes running from the throat down on to the breast. The tiniest heron in the region, appearing more like a large rail in the field. Most easily confused with Greenbacked Heron.
SEXES alike. IMM. is similar to ad. but head and back feathers scalloped with buff, breast more rufous. HABITAT. Freshwater ponds and lakes surrounded by trees, and especially in flooded woodlands. STATUS. Summer visitor. CALL. A barking 'ra-ra-ra-ra-ra...' at the start of breeding, otherwise silent. (Dwergrietreier)

LITTLE BITTERN *Ixobrychus minutus* (78) 36 cm
Differs from smaller Dwarf Bittern by having conspicuous whitish wing patches and less striping on throat and breast. Two races occur in the region, one a fairly common non-breeding migrant (I.m. minutus) and the other an uncommon and localized resident (I.m. payesii) which is smaller and subject to local movements.
FEMALE is browner than male. IMM. resembles female, but is much more heavily streaked below; distinguished from Greenbacked Heron by smaller size and green (not orange) legs. HABITAT. Thick reedbeds. STATUS. Uncommon resident and summer visitor. Solitary breeder. CALL. A short bark, 'rao', uttered at intervals of a few seconds, at the start of breeding. (Woudapie)

BITTERN

BITTERN

BLACKCROWNED NIGHT HERON

br.

imm.

imm.

ad.

imm.

GREENBACKED HERON

GREENBACKED
HERON

ad.

ad.

DWARF BITTERN

ad.

imm.

male ad.
minutus

male ad.
payesii

LITTLE BITTERN

female ad.

imm.

male ad.

female ad.

imm.

63

BLACK STORK *Ciconia nigra* (84) 97 cm

A large, glossy black stork with a white belly and undertail. Distinguished from the smaller Abdim's Stork by the black rump and lower back, and by the red bill and legs. SEXES alike. IMM. is a browner version of ad. and has a yellowish bill and legs. HABITAT. Feeds in streams and ponds. Also occurs along the coast in estuaries and lagoons. STATUS. Uncommon resident. Nests solitarily on cliff ledges. CALL. Silent except on nest when loud whining and bill clapping are given. (Grootswartooievaar)

ABDIM'S STORK *Ciconia abdimii* (85) 76 cm

Distinguished from larger Black Stork by having a white lower back and rump, greenish legs with a pink ankle, and a greenish bill. In flight, the legs do not project as far beyond the end of the tail as they do in Black Stork. SEXES alike. IMM. duller than ad. HABITAT. Open fields and agricultural lands, often in the company of White Storks. STATUS. Common summer visitor, usually in large flocks. CALL. Usually silent in the region; a weak two-note whistle at roosts. (Kleinswartooievaar)

WHITE STORK *Ciconia ciconia* (83) 102 cm

Most resembles Yellowbilled Stork but differs by having a red bill and legs, and an all-white tail. Legs are often white because the birds excrete on them to lose body heat. SEXES alike. IMM. has a darker bill and legs, and white plumage tinged with brown. HABITAT. Grassland, vleis, cultivated lands and pastures. STATUS. Common summer visitor. Small breeding population in the southern Cape. CALL. Silent except on nest when loud whining and bill clapping are given. (Witooievaar)

YELLOWBILLED STORK *Mycteria ibis* (90) 95 cm

The long, slightly decurved yellow bill is diagnostic. During the breeding season the naked facial skin is red and the wing coverts and back are tinged pink. In flight appears similar to White Stork but differs by having a black tail. SEXES alike. IMM. like ad. but lacks the pink wash, and its head and neck are greyish (not white). HABITAT. Lakes, large rivers and estuaries. STATUS. Common resident in the north but rare summer visitor further south. CALL. Normally silent except during breeding season when it gives loud squeaks and hisses. (Nimmersat)

BLACK STORK

ad.

ad.

imm.

ABDIM'S STORK

ABDIM'S STORK

ad.

imm.

WHITE STORK

ad.

ad.

imm.

YELLOWBILLED
STORK

YELLOWBILLED STORK

ad.

imm.

YELLOWBILLED STORK

br.

MARABOU STORK *Leptoptilos crumeniferus* (89) 150 cm

The huge size, unfeathered head and neck, combined with the massive bill, render this species unmistakable. In flight the black wings contrast with the white body and the head is tucked into the shoulders.
SEXES alike. IMM. like ad. but has head and neck covered with a sparse woolly down. HABITAT. Not often seen outside major game reserves where it scavenges at game kills, refuse dumps and abattoirs. STATUS. Uncommon resident. Usually flocks. CALL. A low, hoarse, croak is given when alarmed. Claps bill when displaying. (Maraboe)

SADDLEBILLED STORK *Ephippiorhynchus senegalensis* (88) 145 cm

Unlikely to be confused with any other stork species because of its large size and its unusual red and black banded bill, and the yellow 'saddle' at the bill base.
MALE has brown eyes and a small yellow wattle. FEMALE has yellow eyes and lacks wattle. IMM. is grey instead of black, its neck and head are brown, and it lacks the yellow 'saddle' at the bill base. HABITAT. Fresh water, dams, pans, rivers and floodplains. STATUS. Uncommon resident; usually solitary or in pairs. CALL. Normally silent except for bill clapping during display. (Saalbekooievaar)

OPENBILLED STORK *Anastomus lamelligerus* (87) 94 cm

A large black stork with a pale ivory-coloured bill which has a diagnostic wide, nutcracker-like gap between the mandibles.
SEXES alike. IMM. is duller version of ad. and lacks the bill gap, which develops with maturity. HABITAT. Freshwater lakes and dams. STATUS. Uncommon visitor, mainly in summer. CALL. Seldom heard; a croaking 'honk'. (Oopbekooievaar)

WOOLLYNECKED STORK *Ciconia episcopus* (86) 85 cm

The combination of the glossy black plumage, white woolly neck, and white belly and undertail are distinctive.
SEXES alike. IMM. is like ad. but the glossy black is replaced by brown and the black forehead extends further back on the crown. HABITAT. Usually near fresh water: lagoons, ponds and rivers. STATUS. Uncommon resident. Solitary, in pairs, and occasionally in flocks. CALL. Seldom heard; a harsh croak. (Wolnekooievaar)

MARABOU STORK

soaring

ad.

SADDLEBILLED STORK

female

male

imm.

male

female

OPENBILLED STORK

ad.

imm.

WOOLLYNECKED STORK

ad.

imm.

WOOLLYNECKED STORK

GREATER FLAMINGO *Phoenicopterus ruber* (96) 127 cm

Very long legs and long neck characteristic. In flight shows brilliant red patches in the forewings. Differs from Lesser Flamingo by being larger, paler pink and by having a pink bill with a black tip.
SEXES alike. IMM. is sandy brown. Its grey and black bill distinguishes it from the imm. Lesser. JUV. is browner, becoming paler with age. HABITAT. Shallow freshwater lakes, salt pans, estuaries and open coast. STATUS. Common but nomadic resident; sometimes occurs in huge concentrations. CALL. 'Honk, honk', sounding not unlike a farmyard goose. (Grootflamink)

LESSER FLAMINGO *Phoenicopterus minor* (97) 100 cm

Distinguished from Greater Flamingo by being much smaller and having a dark red bill which appears all black when seen at long range. Head, neck and body plumage very variable but normally far redder than Greater Flamingo, with a larger expanse of crimson in the wings.
SEXES alike. IMM. differs from imm. Greater Flamingo by being smaller, having a darker, stubbier bill and greyish-brown body coloration. JUV. is browner, becoming paler with age. HABITAT. Freshwater lakes, salt pans and estuaries, usually in the company of Greater Flamingo. STATUS. Common but nomadic resident. CALL. A goose-like honking. (Kleinflamink)

AFRICAN SPOONBILL *Platalea alba* (95) 90 cm

The long, flattened, spoon-shaped grey and red bill is diagnostic. In flight differs from similarly sized white egrets by holding its neck outstretched, not tucked into the shoulders. Feeds with a characteristic side-to-side sweeping motion of the bill.
MALE has a longer bill than that of the female. IMM. has a yellowish-horn bill and dark-tipped flight feathers. HABITAT. Freshwater lakes, floodplains and estuaries. STATUS. Common resident with local movements. CALL. A low 'kaark'. In breeding colonies emits various grunts and claps bill. (Lepelaar)

HAMERKOP *Scopus umbretta* (81) 56 cm

A dark brown, long-legged bird with a heavy crest and flattened bill. The hammer-shaped profile of the head renders this bird unmistakable. In flight, its shape and barred tail lend a hawk-like appearance, but the long bill and legs rule out confusion with any bird of prey.
SEXES alike. IMM. like ad. HABITAT. Freshwater dams, lakes and rivers. Nest is a characteristic, huge domed structure of sticks, with small side entrance, usually in a sturdy tree or on a cliff ledge. STATUS. Common resident. CALL. A sharp 'kiep' in flight; a jumbled mixture of querulous squawks and frog-like croaks during courtship. (Hamerkop)

GREATER FLAMINGO

ad.

ad.

sub-ad.

imm.

br.

LESSER FLAMINGO

ad. non-br.

imm.

GREATER
FLAMINGO

LESSER
FLAMINGO

GREATER

LESSER

GREATER
FLAMINGO

ad.

ad.

juv.

ad.

ad.

juv.

LESSER FLAMINGO

AFRICAN SPOONBILL

ad.

imm.

ad.

HAMERKOP

HADEDA IBIS *Bostrychia hagedash* (94) 76 cm
A drab, greyish-brown bird which at close range shows glossy bronze wing coverts.
The face is grey and a white stripe runs from the bill base to below and behind the
eye. The long, dark, decurved bill has a red ridge on the upper mandible.
SEXES alike. IMM. lacks the red on bill and the bronzing on wings. HABITAT. Diverse:
forest clearings, woodland, savanna, open grassland and farmland. STATUS. Common
resident. Usually in small parties. CALL. One of the most familiar calls in certain parts
of Africa. Noisy in flight, uttering a loud 'ha-ha-ha-dah-da'. (Hadeda)

SOUTHERN BALD IBIS *Geronticus calvus* (92) 78 cm
Differs from the smaller Glossy Ibis by having a bald red head with a white face, a
long, decurved red bill and red legs and feet. General colour is glossy blue-black with
coppery patches on forewings.
SEXES alike but male has longer bill. IMM. has duller plumage with the head covered in
short light brown feathers and has the red on the bill confined to the base. Legs are
brown (not red as in ad.) and the coppery patches on the forewings are absent.
HABITAT. Short-grazed or burnt upland grassland. Breeds on cliffs. STATUS. Locally
common resident; endemic. Found in flocks. CALL. A high-pitched wheezing call.
(Kalkoenibis)

GLOSSY IBIS *Plegadis falcinellus* (93) 65 cm
The smallest ibis of the region. Appears black when seen at long range, but closer
views show the head, neck and body to be a dark chestnut and the wings, back and
tail a dark glossy green with bronze and purple highlights.
SEXES alike. IMM. has the glossy areas of ad. but the remainder of the body plumage is
a dull, sooty brown; shows a pale spot at the base of the bill. HABITAT. Invariably associated with water: dams, pans, vleis and flooded grassland. STATUS. Locally common
resident. CALL. Normally silent. A low, guttural 'kok-kok-kok' given in breeding
colonies. (Glansibis)

SACRED IBIS *Threskiornis aethiopicus* (91) 90 cm
A white bird with an unfeathered black head and neck, and a long, decurved black
bill. The scapular feathers are blue-black and flight feathers are black tipped, giving a
narrow black edge to the wing. During breeding, the naked skin on the underwing
turns scarlet and the flank feathers yellow. Often flies in V-formation.
SEXES alike but male is longer billed. IMM. differs from ad. by having white feathering
on the neck. HABITAT. Ranges from offshore islands and estuaries to grassland and
vleis. Regular at man-made wetlands and croplands. STATUS. Common resident.
CALL. Loud croaking at breeding colonies. (Skoorsteenveër)

ad.

HADEDA IBIS

imm.

ad.

SOUTHERN BALD IBIS

imm.

ad.

GLOSSY IBIS

imm.

br.

br.

imm.

SACRED IBIS

male

SPURWINGED GOOSE *Plectropterus gambensis* (116) 100 cm
A large black goose with variable amounts of white on the throat, neck and belly. In flight the large white area in the forewing distinguishes this species from Knobbilled Duck.
MALE is up to twice the size of the female, and its facial skin extends behind the eye. IMM. like ad. but browner. HABITAT. Frequents water bordered by grassland and agricultural areas. Feeds ashore, often at night, on grasses and other vegetable matter. STATUS. Common resident. CALL. Utters a feeble, wheezy whistle in flight. (Wildemakou)

EGYPTIAN GOOSE *Alopochen aegyptiacus* (102) 70 cm
A large, brown bird which has a dark brown mask around the eye, and a brown patch on the breast which is distinctive in flight.
Compared with South African Shelduck it has a longer neck and legs, and a thin dark line running through the white forewing is visible in flight. SEXES alike. IMM. lacks the brown mask and breast patch and the forewing is not pure white. HABITAT. Almost any freshwater habitat but frequently feeds in fields. STATUS. Very common resident. CALL. The male hisses, female utters a grunting honk; both give rapid repeated honks at take-off. (Kolgans)

SOUTH AFRICAN SHELDUCK *Tadorna cana* (103) 64 cm
A large, russet-coloured duck with black bill and legs.
MALE has a diagnostic grey head. FEMALE has a variable white and grey head, whereas Whitefaced Duck (p. 74) has a white and black head. In flight both sexes show white forewings but no black dividing line as seen in Egyptian Goose. IMM. like ad. HABITAT. Freshwater lakes and dams in drier areas. Nests underground in a mammal burrow. STATUS. Common resident; endemic. CALL. Various honks and hisses. (Kopereend)

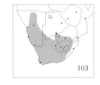

KNOBBILLED DUCK *Sarkidiornis melanotos* (115) 73 cm
This large duck with its grey speckled head and contrasting blue-black and white plumage is unmistakable in the region. In flight the wings are black with no markings, although female shows a little white on the lower back.
MALE is larger than the female and has a rounded protuberance on the bill which enlarges conspicuously during the breeding season. FEMALE lacks bill development of breeding male and is smaller. IMM. like female but has dark speckling on the white areas. HABITAT. Mainly on pans and dams in woodland and along larger rivers in the north. Nests in a large hole in a tree. STATUS. Mainly a summer visitor. Widely distributed but nomadic, more common to the north. CALL. Whistles, but usually silent. (Kobbeleend)

SPURWINGED GOOSE

northern race

SPURWINGED GOOSE

SPURWINGED GOOSE

imm.

EGYPTIAN GOOSE

ad.

SOUTH AFRICAN SHELDUCK

male

SOUTH AFRICAN SHELDUCK

female

KNOBBILLED DUCK
male br.

WHITEFACED DUCK *Dendrocygna viduata* (99) 48 cm
A distinctive, long-necked duck with a diagnostic white face. Differs from larger South African Shelduck (p. 72) by lacking grey on the head. Like Fulvous Duck, it stands very erect and is highly gregarious, but it can be distinguished from that species in flight by the lack of white on the rump. At times the white face can be stained a muddy brown.
SEXES alike. IMM. lacks white face. HABITAT. Almost any expanse of water but spends much time ashore. STATUS. Common resident. CALL. A characteristic three-note whistle, the last two notes being closer together. (Nonnetjie-eend)

FULVOUS DUCK *Dendrocygna bicolor* (100) 46 cm
Similar in shape to Whitefaced Duck but has a golden brown face. Shows a dark line down the hind nape and neck and has conspicuous white flank stripes. In flight, distinguished from Whitefaced Duck by its white horseshoe-shaped rump contrasting with the dark upperparts.
SEXES alike. IMM. distinguished from imm. Whitefaced Duck by white on flanks and rump. HABITAT. Freshwater lakes and dams. STATUS. Locally common resident; less abundant than Whitefaced Duck. CALL. A soft, double-syllable whistle. (Fluiteend)

WHITEBACKED DUCK *Thalassornis leuconotus* (101) 43 cm
A mottled brown, hump-backed, large-headed duck. When swimming the most diagnostic feature of this species is the pale patch at the base of the bill. Only in flight is the white back seen.
MALE, FEMALE and IMM. are similar. HABITAT. Fresh water, typically among floating vegetation. STATUS. Locally common resident. CALL. A low-pitched whistle, rising on the second syllable. (Witrugeend)

PYGMY GOOSE *Nettapus auritus* (114) 33 cm
The orange body, white face and dark greenish upperparts are diagnostic. In flight, the white secondaries are distinctive. Difficult birds to see as they frequently sit motionless in floating vegetation.
MALE has highly contrasting head markings with vertical black ear-stripe. FEMALE's head tends to be more speckled, lacks ear-stripe. IMM. resembles female. HABITAT. Prefers freshwater areas with floating vegetation, especially *Nymphaea*. Nests in a hole in a tree. STATUS. Locally common resident. CALL. A soft, repeated 'tsui-tsui'. (Dwerggans)

SOUTHERN POCHARD *Netta erythrophthalma* (113) 50 cm
A dark brown duck. In flight both sexes show a distinct white wing bar. Sits low in the water with its tail submerged.
MALE is superficially similar to male Maccoa Duck but has fairly uniform blackish-brown plumage with a glossy sheen, a pale blue bill and bright red eyes. FEMALE is dark brown with a pale patch at the bill base and a pale crescent extending down from the eye. IMM. resembles female. HABITAT. Lakes, dams and vleis. STATUS. Common resident. CALL. Male makes a whining sound, female quacks. (Bruineend)

MACCOA DUCK *Oxyura maccoa* (117) 46 cm
In flight, the upperwing is uniform dark brown. Sits very low in the water with its stiff tail often cocked at a 45 degree angle. Male has a chestnut body, large black head and a bright cobalt blue bill. (The male Southern Pochard has a smaller brown head and duller bill.) In eclipse plumage resembles female.
FEMALE is dark brown with a pale cheek, under which is a dark line. This gives the impression of a pale stripe running from the bill beyond the eye: in comparison, the female Southern Pochard has a pale vertical crescent behind the eye. IMM. resembles female. HABITAT. A diving species of quieter waters that have surface vegetation. STATUS. Resident. Thinly distributed throughout; absent from the desert regions and eastern lowlands. CALL. A peculiar nasal trill. (Bloubekeend)

ad.

WHITEFACED DUCK

imm.

FULVOUS DUCK

WHITEBACKED DUCK

male   PYGMY GOOSE

female

SOUTHERN POCHARD

male

SOUTHERN
POCHARD

male imm.

female

MACCOA DUCK

male

female

YELLOWBILLED DUCK *Anas undulata* (104) 54 cm
The rich yellow bill with a black patch on the upper mandible is distinctive. From a distance, plumage appears dark but less so than that of African Black Duck. In flight it shows a blue-green speculum narrowly edged with white.
SEXES alike. IMM. duller than ad. HABITAT. Virtually any area of open fresh water, also estuaries, often in flocks. STATUS. Common resident. CALL. Male's call is a rasping hiss, female quacks. (Geelbekeend)

AFRICAN BLACK DUCK *Anas sparsa* (105) 56 cm
A dark-billed, dark-plumaged duck with white speckles on back and bright orange legs and feet.
In flight, might be confused with Yellowbilled Duck as it also has a blue-green speculum edged with white, but the underwing is whitish (not grey as in the Yellowbilled). When sitting in the water it appears long bodied. SEXES alike but female smaller. IMM. is paler, with a whitish belly. HABITAT. Prefers fast-moving streams and rivers. STATUS. Widespread resident. CALL. 'Quack', especially in flight. Male gives a high-pitched, weak whistle. (Swarteend)

MALLARD *Anas platyrhynchos* (923) 58 cm
Male is unmistakable with a bottle-green glossy head, white ring around the neck and a chestnut breast.
When in eclipse plumage resembles female. Domesticated form of Mallard is the Khaki Campbell which looks very similar but is much larger and has a khaki-coloured (not grey) back. FEMALE very similar to Yellowbilled Duck but lacks the yellow bill of that species. IMM. resembles female. HABITAT. Any area of open water. STATUS. Resident; feral populations on the Witwatersrand and in the south-western Cape. CALL. Male and female call similar to that of Yellowbilled Duck. (Mallard)

CAPE SHOVELLER *Anas smithii* (112) 53 cm
Both sexes distinguished from other ducks, except European Shoveller, by the long, black, spatulate bill. The plumage is finely speckled grey-brown and the legs are a rich orange in colour.
MALE has a paler head and yellower eyes than female. FEMALE is darker and greyer than European Shoveller, especially around the head and neck. IMM. resembles female. HABITAT. Fresh water, preferably with surface vegetation. STATUS. Resident; endemic. Abundant in the Cape and Highveld region. CALL. 'Quack', and a continuous rasping. (Kaapse Slopeend)

EUROPEAN SHOVELLER *Anas clypeata* (111) 53 cm
Breeding plumage of male is unmistakable: green head, white breast and chestnut belly. Very rapid, direct flight shows powder-blue forewing similar to that of Garganey (p. 78), but the latter is smaller and lacks the large bill. In both sexes, European Shoveller has a heavier, longer and more spatulate bill than that of Cape Shoveller.
MALE in eclipse plumage resembles female. FEMALE differs from Cape Shoveller by being speckled brown and much paler overall, especially around the head and neck. IMM. resembles female. HABITAT. Inland water bodies. STATUS. Most sightings are probably of escaped aviary birds, but true vagrants may occasionally occur in Zimbabwe, Namibia, Mozambique and the Transvaal. CALL. Male gives a nasal 'crook, crook', female quacks. (Europese Slopeend)

YELLOWBILLED DUCK

AFRICAN BLACK DUCK

male MALLARD female

CAPE SHOVELLER

female male

male EUROPEAN SHOVELLER female

PINTAIL *Anas acuta* (109) 47 cm
Male is striking with a dark-chocolate brown head and a white stripe running down the side of the neck to the white breast. In eclipse plumage it resembles the female.
FEMALE is similar to Yellowbilled Duck (p. 76) but has a dark bill, paler plumage, brown speculum with a white trailing edge, and a long, slender neck and body. The tail is pointed in both sexes, but the male's is longer in breeding plumage. IMM. resembles female. HABITAT. Inland water bodies. STATUS. Most sightings are probably of escaped aviary birds, but vagrants may occasionally occur in the northern parts of the subregion. CALL. Male's call is a soft nasal honk, female quacks. (Pylsterteend)

GARGANEY *Anas querquedula* (110) 38 cm
Male has an obvious white eyebrow stripe on a dark brown head. The brown breast is sharply demarcated by the white belly and pale grey flanks; the black and white stripes on the back are conspicuous.
MALE in eclipse plumage resembles female but has a more pronounced eyebrow stripe. FEMALE, which is speckled mid-brown, is larger than Hottentot Teal and lacks the dark cap. In flight both sexes show the pale blue forewings and green speculum also found in Cape and European Shovellers (p. 76), but lack their heavy bills. IMM. resembles female. HABITAT. Inland water bodies. STATUS. Rare summer vagrant. CALL. A nasal 'quack' and some harsh rattles. (Somereend)

CAPE TEAL *Anas capensis* (106) 46 cm
The palest duck of the region. At close range, the combination of a speckled head and pink bill is diagnostic.
Distinguished from Redbilled Teal by the uniformly coloured head and lack of a dark cap. In flight shows a dark greenish speculum surrounded by white. Usually occurs in mixed flocks. SEXES alike. IMM. pale grey. HABITAT. Any area of open fresh or saline water. STATUS. Resident. Occurs throughout except in the north-east, most common in the dry west. CALL. A thin whistle usually given in flight. (Teeleend)

REDBILLED TEAL *Anas erythrorhyncha* (108) 48 cm
The combination of dark cap, pale cheeks and red bill is diagnostic. Larger than Hottentot Teal which has a blue (not red) bill. Dark cap distinguishes it from Cape Teal. In flight the secondaries are pale and the lack of the dark green speculum precludes confusion with Hottentot Teal.
SEXES alike. IMM. is duller than ad. HABITAT. Occurs in mixed flocks on fresh water. STATUS. Very common resident. CALL. Male gives a soft, nasal whistle, female quacks. (Rooibekeend)

HOTTENTOT TEAL *Anas hottentota* (107) 35 cm
A diminutive species resembling Redbilled Teal from which it differs by having a blue (not red) bill, and a dark smudge on its creamy cheeks. In flight shows a green speculum with a white trailing edge and a black and white underwing.
SEXES alike. IMM. duller than ad. HABITAT. Mainly inland on small water bodies, often close to floating vegetation. STATUS. Locally common resident. CALL. Soft quacks. (Gevlekte Eend)

PINTAIL

male

female

GARGANEY

male

male
eclipse plumage

female

CAPE TEAL

REDBILLED TEAL

HOTTENTOT TEAL

SPURWINGED GOOSE

EGYPTIAN GOOSE

SOUTH AFRICAN SHELDUCK

KNOBBILLED DUCK

female

male non-br.

male

female

EGYPTIAN GOOSE

SOUTH AFRICAN SHELDUCK

KNOBBILLED DUCK

SPURWINGED GOOSE

WHITEFACED DUCK

FULVOUS DUCK

HOTTENTOT TEAL

REDBILLED TEAL

CAPE TEAL

MALLARD

WHITEBACKED DUCK

male

female

female

GARGANEY

EUROPEAN SHOVELLER

male

female

male

female

imm.

PINTAIL
male

YELLOWBILLED
DUCK

AFRICAN BLACK
DUCK

male

CAPE SHOVELLER

female

male

female

PYGMY
GOOSE

male

female

MACCOA DUCK

SOUTHERN
POCHARD

male

81

LAPPETFACED VULTURE *Torgos tracheliotus* (124) 100 cm
At close range the bare red skin on face and throat is diagnostic. In flight, the white thighs and white bar running along the forepart of the underwing from the body to the carpal joint are conspicuous.
SEXES alike. IMM. is dark brown all over and most closely resembles Hooded Vulture (p. 84) but is almost twice the size. HABITAT. Thornveld; mainly in drier regions. The common vulture in the Namib desert. Nests on tree-tops; solitarily or in small, scattered colonies. STATUS. Resident; rare outside major game reserves. Threatened. CALL. Unknown. High-pitched whistles recorded during display. (Swartaasvoël)

WHITEHEADED VULTURE *Trigonoceps occipitalis* (125) 80 cm
In the region, the only dark vulture with large white wing patches. These patches are confined to the secondaries and are white in the female and off-white to grey in the male. The triangular-looking head and the neck are white, the naked face is pink, and the bill is orange with a blue base.
IMM. is dark brown and distinguishable in flight from imm. Lappetfaced Vulture and imm. Hooded Vulture (p. 84) by the narrow white line between flight feathers and wing coverts. HABITAT. Thornveld and savanna. Nests on tree-tops; solitary. STATUS. Uncommon resident; rare outside major game reserves. CALL. High-pitched chittering recorded when feeding. (Witkopaasvoël)

CAPE VULTURE *Gyps coprotheres* (122) 115 cm
Difficult to distinguish from Whitebacked Vulture. When seen together, Cape Vulture is much larger and (in ad.) much paler in appearance. Under ideal viewing conditions, two bare patches of blue skin at the base of the neck are diagnostic.
SEXES alike. IMM. not readily distinguished from imm. Whitebacked Vulture unless size can be compared. HABITAT. Grassland, savanna and semi-desert. Nests on cliff ledges, in colonies. STATUS. Resident; endemic. Threatened. The most common vulture in the Drakensberg and Transkei. CALL. Cackling and hissing noises given when feeding at carcasses, and at the nest. (Kransaasvoël)

WHITEBACKED VULTURE *Gyps africanus* (123) 95 cm
If seen from above, ad. has white lower back which contrasts with dark upperwing. Smaller than Cape Vulture and has a strongly contrasting leading/trailing edge to its underwing.
SEXES alike. IMM. Smaller size distinguishes it from imm. Cape Vulture. HABITAT. Savanna. Nests on tree-tops in small colonies. STATUS. Resident. The most frequently seen vulture in bushveld game reserves. CALL. Harsh cackles and hisses when feeding and at the nest. (Witrugaasvoël)

ad.

LAPPETFACED VULTURE

imm.

ad.

WHITEHEADED VULTURE

female

male

WHITEHEADED VULTURE

female

CAPE VULTURE

ad.

imm.

ad.

imm.

WHITEBACKED VULTURE

ad.

imm.

BEARDED VULTURE *Gypaetus barbatus* (119) 110 cm
Shape in flight is unlike any other vulture in the region: the long, narrow, pointed wings and long, wedge-shaped tail impart falcon-like proportions. Ad. is mainly dark above with rufous underparts and has a black mask across the face, terminating in a black 'beard'. (The 'beard' is not usually visible except at close quarters.)
SEXES alike. IMM. is dark brown all over with underparts paling as it ages. HABITAT. Remote high mountains; usually not found below 2 000 m. Confined to the Drakensberg. Nests on cliff ledges; solitary. STATUS. Scarce resident; range has contracted in the past 50 years. CALL. Silent except for high-pitched whistling during display. (Baardaasvoël)

PALMNUT VULTURE *Gypohierax angolensis* (147) 60 cm
This small black and white vulture is likely to be confused only with Egyptian Vulture, from which it differs by having extensive white in the primaries (all black in Egyptian Vulture), and by its tail being black and straight-ended (not white and wedge-shaped).
SEXES alike. IMM. resembles Hooded Vulture but is smaller and has a feathered (not bare) throat and neck. HABITAT. Coastal forests in the vicinity of raffia palms. STATUS. Rare, localized resident; restricted to Zululand and further north; also large inland rivers in the north-west and the Okavango delta. Vagrant elsewhere. CALL. In flight sometimes utters a 'kok-kok-kok'. (Witaasvoël)

EGYPTIAN VULTURE *Neophron percnopterus* (120) 62 cm
Ad. could be confused with similar black and white Palmnut Vulture but has all-black primaries and a white, wedge-shaped tail.
SEXES alike. IMM. in flight looks like diminutive imm. Bearded Vulture, but has a bare face and a long, thin bill. Differs from imm. Palmnut and Hooded Vultures by its long, wedge-shaped tail. HABITAT. Grassland, savanna, semi-desert; usually found at kills in game reserves. STATUS. Formerly a localized breeding resident, now a rare vagrant with most recent sightings from Transkei, Namibia and Transvaal. CALL. Soft grunts and hisses when excited. (Egiptiese Aasvoël)

HOODED VULTURE *Necrosyrtes monachus* (121) 70 cm
A small brown vulture which could be confused with imm. Palmnut and Egyptian Vultures. Distinguished from the former by its larger size, and by having down (not feathers) on the head and neck. Unlike this species, the imm. Egyptian Vulture has a long, wedge-shaped (not square) tail, yellowish (not pink) facial skin and elongated nape feathers.
SEXES alike. IMM. darker, with blackish-brown head. HABITAT. Savanna; found mostly in game reserves in the north. STATUS. Uncommon resident. CALL. Normally silent. Emits soft whistling calls at nest. (Monnikaasvoël)

BEARDED VULTURE
imm.

ad.

BEARDED VULTURE

ad.

imm.

PALMNUT
VULTURE

PALMNUT VULTURE

ad.

imm.

ad.

EGYPTIAN VULTURE

imm.

EGYPTIAN VULTURE

ad.

imm.

HOODED VULTURE

HOODED VULTURE

ad.

imm.

ad.

85

HOODED VULTURE
ad.

HOODED VULTURE
imm.

EGYPTIAN VULTURE
ad.

EGYPTIAN VULTURE
imm.

showing first
white of ad. plumage

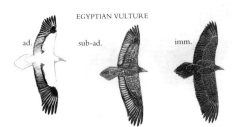

EGYPTIAN VULTURE

ad.   sub-ad.   imm.

PALMNUT VULTURE

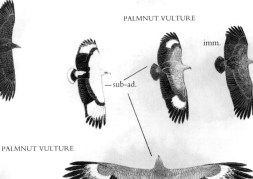

imm.

sub-ad.

PALMNUT VULTURE

sub-ad.

SECRETARYBIRD

86

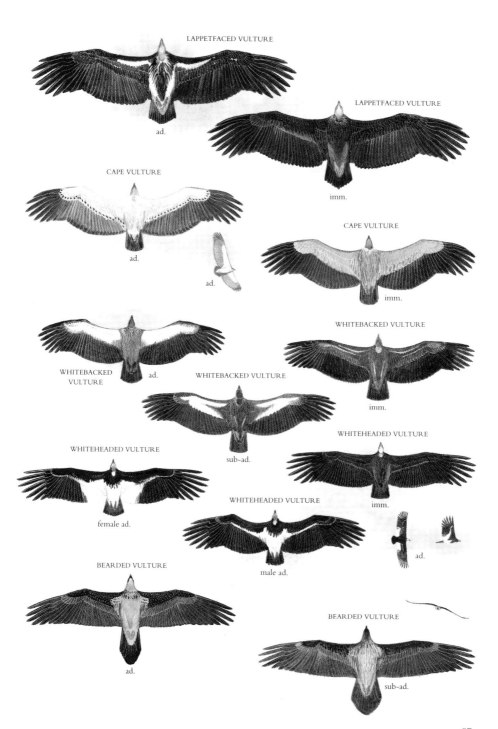

LAPPETFACED VULTURE
ad.

LAPPETFACED VULTURE
imm.

CAPE VULTURE
ad.

CAPE VULTURE
imm.

ad.

WHITEBACKED VULTURE
imm.

WHITEBACKED
VULTURE
ad.

WHITEBACKED VULTURE
sub-ad.

WHITEHEADED VULTURE
imm.

WHITEHEADED VULTURE
female ad.

WHITEHEADED VULTURE
male ad.

ad.

BEARDED VULTURE
ad.

BEARDED VULTURE
sub-ad.

AFRICAN FISH EAGLE *Haliaeetus vocifer* (148) 63-73 cm

Apart from its diagnostic call, the ad. African Fish Eagle is unmistakable with its white head and breast, chestnut belly and forewings, black underwing coverts and white tail. Overall impression in flight is of a large, broad-winged eagle with a short tail. SEXES alike but female larger. IMM. identifiable by general dark brown coloration with white streaks on head and throat, white patches in flight feathers, and diagnostic white tail with dark terminal band. HABITAT. Aquatic: large rivers, lakes and dams. Coastal in some regions where it frequents estuaries and lagoons. Found throughout except in the extreme dry west. STATUS. Locally common resident. CALL. A characteristic ringing 'kyow-kow-kow', male higher pitched; often in duet. (Visarend)

OSPREY *Pandion haliaetus* (170) 55-69 cm

Flight outline resembles that of a huge gull with pale underwings, black patches at carpal joints and diagnostic black mask on white head. Might be confused with imm. African Fish Eagle found in similar habitat but the latter is a larger bird with broad wings and a very short tail. SEXES alike. IMM. like ad. HABITAT. Inland freshwater bodies, estuaries and lagoons, rarely fishing over open sea. Found throughout the south and east but absent from the west, except for vagrants. STATUS. Uncommon visitor, chiefly in summer. CALL. Usually silent when in Africa. (Visvalk)

BATELEUR *Terathopius ecaudatus* (146) 55-70 cm

The most easily identified eagle of the region. The black, white and chestnut plumage combined with diagnostic wing shape and very short tail render this bird unmistakable. Flight action is also diagnostic: with long wings held slightly angled, rarely flapping, it flies direct, canting from side to side. Less common colour form has cream back and tail. MALE has broad black trailing edge to wing. FEMALE has narrow black trailing edge to wing. IMM. is a uniform brown and is distinguished from all other brown eagles by its flight action and very short tail. Sex of imms. can be determined by the extent of brown on the trailing edge of the underwing. HABITAT. Savanna. STATUS. Resident; in the east, restricted to major game reserves, where common. CALL. A loud bark, 'kow-wah'. (Berghaan)

ad.

imm.

female

male

AFRICAN FISH EAGLE

imm.

OSPREY

BATELEUR
imm.

OSPREY

female

BATELEUR

male

BATELEUR

male

female

female imm.

89

BROWN SNAKE EAGLE *Circaetus cinereus* (142) 70-76 cm

Ad. distinguished from all other dark brown eagles by having unfeathered creamy-white legs. At rest, it appears unusually large headed with big yellow eyes. In flight the dark brown underwing coverts contrast with white primaries and secondaries.
SEXES alike. IMM. resembles ad. and differs from imm. Blackbreasted Snake Eagle by being darker brown, and by the lack of barring on flight feathers. HABITAT. Savanna, avoiding open grassland and forests. STATUS. Locally common to rare resident; nomadic within subregion. CALL. Rarely calls. A croaking 'hok-hok-hok-hok' is uttered in flight. (Bruinslangarend)

BLACKBREASTED SNAKE EAGLE *Circaetus gallicus* (143) 63-68 cm

In flight, ad. resembles most closely the ad. Martial Eagle (p. 96) but differs by having white underwings, with primaries and secondaries barred black. At rest the large, dark-coloured head shows exceptionally large, bright yellow eyes. Lacks black spots of Martial Eagle on lower breast and belly.
SEXES alike but female larger. IMM. differs from ad. and the imm. Brown Snake Eagle by being a rich rufous when recently fledged, becoming pale brown below with pale underwing and undertail, both lightly barred. HABITAT. Frequents a wide range of habitats, from desert to savanna. STATUS. Locally common to scarce resident; nomadic within the subregion. CALL. Rarely calls: a melodious whistle 'kwo-kwo-kwo-kweeu'. (Swartborsslangarend)

SOUTHERN BANDED SNAKE EAGLE *Circaetus fasciolatus* (144) 55-60 cm

Ad. resembles ad. Cuckoo Hawk (p. 110) but is much larger, with a large, rounded head and a relatively short tail. In flight distinguished from Western Banded Snake Eagle by its darker underwings and four (not two) black bars on tail.
SEXES alike. IMM. dark brown above, pale with dark streaks on face, throat and upper breast below. HABITAT. Coastal evergreen forests, riverine forests and open woodland in marshy areas. STATUS. Uncommon resident. CALL. A harsh 'crok-crok-crok' and high-pitched 'ko-ko-ko-ko-keear'. (Dubbelbandslangarend)

WESTERN BANDED SNAKE EAGLE *Circaetus cinerascens* (145) 55-60 cm

Differs from similar Southern Banded Snake Eagle by being stockier, less heavily barred below, and by having a shorter tail with a diagnostic broad white band across the middle, visible both in flight and at rest. In flight the tail band and white (not barred) underwings differentiate it from Southern Banded Snake Eagle.
SEXES alike. IMM. paler than ad. and not easily distinguishable from the imm. Southern Banded Snake Eagle. HABITAT. Woodland fringing large tropical rivers. STATUS. Uncommon resident. CALL. A high-pitched 'kok-kok-kok-kok-kok'. (Enkelbandslangarend)

BROWN SNAKE EAGLE

ad.

ad.

ad.

BLACKBREASTED
SNAKE EAGLE

ad.

ad.

imm.

imm.

SOUTHERN BANDED SNAKE EAGLE

ad.

ad.

ad.

WESTERN BANDED SNAKE EAGLE

ad.

ad.

ad.

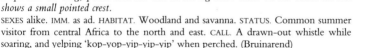 EAGLES

See also pages 94-95

STEPPE EAGLE *Aquila nipalensis* (133) 65–80 cm

Plumage variable but tail always strongly barred. Ad. usually uniform dark brown. Imms., which are much more common in the subregion, are lighter brown with two prominent light bars along the wing, a light U-shaped rump and light panels in the outer wing. At close range and if clearly seen, the yellow gape is long and extends behind the eye in the race A.n. nipalensis, *whereas the gape of the race* A.n. orientalis *extends behind the middle of the eye, but not to the back of the eye. Gape of Tawny Eagle extends only to the middle of the eye.*

Although similar in plumage, *A.n. nipalensis* is larger than *A.n. orientalis* and appears longer winged in flight. Structural differences between the two suggest that they may be distinct species. SEXES alike. HABITAT. Thornveld and semi-desert regions. STATUS. An erratic but sometimes common summer visitor to the north. Often gregarious. CALL. Silent on its wintering grounds. (Steppe-arend)

TAWNY EAGLE *Aquila rapax* (132) 65–80 cm

Easily confused with migrant Steppe Eagle which is similar in size and shape. At close range the gape length is diagnostic; in Tawny Eagle it extends only to below the middle of the eye. Confusion possible in the gape length of Steppe Eagle race A.n. orientalis. *Unbarred to faintly barred tail diagnostic.*

Plumage variable: mostly birds are uniform tawny coloured, but they can range from streaked dark brown to pale buff in colour. FEMALE usually darker than male. IMM. rufous brown fading to buff as sub-adult. HABITAT. Thornveld and semi-desert areas. STATUS. Resident and local migrant. Common in the major game reserves but thinly distributed elsewhere. CALL. Seldom calls: a sharp bark 'kyow'. (Roofarend)

LESSER SPOTTED EAGLE *Aquila pomarina* (134) 61–66 cm

A small dark eagle of buzzard-like proportions. Differs from Wahlberg's Eagle by having a short, rounded tail. At rest the tightly feathered legs appear unusually thin.

SEXES alike. IMM. from above very similar to imm. Steppe Eagle, showing white bases to primaries, white edging to coverts and secondaries, a 'U'-shaped white rump and sometimes a white patch on the back. HABITAT. Often seen in company of Steppe Eagles in savanna. STATUS. Uncommon summer visitor. CALL. Silent when in the region. (Gevlekte Arend)

WAHLBERG'S EAGLE *Aquila wahlbergi* (135) 55–60 cm

Usually brown but has pale and intermediate colour forms. The flight shape is diagnostic with long, straight-edged wings and a long, narrow, square-ended tail. Pale form birds could be confused with pale form Booted Eagle (p. 98) but differ in flight shape and the long, pencil-thin tail and in having more white on the head. At rest shows a small pointed crest.

SEXES alike. IMM. as ad. HABITAT. Woodland and savanna. STATUS. Common summer visitor from central Africa to the north and east. CALL. A drawn-out whistle while soaring, and yelping 'kop-yop-yip-yip-yip' when perched. (Bruinarend)

STEPPE EAGLE
(*A.n. nipalensis*)

STEPPE EAGLE
(*A.n. orientalis*)

TAWNY EAGLE

STEPPE EAGLE
(*A.n. nipalensis*)
imm.

STEPPE EAGLE
(*A.n. orientalis*)
imm.

TAWNY EAGLE
rufous form
imm.

LESSER SPOTTED EAGLE
imm.

TAWNY EAGLE
pale form
imm.

WAHLBERG'S EAGLE
dark form
imm.

WAHLBERG'S EAGLE
pale form
imm.

STEPPE EAGLE   (*A.n. nipalensis*)   imm.

LESSER SPOTTED EAGLE   imm.

STEPPE EAGLE   (*A.n. orientalis*)   imm.

WAHLBERG'S EAGLE   dark form imm.

TAWNY EAGLE   imm.

See also page 92

tail feathers

STEPPE
EAGLE

TAWNY
EAGLE

STEPPE EAGLE
A.n. nipalensis ad.

STEPPE EAGLE
A.n. orientalis ad.

A.n. nipalensis ad.

STEPPE EAGLE

A.n. orientalis ad.

TAWNY EAGLE
dark form

TAWNY EAGLE
dark form

TAWNY EAGLE
medium/pale form

TAWNY EAGLE
medium/pale form

TAWNY EAGLE
very pale form

TAWNY EAGLE
pale form

TAWNY EAGLE
streaked form

STEPPE EAGLE
nipalensis

ad.

STEPPE EAGLE
A.n. nipalensis imm.

STEPPE EAGLE
orientalis

ad.

TAWNY EAGLE

ad.

STEPPE EAGLE
A.n. orientalis imm.

TAWNY EAGLE
ad.

LESSER SPOTTED EAGLE
imm.

LESSER SPOTTED EAGLE
ad.

LESSER
SPOTTED
EAGLE
imm.

LESSER SPOTTED EAGLE
sailing

LESSER
SPOTTED EAGLE
ad.

slow glide

STEPPE EAGLE
A.n. orientalis
imm.

fast glide

LESSER
SPOTTED EAGLE

WAHLBERG'S
EAGLE

WAHLBERG'S EAGLE
dark form

WAHLBERG'S EAGLE

WAHLBERG'S EAGLE
buff form

dark-headed
form

dark form

WAHLBERG'S EAGLE
pale form

darkish form

WAHLBERG'S
EAGLE

buff form

buff form

WAHLBERG'S EAGLE

pale form

WAHLBERG'S EAGLE

95

MARTIAL EAGLE *Polemaetus bellicosus* (140) 78-83 cm
The dark head, throat and upper breast combined with white, lightly spotted breast and belly, and very dark underwings are diagnostic in this huge eagle. From beneath, the ad. Blackbreasted Snake Eagle (p. 90) resembles this species but has a white underwing barred with black on primaries and secondaries.
SEXES alike but female larger. IMM. differs from imm. Crowned Eagle by being whiter, having unspotted flanks and the underwings finely (not broadly) barred. HABITAT. Mainly a savanna species but frequents a wide range of habitats, from desert to forest edge. STATUS. Uncommon resident; scarce outside large reserves. CALL. Display call consists of a rapid 'klooee-klooee-klooee'. (Breëkoparend)

BLACK EAGLE *Aquila verreauxii* (131) 75-95 cm
Adult unmistakable. In flight wings narrow at base, broadening in middle, and white back and wing panels contrasting with black plumage are characteristic.
SEXES alike except female larger and more extensively white on back. IMM. best recognized by characteristic flight shape: mottled light and dark brown with diagnostic rufous crown and nape which contrast with darker face and throat. HABITAT. Mountainous regions where there are cliffs and its major prey, dassies. STATUS. Locally common to scarce resident. CALL. Rarely calls; a melodious 'keee-uup'. (Witkruisarend)

CROWNED EAGLE *Stephanoaetus coronatus* (141) 80-90 cm
The dark coloration, and combination of large size and hawk-like appearance, especially in flight, identify this species.
Ad. is dark grey above and rufous below, with breast and belly heavily mottled black. In flight shows well-rounded wings and a long barred tail. The underwing is rufous, with primaries and secondaries heavily barred black. SEXES alike but female larger. IMM. similar to imm. Martial Eagle but is creamy white in front and differs in shape, has dark speckling on flanks and legs, and the tail and underwing are heavily barred. HABITAT. Evergreen forest and tree galleries along large rivers. STATUS. Locally common resident. CALL. A very vocal species: utters a ringing 'kewee-kewee-kewee' call in flight. Male's call higher pitched than female's. (Kroonarend)

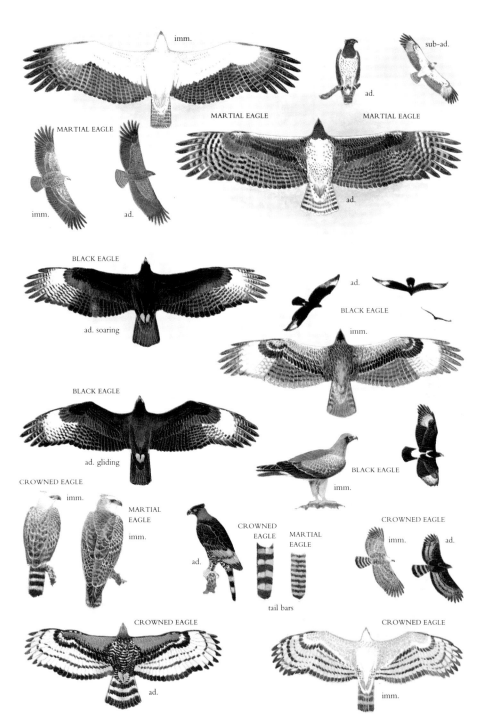

imm.

sub-ad.

ad.

MARTIAL EAGLE

MARTIAL EAGLE

MARTIAL EAGLE

imm.   ad.

ad.

BLACK EAGLE

ad.

ad. soaring

BLACK EAGLE

imm.

BLACK EAGLE

ad. gliding

BLACK EAGLE

imm.

CROWNED EAGLE

imm.

MARTIAL
EAGLE

imm.

CROWNED
EAGLE

MARTIAL
EAGLE

CROWNED EAGLE

imm.   ad.

ad.

tail bars

CROWNED EAGLE

ad.

CROWNED EAGLE

imm.

AFRICAN HAWK EAGLE *Hieraaetus fasciatus* (137) 66-74 cm

Ad. likely to be confused only with smaller Ayres' Eagle: is less boldly marked below, has white, unspotted thighs; in flight underwing mainly white (dark and heavily barred in Ayres'), and upperwing dark brown with distinctive white panels at base of primaries (uniform dark upperwing in Ayres').
SEXES alike but female is larger. IMM. has underwing coverts and underbody rufous, lightly streaked with black; above, browner than ad. and lacks conspicuous terminal tail bar. Easily confused with imm. Black Sparrowhawk (p. 114) but has feathered (not bare) legs. HABITAT. Woodland and savanna in hilly and flat country. STATUS. Thinly distributed resident. CALL. Seldom calls: a whistled musical 'klee-klee-klee'. (Afrikaanse Jagarend)

LONGCRESTED EAGLE *Lophaetus occipitalis* (139) 52-58 cm

The combination of dull black plumage and long wispy crest renders this eagle unmistakable. In flight shows conspicuous white bases to primaries and secondaries, and a black and white barred tail. Flight action is fast and direct on stiffly held wings with shallow wing beats.
MALE has white leggings and longer crest than female which has brown or brown and white mottled leggings. IMM. very like ad. but has short crest and grey (not yellow) eyes. HABITAT. Well-wooded country (plantations) and forest edges, especially where marshy. STATUS. Common resident. CALL. High-pitched scream 'kee-ah' given during display flight or when perched. (Langkuifarend)

AYRES' EAGLE *Hieraaetus ayresii* (138) 45-55 cm

The bold black spotting on the white underparts, extending on to the belly and legs, helps differentiate this species from the larger African Hawk Eagle. The underwing is heavily barred and the underwing coverts are heavily blotched. Upperwing uniform dark brown in contrast to African Hawk Eagle's which shows pale panels in the outer wing. Head usually dark brown but variable, may even be white.
SEXES alike but female larger than male. IMM. has more heavily barred underwing than imm. African Hawk Eagle. HABITAT. Well-wooded country. STATUS. Resident in north, summer visitor in south. Uncommon to rare. CALL. Normally silent but when displaying it utters a shrill 'pueep-pip-pip-pueep'. (Kleinjagarend)

BOOTED EAGLE *Hieraaetus pennatus* (136) 46-53 cm

This small, buzzard-sized eagle has pale and dark colour forms: in both of these it differs from Wahlberg's Eagle (p. 92) by its shorter, broader tail and broader wings. Underparts and underwing coverts whitish in pale colour form; dark form is uniformly dark brown below with paler brown tail. From above, a small white patch is visible at the base of the forewing, giving the impression of a pair of white 'braces'. The dark brown on head and face extends well below the eyes and contrasts with the small white throat.
SEXES alike. IMM. as ad. HABITAT. Fynbos, Karoo, semi-desert, usually in mountainous country. STATUS. Uncommon resident and summer visitor. A small number breed in the south and west. CALL. High-pitched 'kee-keeee' or 'pee-pee-pee-pee'. (Dwergarend)

AFRICAN HAWK EAGLE
ad.

AFRICAN HAWK EAGLE
imm.

AFRICAN
HAWK EAGLE
ad.

ad.

imm.

LONGCRESTED
EAGLE

LONGCRESTED EAGLE
ad.

AYRES' EAGLE
ad.
dark form

sub-ad.

AYRES' EAGLE
ad.

AYRES' EAGLE
ad.

AYRES' EAGLE
imm.

AYRES' EAGLE
ad.

imm.

BOOTED EAGLE

rufous form

medium-dark
form

pale form

pale form

BOOTED EAGLE

pale form
BOOTED EAGLE

dark form

BOOTED EAGLE

pale form

pale form

99

 BUZZARDS

HONEY BUZZARD *Pernis apivorus* (130) 56 cm
Like Steppe Buzzard (p. 102) which it resembles, this species is very variable in colour, but it differs by having two broad black bars at the base of its tail (not easily seen) and a broad, dark terminal tail band. More slender in appearance than Steppe Buzzard with a smaller, more compact head. At close range the scaly feathering which covers the face is diagnostic.
SEXES alike. IMM. lacks diagnostic tail pattern of ad. but the general shape and small head should help distinguish it from Steppe Buzzard. HABITAT. Found mostly in woodland. STATUS. An annual but rare summer visitor. CALL. 'Meeuuw', a higher pitched call than that of Steppe Buzzard. (Wespedief)

JACKAL BUZZARD *Buteo rufofuscus* (152) 45-53 cm
Ad. has dark grey upperparts with bright chestnut breast and barred black and white belly. In flight vaguely resembles ad. Bateleur (p. 88) but the longer, rufous tail and more flapping flight action eliminate confusion. Jackal Buzzards with white breasts can be distinguished from Augur Buzzard by their dark underwing coverts.
SEXES alike. IMM. easily mistaken for Steppe Buzzard (p. 102) but has larger, broader wings and a pale, unbarred tail. HABITAT. Generally confined to mountain ranges and adjacent grassland. STATUS. Locally common resident; endemic. CALL. A loud, drawn-out 'weeaah-ka-ka-ka', much like the yelp of Blackbacked Jackal. (Rooiborsjakkalsvoël)

AUGUR BUZZARD *Buteo augur* (153) 45-53 cm
Similar in shape and overall structure to Jackal Buzzard but differs by having white throat, breast and belly, and white underwing coverts. Some Jackal Buzzards show white breasts but their dark underwing coverts should eliminate confusion with Augur Buzzard.
FEMALE has black on lower throat. IMM. brown above, buffy below with darker brown streaking. HABITAT. Mountain ranges and hilly country in woodland, savanna and desert. STATUS. Common resident. CALL. A harsh 'kow-kow-kow-kow' during display. (Witborsjakkalsvoël)

LONGLEGGED BUZZARD *Buteo rufinus* (151) 51-66 cm
As with other buzzards, plumage is very variable. However, this species is large and bulky, and hovers occasionally in flight. The combination of dark belly, pale head, and longer and broader wings also distinguishes this from Steppe and Forest Buzzards (p. 102). Other useful identification characters are the white unmarked primaries with black wing tips and trailing edge, and the pale, almost translucent tail in the typical ad.
SEXES alike. IMM. indistinguishable from other imm. buzzards unless direct comparison of size and shape is made. HABITAT. Open grassland and semi-desert. STATUS. Rare summer vagrant to the north-west. CALL. Typical buzzard 'pee-ooo'. (Langbeenjakkalsvoël)

imm. pale form

ad.
dark form

imm.
dark form

HONEY BUZZARD

pale form

ad.
pale form

imm. undertail

ad. undertail

pale form

ad.

JACKAL BUZZARD

imm.

ad.

ad.

ad.

AUGUR BUZZARD

male ad.

female ad.

imm.

male ad.

female ad.

imm.

LONGLEGGED BUZZARD

ad.

FOREST BUZZARD *Buteo tachardus* (150) 45-50 cm
Very similar to Steppe Buzzard in size and plumage; distinguished from Steppe Buzzard by having tear-shaped streaks on the underparts but no barring on flanks.
SEXES alike. IMM. distinguished from imm. Steppe Buzzard by mostly white front and by flank streaks being tear-shaped. HABITAT. Evergreen forests and forest edges. Has adapted to exotic eucalyptus and pine plantations. STATUS. Locally common resident. CALL. A gull-like 'pee-ooo'. (Bergjakkalsvoël)

STEPPE BUZZARD *Buteo buteo* (149) 45-50 cm
Plumage varies from pale brown through to almost black. It is generally darker below than Forest Buzzard, and occurs mostly in different habitats. Frequently seen perched on telephone poles along roads and freeways.
SEXES alike. IMM. as ad., but has yellow (not brown) eyes and a narrower terminal tail bar. HABITAT. Open country, avoiding desert and well-wooded regions. STATUS. Common summer visitor. CALL. A gull-like 'pee-ooo'. (Bruinjakkalsvoël)

GYMNOGENE *Polyboroides typus* (169) 60-66 cm
Ad. could be confused with the Chanting Goshawks (p. 108), but the broad floppy wings and single central white tail band are distinctive. Legs yellow (not red). Close views reveal bare yellow facial skin and elongated nape feathers.
SEXES alike. IMM. has variable brown plumage with no diagnostic markings but the small head and broad wings, combined with the lazy manner of flight, help identification. At close range the imm. shows bare greyish facial skin. HABITAT. Forests, riverine forests and open broadleafed woodland. STATUS. Common to scarce resident. CALL. During the breeding season it utters a whistled 'suuu-eeee-ooo'. (Kaalwangvalk)

FOREST BUZZARD
imm.
ad.

FOREST BUZZARD
ad.
imm.

imm.
ad.

FOREST BUZZARD
imm.
ad.

STEPPE BUZZARD
imm.
ad. rufous form
ad.

STEPPE BUZZARD
imm.

STEPPE BUZZARD
imm.
ad.
rufous form
imm.
grey form
ad.
grey form

STEPPE
BUZZARD
ad.
ad.

STEPPE BUZZARD
ad.

imm.
ad.

sub-ad.
imm.

GYMNOGENE

sub-ad.
imm.

display
ad.

103

HARRIERS *See also pages 126-127*

AFRICAN MARSH HARRIER *Circus ranivorus* (165) 45-50 cm

Ad. differs from female European Marsh Harrier by lacking the well-demarcated white crown and throat, and by having barring on flight feathers and tail. Distinguished from female Pallid and Montagu's Harriers (p. 106) by its larger size, broader wings and lack of a white rump.
SEXES alike. IMM. has pale creamy head and creamy leading edge to upperwing. Could be confused with female European Marsh Harrier but shows a pale bar across the breast and has barred flight feathers and tail. HABITAT. Marshland and flooded grassland and adjacent fields. STATUS. Locally common resident. CALL. Normally silent except during breeding season, when a variety of chattering notes is uttered. (Afrikaanse Paddavreter)

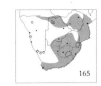

EUROPEAN MARSH HARRIER *Circus aeruginosus* (164) 48-55 cm

Male easily identifiable by brownish body contrasting with grey on wings and unbarred grey tail. Female is dark brown with creamy white cap and throat, white-edged forewings, and unbarred brown tail. Imm. African Marsh Harrier, in worn and abraded plumage, can also show pale forehead and leading edge to wings but has barred flight feathers and tail and a pale band across the breast.
IMM. similar to female or can lack white on crown and forewings. HABITAT. Confined to marshy areas and adjoining fields. STATUS. Rare summer visitor. CALL. Silent in the region. (Europese Paddavreter)

BLACK HARRIER *Circus maurus* (168) 48-53 cm

The pied plumage of the ad. renders this harrier unmistakable.
SEXES alike. IMM. resembles the imm. and female of the Pallid and Montagu's Harriers (p. 106), but differs by having white undersides to secondaries, primaries barred with brown, and a barred white and brown tail. HABITAT. Open grassland, scrub, and semi-desert and mountainous regions. STATUS. Uncommon resident in southern Cape, but outside the breeding season it wanders to northern and central regions. Endemic. CALL. A 'pee-pee-pee-pee' call is given during display and a harsh 'chak-chak-chak' when alarmed. (Witkruispaddavreter)

wing feather

AFRICAN MARSH HARRIER

ad.

ad.

ad.

imm.

ad.

imm.

AFRICAN MARSH HARRIER   ad.

imm.

EUROPEAN
MARSH HARRIER

female

male ad.
EUROPEAN MARSH HARRIER

male

female ad.

female imm.

male ad.

male ad.

EUROPEAN MARSH HARRIER

imm.

ad.

BLACK HARRIER   ad.

ad.

ad.

imm.

ad.

BLACK HARRIER

105

MONTAGU'S HARRIER *Circus pygargus* (166) 41-46 cm

Male differs from male Pallid Harrier by larger size, grey throat and upper breast, bulkier shape, streaks on belly and flanks, and a conspicuous black bar on secondaries visible in flight from above. Secondaries lightly barred from below (unmarked in Pallid Harrier).
FEMALE and IMM. virtually inseparable except at close quarters from female and imm. Pallid Harriers. Dark markings on head restricted to crescent on ear coverts and very small, dark eye-stripe. Lacks a pale collar behind the ear covert crescent. HABITAT. Grassland and savanna. STATUS. Uncommon summer visitor. CALL. Silent in the region. (Bloupaddavreter)

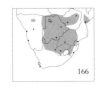

PALLID HARRIER *Circus macrourus* (167) 38-46 cm

Smaller, and daintier in flight, than Montagu's Harrier. Male easily recognized by very pale grey body and plain grey upperwings with a wedge-shaped black patch at the wing tips. Distinguished from male Montagu's Harrier by absence of streaking on belly and flanks and lack of black bar on secondaries.
FEMALE and IMM. Pallid and Montagu's Harriers are not easily distinguishable in the field unless a close view is obtained. The female and imm. of Pallid Harrier show whitish cheeks with a dark line through the eye and a black crescent behind the ear, a pattern lacking in the female and imm. Montagu's Harrier. Pallid Harrier typically shows a pale collar, lacking in Montagu's. HABITAT. Grassland and savanna. STATUS. Uncommon to rare summer visitor. CALL. Silent in the region. (Witborspaddavreter)

BLACKSHOULDERED KITE *Elanus caeruleus* (127) 33 cm

A small, easily identified grey and white raptor with diagnostic black shoulder patches. Has a characteristic habit of hovering and, when perched, it often wags its white tail up and down.
SEXES alike. IMM. is more buffy than ad. with brown-washed back and dark shoulders. HABITAT. Found in a wide range of open habitats but most common in agricultural areas, often seen perched on telephone poles and lines. STATUS. Common resident with local movements. CALL. A high-pitched whistle 'peeeu', a soft 'weep' and rasping 'wee-ah'. (Blouvalk)

MONTAGU'S HARRIER

male ad.

female

female

MONTAGU'S
HARRIER

imm.

female

PALLID
HARRIER

imm.

female
sub-ad.

male ad.

imm.

MONTAGU'S
HARRIER

female ad.

MONTAGU'S HARRIER
imm.

PALLID HARRIER

imm.

female
sub-ad.

female
ad.

PALLID HARRIER

imm.

male ad.

male ad.

female

imm.

Pallid female ad.

Comparison of length
of primaries on
the folded wing

PALLID HARRIER

Montagu's female ad.

BLACKSHOULDERED KITE

BLACKSHOULDERED KITE

imm.

imm.

BLACKSHOULDERED KITE

ad.

ad.

ad.

ad.

PALE CHANTING GOSHAWK *Melierax canorus* (162) 54-63 cm
Confusion only arises with Dark Chanting Goshawk where their ranges overlap.
This species is paler grey, especially on the forewings, and has a white rump and
white secondaries.
SEXES alike. IMM. is paler than imm. Dark Chanting Goshawk and has white (not
barred) rump. Superficially resembles a female harrier, but broader wings, flight action
and long legs should eliminate confusion. HABITAT. The common roadside hawk of
arid areas. STATUS. Common resident; near-endemic. CALL. A melodious piping
'kleeuu-kleeuu-klu-klu-klu', usually uttered at dawn. (Bleeksingvalk)

DARK CHANTING GOSHAWK *Melierax metabates* (163) 50-56 cm
Darker grey than Pale Chanting Goshawk. At rest the grey forewing does not contrast
with the rest of the wing as in Pale Chanting Goshawk. Rump and secondaries are
grey (not white).
SEXES alike. IMM. has a darker brown breast band than imm. Pale Chanting Goshawk
and has a barred grey-brown rump. HABITAT. Thornveld and open broadleafed woodland. Range overlaps narrowly with that of Pale Chanting Goshawk. STATUS. Scarce
resident. CALL. Piping call similar to that of Pale Chanting Goshawk, 'kleeu-kleeu-
klu-klu'. (Donkersingvalk)

YELLOWBILLED KITE *Milvus parasitus* (126b) 56 cm
Same size and shape as Black Kite, with much the same 'jizz'. Differs from Black
Kite in ad. plumage by having a bright yellow bill and more deeply forked tail.
SEXES alike. IMM. has black bill and buffy feather margins. HABITAT. The common kite
seen around human habitation. STATUS. Locally abundant breeding summer visitor.
CALL. Similar to that of Black Kite. (Geelbekwou)

BLACK KITE *Milvus migrans* (126a) 56 cm
Differs from similarly sized Steppe Buzzard (p. 102) by longer, forked tail and nar-
rower wings which are more acutely angled backwards in flight. Although much the
same size, African Marsh Harrier (p. 104) has a longer, square-ended tail and flies
with wings canted up; Black Kite has floppy flight action and twists its long tail for
steering. Differs from Yellowbilled Kite by having a black bill (but yellowish cere), a
paler, greyer head and a less deeply forked tail.
SEXES alike. IMM. has buffy feather margins. HABITAT. Diverse; from forest edge to
savanna and semi-desert. Often found in flocks at termite emergences. STATUS.
Locally common non-breeding summer visitor. CALL. A high-pitched shrill whinnying.
(Swartwou)

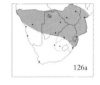

PALE CHANTING
GOSHAWK

ad.

ad.

imm.

imm.

imm.

ad.

ad.

ad.

imm.

DARK
CHANTING
GOSHAWK

ad.

imm.

YELLOWBILLED KITE

ad.

ad.

ad.

BLACK KITE

BLACK KITE
ad.

imm.

imm.

BLACK KITE   ad.

109

CUCKOO HAWK *Aviceda cuculoides* (128) 40 cm

Superficially resembles male African Goshawk (p. 114) but has a crest, a grey throat and upper breast which form a clearly defined bib, a heavily rufous-barred breast and belly, and short legs. In flight has long wings (not short and rounded as in African Goshawk) with rufous underwing coverts.
SEXES alike except in eye colour: female's are yellow and male's red or brown. IMM. resembles imm. African Goshawk and imm. Little Sparrowhawk (p. 112) but is larger, with shorter legs, a small crest and in flight, pointed (not rounded) wings. HABITAT. Mature woodland, riparian forest and evergreen forest fringes. STATUS. Uncommon resident. CALL. A loud, far-carrying 'teee-oooo' whistle and a shorter 'tittit-eooo'. (Koekoekvalk)

LIZARD BUZZARD *Kaupifalco monogrammicus* (154) 35-37 cm

Larger and bulkier than the similar Gabar Goshawk (p. 112), this bird has a white throat with a black line down the centre, a white rump and a broad white tail bar (or, rarely, two tail bars).
SEXES alike. IMM. similar to ad. but has paler cere and legs. HABITAT. Open broadleafed woodland and thornveld in the east and north. STATUS. Common to scarce resident and local migrant. CALL. Noisy in the breeding season: a whistled 'peoo-peoo' and a melodious 'klioo-klu-klu-klu-klu'. (Akkedisvalk)

PYGMY FALCON *Polihierax semitorquatus* (186) 18-20 cm

Its small size is distinctive. Shrike-like, it sits very upright on an exposed perch and hawks lizards and insects.
MALE is grey above and white below, FEMALE has chestnut back. IMM. as female but with dull brown back. HABITAT. Dry thornveld and semi-desert regions. Breeds in a chamber of Sociable Weaver nest, leaving a telltale whitewashed rim around the nest entrance. STATUS. Uncommon to locally common resident. CALL. Noisy; a 'chip-chip' and a 'kik-kik-kik-kik' call. (Dwergvalk)

ad.

crown
pattern

CUCKOO HAWK

ad.

imm.

imm.

ad.

CUCKOO HAWK

imm.

ad.

imm.

ad.

LIZARD BUZZARD

ad.

2-banded tail

LIZARD BUZZARD

PYGMY FALCON

male

PYGMY FALCON

female

male

female

male

OVAMBO SPARROWHAWK *Accipiter ovampensis* (156) 33-40 cm
Distinguished from similar Little Banded Goshawk by brown (not red) eye, by grey (not rufous) barring on front and by white vertical flecks on black and grey barred tail. Cere and legs usually yellow, but can be orange or red. Rare melanistic form differs from the melanistic form of Gabar Goshawk in having white vertical flecks in tail and lacking whitish webbing in rectrices of latter.
SEXES alike except in size; female larger. IMM. has two forms: the dark form differs from ad. Redbreasted Sparrowhawk (p. 114) by its rufous (not dark grey) head, and by its pale eyebrow. Other form is beige with distinctive broad pale eyebrow. Uppertail of both is as in ad. HABITAT. Tall woodland, avoiding forests and desert areas, and has adapted to exotic plantations, favouring poplars. STATUS. Locally common to rare resident. CALL. A soft 'keeep-keeep-keeep' is given when breeding. (Ovambosperwer)

GABAR GOSHAWK *Micronisus gabar* (161) 30-34 cm
Distinguished by its grey throat and breast, red cere and legs. Could be confused with Lizard Buzzard (p. 110) but that species has a white throat with a central stripe and a broad white tail band. Melanistic form Gabar Goshawk differs from melanistic form Ovambo Sparrowhawk by having white webbing in rectrices and lacking white vertical flecks in tail.
SEXES alike except in size; female larger. IMM. differs from other imm. hawks by its white rump. HABITAT. Savanna, especially thornveld and semi-arid habitats. STATUS. Locally common to scarce resident. CALL. A high-pitched whistling 'kik-kik-kik-kik-kik'. (Kleinsingvalk)

LITTLE BANDED GOSHAWK *Accipiter badius* (159) 28-30 cm
Lacks the white rump and tail spots of Little Sparrowhawk. Differs from Ovambo Sparrowhawk by its rufous (not grey) barring below, cherry-red (not brown) eye, and unbarred tail (when seen closed).
SEXES alike. IMM. most like imm. Gabar (both brown with streaked breast and barred belly) but lacks white rump. HABITAT. Savanna and tall woodland. STATUS. Common to scarce resident, with local movements. CALL. Male's call is a high-pitched 'keewik-keewik-keewik', female's call is a softer 'kee-uuu'. (Gebande Sperwer)

LITTLE SPARROWHAWK *Accipiter minullus* (157) 23-25 cm
Ad. distinguished from Little Banded Goshawk by its white rump and two white spots on the uppertail. Most like male African Goshawk (p. 114) but has white rump and lacks grey cere.
SEXES alike except in size; female larger. IMM. similar to imm. male African Goshawk in colour but is smaller, has a yellow eye, and lacks the grey cere. HABITAT. Diverse; frequents forests, woodland, savanna and has adapted to exotic plantations. Secretive. STATUS. Common to scarce resident. CALL. A high-pitched 'tu-tu-tu-tu-tu' is uttered by the male during the breeding season. Female has a softer 'kew-kew-kew'. (Kleinsperwer)

male imm.
pale form

male imm.
dark form

OVAMBO SPARROWHAWK

female ad.

GABAR GOSHAWK

female imm.

male ad.

GABAR GOSHAWK

male ad.
melanistic form

LITTLE BANDED GOSHAWK

male ad.

female ad.

LITTLE SPARROWHAWK

male ad.

male imm.

female imm.

113

 HAWKS *See also pages 128-129*

BLACK SPARROWHAWK *Accipiter melanoleucus* (158) 46-58 cm

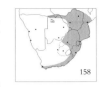

The largest accipiter of the region. The black and white plumage and large size render this species unmistakable. A rare melanistic form occurs but it has a white throat and this, combined with size, should preclude confusion with melanistic forms of Ovambo Sparrowhawk (p. 112) and Gabar Goshawk (p. 112).
MALE is smaller than female. IMM. has both pale and rufous forms. Pale form may be confused with imm. African Goshawk but is much larger. Rufous form resembles imm. African Hawk Eagle (p. 98) but has more heavily streaked underparts, un-feathered tarsi and a different shape and flight action. HABITAT. Forests and kloofs. Has adapted to exotic plantations. STATUS. Locally common resident. CALL. Normally silent except when breeding. Male's call is a 'keeyp', female's call is a repeated short 'kek'. (Swartsperwer)

AFRICAN GOSHAWK *Accipiter tachiro* (160) 36-39 cm

Wholly barred on front, no white on rump, yellow eye and grey cere distinguish ad. from other similar-looking hawks. Sexes highly dimorphic; small males bluish-grey above, barred rufous below with two white spots in the tail (like Little Sparrowhawk, p. 112); large females brown above, brown barred below, lack tail spots.
IMM. boldly spotted on front, distinguished from imm. Little Sparrowhawk by grey cere and from imm. Cuckoo Hawk (p. 110) by smaller size, longer legs and lack of a crest. HABITAT. Evergreen and riverine forests, tall mature woodland and well-wooded suburbia. STATUS. Common resident. CALL. Noisy; usually detected by a short 'whit' or 'chip' uttered on the wing or while perched. Female has mewing 'keeuuu' call. (Afrikaanse Sperwer)

REDBREASTED SPARROWHAWK *Accipiter rufiventris* (155) 33-40 cm

Ad. identified by uniformly rufous underparts, slate grey upperparts, and the lack of white on the rump.
SEXES alike except in size; female larger. IMM. plumage variable; generally darker above and more mottled below than imm. Ovambo Sparrowhawk (p. 112), which lacks the uniform dark cap, showing only a dark spot behind the eye. HABITAT. Montane grassland/forest mosaics; adapted to exotic plantations and has extended its range in the Karoo and on the highveld where these occur. STATUS. Locally common to rare resident. CALL. A sharp, staccato 'kee-kee-kee-kee-kee' during display. (Rooiborssperwer)

BLACK SPARROWHAWK

female ad.

male imm.

AFRICAN GOSHAWK

female sub-ad.

male ad.

male imm.

breast feather 'spot'

REDBREASTED SPARROWHAWK

male imm.

female ad.

115

FALCONS *See also pages 130-131*

LANNER FALCON *Falco biarmicus* (172) 40-45 cm
The rufous forehead and crown, and pinkish unmarked underparts, distinguish this species from Peregrine Falcon. It also has broader, more rounded wings, a longer tail and a floppier, less dynamic flight action than Peregrine Falcon.
SEXES alike except in size; female larger. IMM. much paler than imm. Peregrine with less streaking on underparts and a pale creamy or rufous crown. HABITAT. A wide range of habitats, from mountainous terrain to deserts and open grassland. Avoids forests. STATUS. Common to scarce resident. CALL. A harsh 'kak-kak-kak-kak-kak', similar to a Peregrine's call. Also makes whining and chopping notes. (Edelvalk)

PEREGRINE FALCON *Falco peregrinus* (171) 34-38 cm
Confusable with Lanner and Taita Falcons. Differs from Lanner by smaller size, black forehead and crown, and white breast with underparts finely barred black. It is swifter and more agile than Lanner Falcon, and has more pointed wings and a relatively short tail. Taita Falcon is smaller, has rufous underparts and two rufous patches on nape.
SEXES alike except for size; female larger. IMM. is darker than imm. Lanner Falcon and has forehead and crown dark brown (not rufous). HABITAT. High cliffs and gorges, both coastal and inland. STATUS. Scarce or rare resident and visitor: the larger and paler northern hemisphere race *calidus* visits in summer and may occur anywhere, but is scarce. CALL. A raucous 'kak-kak-kak-kak-kak' is uttered around nesting cliff; also makes whining and chopping notes. (Swerfvalk)

TAITA FALCON *Falco fasciinucha* (176) 28-30 cm
This small, robustly built falcon is shaped like a Peregrine and, in flight, shows the dash and speed of that species. In coloration it resembles an African Hobby (p. 118) but differs by having rufous patches on the nape, and a white throat which contrasts with black moustachial stripes.
SEXES alike. IMM. similar to ad. but has buff edges to back feathers. HABITAT. High cliffs and gorges. STATUS. Rare resident. CALL. A high-pitched 'kree-kree-kree' and 'kek-kek-kek'. (Teitavalk)

REDNECKED FALCON *Falco chicquera* (178) 30-36 cm
Ad. unmistakable with its chestnut crown and nape, and dark brown moustachial stripes on white cheeks.
SEXES alike. IMM. has a dark brown head, two buff patches on nape, and pale rufous underparts finely barred with brown. HABITAT. Palm savanna and arid thornveld. STATUS. Uncommon resident. CALL. A shrill 'ki-ki-ki-ki-ki' during breeding season. (Rooinekvalk)

LANNER FALCON

tail

female ad.

ad.

ad.

ad. imm.

imm.

PEREGRINE FALCON

PEREGRINE FALCON

imm.

ad.

female ad.

tail

imm.

PEREGRINE FALCON

(same scale)

imm.

ad.

calidus
female
ad.

female
ad.

ad. imm.

TAITA FALCON

ad.

ad.

ad. imm.

ad.

TAITA FALCON

ad.

REDNECKED FALCON

ad.

ad.

imm.

117

 FALCONS, HAWKS *See also pages 130-131*

ELEONORA'S FALCON *Falco eleonorae* (177) 38 cm
Pale form distinguished from imm. Peregrine Falcon (p. 116) by its rufous, heavily streaked underparts, and longer wings and tail. Differentiated from European Hobby by larger size, rufous underparts and dark underwing. Dark form most likely to be confused with Sooty Falcon (p. 120) but is larger, darker, longer tailed, has darker underwing coverts and has greenish (not chrome yellow) legs and feet.
SEXES alike except that male's cere is yellow, female's is blue. IMM. differs from imm. Peregrine by having a rufous wash and darker underwing. HABITAT. Open broadleafed woodland and adjoining grassland. STATUS. Rare vagrant during late summer. CALL. Silent in the region. (Eleonoravalk)

EUROPEAN HOBBY *Falco subbuteo* (173) 28-35 cm
In flight the long pointed wings and relatively short tail give this species a swift-like appearance. It has the breast heavily streaked and has conspicuous rufous leggings and vent. Distinguished from similarly shaped African Hobby by rufous front of that species. Larger, darker backed, and more heavily streaked in front than female and imm. Eastern Redfooted Falcon (p. 122).
SEXES alike. IMM. lacks rufous vent and leggings. HABITAT. Broadleafed woodland and savanna. Avoids forests and deserts. Often found near open water. STATUS. Uncommon summer visitor. CALL. Silent in the region. (Europese Boomvalk)

AFRICAN HOBBY *Falco cuvierii* (174) 28-30 cm
Resembles European Hobby but is smaller, has an unstreaked rufous breast and underparts. Might be mistaken for Taita Falcon (p. 116) which is more robust and has rufous nape markings and a white throat.
SEXES alike. IMM. shows a streaked front. HABITAT. Open broadleafed woodland, forests and adjoining open country. STATUS. Rare summer visitor. CALL. A high-pitched 'kik-kik-kik-kik' in display. (Afrikaanse Boomvalk)

BAT HAWK *Macheiramphus alcinus* (129) 45 cm
A dark brown bird, appearing black in the field, with a varying amount of white visible on throat and abdomen. Falcon-shaped in flight and could easily be mistaken for a Lanner or Peregrine Falcon (p. 116) if seen in twilight when colours are not discernible, but has thinner body and longer wings. At close quarters white legs, eyelids and nape patches distinctive.
SEXES alike. IMM. shows more white on the underparts. HABITAT. Woodland, including plantations, and savanna. Crepuscular and nocturnal, roosting in thick foliage during the day. Easily overlooked. STATUS. Rare resident. CALL. A high-pitched whistling, reminiscent of a dikkop. (Vlermuisvalk)

ad.

ELEONORA'S FALCON

male ad.

ad.   imm.

ad.
dark form

imm.

ad.   ad.

ad.   imm.

EUROPEAN HOBBY

AFRICAN HOBBY

ad.   imm.

imm.

ad.   imm.

imm. pale form

ad.

BAT HAWK

119

SOOTY FALCON *Falco concolor* (175) 32-35 cm

Most like Grey Kestrel which is squatter and shorter winged (wings do not extend beyond tail when perched), and Dickinson's Kestrel, which has a paler head and rump. Differs from ad. male Western Redfooted Falcon (p. 122) by lack of chestnut vent and by chrome-yellow (not red) legs and cere. Flight shape like European Hobby (p. 118) but wings are longer.
SEXES alike. IMM. has shape of ad. but is buffy below, heavily streaked with grey. Moustachial streak less pronounced than in European Hobby (p. 118). HABITAT. Well-wooded coastal areas. STATUS. Rare summer visitor to east coast, vagrant elsewhere. CALL. Silent in southern Africa. (Roetvalk)

DICKINSON'S KESTREL *Falco dickinsoni* (185) 28-30 cm

The combination of a grey body contrasting with a very pale grey head and pale grey rump should rule out confusion with any other grey falcon in the region.
SEXES alike. IMM. very similar to ad. but has white barring on flanks. HABITAT. Open palm and woodland savanna, often in the vicinity of baobab trees. STATUS. Scarce resident. CALL. High-pitched 'keee-keee-keee'. (Dickinsonse Valk)

GREY KESTREL *Falco ardosiaceus* (184) 30-33 cm

Distinguished from Sooty Falcon by shorter, broader wings, and stockier, more robust build. At rest the wings do not reach the tip of the square tail. An entirely grey falcon, it lacks the pale head and rump of Dickinson's Kestrel.
SEXES alike. IMM. like ad., slightly suffused with brown. HABITAT. Savanna, especially where there are palms present. STATUS. Rare and localized in the extreme north-west. CALL. Silent when in the region. (Donkergrysvalk)

See also pages 130-131

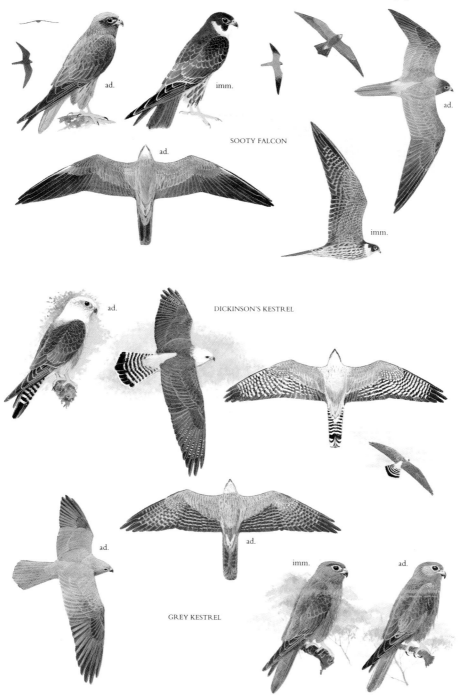

ad.

imm.

SOOTY FALCON

ad.

ad.

imm.

DICKINSON'S KESTREL

ad.

ad.

ad.

GREY KESTREL

ad.

ad.

imm.

ad.

EASTERN REDFOOTED FALCON *Falco amurensis* (180) 30 cm
Ad. male's slate plumage contrasts with the diagnostic white underwing coverts.
FEMALE and IMM. resemble European Hobby (p. 118) but have a white forehead and pale grey crown. Female lacks the rufous crown, nape and underparts of female Western Redfooted Falcon. Imm. resembles female but is even paler on the crown. HABITAT. Open grassland. Roosts communally in tall trees in towns. STATUS. Common summer visitor. CALL. A shrill chattering, heard at roosts. (Oostelike Rooipootvalk)

WESTERN REDFOOTED FALCON *Falco vespertinus* (179) 30 cm
The combination of slate-grey plumage with chestnut vent is diagnostic in the male. It lacks the white underwing coverts of Eastern Redfooted Falcon.
FEMALE differs from female Eastern Redfooted Falcon by having rufous crown, nape and buffy underparts. IMM. might be confused with European Hobby (p. 118) but differs by having pale crown, pale underparts and a much paler underwing with a dark trailing edge. HABITAT. Open grassland and arid savanna. STATUS. Common to rare summer visitor. CALL. A shrill chattering, heard at roosts. (Westelike Rooipootvalk)

LESSER KESTREL *Falco naumanni* (183) 30 cm
Male differs from ad. Rock Kestrel by its unspotted chestnut back, grey secondaries and spotted, buff-coloured front.
FEMALE and IMM. similar to imm. Rock Kestrel but are paler below, especially on the underwing. HABITAT. Open grassland and agricultural areas. Roosts communally in tall trees in towns. STATUS. Common summer visitor. CALL. Silent in the region. (Kleinrooivalk)

ROCK KESTREL *Falco tinnunculus* (181) 33-39 cm
Differs from male Lesser Kestrel by having a spotted chestnut back and wings, lacking grey on secondaries and having the underwing spotted and barred (not silvery white). Differs from Greater Kestrel by grey head, more rufous colour, smaller size, spotted (not barred) back, and more heavily marked underwing.
SEXES alike except on tail, where female has narrow bands which male lacks. IMM. differs from female and imm. Lesser Kestrel, as that species is slimmer, paler below, especially on underwing. HABITAT. Diverse, but usually in mountainous or rocky terrain. STATUS. Common resident with local movements. CALL. High-pitched 'kik-kik-kik'. (Kransvalk)

GREATER KESTREL *Falco rupicoloides* (182) 36-40 cm
At close range the diagnostic whitish eye is obvious.
Larger and paler brown than Rock Kestrel with whitish underwing; distinguished from female Lesser Kestrel by a grey, barred tail, and lack of moustachial stripes. SEXES alike. IMM. has rufous, barred tail and a dark eye. HABITAT. Arid savanna to desert. STATUS. Locally common resident. CALL. During display a shrill, repeated 'kee-ker-rik' is given. (Grootrooivalk)

male

female

male

EASTERN REDFOOTED FALCON

male

female

imm.

male

female

male

WESTERN REDFOOTED FALCON

male

female

imm.

female

male

female

male

LESSER KESTREL

male

female

GREATER KESTREL

ad.

ad.

male

female

male

imm. tail

ROCK KESTREL

male

male tail

female

male

GREATER KESTREL

imm.

HONEY BUZZARD

female ad.

imm. dark form

male ad.
pale form

imm. pale form

ad.

HONEY BUZZARD

HONEY BUZZARD   male ad.

sailing

STEPPE BUZZARD   soaring

JACKAL BUZZARD   AUGUR BUZZARD   AUGUR BUZZARD

imm.   imm.   male ad.   female ad.

imm.

JACKAL BUZZARD

ad. pale form

imm.

JACKAL BUZZARD

sub-ad.

imm.

ad.

JACKAL
BUZZARD

AUGUR BUZZARD

imm.

AUGUR BUZZARD

ad.   AUGUR   imm.
             BUZZARD

male ad.

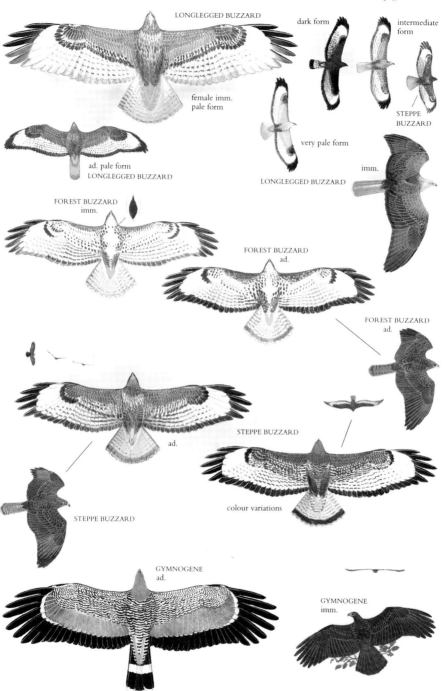

See also pages 100-102

LONGLEGGED BUZZARD

dark form

intermediate form

female imm. pale form

STEPPE BUZZARD

very pale form

ad. pale form
LONGLEGGED BUZZARD

LONGLEGGED BUZZARD

imm.

FOREST BUZZARD
imm.

FOREST BUZZARD
ad.

FOREST BUZZARD
ad.

ad.

STEPPE BUZZARD

colour variations

STEPPE BUZZARD

GYMNOGENE
ad.

GYMNOGENE
imm.

125

ad.

AFRICAN MARSH HARRIER

female

EUROPEAN MARSH HARRIER

BLACK HARRIER   imm.

BLACK HARRIER
imm.

MONTAGU'S HARRIER

male ad.

imm.
moulting
into ad.
plumage

male melanistic form

PALLID HARRIER

male ad.

young male
in worn plumage

male ad.
in worn
plumage

BLACKSHOULDERED KITE
ad.

ad.

PALE CHANTING GOSHAWK
ad.

PALE CHANTING GOSHAWK
imm.

DARK CHANTING GOSHAWK
ad.

DARK CHANTING GOSHAWK
imm.

YELLOWBILLED KITE
imm.

MARSH HARRIERS

BLACK KITE

BLACK KITE
ad.

See also pages 110-112

CUCKOO HAWK

imm.

imm.

ad.

ad.

male

female

ad.

LIZARD BUZZARD
ad.

PYGMY FALCON

OVAMBO SPARROWHAWK

female ad.

male ad.
melanistic form

OVAMBO SPARROWHAWK

OVAMBO SPARROWHAWK

male imm.

female ad.

female imm.

LITTLE BANDED GOSHAWK

male ad.

LITTLE BANDED
GOSHAWK

female imm.

male ad.

male imm.

See also pages 112-114

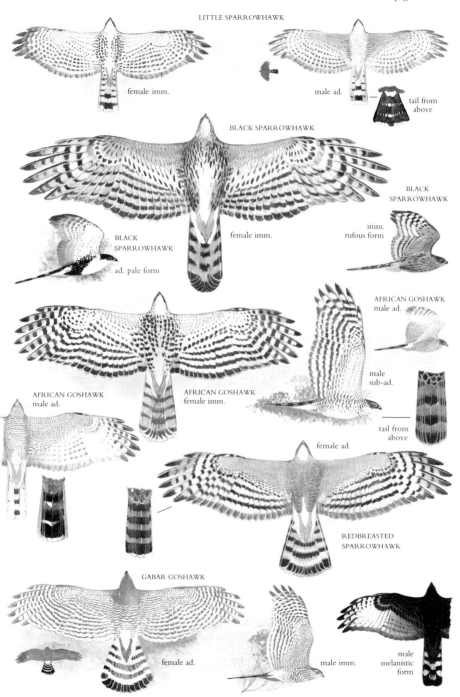

LITTLE SPARROWHAWK

female imm.

male ad.

tail from above

BLACK SPARROWHAWK

BLACK SPARROWHAWK

BLACK SPARROWHAWK
ad. pale form

female imm.

imm. rufous form

AFRICAN GOSHAWK
male ad.

male sub-ad.

AFRICAN GOSHAWK
male ad.

AFRICAN GOSHAWK
female imm.

tail from above

female ad.

REDBREASTED SPARROWHAWK

GABAR GOSHAWK

female ad.

male imm.

male melanistic form

129

See also pages 116-118

PEREGRINE FALCON

female imm.

LANNER FALCON
female imm.

TAITA FALCON
ad.

REDNECKED FALCON
imm.

ELEONORA'S FALCON

female imm.

ad.

ad. dark form

EUROPEAN HOBBY

ad.

AFRICAN HOBBY

ad.

BAT HAWK
ad.

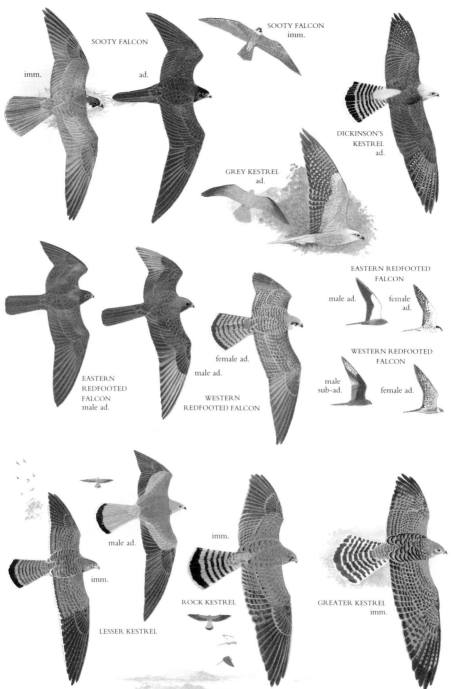

See also pages 120-122

131

REDBILLED FRANCOLIN *Francolinus adspersus* (194) 35-38 cm
The combination of dull red bill and legs and the yellow eye-ring is diagnostic.
FEMALE lacks the spurs of the male. IMM. lacks the yellow around the eye. HABITAT.
Dry thornveld and open broadleafed woodland. In the dry west it is the typical
francolin of seasonal riverbeds and associated riverine vegetation. Feeds freely in the
open and is less skulking than other francolins. STATUS. Locally common resident;
near-endemic. CALL. A loud, harsh 'chaa-chaa-chek-chek' is uttered at dawn and
dusk. (Rooibekfisant)

SWAINSON'S FRANCOLIN *Francolinus swainsonii* (199) 38 cm
*Bare red face, black bill and black legs distinguish this species from all other francolins
in the region.*
FEMALE lacks the spurs of the male. IMM. has red on face reduced and paler than ad.
HABITAT. Dry thornveld and agricultural lands. Seen in small groups of three to five.
STATUS. Common resident. CALL A raucous 'krraae-krraae-krraae' given by males at
dawn and dusk. (Bosveldfisant)

REDNECKED FRANCOLIN *Francolinus afer* (198) 36 cm
*Similar to Swainson's Francolin in having bare red skin on throat and around eyes
but has red (not black) legs and bill and conspicuous white striping on flanks.
Different races vary in the amount of white on face and underparts.*
FEMALE lacks the spurs of the male. IMM. like ad. HABITAT. Evergreen temperate
forests, their edges and adjoining grassland. STATUS. Common resident. CALL. A loud
'kwoor-kwoor-kwoor-kwaaa' given at dusk and dawn. (Rooikeelfisant)

CAPE FRANCOLIN *Francolinus capensis* (195) 42 cm
*Distinguished from all other large, dark francolins by having pale cheeks which con-
trast with a dark cap. Lacks any red on throat or around the eyes and ad. shows a
greyish-horn bill. Has diffuse white streaking on lower belly.*
MALE has a spur, female has only a reduced spur. IMM. like ad. HABITAT. The common
francolin of fynbos. Has adapted to wheatfields. STATUS. Common resident; endemic.
CALL. A loud, screeching 'cackalac-cackalac-cackalac'. (Kaapse Fisant)

NATAL FRANCOLIN *Francolinus natalensis* (196) 35 cm
*Similar to the larger Rednecked Francolin but does not have bare red skin around the
eyes and on the throat. Generally brown above and barred and speckled black and
white below.*
SEXES alike. IMM. similar to ad. but has less speckling below and is darker brown on
breast and back. HABITAT. Wooded habitat, especially thickets of bush along rivers and
on hill slopes. STATUS. Common resident; near-endemic. CALL. A raucous, unmusical
screeching. (Natalse Fisant)

REDBILLED
FRANCOLIN

male ad.

ad.

imm.

SWAINSON'S FRANCOLIN

imm.

male ad.

REDNECKED FRANCOLIN

castaneiventer
male ad.

notatus
female ad.

lehmanni
female ad.

swynnertoni
male ad.

REDNECKED
FRANCOLIN

cunensis
male ad.

CAPE
FRANCOLIN
male ad.

NATAL FRANCOLIN
male ad.

133

ORANGE RIVER FRANCOLIN *Francolinus levaillantoides* (193) 35 cm
This species is slightly smaller than the very similar Redwing Francolin: it differs by having a thin, dark necklace which never broadens to form a dark breast band. There are many races which vary greatly in coloration. Distinguished from Shelley's Francolin by lack of black barring on belly, and from Greywing Francolin by the white (not grey-freckled) throat.
SEXES alike. IMM. resembles ad. HABITAT. Open grassland to bush or shrub savanna. STATUS. Locally common resident; near-endemic. CALL. A melodious, often repeated 'kibitele', mostly at dawn. (Kalaharipatrys)

REDWING FRANCOLIN *Francolinus levaillantii* (192) 38 cm
The black-speckled necklace on the breast is much broader than in any other francolin. It forms a distinct breast band, which distinguishes this species from Orange River Francolin.
SEXES alike. IMM. paler than ad. but still shows dark breast band. HABITAT. Grassland and fields in mountainous terrain, usually on lower slopes and in valleys. STATUS. Locally common resident. CALL. A melodious piping 'too-queequee', sometimes preceded by several short 'tok' notes. (Rooivlerkpatrys)

GREYWING FRANCOLIN *Francolinus africanus* (190) 33 cm
A mainly grey francolin, easily identified by its grey freckled throat, not white or buff as in other grassland francolins.
SEXES alike. IMM. is duller version of ad. but still displays throat character. HABITAT. Upland grassland and fynbos. STATUS. Common resident; endemic. CALL. A multi-syllabled whistling call starting with a series of 'pi' notes and ending with an explosive 'wip, ki-peeo'. (Bergpatrys)

SHELLEY'S FRANCOLIN *Francolinus shelleyi* (191) 33 cm
The chestnut-striped breast and flanks, and black and white barred belly are diagnostic. Throat white, edged black.
SEXES alike. IMM. resembles ad. but has throat streaked brown. HABITAT. Savanna, especially associated with rocky ground. STATUS. Locally common resident. CALL. A rhythmic 'tilitileeo', repeated many times at dawn and dusk. (Laeveldpatrys)

ORANGE RIVER FRANCOLIN

levaillantoides

langi

pallidior

REDWING FRANCOLIN

neck feather

GREYWING FRANCOLIN

neck feather

SHELLEY'S FRANCOLIN

belly pattern

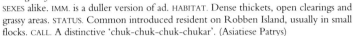

CHUKAR PARTRIDGE *Alectoris chukar* (187) 33 cm

Totally unlike any francolin in the region. The creamy white throat with broad black border and barred chestnut, black and white flanks, are diagnostic. Shelley's Francolin (p. 134) has a white throat bordered by a dark necklace but lacks the bright vertical barring on flanks.

SEXES alike. IMM. is a duller version of ad. HABITAT. Dense thickets, open clearings and grassy areas. STATUS. Common introduced resident on Robben Island, usually in small flocks. CALL. A distinctive 'chuk-chuk-chuk-chukar'. (Asiatiese Patrys)

CRESTED FRANCOLIN *Francolinus sephaena* (189) 33-35 cm

The dark cap with contrasting broad white eyebrow stripe and dark-striped chest are diagnostic in all races. The tail is frequently held cocked at a 45 degree angle, imparting a bantam-like appearance.

FEMALE less boldly marked than male. IMM. as female, but paler. HABITAT. Woodland and savanna, especially in thornveld. STATUS. Common resident. CALL. A rattling 'chee-chakla, chee-chakla' by birds calling in duet. (Bospatrys)

COQUI FRANCOLIN *Francolinus coqui* (188) 28 cm

Male is the only francolin in the region to have a plain buffy head with a contrasting darker crown. Smaller than other francolins, except Hartlaub's.

FEMALE resembles Shelley's Francolin (p. 134) but has a broad white eye-stripe which runs behind the eye and on to the neck, and lacks chestnut striping on breast and flanks. IMM. resembles the ad. of the respective sex. HABITAT. Woodland, savanna and fringing open areas; favours sandy soils. STATUS. Common resident. CALL. Common call: two-syllabled 'co-qui'; less frequently heard 'kraak, kara-ka ka'. (Swempie)

HARTLAUB'S FRANCOLIN *Francolinus hartlaubi* (197) 26 cm

The smallest francolin of the region, its size approximates that of the female Coqui Francolin.

MALE is easily identified by its dark cap contrasting with a distinct white eyebrow, large decurved bill and pale underparts heavily streaked with brown. FEMALE is a dull orange-brown bird lacking distinguishing features other than the large bill. IMM. female is a drab version of the ad. female while the imm. male shows a white eyebrow. HABITAT. Boulder-strewn slopes and rocky outcrops in hilly and mountainous regions. Often seen in small groups scurrying over rocks. STATUS. Uncommon, localized resident. CALL. A 'wa-ak-ak-ak-ak' alarm call. A very distinct duet uttered at dawn. (Klipfisant)

CHUKAR PARTRIDGE

rovuma
male ad.

CRESTED FRANCOLIN

male ad.

CRESTED FRANCOLIN

imm.

sephaena

COQUI FRANCOLIN

male

female

male

HARTLAUB'S FRANCOLIN

female

COMMON PEAFOWL *Pavo cristatus* (924) 120 cm (male)
Both male and female are unmistakable. The species is included here on the admission to the subregion list of a feral population living on Robben Island, Cape Province. (Pou)

HELMETED GUINEAFOWL *Numida meleagris* (203) 56 cm
The grey body, flecked with white, the naked blue and red head and bare casque on the crown render this large gamebird unmistakable.
MALE has longer casque than female. IMM. like ad. but has a less-developed casque on crown, browner body coloration with white flecking enlarged on neck feathering. HABITAT. Grassland, broadleafed woodland, thornveld and agricultural land. STATUS. Common resident. May flock in hundreds. CALL. A loud, repeated 'krrdii-krrdii-krrdii-krrdii' and a 'kek-kek-kek-kek' alarm note. (Gewone Tarentaal)

CRESTED GUINEAFOWL *Guttera pucherani* (204) 50 cm
A black guineafowl finely spotted with white, and having a tuft of curly black feathers on the crown. The naked face is blue-grey with a large bare white patch on ears and nape. In flight shows a white stripe on primaries.
SEXES alike. IMM. is mottled and barred above and below. HABITAT. Montane, riparian, dune and coastal forests. STATUS. Uncommon and localized resident. CALL. A 'chik-chik-chil-chrrrr' is given by males. A soft 'keet-keet-keet' contact call is uttered by groups foraging on the forest floor. (Kuifkoptarentaal)

GROUND HORNBILL *Bucorvus leadbeateri* (463) 90 cm
Unmistakable, turkey-sized black bird with conspicuous red face and throat patches and a large, black, decurved bill. Toes distinctively arched. In flight shows broad white wing patches.
FEMALE is distinguished from the male by having a blue throat patch. IMM. differs from ad. by having a yellow (not red) face and throat patch. HABITAT. Savanna, woodland and grassland with adjoining forests. STATUS. Resident; mainly confined to large reserves and national parks. Threatened in many parts of its range. CALL. A loud, booming 'ooomph ooomph' early in the morning. (Bromvoël)

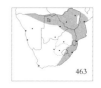

OSTRICH *Struthio camelus* (1) H 2 m
By far the largest (flightless) bird of the region. Male is black with a grey neck, predominantly white wings and a pale chestnut tail. In female, body feathering and tail are brown, the wings off-white.
IMM. resembles a small female. Chick resembles a korhaan but has a flattened bill and thick legs. HABITAT. Feral stock found on farms virtually throughout the region. STATUS. The only genuine wild ostriches occur in northern Namibia and the Kalahari. All others are descended from hybrids bred for the feather trade. CALL. Nocturnal; a booming leonine roar. (Volstruis)

COMMON PEAFOWL   male

female

ad.

CRESTED GUINEAFOWL

HELMETED GUINEAFOWL

imm.

ad.

imm.

GROUND HORNBILL

female

imm.

OSTRICH

female

male

GROUND HORNBILL

chick

BLUE QUAIL *Coturnix adansonii* (202) 15 cm
The smallest quail of the region, similar in size to the buttonquail.
MALE unmistakable: black and white face and throat pattern, rufous upperparts, and blue underparts which, in flight, appear black. FEMALE and IMM. on the ground can be distinguished from other quail by their barred underparts. HABITAT. Damp and flooded grassland in lightly wooded areas. STATUS. Rare summer visitor. CALL. Described as a high-pitched whistle 'teee-ti-ti'. (Bloukwartel)

HARLEQUIN QUAIL *Coturnix delegorguei* (201) 18 cm
Male much darker in appearance than Common Quail and differs from Common and Blue Quail by its chestnut underparts with black streaks.
FEMALE and IMM. are pale versions of male but are almost indistinguishable from Common Quail in flight. HABITAT. Grassland, damp fields, and open savanna. STATUS. Sporadic summer visitor, locally abundant in some years. CALL. High-pitched 'wit, wit-wit' similar to that of Common Quail, but more metallic in tone. A squeaky 'kree-kree' in flight. (Bontkwartel)

COMMON QUAIL *Coturnix coturnix* (200) 18 cm
A small gamebird usually seen in flight, when its dumpy body and whirring wings attract attention. On the ground runs swiftly through the grass in a hunched position.
MALE has black or russet throat but lacks the chestnut and black underparts of male Harlequin Quail. FEMALE and IMM. are much paler below than female Harlequin Quail. HABITAT. Grassland and fields. STATUS. Locally abundant summer visitor. CALL. A high-pitched 'whit wit-wit', repeated at intervals, more mellow than that of Harlequin Quail; a 'crwee-crwee' in flight. (Afrikaanse Kwartel)

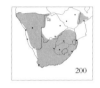

KURRICHANE BUTTONQUAIL *Turnix sylvatica* (205) 14 cm
In flight the lack of dark rump and back distinguish this species from Blackrumped Buttonquail. On the ground the black flecks on the sides of the breast and flanks, pale eye, and the absence of chestnut on the face, are diagnostic.
FEMALE is larger and more boldly marked than the male. IMM. is similar to male. HABITAT. Open grassland, old fields and open savanna. STATUS. Resident, with local movements. The most frequently encountered buttonquail throughout the region, except in the south and south-west. CALL. A low-pitched hoot 'hmmmmmm', repeated at intervals. (Bosveldkwarteltjie)

BLACKRUMPED BUTTONQUAIL *Turnix hottentotta* (206) 14 cm
This and Kurrichane Buttonquail, unless clearly seen, are difficult to distinguish. In flight, this species shows a diagnostic dark back and rump which contrast with paler wings. At rest ginger face and throat and dark eye distinguish it from Kurrichane Buttonquail. Both species are noticeably smaller than the similar Coturnix quail and appear to buzz through the air when put to flight.
FEMALE lacks ginger face. IMM. spotted across breast. HABITAT. Edges of vleis and moist grassland in hilly and mountainous areas. STATUS. Resident and summer visitor. A rare and little-known species considered to be endangered in southern Africa. CALL. A flufftail-like 'oooooop-oooooop'. (Kaapse Kwarteltjie)

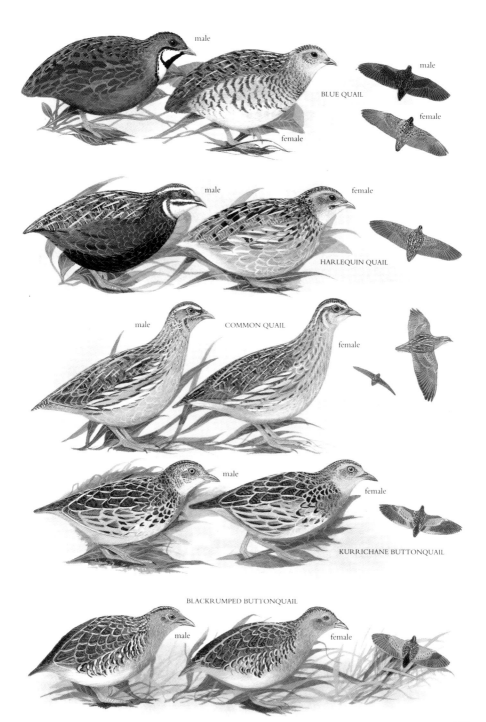

male

BLUE QUAIL

male

female

female

male

female

HARLEQUIN QUAIL

male

COMMON QUAIL

female

male

female

KURRICHANE BUTTONQUAIL

BLACKRUMPED BUTTONQUAIL

male

female

AFRICAN FINFOOT *Podica senegalensis* (229) 63 cm
When swimming, the head shape and submerged body suggest a Darter (p. 52), but this species differs by having a much shorter, stouter neck and a red bill. Out of the water the bright reddish-orange feet and legs are conspicuous.
MALE is greyer and darker headed than female. IMM. resembles female. HABITAT. Densely vegetated rivers with overgrown banks. A shy, furtive species. STATUS. Uncommon resident. CALL. Normally silent except for a short, frog-like 'krork'. (Watertrapper)

REDKNOBBED COOT *Fulica cristata* (228) 44 cm
A black, duck-like bird with a white bill and a white unfeathered forehead. The two red knobs on the forehead swell and become more noticeable during the breeding season.
SEXES alike. IMM. is dull brown and differs from the smaller imm. Moorhen by lacking white undertail coverts. HABITAT. Dams, pans and lakes; virtually any stretch of fresh water except fast-flowing rivers. STATUS. Common to abundant resident. CALL. A harsh, metallic 'claak'. (Bleshoender)

MOORHEN *Gallinula chloropus* (226) 32 cm
Unlike the glossy purple and green Lesser and American Purple Gallinules (p.144), the Moorhen is a dull, sooty black, and also differs by having greenish-yellow legs and a red frontal shield. Bolder than Lesser Moorhen and the gallinules, it swims freely in patches of open water.
SEXES alike. IMM. is distinguished from imm. Lesser Moorhen by its larger size and grey (not buffy) colour. HABITAT. Virtually any stretch of fresh water surrounded by reeds and tall grasses. STATUS. Common resident. CALL. A sharp 'krrik'. (Grootwaterhoender)

LESSER MOORHEN *Gallinula angulata* (227) 24 cm
Similar to Moorhen but is smaller, lacks conspicuous white flank feathers, and has a mainly yellow (not red) bill. Far more secretive than Moorhen.
SEXES alike. IMM. is sandy buff with dull yellowish-green bill and legs. Differs from imm. Moorhen which is grey-coloured. HABITAT. Flooded grassland, and small, secluded ponds. Skulking and usually heard rather than seen. STATUS. Locally common, but erratic, summer visitor. CALL. A series of hollow notes 'do do do do do do do'. (Kleinwaterhoender)

imm.

female

AFRICAN FINFOOT

male

juv.

imm.

REDKNOBBED COOT

ad.

MOORHEN

ad.

imm.

ad.

LESSER MOORHEN

undertail

imm.

ad.

sub-ad.

PURPLE GALLINULE *Porphyrio porphyrio* (223) 46 cm
The large size, massive red bill and frontal shield, red legs and toes combined with its general purplish coloration and turquoise neck and breast, are unmistakable. Imm. Lesser Gallinule is half the size and has a green or blue (but not red) frontal shield.
SEXES alike. IMM. is dull brown and has a massive, dull reddish-brown bill. HABITAT. Reedbeds, sedge marshes and flooded grassland. STATUS. Common resident. CALL. Variety of harsh shrieks, wails, and booming notes. (Grootkoningriethaan)

LESSER GALLINULE *Porphyrula alleni* (224) 25 cm
Easily distinguished from Purple Gallinule by smaller size, dark colour and green or blue shield, from American Purple Gallinule by red (not yellow) legs and lack of yellow tip to bill.
MALE in breeding condition has a blue frontal shield, the female's is lime-green. Non-breeding birds of both sex have dull brown shields. IMM. differentiated from imm. Moorhen (p. 142) by pale, fleshy coloured (not greenish-brown) legs, and by lacking the white stripes along flanks. Very similar to imm. American Purple Gallinule but that species has olive-coloured legs. HABITAT. Flooded grassland. STATUS. Locally common summer visitor. CALL. Six or more rapidly uttered sharp clicks 'duk duk duk duk duk duk'. (Kleinkoningriethaan)

AMERICAN PURPLE GALLINULE *Porphyrula martinica* (225) 33 cm
Similar to Purple Gallinule but is smaller, has bright yellowish-green (not red) legs and a yellow tip to its bill. Size, yellow legs and bill colour distinguish ad. from Lesser Gallinule. Frontal shield pale chalky blue.
SEXES alike. IMM. differs from imm. Moorhen (p. 142) by lack of white stripes on flanks and has olive (not green) legs. IMM. Lesser Gallinule very similar but that species has flesh-coloured legs. HABITAT. Usually thick reedbeds but virtually anywhere, some having been found walking along roads and beaches in an exhausted state. STATUS. Rare vagrant during autumn and winter to the west coast, with one record from the Natal coast. CALL. Silent when in southern Africa. (Amerikaanse Koningriethaan)

BLACK CRAKE *Amaurornis flavirostris* (213) 20 cm
Ad. is unmistakable with jet black coloration, bright yellow bill, red eyes and legs. A noisy bird, more often heard than seen, but it frequently ventures into the open.
SEXES alike but male slightly larger. IMM. is a grey version of ad. and has a black bill and dull red to black legs. HABITAT. Marshes and swamps with a thick cover of reedbeds and other aquatic vegetation. STATUS. Common resident. CALL. A throaty 'chrrooo' and rippling trill 'weet-eet-eet-eet', uttered in duet. (Swartriethaan)

AFRICAN JACANA *Actophilornis africanus* (240) 28 cm
Unmistakable. A rufous bird with a white neck and yellow upper breast, and a con-trasting black and white head which highlights the blue frontal shield. The extremely long toes and nails which enable it to walk over floating vegetation are easily visible.
SEXES alike but female larger. IMM. is paler than ad., lacking frontal shield, and having a white belly. Easily confused with Lesser Jacana, but very much larger and lacks white secondaries. HABITAT. Wetlands with floating vegetation, especially waterlilies. STATUS. Locally common resident. CALL. Noisy; a sharp, ringing 'krrrek', rasping 'krrrrrk', and barking 'yowk-yowk'. (Grootlangtoon)

LESSER JACANA *Microparra capensis* (241) 15 cm
Much smaller than African Jacana, it has a white belly, breast and throat but other-wise is pale brownish. Resembles imm. African Jacana but much smaller and in flight shows white on the trailing edges of the secondaries which contrast with the primaries.
SEXES alike. IMM. as ad. HABITAT. River floodplains, lagoons and bays in wetlands with emergent grass and sedge. STATUS. Uncommon resident with local movements. CALL. A soft, flufftail-like 'poop-oop-oop-oop'; a scolding 'ksh-ksh-ksh' and a high-pitched 'tititititi'. (Dwerglangtoon)

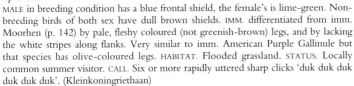

sub-ad.

ad.

ad.

PURPLE GALLINULE

sub-ad.

imm.

imm.

LESSER GALLINULE

imm.

ad.

imm.

ad.

imm.

AMERICAN
PURPLE GALLINULE

imm.

BLACK CRAKE

ad.

ad.

ad.

ad.

LESSER JACANA

ad.

AFRICAN JACANA

ad.

imm.

imm.

145

AFRICAN RAIL *Rallus caerulescens* (210) 37 cm
A distinctive species with a long, slightly decurved red bill and red legs, a blue-grey throat and breast, black and white barred flanks and undertail, and dull chestnut upperparts. More frequently seen than other rails and crakes, readily venturing out into the open, especially in early morning.
SEXES alike but male longer billed. IMM. has a long brown bill and a buff throat and breast. HABITAT. Marshes, thick reedbeds and flooded grassland. STATUS. Common resident. CALL. A high-pitched, trilling whistle 'trrreee-tee-tee-tee-tee-tee'. (Grootriethaan)

CORNCRAKE *Crex crex* (211) 35 cm
Much paler and more sandy coloured than the smaller African Crake. Rarely seen except when flushed, when it flies away on whirring wings, legs dangling, showing its diagnostic, conspicuous chestnut-orange wing coverts.
SEXES alike. IMM. similar to ad. HABITAT. Rank grassland, lightly wooded, grassy areas, and vlei margins. STATUS. Uncommon summer visitor. CALL. Silent in Africa. (Kwartelkoning)

SPOTTED CRAKE *Porzana porzana* (214) 20 cm
Most likely to be confused with African Crake but has a predominantly yellow bill, and obvious white spots and stripes on upperparts. When flushed, shows a distinctive white leading edge to the wing, and the diagnostic greenish-coloured legs and the barring on the flanks (less bold than on African Crake) can be seen. When on the ground, the bird flicks its tail, showing the buffy undertail coverts.
SEXES alike. IMM. similar to ad. HABITAT. Flooded grassland. STATUS. Rare summer visitor. Secretive and easily overlooked. CALL. Silent in Africa. (Gevlekte Riethaan)

AFRICAN CRAKE *Crex egregia* (212) 22 cm
Distinguished from African Rail by its short stubby bill, and from Spotted Crake by its unmarked breast and neck and more boldly barred flanks and belly. When flushed, the bird flies a short distance, legs dangling, showing clearly the brown mottled upperparts and black and white barred flanks.
SEXES alike. IMM. resembles ad. and although browner in appearance, still shows black and white barred flanks. HABITAT. Damp grassland and vleis. Has adapted to sugarcane plantations bordering rivers and dams. STATUS. Uncommon to locally common summer visitor. CALL. A monotonous, hollow-sounding series of notes 'krrr-krrr-krrr'. (Afrikaanse Riethaan)

STRIPED CRAKE *Aenigmatolimnas marginalis* (216) 20 cm
The rich brown upperparts with long white stripes on the back and wings are obvious characters in the male. Undertail and flanks are russet; flanks are not barred.
FEMALE differs markedly from male by having a blue-grey breast and belly but still shows the rich russet flanks and undertail. IMM. resembles male. HABITAT. Seasonally flooded grassland and marshes. STATUS. An erratic and localized summer visitor. CALL. A rapid 'tik-tik-tik-tik-tik...' which may continue for a minute or more. (Gestreepte Riethaan)

BAILLON'S CRAKE *Porzana pusilla* (215) 18 cm
The smallest crake in the region, similar to a flufftail in size. Resembling a diminutive African Crake, it differs by having warm brown upperparts flecked and spotted with white and less contrasting black and white barring on flanks and undertail.
SEXES alike. IMM. resembles ad. but paler, and mottled and barred below. HABITAT. Vlei margins, thick reedbeds, flooded grassland and flooded broadleafed woodland with tall grass. Rarely seen in the open except at dawn or dusk. STATUS. Uncommon resident with local movements. CALL. A soft 'qurrr-qurrr' and various frog-like croaks. (Kleinriethaan)

ad.

undertail

imm.

ad.

AFRICAN RAIL

CORNCRAKE

SPOTTED CRAKE

AFRICAN CRAKE

STRIPED CRAKE

STRIPED
CRAKE

female

imm.

male

BAILLON'S CRAKE

ad.

imm.

147

REDCHESTED FLUFFTAIL Sarothrura rufa (217) 16 cm
Male is the only flufftail in the region to have the rufous head colour extend to the
lower breast. In flight distinguished from Striped Flufftail by its black (not red) tail.
FEMALE distinguished from female Striped Flufftail by appearing much blacker and
larger, with a floppier, less deliberate flight. IMM. resembles female. HABITAT. Thick
stands of reeds and tall water grasses, marshes and small vleis. STATUS. Common resident. CALL. A low, hoot 'woop' repeated at intervals of about one second, a more
rapid 'gu-duk, gu-duk, gu-duk' and a ringing 'tuwi-tuwi-tuwi'. (Rooiborsvleikuiken)

STRIPED FLUFFTAIL Sarothrura affinis (221) 15 cm
On the ground, the male's plain chestnut tail is diagnostic and distinguishes it from
the male Whitewinged Flufftail, which has a barred chestnut and black tail.
FEMALE differs from female Redchested Flufftail by being smaller, much swifter on the
wing and having the tail suffused with chestnut. IMM. resembles female. HABITAT.
Upland grassland in mountainous regions; sometimes associated with vleis. STATUS.
Locally common resident. CALL. A low, long hoot 'oooooop' lasting about a second
and repeated at two-second intervals. (Gestreepte Vleikuiken)

STREAKYBREASTED FLUFFTAIL Sarothrura boehmi (219) 15 cm
In the male, the chestnut head and neck contrasting with the very pale throat are dia-
gnostic characteristics. Most likely to be confused with Redchested Flufftail but, when
flushed, appears much paler and it can be seen that the chestnut on the head does not
extend on to the lower breast.
FEMALE and IMM. are much paler below than female Redchested Flufftail. HABITAT.
Seasonally flooded grassland. Rarely seen; usually detected by its call. STATUS.
Uncommon and localized summer visitor in Zimbabwe; vagrant elsewhere. CALL.
Low hoot 'gawooo', repeated at half-second intervals 20-30 times. (Streepbors-
vleikuiken)

LONGTOED FLUFFTAIL Sarothrura lugens (220) 15 cm Not illustrated
The one putative record of this central African species, from the Eastern Highlands of
Zimbabwe, is now considered to be a mis-identification of Redchested Flufftail.

WHITEWINGED FLUFFTAIL Sarothrura ayresi (222) 14 cm
When flushed, both sexes show diagnostic square white panels on the secondaries.
Flight is very fast and direct with whirring wing beats, ending with a plunge into the
vegetation. On the ground, a thin white line is noticeable on the outer web of the first
primary. Distinguished from Striped Flufftail by this white line, and by the barred
black and chestnut tail.
FEMALE and IMM. differ from all other female and imm. flufftails by the white wing
panel. HABITAT. Upland marshes and vleis, where sedges and aquatic grasses grow in
shallow water. STATUS. Rare, erratic and localized in occurrence. CALL. A low, deep
hoot, repeated in duet. (Witvlerkvleikuiken)

BUFFSPOTTED FLUFFTAIL Sarothrura elegans (218) 16 cm
In the male, the dark body is more speckled than other flufftails' and the chestnut
extends only as far as the upper breast, not on to the lower breast and back as in
Redchested Flufftail.
MALE, if seen on the forest floor, gives the impression of a small, plump, chestnut-
headed bird, heavily spotted with golden buff. FEMALE and IMM. are buff breasted,
barred brown, and dark brown above. HABITAT. Evergreen forests, coastal scrub, and
well-wooded gardens. STATUS. Common resident. CALL. A low, foghorn-like
'dooooooo' given mainly at night and on overcast days. (Gevlekte Vleikuiken)

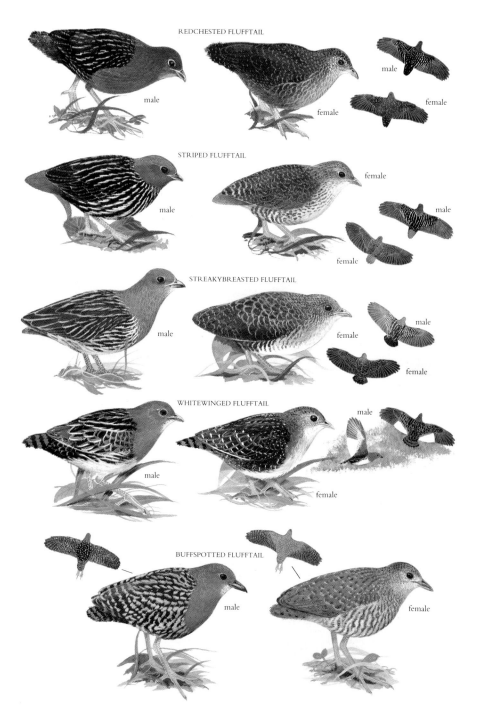

REDCHESTED FLUFFTAIL

male

female

male

female

STRIPED FLUFFTAIL

male

female

male

female

STREAKYBREASTED FLUFFTAIL

male

female

male

female

WHITEWINGED FLUFFTAIL

male

male

female

BUFFSPOTTED FLUFFTAIL

male

female

SOUTHERN CROWNED CRANE *Balearica regulorum* (209) 105 cm
Unlikely to be confused with any other species. In flight the large white upperwing patches are diagnostic. During the non-breeding season may be found in mixed flocks with Blue Cranes.
SEXES alike. IMM. lacks the large, unfeathered, white face patch and the bristly crown is less well developed. HABITAT. Marshes, dams and adjoining grassland, and agricultural lands. STATUS. Common but localized resident. CALL. A trumpeting flight call 'may hem' and a deep 'huum huum' when breeding. (Mahem)

WATTLED CRANE *Grus carunculatus* (207) 120 cm
This enormous crane with its long, white feathered wattles is unmistakable. Even at very long range can be easily identified by its dark face, and white head and neck contrasting with black underparts.
SEXES alike. IMM. has white (not grey) crown until a year old. HABITAT. Upland vleis and marshes and adjoining grassland. Usually found in pairs or small groups, but non-breeding birds sometimes gather in flocks of 50 or more. STATUS. Rare resident; endangered. CALL. Seldom calls: a loud 'kwaarnk'. (Lelkraanvoël)

BLUE CRANE *Anthropoides paradisea* (208) 100 cm
The large head, long slender neck and elongated, trailing inner secondaries are diagnostic of this species.
SEXES alike. IMM. lacks the long inner secondaries and is paler grey, especially on the head. HABITAT. Vleis, grassland, Karoo scrub and agricultural lands. Found in small groups or in pairs but non-breeding birds gather in large flocks which sometimes contain several hundred birds. STATUS. Common resident; endemic. CALL. A loud, nasal 'kraaaank'. (Bloukraanvoël)

SECRETARYBIRD *Sagittarius serpentarius* (118) 140 cm
This bird's peculiar shape and long legs render it likely to be confused only with a crane at long range. In flight the two elongated central tail feathers project well beyond the tail and the legs, producing an unmistakable flight shape. The black 'leggings' are conspicuous.
SEXES alike. IMM. resembles ad. but has a shorter tail and yellow (not red) bare facial skin. HABITAT. Savanna and open grassland from coastal regions to high altitudes. Avoids thick bush and forests. STATUS. Uncommon to locally common resident, now absent from many settled areas. CALL. Normally silent but during aerial display utters a deep croak. (Sekretarisvoël)

SOUTHERN CROWNED CRANE

WATTLED CRANE

imm.

BLUE CRANE

BLUE CRANE

SECRETARYBIRD

SECRETARYBIRD

imm.

151

KORI BUSTARD *Ardeotis kori* (230) 135 cm
The largest bustard of the region. The size, dark crest and lack of any rufous on the hind neck and upper mantle are diagnostic. In flight distinguished from Stanley's and Ludwig's Bustards by its uniformly speckled grey upperwing, lacking white markings.
Displaying MALE balloons out breast feathers. FEMALE is similar to male but noticeably smaller. IMM. resembles female. HABITAT. Dry thornveld, grassland and semi-desert, usually near the cover of trees. STATUS. Resident but with nomadic local movements. Numbers much reduced by hunting and habitat destruction in some regions and now uncommon in many regions outside major game reserves. CALL. A deep, resonant 'oom-oom-oom' is given by the male during the breeding season. (Gompou)

STANLEY'S BUSTARD *Neotis denhami* (231) 104 cm
The dark cap, pale grey foreneck and breast, and conspicuous white wing markings are diagnostic in the male. The similar Ludwig's Bustard has a dark throat and foreneck, and has less white in the wing.
MALE is considerably larger than the female with a darker, plainer back. Displaying male inflates throat and forms a conspicuous balloon of white feathers. FEMALE and IMM. have less white in the wings and have brown speckling on the neck. HABITAT. Recently burnt fynbos, open grassland and agricultural land. STATUS. Uncommon resident at the coast; inland populations tend to move to lower altitudes during winter. CALL. Largely silent. (Veldpou)

LUDWIG'S BUSTARD *Neotis ludwigii* (232) 90 cm
Most likely to be confused with Stanley's Bustard but differs by having a dark brown neck and breast and having far less white in the wings.
BREEDING MALE has similar display to Stanley's Bustard, but balloon grey (not white). FEMALE noticeably smaller than male. IMM. paler on the head and neck than ad. HABITAT. Much drier regions than Stanley's Bustard and largely restricted to the Karoo and Namib desert. STATUS. Nomadic near-endemic, uncommon to locally common in its range. CALL. In display, the male gives an explosive, far-carrying 'woodoomp' repeated every 15-30 seconds. (Ludwigse Pou)

display

KORI BUSTARD

upperwing

male female

female nape

upperwing

male

STANLEY'S BUSTARD

STANLEY'S BUSTARD

male nape

male

female

male

LUDWIG'S BUSTARD

male

LUDWIG'S BUSTARD

RÜPPELL'S KORHAAN *Eupodotis rueppellii* (236) 58 cm

Confusable only with Karoo Korhaan from which it differs by being much paler on the back, by having a conspicuous black line down the centre of the foreneck on to the breast, and by its contrasting black and white facial markings.

MALE is more boldly marked than female, especially on head and throat. IMM. resembles female. HABITAT. Gravel plains and scrub desert of Namibia. STATUS. Common resident; near-endemic. Usually encountered in small groups. CALL. Similar to that of Karoo Korhaan but slightly higher pitched. (Woestynkorhaan)

KAROO KORHAAN *Eupodotis vigorsii* (235) 58 cm

Plumage variable but is generally greyish brown on the back, with a greyer head and neck and a black throat patch. Similar to Rüppell's Korhaan but is darker on the back and lacks the black line down the centre of the foreneck from the throat to the breast and the contrasting black and white facial markings.

FEMALE has a less well-developed throat patch and more mottled wing coverts. IMM. as female. HABITAT. Desert and semi-desert of the Karoo, and wheatfields and pastures in the southern Cape. STATUS. Common resident; endemic. Usually found in groups of two or three. CALL. A deep, rhythmical frog-like two or three syllable 'kraak-rak' or 'crrok-rak-rak', with the accent on the deeper first syllable, is given repeatedly at dawn and dusk. Pairs call in duet. (Vaalkorhaan)

BLUE KORHAAN *Eupodotis caerulescens* (234) 56 cm

The blue underparts of this species are diagnostic and it is the only korhaan to show blue in the wings in flight.

MALE has white ear coverts, FEMALE has brown ear coverts and those of IMM. are blackish. HABITAT. Open short grassland extending marginally into the semi-desert eastern Karoo. STATUS. Locally common resident; endemic. Usually located early in morning when males call. Very wary, running off at close approach before finally taking flight, calling loudly. CALL. A deep discordant 'krok-kaa-krow' given repeatedly at dawn and dusk. (Bloukorhaan)

WHITEBELLIED KORHAAN *Eupodotis cafra* (233) 52 cm

In the male the combination of blue foreneck and white belly is diagnostic.

FEMALE and IMM. have brown necks and resemble the female Blackbellied Korhaan (p. 156), as both species have white underparts, but Whitebellied Korhaan differs by lacking the long neck and legs, and black underwing coverts of Blackbellied Korhaan. HABITAT. Open grassland or lightly wooded savanna; requires taller grass than most other korhaans. STATUS. Uncommon resident. CALL. A rhythmical crowing 'takwarat' is given repeatedly at dawn and dusk. (Witpenskorhaan)

upperwing

male

RÜPPELL'S KORHAAN

female

male

male

KAROO KORHAAN

male

KAROO
KORHAAN

female
upperwing

BLUE KORHAAN

male

upperwing

female

WHITEBELLIED KORHAAN
upperwing

female

male

WHITEBELLIED KORHAAN

male

BLACKBELLIED KORHAAN *Eupodotis melanogaster* (238) 64 cm
The long, thin neck and legs are diagnostic. The back of both sexes is spotted and barred. The male has a black throat, with a black line down the centre of the foreneck to the breast, and the underwings are black.
MALE in its slow display flight shows striking and diagnostic large white patches in the primaries, secondaries and underwing coverts. FEMALE is plainer with a brown head and neck, and white underparts. The female can be told from other korhaans in flight by its combination of white underparts, and black underwing coverts. IMM. resembles female. HABITAT. Woodland and tall open grassland. STATUS. Uncommon and easily overlooked resident. CALL. A short, sharp 'chikk', followed by a 'pop'. (Langbeen-korhaan)

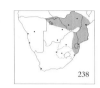

REDCRESTED KORHAAN *Eupodotis ruficrista* (237) 50 cm
The red crest is rarely seen unless a displaying male is observed in which case elongated rufous feathers are erected to form a crest resembling that of Crowned Crane (p. 150).
Both sexes have a black belly. MALE in courtship display flies straight up, then suddenly tumbles and plummets towards the ground, before gliding off and settling. FEMALE has a mottled brown crown and neck. Readily distinguished from female Northern Black Korhaan by chevron-shaped markings (not barring) on back. IMM. resembles female. HABITAT. Dry woodland and semi-desert Kalahari grassland and thornveld. STATUS. Common resident. CALL. The male's protracted call is a characteristic sound of the bushveld in summer. It starts with a series of clicks 'tic-tic-tic' which builds into an extended series of loud, piping whistles 'pi-pi-pi ... pipity-pipity'. (Boskorhaan)

NORTHERN BLACK KORHAAN *Eupodotis afroides* (239b) 52 cm
Differs from Southern Black Korhaan by showing conspicuous white flashes in the primaries in flight.
FEMALE resembles female Southern Black Korhaan. Separated from female Redcrested Korhaan by barring (not chevron-shaped markings) on upperparts. IMM. resembles female. HABITAT. Open grassland and scrub. STATUS. Common resident; endemic. CALL. Similar to that of Southern Black Korhaan. (Witvlerkswartkorhaan)

SOUTHERN BLACK KORHAAN *Eupodotis afra* (239a) 52 cm
The most easily recognized small korhaan with its black underparts and bright yellow legs.
During MALE'S display flight, the legs dangle as the bird 'parachutes' slowly to the ground, continually giving its harsh call. FEMALE has a brown head and neck, which are heavily marked, and barred upperparts. IMM. striped on head and neck. HABITAT. Coastal and strandveld fynbos. STATUS. Common resident; endemic. CALL. Male gives a raucous and repeated 'kerrrak-kerrrak-kerrrak', both in flight and on the ground. (Swartkorhaan)

male upperwing

female

male

female

male

BLACKBELLIED
KORHAAN

female

male

male
display

REDCRESTED KORHAAN

male

male upperwing

female

male

female

SOUTHERN
BLACK KORHAAN

female

male

female

NORTHERN
BLACK KORHAAN

male upperwing

male upperwing

CRAB PLOVER *Dromas ardeola* (296) 38 cm

A large, predominantly white wader with extensive black patches on its back and upperwings. The black, dagger-shaped bill is proportionally very heavy and thick for a bird of this size. Legs are long and greyish, extending well beyond the tail in flight.
SEXES alike. IMM. more grey than ad. on upperwings and tail; grey back and streaking on crown and hindneck. HABITAT. Coastal areas and estuaries, especially muddy mangrove stands which are rich in crabs. STATUS. Non-breeding summer visitor; regular only in Mozambique, uncommon and erratic in northern Natal with two records from the eastern Cape. CALL. Variety of metallic calls while foraging: 'kwa-daaaa-dak', 'kwa-da-dak' or 'grr-kwo-kwo-kwo-kwo'. Flight call a two-note 'kwa-da'. (Krapvreter)

AFRICAN BLACK OYSTERCATCHER *Haematopus moquini* (244) 44 cm

An easily identified, large, all-black wader with a bright orange bill and eye-ring and dull pink legs. Some ads. have small white patches on the underparts. In flight, wings are all black with no bars.
SEXES alike. IMM. duller, appearing faintly buff-scaled, with a duller orange bill, tipped brown. Legs grey or greyish pink. HABITAT. Strictly coastal, may be encountered along any shoreline, estuary or lagoon from central Transkei to northern Namibia. Usually in pairs or small flocks. STATUS. Common on rocky islands and the adjacent mainland; vagrant to coastal Natal. Endemic. CALL. A 'klee-kleeep' call, similar to that of European Oystercatcher, and a fast 'peeka-peeka-peeka' alarm call. Display calls more complex, including rapid trilling. (Swarttobie)

EUROPEAN OYSTERCATCHER *Haematopus ostralegus* (243) 43 cm

Smaller and more slender than African Black Oystercatcher, this large, pied wader has white underparts and a bold white wing bar. Bill orange, legs pink. The broad white wing bar, white rump and base of the tail are visible in flight.
SEXES alike. IMM. and most NON-BREEDING ADS. have a white throat crescent. Bill and legs duller than ad.'s, and black feathering tinged brown. HABITAT. Open coast, estuaries and coastal lagoons. STATUS. Rare summer visitor to all coasts, most records from the eastern Cape and Namibia, especially Walvis Bay. CALL. A sharp, high-pitched 'klee-kleep'. (Bonttobie)

BLACKWINGED STILT *Himantopus himantopus* (295) 38 cm

A large, black and white wader with very long, red legs and a thin, pointed black bill. In flight the black underwings contrast with the white underparts, and the long legs trail conspicuously.
SEXES alike but female may be duller black on wings. Head and neck markings variable in both sexes, from pure white to predominantly dusky. IMM. has grey nape, dull black wings and greyish-pink legs. HABITAT. Estuaries, marshes, vleis, saltpans and flooded ground. STATUS. Common resident and local nomad. CALL. A harsh, short 'kik-kik', especially when alarmed. Very vocal in defence of nest and young. (Rooipootelsie)

AVOCET *Recurvirostra avosetta* (294) 42 cm

An unmistakable white and black wading bird with a long, very thin, upturned bill and a black cap and hindneck. In flight the pied pattern is striking, with three black patches on each upperwing. Underwing black only at tip. Long bluish-grey legs extend beyond the tail in flight.
SEXES alike. IMM. has the black replaced by mottled brown. HABITAT. Lakes, estuaries, vleis, saltpans and temporary pools, coastally and inland. Feeds in water, using a sweeping side-to-side bill movement or by upending, duck-style, in deeper water. Usually in small flocks. STATUS. Common and widespread resident and local nomad. CALL. A clear 'kooit', also a 'kik-kik' alarm call. (Bontelsie)

ad.

CRAB PLOVER

imm.

ad. non-br.

ad.

AFRICAN BLACK
OYSTERCATCHER

imm.

EUROPEAN
OYSTERCATCHER

ad.

imm.

ad.

BLACKWINGED STILT

AVOCET

ad.

imm.

 PLOVERS *See also pages 186-187*

RINGED PLOVER *Charadrius hiaticula* (245) 16 cm
A small, short-legged, dark plover with a white collar above a blackish-brown breast band which is often incomplete in non-breeding plumage. Distinguished from Sand and Mongolian Plovers (p. 162) by combination of collar, smaller size, slighter bill, usually orange at the base, and orange-yellow legs. In flight, narrow white wing bar and collar are conspicuous.
SEXES alike. IMM. has duller plumage overall; breast band incomplete. HABITAT. Coastal and inland wetlands, preferring patches of soft, fine mud. STATUS. Common summer visitor, some overwinter. CALL. A fluty 'tooi'. (Ringnekstrandkiewiet)

THREEBANDED PLOVER *Charadrius tricollaris* (249) 18 cm
The black double breast band, grey cheeks and conspicuous red eye-ring and base to the bill are distinctive. In flight the tail shows white outer tips and edges; very narrow white wing bar. Rump and tail appear elongate in flight, resembling Ringed Plover.
SEXES alike. IMM. duller version of ad., lacking the red eye-ring. HABITAT. On most waterbodies with sandy or pebbly margins. Rare on open coast. STATUS. Widespread and common resident. CALL. A penetrating, high-pitched 'weee-weet' whistle. (Driebandstrandkiewiet)

KITTLITZ'S PLOVER *Charadrius pecuarius* (248) 16 cm
The black forehead line that extends behind the eye to the nape is distinctive when this species is breeding. The breast is variably creamy-buff to chestnut and there is a dark shoulder patch.
Head less well marked in NON-BREEDING plumage, with pale buffy ring around crown extending to nape. Dark eye patch at all times. SEXES alike. IMM. distinguished from imm. Whitefronted Plover (p. 162) by broad buffy eyebrow stripe extending into buffy nape. HABITAT. Found throughout in dried muddy or short grassy areas near water, also on mudflats in estuaries and coastal lagoons. STATUS. Common resident and local nomad. CALL. A short, clipped trill 'kittip'. (Geelborsstrandkiewiet)

CASPIAN PLOVER *Charadrius asiaticus* (252) 22 cm
In breeding plumage differs from Mongolian and Sand Plovers (p. 162) by having a black lower border to the chestnut breast band, an obvious pale eyebrow stripe and in lacking an extensive dark eye-patch. In all other plumages it has a complete (or virtually complete) grey-brown wash across the breast, and a broad buffy eyebrow stripe. Bill is small and thin. In flight lacks distinct white areas on the upperparts, but pale bases to inner primaries are usually visible. Distinguished from non-breeding American and Pacific Golden Plovers (p. 172) by uniform upperwings and smaller size. Usually in flocks.
MALE brighter than female in breeding dress. IMM. similar to non-breeding ad. but buffy tips to mantle feathers give scaled appearance. HABITAT. Sparsely grassed areas and wetland fringes. STATUS. Scarce summer visitor; patchily distributed, mainly in the north. CALL. A clear, whistled 'tooeet'. (Asiatiese Strandkiewiet)

RINGED PLOVER

br.

ad. non-br.

imm.

THREEBANDED PLOVER

KITTLITZ'S PLOVER

imm.

KITTLITZ'S PLOVER

br.

ad. non-br.

CASPIAN PLOVER

male br.

ad. non-br.

161

CHESTNUTBANDED PLOVER *Charadrius pallidus* (247) 15 cm
The smallest, palest plover of the region. Ad. has a thin, chestnut breast band,
extending in a thin line on to the crown in the male.
MALE also has neat black markings on forehead and lores, which are replaced by grey
in the female. Distinguished from larger Whitefronted Plover by breast band and lack
of a white collar. IMM. lacks black and chestnut coloration; breast band is duller and
usually incomplete. HABITAT. Predominantly salt pans in summer, some moving to
estuaries and coastal wetlands in winter. STATUS. Uncommon, localized resident. CALL.
A single 'prrp' or 'tooit'. (Rooibandstrandkiewiet)

KENTISH PLOVER *Charadrius alexandrinus* (908) 16 cm
Ad. in breeding plumage distinguished from closely related Whitefronted Plover by
chestnut crown and nape and a small black patch extending from the shoulder to the
sides of the breast.
SEXES alike. NON-BREEDING birds and IMM. virtually impossible to distinguish from
imm. Whitefronted Plover but appear more slender and attenuated in the body.
HABITAT. Coastal wetlands and sandy beaches. STATUS. Very rare vagrant. Occurrence
in the region based on a single beached specimen from Namibia. CALL. A short, sharp
'wiiit', similar to that of Whitefronted Plover. (Alexandria Strandkiewiet)

WHITEFRONTED PLOVER *Charadrius marginatus* (246) 18 cm
A pale plover, superficially resembling Chestnutbanded Plover, but slightly larger with
a white collar and lacking a complete breast band. Paler than Kittlitz's Plover
(p. 160) and lacks the dark head markings, but may have a thin black line through
the eye and across the forehead. It is also lighter-coloured, and smaller than
Mongolian Plover. Birds in the north-east of the region are consistently buffier below.
SEXES alike. NON-BREEDING birds and IMM. greyer, lacking black markings on the
head. Breast usually white with small, dusky lateral patches. HABITAT. Sandy and
rocky shores, muddy coastal areas and larger inland rivers and pans. STATUS. Common
resident. CALL. A clear 'wiiit', but also a 'tukut' alarm call. (Vaalstrandkiewiet)

SAND PLOVER *Charadrius leschenaultii* (251) 22 cm
Very similar to Mongolian Plover, but stands taller, has a bigger body and a longer,
more robust bill. Differs from Whitefronted Plover by much larger size and lack of a
white collar. Caspian Plover (p. 160) is smaller billed and lacks extensive white on
the sides of the rump.
In BREEDING plumage, the brown shoulder patches become rufous and extend across
the breast, but not as extensively as in Mongolian Plover. Leg colour variable, usually
greyish green, very rarely black (cf. Mongolian Plover). In flight, more extensive
white on sides of rump and dark subterminal tail band aid separation from Mongolian
Plover. SEXES alike in non-breeding plumage, MALE brighter in breeding plumage.
IMM. has upperparts fringed buff. HABITAT. Coastal wetlands. STATUS. Uncommon to
locally common summer visitor, most regular in the east. CALL. A short musical trill.
(Grootstrandkiewiet)

MONGOLIAN PLOVER *Charadrius mongolus* (250) 19 cm
Confusion possible with Sand Plover, but is shorter legged, smaller bodied and has a
shorter, less robust bill. Both ad. Whitefronted and Kittlitz's Plovers (p. 160) are
smaller and have a pale collar. In breeding plumage, the rufous breast band is more
extensive than that of Sand Plover. Legs almost always dark grey or black. In flight,
little colour contrast between tail, rump and back.
SEXES alike in non-breeding plumage. IMM. has upperparts fringed buff. HABITAT.
Coastal wetlands. STATUS. Fairly common summer visitor to coasts of Mozambique
and Natal, vagrant to the Cape and Namibia. CALL. 'Chittick'. (Mongoolse Strandkiewiet)

CHESTNUTBANDED PLOVER

male ad.

female ad.

imm.

KENTISH PLOVER

ad. non-br.

male ad.
non-br.
worn plumage

WHITEFRONTED PLOVER

br.

ad. non-br.

imm.

SAND PLOVER

male br.

ad. non-br.

MONGOLIAN PLOVER

male br.

ad. non-br.

163

CROWNED PLOVER *Vanellus coronatus* (255) 30 cm
A large, unmistakable plover with its black cap interrupted by a white 'halo'. Legs and basal part of the bill bright reddish. Sandy brown breast separated from white belly by a black band.
SEXES alike. IMM. much like ad., but less strikingly marked. Upperparts more scalloped and legs paler; crown barred buff. HABITAT. Short grassland (either grazed or burnt); also on golf courses, playing fields and fallow land. Aggregates in small flocks, especially when not breeding. Regularly associates with Blackwinged Plovers where their ranges overlap. STATUS. Common resident. CALL. A noisy species, uttering a loud, grating 'kreep', day and night. (Kroonkiewiet)

BLACKWINGED PLOVER *Vanellus melanopterus* (257) 27 cm
Similar to Lesser Blackwinged Plover, but is larger and more heavily built, with more white on the forehead extending back almost to the eye, and a broader black border separating breast from belly. In flight from above distinguished from Lesser Blackwinged Plover by a broad white wing bar and a black trailing edge to the secondaries, and from below by a black (not white) trailing edge to the secondaries.
SEXES alike. IMM. browner, with buff edges to back and wing feathers. HABITAT. Short grassland, both coastal and upland. Frequently associates with Crowned Plovers. STATUS. Uncommon resident and local migrant, with movements between uplands and the coast. CALL. A shrill, piping 'ti-tirree', higher pitched than that of Lesser Blackwinged Plover. (Grootswartvlerkkiewiet)

LESSER BLACKWINGED PLOVER *Vanellus lugubris* (256) 22 cm
Closely resembles Blackwinged Plover but is smaller, has a narrow black border to the breast, less white on the forehead and a slight greenish tinge to the upperparts. In flight both upper- and underwings show completely white secondaries.
SEXES alike. IMM. less clearly marked than ad.; upperparts spotted buff. HABITAT. Dry, open, short grass areas in savanna. STATUS. Uncommon resident and local migrant. CALL. A clear double-note 'teeyoo, tee-yoo'. (Kleinswartvlerkkiewiet)

CROWNED PLOVER

ad.

imm.

ad.

BLACKWINGED PLOVER

ad.

imm.

ad.

LESSER
BLACKWINGED
PLOVER

ad.

imm.

ad.

WATTLED PLOVER *Vanellus senegallus* (260) 35 cm
The largest Vanellus plover of the region. Has smaller yellow wattles than White-crowned Plover, from which it also differs by having a dark breast bordered by a black line on the belly, and streaked (not grey) sides to the head. The white on the head is restricted to the forecrown and forehead, unlike Whitecrowned Plover in which the white stripe extends to the nape. In flight this species does not have the startling white-winged appearance of Whitecrowned Plover, but does have an obvious pale wing bar.
SEXES alike. IMM. as ad., but with much reduced wattles and less distinct head markings. HABITAT. Damp grassland and wetland fringes. STATUS. Fairly common resident. CALL. A high-pitched, ringing 'keep-keep'; regularly calls at night. (Lelkiewiet)

WHITECROWNED PLOVER *Vanellus albiceps* (259) 30 cm
This large plover with its distinctive pendulous, yellow wattles might be confused with Wattled Plover which has a dark (not white) breast. Whitecrowned Plover is also distinguished by a white stripe running from forehead to nape. In flight the upperwings appear very white, with only the outermost primaries and inner coverts being black. Underwings mostly white. Tail predominantly black.
SEXES alike. IMM. similar to ad., but with a brownish crown and barring on the upperparts. Wattles smaller. HABITAT. Sandbanks and sandbars of major rivers. STATUS. Locally common resident. CALL. A repeated, ringing 'peek-peek'. (Witkopkiewiet)

LONGTOED PLOVER *Vanellus crassirostris* (261) 30 cm
The only plover in the region to have a white face, throat and foreneck. The black nape extends down the sides of the neck to form a broad breast band. Very striking in flight, with a grey back and all-white wings except for black outer primaries. Tail black, rump white. Legs and basal portion of bill reddish.
SEXES alike. IMM. as ad. with buffy mottling on upperparts. HABITAT. Well-vegetated vleis, marshes and river floodplains. STATUS. Locally common resident. CALL. A repeated high-pitched 'pink-pink'. (Witvlerkkiewiet)

BLACKSMITH PLOVER *Vanellus armatus* (258) 30 cm
This large, black, white and grey bird is the easiest plover to identify in the region, and its bold pattern makes it easily distinguishable in flight.
SEXES alike. IMM. duller than ad., with greyish-brown feathering replacing the black, and brown streaking on the crown. Often in flocks when not breeding. HABITAT. Damp areas of wetland margins and adjoining grassland and fields. STATUS. Common resident. CALL. A very vocal species with a loud, ringing 'tink, tink, tink' alarm call. (Bontkiewiet)

166

WATTLED PLOVER

WHITECROWNED
PLOVER

LONGTOED PLOVER

imm.

BLACKSMITH PLOVER

ad.

ad.

imm.

KNOT *Calidris canutus* (271) 25 cm
This short-legged, dumpy and rather plain wader differs from the smaller Curlew Sandpiper by its shorter, straight bill, and greenish (not grey) legs. It is much smaller than Grey Plover (p. 172) which has a speckled (not uniformly grey) back, and a short bill. In flight a pale wing bar is visible and the rump is flecked pale grey.
In BREEDING plumage, the entire underparts, except for the underwing, are deep chestnut and the upperparts are spangled gold and black. MALE brighter than female in breeding dress. IMM. slightly browner than ad. HABITAT. Gregarious at estuaries and coastal lagoons, occasionally inland. STATUS. Locally common summer visitor, regularly overwinters. CALL. A nondescript 'knut'. (Knoet)

CURLEW SANDPIPER *Calidris ferruginea* (272) 19 cm
The only small, plain greyish wader with an obviously decurved bill. In flight, has a squarish white rump, variably scalloped pale grey.
In BREEDING plumage, the rump becomes blotched and the underparts and face rufous; male brighter than female. SEXES alike in NON-BREEDING plumage. IMM. has buffy edging to mantle feathers. HABITAT. Coastal and freshwater wetland, usually in flocks. STATUS. Very common summer visitor, regularly overwinters. CALL. A short trill, 'chirrup'. (Krombekstrandloper)

DUNLIN *Calidris alpina* (273) 18 cm
The bill is less evenly curved than that of Curlew Sandpiper, from which it also differs by smaller size, less conspicuous eyebrow stripe, and by a blackish centre line through the rump. Broadbilled Sandpiper is smaller, has shorter, paler legs (Dunlin's legs are black), striped head markings and a flattened bill tip.
In BREEDING and transitional plumage has a black patch on the belly and chestnut feathering on the back. SEXES alike. IMM. similar to non-breeding ad. HABITAT. Coastal wetlands. STATUS. Very rare vagrant. CALL. A weak 'treep'. (Bontstrandloper)

SANDERLING *Calidris alba* (281) 19 cm
In non-breeding plumage the palest sandpiper of the region. It has a rather short, stubby black bill and a dark carpal patch. Similar to the dark-shouldered Broadbilled Sandpiper but is larger, heavier- and shorter-billed and lacks head stripes.
In BREEDING plumage wing and back feathers are black with chestnut centres and there is a broad, diffuse chestnut breast band streaked black. In flight shows a distinct white wing bar and dark centre line through the white rump and tail. SEXES alike. IMM. resembles non-breeding ad. HABITAT. Mainly sandy beaches, also rocky coasts, estuaries and lagoons; sometimes inland, especially during migration. STATUS. Common summer visitor. CALL. A single, decisive 'wick'. (Drietoonstrandloper)

BROADBILLED SANDPIPER *Limicola falcinellus* (283) 17 cm
A small, markedly short-legged wader distinguished from Little Stint (p. 170) by its relatively long bill which droops slightly at the flattened tip. The legs are dark grey, sometimes greenish. There is a dark shoulder patch which is less pronounced than in Sanderling. The whitish double eyebrow stripe is diagnostic.
In BREEDING plumage the upperparts become blackish with narrow buffy feather margins. SEXES alike. IMM. resembles non-breeding ad. HABITAT. Vleis, lakes and estuaries. STATUS. Rare but regular summer visitor. CALL. A low-pitched, short trill, 'drrrt'. (Breëbekstrandloper)

PECTORAL SANDPIPER *Calidris melanotos* (279) 19 cm
The abrupt division between the streaked breast and the white underparts is distinctive. Larger than the stints, it is longer-necked with a dark-capped appearance and darker upperparts. The legs are yellowish or greenish. Baird's Sandpiper (p. 170) has a black bill and legs, and the much larger Ruff (p. 172) lacks the breast marking.
SEXES alike. IMM. like ad. HABITAT. Margins of estuaries and freshwater wetlands. STATUS. Rare but widely recorded summer visitor. CALL. A low trill, 'prrt'. (Geelpootstrandloper)

KNOT

ad. non-br.

br.

CURLEW SANDPIPER

ad. non-br.

br.

DUNLIN

ad. non-br.

ad. non-br.

SANDERLING

br.

ad. non-br.

from above

BROADBILLED SANDPIPER

imm.

PECTORAL SANDPIPER
ad. non-br.

WHITERUMPED SANDPIPER *Calidris fuscicollis* (277) 17 cm
This small, rather plain sandpiper has a white rump like Curlew Sandpiper (p. 168),
but is smaller and has a shorter, straighter bill. Shape and posture resemble Baird's
Sandpiper, but easily separated in flight by white rump.
SEXES alike. IMM. as ad., but crown chestnut and dark back feathers broadly fringed
chestnut. HABITAT. Wetlands. STATUS. Rare summer vagrant. CALL. A thin, mouse-
like 'jeep'. (Witrugstrandloper)

BAIRD'S SANDPIPER *Calidris bairdii* (278) 17 cm
Larger than the stints; long wings extend well beyond the tail at rest, giving an elong-
ated appearance. Distinguished by its scaled, essentially brown, rarely grey, upper-
parts, and by light vertical streaking on the breast. Legs black, sometimes tinged
green. Ruff (p. 172) also has scaled wing coverts but is much larger, has white sides
to the rump and very rarely has black legs.
SEXES alike. IMM. like non-breeding ad. HABITAT. Open shore and wetland margins.
STATUS. Very rare vagrant. CALL. A short trill, 'kreep'. (Bairdse Strandloper)

LITTLE STINT *Calidris minuta* (274) 14 cm
Very similar to Rednecked Stint, but latter has a shorter, stubbier bill. In breeding
plumage, lacks the rufous chin of Rednecked Stint. Temminck's Stint has olive (not
black) legs, plainer upperparts and white (not grey) outer tail feathers. Longtoed Stint
has darker upperparts, a thinner bill and greenish-yellow legs. Broadbilled Sandpiper
and Dunlin (p. 168) have longer bills which droop very slightly at the tip, and the
former shows a dark shoulder at rest. Narrow white wing bar and white sides to rump
obvious in flight.
SEXES alike. IMM. similar to non-breeding ad. HABITAT. Coastal and freshwater wetlands; typically forages in flocks and has a very rapid feeding action. STATUS. Common
summer visitor; few overwinter. CALL. A short, sharp 'schit'. (Kleinstrandloper)

REDNECKED STINT *Calidris ruficollis* (276) 14 cm
Extremely difficult to distinguish from Little Stint except in breeding plumage when
the throat, neck and cheeks become rufous. In all other plumages, Rednecked Stint's
bill is shorter and stubbier.
In NON-BREEDING plumage it is very pale, with the wing coverts and back feathers
being uniformly pale grey with dark feather shafts. Separated from Temminck's and
Longtoed Stints by black (not greenish or yellowish) legs. SEXES alike. IMM. like non-
breeding ad. HABITAT. Usually with Little Stints or Curlew Sandpipers at vleis, dams,
estuaries or bays. STATUS. Rare summer visitor. May be more regular and widespread
than currently realized. CALL. A short 'chit' or 'prrp'. (Rooinekstrandloper)

TEMMINCK'S STINT *Calidris temminckii* (280) 14 cm
More elongate in appearance than Little Stint. Distinguished by greenish legs, white
outer tail feathers and uniform grey-brown upperparts. Longtoed Stint generally has
yellow legs and is much darker and browner above.
SEXES alike. IMM. as ad., but upperparts scaled buff. HABITAT. Wetland margins with
short grass or reeds. Could occur on any vlei, dam or estuary. STATUS. Rare summer
vagrant. CALL. A shrill 'prrrrtt'. (Temminckse Strandloper)

LONGTOED STINT *Calidris subminuta* (275) 14 cm
Separated from Little and Rednecked Stints by its darker brown and more scalloped
upperparts, yellow (not black) legs and more slender bill. Some Temminck's Stints
have yellow legs but they have plainer, paler upperparts and white (not greyish) edges
to the tail. Only at very close range can the long toes be seen.
SEXES alike. IMM. more brightly patterned than ad. HABITAT. Liable to occur on any
water body. STATUS. Rare summer vagrant. CALL. Not recorded in the region.
Reported from elsewhere as a soft 'chirrup'. (Langtoonstrandloper)

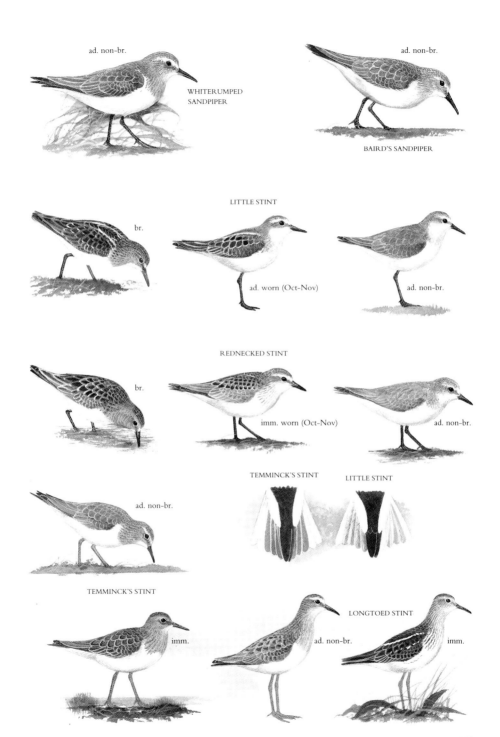

ad. non-br.

WHITERUMPED
SANDPIPER

ad. non-br.

BAIRD'S SANDPIPER

LITTLE STINT

br.

ad. worn (Oct-Nov)

ad. non-br.

REDNECKED STINT

br.

imm. worn (Oct-Nov)

ad. non-br.

ad. non-br.

TEMMINCK'S STINT

LITTLE STINT

TEMMINCK'S STINT

imm.

ad. non-br.

LONGTOED STINT

imm.

GREY PLOVER *Pluvialis squatarola* (254) 30 cm
In flight, the whitish underwings, black axillaries and pale rump distinguish it from both American and Pacific Golden Plovers. At rest, has grey (not buff) speckling on the back and wing coverts. In breeding plumage has whitish (not golden) speckling on the back and wings.
In BREEDING plumage, breast, foreneck and sides of face are black and there is a wide white forecrown and eyebrow stripe extending to the sides of the upper breast. SEXES alike. IMM. buffy-yellow markings on upperparts, but distinguished in flight by white (not dark) rump and black axillaries, and by lack of whitish eyebrow stripe extending well behind eye. HABITAT. Open shore and coastal wetlands where there are expanses of sand or mud, also on rocky coasts. STATUS. Common summer visitor, with some overwintering. CALL. A clear 'tluui', lower in pitch in the middle. (Grysstrandkiewiet)

AMERICAN GOLDEN PLOVER *Pluvialis dominica* (253a) 25 cm
Slightly smaller and more delicately proportioned than Grey Plover, with a more upright stance and longer-necked appearance. In non-breeding plumage upperparts dull brown-grey with golden-yellow speckling, and more pronounced whitish eyebrow stripe than Grey or Pacific Golden Plovers. Distinguished in flight from Grey Plover by dark (not pale) rump, greyish underwing and grey (not black) axillaries. Distinguished from Pacific Golden Plover by heavier build, lack of buff or yellow mottling on breast, and feet not projecting beyond the tail in flight.
In BREEDING plumage resembles breeding Grey Plover with golden spangling on upperparts. Distinguished from Pacific Golden Plover in breeding plumage by black underparts extending to undertail and lack of a white flank line. SEXES alike in non-breeding plumage. In breeding plumage the female has less extensive black on the underparts. IMM. has upperparts more scalloped and yellow. HABITAT. Typically in short grassland. Much less coastal in habits than Pacific Golden Plover. STATUS. Rare summer vagrant. CALL. Variable; usually a single or double-note whistle 'oodle-oo'. (Amerikaanse Gouestrandkiewiet)

PACIFIC GOLDEN PLOVER *Pluvialis fulva* (253b) 26 cm
Smaller than Grey and American Golden Plovers; shape and posture similar to American Golden Plover. Distinguished from Grey Plover in flight by dark (not pale) rump, and grey underwings and axillaries. Feet project slightly beyond tail in flight.
In NON-BREEDING plumage more spangled gold above than American Golden Plover, eyebrow stripe buffy and breast suffused buffy. SEXES alike in non-breeding plumage. IMM. has yellow upperparts and breast. HABITAT. Coastal mud- and sandflats, also on inland grassland. STATUS. Rare summer vagrant. CALL. Not known to differ from American Golden Plover. (Stille Oseean-Gouestrandkiewiet)

RUFF *Philomachus pugnax* (284) m=30 cm, f=24 cm
Scaling of upperparts is conspicuous. The black bill may show an orange or reddish base, and the colour of the legs is variable, often orange or reddish. Similar to Redshank which lacks the scaled upperparts and has striking white secondaries. In flight, the white, oval patch on either side of the dark rump is diagnostic.
MALES sometimes have a white head and neck during the non-breeding season. IMM. resembles non-breeding ad. HABITAT. Vleis, lakes, estuaries and adjacent grassy areas. STATUS. Common summer visitor throughout, often in large flocks. Some overwinter. CALL. Largely silent in the region. (Kemphaan)

BUFFBREASTED SANDPIPER *Tryngites subruficollis* (282) 18 cm
The only sandpiper with completely buff underparts, predominantly buffy face and heavily buff-scaled upperparts. Crown is spotted. It has a short, straight bill, yellow legs, and a white eye-ring visible at close range. Underwing predominantly white.
SEXES alike. IMM. has paler lower belly. HABITAT. Short grassy areas and wetlands. STATUS. Rare summer vagrant. CALL. Not recorded in the region; reported elsewhere as short, sharp 'tik' or 'chek-chek'. (Taanborsstrandloper)

172

GREY PLOVER

GREY PLOVER

ad. non-br.

br.

PACIFIC GOLDEN
PLOVER
ad. non-br.

br.

AMERICAN GOLDEN
PLOVER
ad. non-br.

br.

RUFF
female imm.

male
colour
variant

RUFF
male ad. non-br.

RUFF

male imm.

ad.

RUFF

ad.

BUFFBREASTED
SANDPIPER

PAINTED SNIPE *Rostratula benghalensis* (242) 24–28 cm
Male distinguished from Ethiopian and Great Snipes by breast pattern, longer legs and shorter, slightly decurved bill. Has a laboured flight action.
FEMALE is more striking than the male, with a chestnut neck and breast, and white eye patch. Both sexes have a conspicuous pale harness extending upwards from the breast. IMM. resembles male. HABITAT. Skulks among reeds in marshes and on the edges of lakes, vleis, dams and seasonally inundated ponds and river floodplains. STATUS. Scarce resident, with local movements. CALL. Male utters a trill, female makes a distinctive, soft, two-syllabled 'wuk–oooooo', repeated monotonously, often after dark. (Goudsnip)

ETHIOPIAN SNIPE *Gallinago nigripennis* (286) 32 cm
The long straight bill and striped head markings distinguish it from all except Great Snipe, from which it is separated by longer bill, barred tail feathers at all ages (imm. only in Great Snipe) and a white (not buff) belly with dark barring restricted to the flanks. Flight is faster and more zig-zag than Great Snipe; generally flies further than Great Snipe when flushed.
SEXES alike. IMM. duller than ad. HABITAT. Extensive marshes and margins of perennial and ephemeral wetlands. STATUS. Common resident and local nomad. CALL. A sucking sound when put to flight, more high-pitched and protracted than Great Snipe. Drumming noise during aerial breeding display is caused by air passing over stiffened outer tail feathers. (Afrikaanse Snip)

GREAT SNIPE *Gallinago media* (285) 35 cm
Likely to be confused with Ethiopian Snipe which has white on the belly, not the buffy wash overlaid with dark barring of this species. Great Snipe differs further in having a shorter, stouter bill and clear white spots on the upperwing coverts. At close quarters, the white outer tail feathers of the ad. can be distinguished; those of Ethiopian Snipe are barred. Flight is heavy and direct.
SEXES alike. IMM. Spots on upperwing coverts are less clearly defined and the outer tail feathers are barred. HABITAT. Marshes and wetland margins, including river floodplains and seasonally inundated wetlands. STATUS. Uncommon to rare summer visitor. Previously more abundant and widespread, now largely confined to the north and east. CALL. Deep, short single or double croak when flushed. Lower pitched than Ethiopian Snipe. (Dubbelsnip)

TURNSTONE *Arenaria interpres* (262) 23 cm
This distinctive, stocky wader has a short black bill and orange legs. In non-breeding plumage the upperparts are blackish with irregular dark markings on the front and sides of the breast.
In BREEDING plumage, often seen before northward migration, the head and neck have a crisp black and white pattern and the inner wings and back take on a warm chestnut colouring. In flight (all plumages) there is a distinct wing bar and parallel white lines running down the centre and sides of the back. The tail has a conspicuous subterminal black band. The underparts, including underwings, are white in all plumages. SEXES alike. IMM. has upperparts browner and more conspicuously scaled. HABITAT. Rocky and sandy shores, estuaries and coastal lagoons. Flicks over small stones and weed with its bill in search of food. Usually in small flocks. Rare inland. STATUS. Common summer visitor, regularly overwinters. CALL. A hard 'kttuck', especially in flight. (Steenloper)

PAINTED SNIPE

female

male

ETHIOPIAN SNIPE

ad.

imm.

GREAT SNIPE

imm.

ad.

TURNSTONE

ad. br.

ad. non-br.

SANDPIPERS *See also pages 190-191*

COMMON SANDPIPER *Tringa hypoleucos* (264) 19 cm
Normally shows an obvious white shoulder in front of the closed wing. Legs dull green. Wood Sandpiper is larger, longer-legged and has pale spotting on the upper-parts. Green Sandpiper is larger and has a white rump and black underwings. Flight comprises bursts of shallow wingbeats on slightly bowed wings, interspersed with short glides. Has a prominent pale wingbar, brown rump and barred sides to the dark tail.
SEXES alike. IMM. resembles ad. HABITAT. Wide range of wetland types, including rivers. STATUS. Common summer visitor. CALL. A very shrill 'ti-ti-ti', higher-pitched and thinner than that of Wood Sandpiper. (Gewone Ruiter)

GREEN SANDPIPER *Tringa ochropus* (265) 23 cm
Resembles Wood and Common Sandpipers but is larger, has darker upperparts which contrast with its square white rump and blackish underwings. Greenshank (p. 178) and Marsh Sandpiper (p. 178) are much longer-legged, longer-billed, paler and lack the black underwings.
SEXES alike. IMM. resembles ad. but is browner. HABITAT. Freshwater wetlands, princip-ally along rivers and at small waterbodies such as sewage ponds. STATUS. Uncommon to rare summer visitor to the north and east; vagrant elsewhere. CALL. A three-note whistle 'tew-a-tew'. (Witgatruiter)

WOOD SANDPIPER *Tringa glareola* (266) 20 cm
Intermediate in size between Common and Green Sandpipers, which it superficially resembles. Distinguished from Green Sandpiper by paler upperparts with pale fleck-ing, grey (not black) underwings, less streaking on the breast and yellower legs. Lacks the white shoulder patch, dark rump and tail, and wing bar of Common Sandpiper and has a different flight action (see Common Sandpiper). Much darker and browner than Greenshank (p. 178) or Marsh Sandpiper (p. 178), and has a square (not trian-gular) white rump. Separated from Lesser Yellowlegs (p. 178) by smaller size, less streaked breast and wings not projecting beyond the tail at rest.
SEXES alike. IMM. resembles ad. but warmer brown above. HABITAT. Occurs at a wide range of wetland types throughout the region, but rare on the coast. STATUS. Common summer visitor, singly or in small flocks. CALL. A very vocal species with a high-pitched, slightly descending 'chiff-iff-iff'. (Bosruiter)

TEREK SANDPIPER *Xenus cinereus* (263) 23 cm
The only small wader with a long, upturned dark brown bill with an orange base and yellow-orange legs. Similar to Curlew Sandpiper (p. 168) in size but has shorter legs. At a distance it appears pale with a dark shoulder. The white trailing edge to the sec-ondaries is clearly visible in flight. Usually feeds singly and roosts communally.
SEXES alike. IMM. like ad. but buffier above. HABITAT. Muddy estuaries and coastal lagoons, especially near mangroves and in areas covered by eel-grass (*Zostera*). Crabs are a major prey and the hunting technique, involving long, rapid attack runs with the bill held nearly horizontal in front of the body, is diagnostic. STATUS. Locally common summer visitor; a few overwinter. CALL. A series of fluty, uniformly pitched 'weet-weet-weet' notes. (Terekruiter)

REDSHANK *Tringa totanus* (268) 25 cm
The red base to the bill and the bright orange-red legs differentiate this species from all waders except Ruff (p. 172) and Spotted Redshank (p. 178). Ruff (which sometimes has orange legs and base to the bill) lacks the triangular white rump and finely barred white tail. Spotted Redshank is paler, and longer-billed. Both Ruff and Spotted Redshank lack the striking white secondaries. At rest, Redshank's wings and back appear plain brownish grey, unlike Ruff's scaled and mottled upperparts.
SEXES alike. IMM. is generally browner than ad., legs and base of bill duller red. HABITAT. Freshwater and coastal wetland margins. STATUS. Rare summer visitor, mainly to the coast and northern wetlands. CALL. 'Tiw-hu-hu', the first syllable being a tone above the others. (Rooipootruiter)

176

COMMON SANDPIPER

GREEN SANDPIPER

WOOD SANDPIPER

ad. non-br.

WOOD SANDPIPER

ad. non-br.

imm.

TEREK SANDPIPER

TEREK SANDPIPER

REDSHANK

REDSHANK

REDSHANK

ad. non-br.

REDSHANK

br.

male br.

 SANDPIPERS *See also pages 190-191*

GREENSHANK *Tringa nebularia* (270) 32 cm
Resembles a large Marsh Sandpiper, but has a heavier, slightly upturned black bill usually with a grey or greenish base. Bartailed Godwit (p. 180) is larger, browner, heavier, has relatively short legs and an upturned bill with a pinkish base. Greenshank distinguished from Greater Yellowlegs by green (not orange-yellow) legs, and flight pattern.
SEXES alike. IMM. similar to ad. HABITAT. Coastal and freshwater wetlands. STATUS. Common summer visitor; regularly overwinters. CALL. A loud, rasping 'chew-chew-chew'. (Groenpootruiter)

LESSER YELLOWLEGS *Tringa flavipes* (902) 28 cm
Closely resembles Wood Sandpiper (p. 176), but is larger and has a more streaked breast. Unlike Wood Sandpiper, wings project noticeably beyond the tail at rest. The legs are yellower than any other similarly-sized wader of the region. Distinguished from Marsh Sandpiper in transitional plumage by relatively short bill and, in flight, by square white rump, not extending on to back.
SEXES alike. IMM. upperparts brown spotted with buff; breast greyish. HABITAT. Small vleis and pans to bays and estuaries. Forages on mud and in waterside vegetation. STATUS. Very rare summer vagrant. CALL. A repeated, ringing 'chew'. (Kleingeelpootruiter)

GREATER YELLOWLEGS *Tringa melanoleuca* (906) 31 cm
Slightly smaller than Greenshank, it has orange-yellow (not yellow or greenish-yellow) legs and a square white rump which does not extend up the back. Upperparts are more obviously spotted than those of Greenshank.
SEXES alike. IMM. resembles ad. HABITAT. Freshwater habitats and estuaries; regularly wades in deep water. STATUS. Very rare summer vagrant. CALL. A loud 'tew-tew-tew-tew', very similar to that of Greenshank. (Grootgeelpootruiter)

MARSH SANDPIPER *Tringa stagnatilis* (269) 23 cm
This pale grey sandpiper resembles Greenshank, but is smaller, has a much thinner, straight black bill, slighter build and proportionally longer legs. Non-breeding Wilson's Phalarope (p. 182) is smaller, has much shorter yellow (not grey-green) legs and a square (not triangular) white rump.
SEXES alike. IMM. resembles ad. HABITAT. Estuaries, coastal lagoons and larger inland waterbodies. STATUS. Common summer visitor throughout. CALL. A high-pitched 'yeup', often repeated rapidly. Superficially resembles that of Greenshank, but higher-pitched and less strident. Also a single 'tchuk'. (Moerasruiter)

SPOTTED REDSHANK *Tringa erythropus* (267) 32 cm
Similar to Redshank (p. 176), but is larger, paler, longer-billed, and lacks the white secondaries. Legs and base of lower mandible are dark reddish, distinguishing it from other waders except Ruff (p. 172). Ruff lacks the white rump and prominent white stripe between bill and eye.
In BREEDING plumage, Spotted Redshank becomes black, finely spotted and scalloped with white. SEXES alike. IMM. resembles non-breeding ad. HABITAT. Vleis, lakes, estuaries, bays and lagoons. STATUS. Rare summer vagrant. CALL. A clear, double-note 'tu wik'. (Gevlekte Rooipootruiter)

ad. non-br.

GREENSHANK

ad. non-br.

imm.

LESSER YELLOWLEGS

GREATER YELLOWLEGS

ad. non-br.

ad. non-br.

secondary feather

secondary feather

MARSH SANDPIPER

SPOTTED REDSHANK

ad. non-br.

ad. non-br.

br.

BARTAILED GODWIT *Limosa lapponica* (288) 38 cm

At rest resembles Blacktailed Godwit, but bill is shorter and slightly upturned, the legs are much shorter and the upperparts are browner and more distinctly marked. In flight, lacks Blacktailed Godwit's white wing bar and has thin brown barring (not a black band) on the tail. The white rump is V-shaped (not square), and extends up the back. Best told from Hudsonian Godwit on underwing colour and flight pattern.
In BREEDING plumage the head, neck and underparts are deep chestnut. SEXES alike, but FEMALE has longer bill. IMM. resembles non-breeding ad. HABITAT. Mainly larger estuaries and coastal lagoons; rare inland. STATUS. Fairly common summer visitor to all coasts; regularly overwinters. CALL. Generally silent, but utters a 'wik-wik' or 'kir-rik' call. (Bandstertgriet)

HUDSONIAN GODWIT *Limosa haemastica* (914) 39 cm

Intermediate in size between Bartailed and Blacktailed Godwits. In non-breeding plumage at rest, confusion most likely with Bartailed Godwit due to generally brown coloration. Only safely told from this species if the subterminal black band on the tail is seen or the two species are side by side. Distinguished from Blacktailed Godwit in flight by smaller white wing bar and conspicuous black underwing coverts (diagnostic).
Differs in BREEDING plumage from Blacktailed Godwit by having dark chestnut below extending to belly and vent, and black underwing coverts. SEXES alike. IMM. like non-breeding ad. HABITAT. Estuaries and coastal lagoons. STATUS. Rare summer vagrant to the Cape. CALL. A sharp 'keeewek-keeewek'. (Amerikaanse Griet).

BLACKTAILED GODWIT *Limosa limosa* (287) 40 cm

The largest godwit of the region. Superficially resembles Bartailed and Hudsonian Godwits, but is markedly larger and at rest differs by having noticeably longer legs, a greyer, unmottled back, and a relatively long, almost straight, pink-based bill. In flight the broad white wing bar and white, black-tipped tail are conspicuous. Distinguished in flight from Hudsonian Godwit by larger wing bar and white (not black) underwing coverts.
In BREEDING plumage, the neck and upper breast are chestnut and the belly is white, barred black. SEXES alike. IMM. resembles non-breeding ad. HABITAT. Large lakes, estuaries and coastal lagoons. Regularly forages in deeper water than Bartailed Godwit. STATUS. Rare summer visitor. CALL. A repeated 'weeka-weeka', especially in flight. (Swartstertgriet)

WHIMBREL *Numenius phaeopus* (290) 43 cm

Apart from Curlew, this is the only large wader in the region with a decurved bill. Whimbrel is much smaller, shorter-billed and darker brown than Curlew, and has parallel pale and dark stripes on the head, with an obvious pale eyebrow stripe. The bill is decurved along its full length whereas Curlew's bill is noticeably decurved towards the tip. In flight the tail is barred dusky brown.
SEXES alike but female larger. IMM. resembles ad. HABITAT. Mainly estuaries, coastal lagoons and, to a lesser extent, open shores. STATUS. Common summer visitor to all coasts; regularly overwinters. CALL. An evenly pitched bubbling call of about seven syllables. Highly vocal in the non-breeding season. (Kleinwulp)

CURLEW *Numenius arquata* (289) 55 cm

A very large wader with an extremely long, decurved bill which is proportionally much longer than Whimbrel's. Curlew is paler overall and lacks Whimbrel's head stripes, although a faint pale eyebrow stripe may be visible. In flight it shows a conspicuous white rump which extends up the back as a white triangle.
SEXES alike but FEMALE larger and has a longer bill. IMM. has a relatively short bill; could be mistaken for Whimbrel at a distance, but lacks the head stripes of that species and is paler. HABITAT. Prefers large estuaries and lagoons: a few birds wander inland. STATUS. Fairly common summer visitor; has decreased in numbers this century. Occurs on all coasts, but rare in the east. CALL. A loud 'cur-lew'. (Grootwulp)

BARTAILED GODWIT

ad. non-br.

imm.

HUDSONIAN GODWIT

ad. non-br.

imm.

ad. non-br.

BLACKTAILED GODWIT

ad. non-br.

ad. non-br.

br.

ad. non-br.

WHIMBREL

ad.

CURLEW

ad.

imm.

181

REDNECKED PHALAROPE *Phalaropus lobatus* (292) 16 cm

Resembles Grey Phalarope but has a darker grey back streaked with white, and a thinner, all-black bill. Grey Phalarope's bill is wide along entire length, Rednecked Phalarope's bill is finely tapered. Wilson's Phalarope has a much longer bill, yellow (not black) legs and lacks a distinct black eye patch. In flight the upperparts are darker than Grey Phalarope's. Rednecked Phalarope's rump is black, fringed white, Grey Phalarope's rump is grey.
In BREEDING plumage it is darker overall and acquires a small chestnut gorget; the chin is white. FEMALE is more brightly coloured than the male in breeding plumage. IMM. similar to non-breeding ad. HABITAT. Any quiet body of water, favouring coastal saltpans and sewage works. STATUS. Rare summer visitor, mainly to coastal regions of Namibia and the Cape. CALL. A low 'tchick' when put to flight. (Rooihalsfraiingpoot)

GREY PHALAROPE *Phalaropus fulicarius* (291) 18 cm

Similar to Rednecked Phalarope but more uniformly pale grey above and has a thicker, sometimes yellow-based bill. Separated from Rednecked Phalarope in flight by grey rump (not black rump fringed white). Wilson's Phalarope is larger, has a longer, thinner bill, lacks the distinct black eye patch and, in flight, has a white (not dark) rump and lacks a wing bar.
In BREEDING plumage the chestnut underparts, white sides to the head and black crown are diagnostic. FEMALE in breeding plumage is more brightly coloured than the male. IMM. resembles non-breeding ad. HABITAT. Usually in small flocks at sea, vagrants ashore. STATUS. Fairly common summer visitor to the western Cape and Namibia, vagrant elsewhere. CALL. A soft, low 'wiit'. (Grysfraiingpoot)

WILSON'S PHALAROPE *Phalaropus tricolor* (293) 22 cm

Distinguished from the other, smaller phalaropes in non-breeding plumage by its longer bill, yellow (not dark) legs and lack of a distinct black eye patch. In flight it differs by having a square white rump, grey tail and no wing bar.
In BREEDING plumage a distinct dark stripe runs through the eye and down the side of the neck, and the sides of the breast and mantle attain a rufous wash. MALE in breeding plumage has dark brown crown. FEMALE in breeding plumage is brighter than male and shows a pale grey crown. IMM. resembles non-breeding ad. HABITAT. Coastal wetlands. Rarely spins while foraging, rather lunges with bill from side to side to retrieve food close to the surface. Sometimes forages by walking at water's edge. STATUS. Summer vagrant to Namibia, the Cape and Natal. CALL. A short, grunting 'grrg'. (Bontfraiingpoot)

REDNECKED PHALAROPE

ad. non-br.

ad. non-br.

REDNECKED PHALAROPE

male br.

female br.

ad. non-br.   from above

ads. worn
(Sept-Oct)

GREY PHALAROPE

from above

GREY PHALAROPE

ad. non-br.

ad. non-br.

ad. non-br.

male br.   female br.

female br.

ad. transitional

imm.

WILSON'S PHALAROPE

WILSON'S PHALAROPE   imm.

ad. non-br.

REDWINGED PRATINCOLE *Glareola pratincola* (304) 25 cm

Ad. in breeding plumage has a buffy-yellow throat edged with a thin black line. In non-breeding plumage collar absent or reduced to a few speckles. Similar to Blackwinged Pratincole but has dark rufous (not black) underwing coverts and appears generally paler. The flight is light and graceful and the white rump and forked tail are conspicuous. SEXES alike. IMM. lacks the clearly defined throat markings of ad. and has buff edges to mantle feathers. Rufous underwing coverts and white trailing edge to secondaries are diagnostic. HABITAT. Wetland margins and open areas near water. STATUS. Locally common breeding summer visitor. CALL. 'Kik-kik', especially in flight. (Rooivlerksprinkaanvoël)

BLACKWINGED PRATINCOLE *Glareola nordmanni* (305) 25 cm

At rest appears darker than Redwinged Pratincole. In flight the white rump contrasts sharply with the rest of the upperparts. Best distinguishing features are the black (not rufous) underwing coverts and the lack of a white trailing edge to the secondaries. Mostly seen in the region in non-breeding plumage when throat collar is absent. SEXES alike. IMM. is drabber and more scalloped on the upperparts, without the black gorget. May have some rufous flecking on underwing coverts. HABITAT. Grassland, fallow lands and edges of wetlands. STATUS. Locally common to abundant summer visitor; nomadic. CALL. An often-repeated single or double-note 'pik'. (Swartvlerk-sprinkaanvoël)

ROCK PRATINCOLE *Glareola nuchalis* (306) 18 cm

Much smaller than Redwinged and Blackwinged Pratincoles. A diagnostic white line extends down from the eye across the lower nape to form a hind collar. The legs and base of the bill are red. Appears very dark in flight with a conspicuous white rump. SEXES alike. IMM. is a dull and lightly buff-speckled version of the ad., but lacks the white hind collar and has darker legs. HABITAT. Large northern rivers, especially the Zambezi, where it frequents stretches of water with exposed flat rocks or sandbars. STATUS. Locally common breeding visitor, July to January. Small numbers may be resident. CALL. A loud, repeated, plover-like 'kik-kik'. (Withalssprinkaanvoël)

REDWINGED PRATINCOLE

br.

ad. non-br.

ad. non-br.

imm.

imm.

br.

BLACKWINGED PRATINCOLE

br.

ad. non-br.

ad. non-br.

ad. non-br.

imm.

ROCK PRATINCOLE

ad.

imm.

ad.

See also pages 158-162

CRAB PLOVER

ad.

ad.

imm.

AFRICAN BLACK
OYSTERCATCHER

ad.

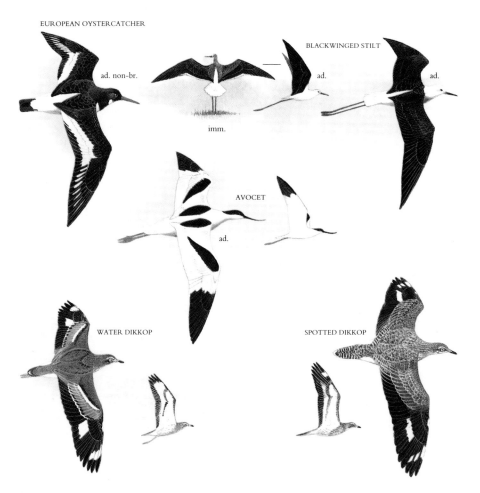

EUROPEAN OYSTERCATCHER

ad. non-br.

imm.

BLACKWINGED STILT

ad.

ad.

AVOCET

ad.

WATER DIKKOP

SPOTTED DIKKOP

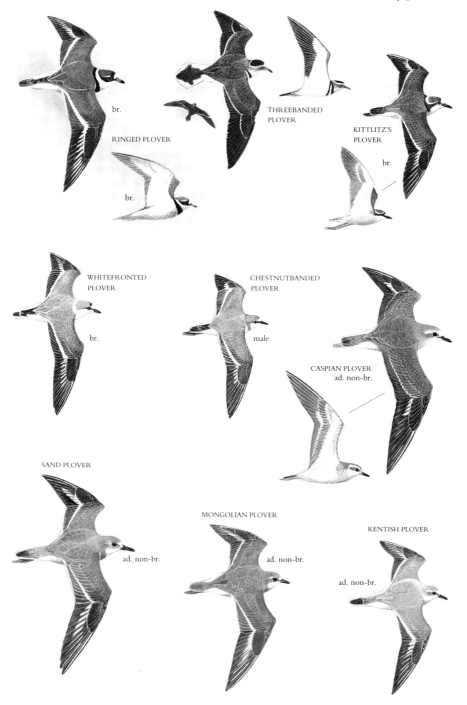

br.

RINGED PLOVER

THREEBANDED
PLOVER

KITTLITZ'S
PLOVER

br.

br.

WHITEFRONTED
PLOVER

CHESTNUTBANDED
PLOVER

br.

male

CASPIAN PLOVER
ad. non-br.

SAND PLOVER

MONGOLIAN PLOVER

KENTISH PLOVER

ad. non-br.

ad. non-br.

ad. non-br.

187

TURNSTONE

ad. non-br.

ad. non-br.

ad. non-br.

LITTLE STINT

REDNECKED STINT

ad. non-br.

moulting
into br.
plumage

imm.
worn (Nov)

TEMMINCK'S STINT

ad. non-br.

LONGTOED STINT

ad. non-br.
fresh plumage

ad. non-br.
worn plumage

SANDERLING

ad. non-br.

ad. non-br.

KNOT

imm.

moulting
into br.
plumage

DUNLIN

ad. non-br.

imm.

ad. non-br.

CURLEW SANDPIPER

ad. non-br.

imm.

CURLEW SANDPIPER
imm.

BROADBILLED SANDPIPER
ad. non-br.

BAIRD'S SANDPIPER
ad. non-br.

WHITERUMPED SANDPIPER

ad. non-br.

PECTORAL SANDPIPER

ad. non-br.

TEREK SANDPIPER
ad. non-br.

COMMON SANDPIPER

low-level flight

GREEN SANDPIPER

ad. non-br.

WOOD SANDPIPER

ad. non-br.

SPOTTED REDSHANK

br.

ad. non-br.

br.

REDSHANK

ad. non-br.

ad. non-br.

GREENSHANK   ad.

MARSH SANDPIPER

ad. non-br.
worn plumage

ad.
worn plumage

GREATER YELLOWLEGS

ad. non-br.   imm.

LESSER YELLOWLEGS

imm.
worn plumage

ad. non-br.

See also pages 168, 170, 172, 180, 182

KNOT
full br.

BARTAILED GODWIT
full br.

CURLEW SANDPIPER

full br.

SANDERLING

full br.

LITTLE STINT

full br.

REDNECKED
PHALAROPE

female

full br.

GREY PLOVER

full br.

BARTAILED GODWIT

HUDSONIAN GODWIT

tail

BLACKTAILED GODWIT

CURLEW

WHIMBREL

AMERICAN GOLDEN PLOVER

GREY PLOVER

PACIFIC
GOLDEN PLOVER

193

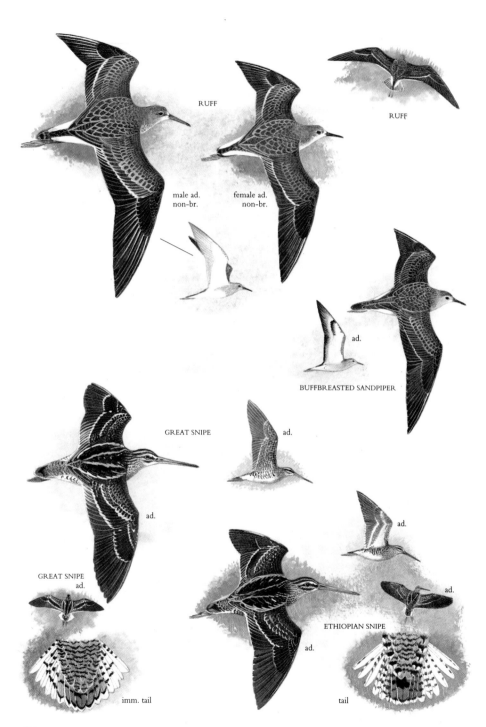

RUFF

RUFF

male ad.
non-br.

female ad.
non-br.

ad.

BUFFBREASTED SANDPIPER

GREAT SNIPE   ad.

ad.

ad.

GREAT SNIPE
ad.

ETHIOPIAN SNIPE

ad.

ad.

imm. tail

tail

194

See also pages 174, 182

PAINTED SNIPE

female

female

female

male

female

REDNECKED PHALAROPE

REDNECKED PHALAROPE
ad. non-br.
fresh plumage
(Sept-Oct)

ad. non-br.
worn
plumage
(Jan-Feb)

ad. non-br.
worn plumage
(Dec)

ad. non-br.
fresh plumage
(Sept-Oct)

GREY PHALAROPE

WILSON'S PHALAROPE

ad. non-br.

ad. non-br.
(Sept-Nov)

ad. non-br.
(Dec-Feb)

ad. non-br.
(Nov-Dec)

SPOTTED DIKKOP *Burhinus capensis* (297) 44 cm
Larger and darker than Water Dikkop, with obviously spotted upperparts. Lacks a wing bar or panel, but has two small white patches on each upperwing visible in flight. Nocturnal.
SEXES alike. IMM. resembles ad. HABITAT. Grassland and savanna. STATUS. Common resident. CALL. A rising then falling 'whiw-whiw-whiw', especially at night. (Dikkop)

WATER DIKKOP *Burhinus vermiculatus* (298) 40 cm
At rest confusion likely only with Spotted Dikkop but is smaller, has a large grey wing panel and narrow white wing bar, and streaked (not spotted) upperparts. The grey wing panel and white wing bar distinguish it in flight. Active mainly at night.
SEXES alike. IMM. resembles ad. HABITAT. River edges, wetlands with suitable cover. Usually in pairs. STATUS. Common resident. CALL. 'Ti-ti-tee-teee-tooo', slowing and dropping in pitch at the end. Usually heard at night. (Waterdikkop)

TEMMINCK'S COURSER *Cursorius temminckii* (300) 20 cm
Confusion likely only with Burchell's Courser from which it is distinguished by being more grey-brown above, having a rufous (not grey) hind crown and a black patch (not bar) on its belly. In flight, the outer tail shows white, and the underwing is black with a narrow white trailing edge to the secondaries.
SEXES alike. IMM. duller, with lightly speckled underparts and scalloped upperparts. HABITAT. Prefers dry, sparsely grassed and recently burned areas. STATUS. Locally common resident and nomad. CALL. A grating 'keerkeer'. (Trekdrawwertjie)

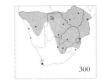

BURCHELL'S COURSER *Cursorius rufus* (299) 23 cm
A plain buff-grey courser with a black and white line extending back from the eye and forming a hind collar. Distinguished from Temminck's Courser by its blue-grey (not rufous) hind crown and nape, and a black bar as opposed to patch on the belly. In flight there is a white bar on the secondaries, and a white tip to the outer tail.
SEXES alike. IMM. mottled above; lower breast markings less well defined than in ad. HABITAT. Dry, sparsely grassed areas. STATUS. Uncommon near-endemic. Distribution erratic and unpredictable. CALL. A harsh, repeated 'wark'. (Bloukopdrawwertjie)

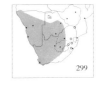

DOUBLEBANDED COURSER *Rhinoptilus africanus* (301) 22 cm
The two narrow black bands ringing the upper breast are diagnostic. Has the plainest head of the local coursers, marked only with a creamy eyebrow stripe. Wing and back feathers are dark with contrasting pale, creamy-buff edges. In flight the uppertail coverts are conspicuously white; inner primaries and all secondaries are chestnut.
SEXES alike. IMM. has chestnut breast bands. HABITAT. Dry open areas, including deserts. STATUS. Common resident. CALL. A thin, falling and rising 'teeu-wee' whistle and repeated 'kee-kee' notes. (Dubbelbanddrawwertjie)

THREEBANDED COURSER *Rhinoptilus cinctus* (302) 28 cm
Neck and breast are ringed by three diagnostic bands, the upper and lower of which are rufous. The white eye-stripe forks behind the eye, extending backwards into a hind collar. In flight, the white uppertail coverts contrast with the dark tail.
SEXES alike. IMM. resembles ad. HABITAT. Dry woodland, especially mopane. Largely nocturnal. STATUS. Uncommon to locally common resident confined to the extreme north. CALL. A repeated 'kika-kika-kika'. (Driebanddrawwertjie)

BRONZEWINGED COURSER *Rhinoptilus chalcopterus* (303) 25 cm
A large, dark, brown and white courser with a broad dusky band across the breast and lower neck, separated from the pale lower breast and belly by a black line. In flight, the white uppertail coverts and wing bars contrast with the dark upperparts.
SEXES alike. IMM. has rufous-tipped feathers. HABITAT. Woodland and savanna. Nocturnal. STATUS. Fairly common resident and summer visitor; subject to local movements. CALL. A ringing 'ki-kooi'. (Bronsvlerkdrawwertjie)

SPOTTED DIKKOP

WATER DIKKOP

TEMMINCK'S
COURSER

BURCHELL'S
COURSER

DOUBLEBANDED
COURSER

THREEBANDED COURSER

BRONZEWINGED COURSER

SUBANTARCTIC SKUA *Catharacta antarctica* (310) 60 cm

The largest skua, this species is heavy-bodied, broad-winged and dark brown in colour. Its large size and relatively short rump and tail distinguish it from imm. Pomarine Skua, which also has a less obvious wing patch. Separated from South Polar Skua by uniform (not contrasting) wings and underparts. Uppertail coverts of imm. Kelp Gull (p. 200) are pale, contrasting with its brown tail; rump and tail of Subantarctic Skua are dark brown.
SEXES alike. IMM. resembles ad. HABITAT. Open seas; regularly scavenges at trawlers. STATUS. Common visitor to all coasts, chiefly during winter. CALL. A soft 'wek-wek' and a loud 'yap-yap'. (Bruinroofmeeu)

SOUTH POLAR SKUA *Catharacta maccormicki* (311) 53 cm

Plumage variable, but dark upperparts and underwing always contrast with paler head, nape and underbody. Both this species and Subantarctic Skua have a white 'window' in the primaries, but the latter species lacks the contrasting plumage and has a larger, heavier bill. Imm. Kelp Gull (p. 200) has a barred (not uniform) brown rump and lacks white primary patch.
SEXES alike. IMM. darker than ad., but also has diagnostic pale collar. HABITAT. Open sea; scavenges at trawlers and pirates other seabirds. STATUS. Vagrant to Cape and Natal waters. CALL. Not recorded in the region. (Suidpoolroofmeeu)

POMARINE SKUA *Stercorarius pomarinus* (309) 50 cm

Most common in pale form, when ad. identified by spoon-shaped (not pointed) central tail feathers, although these are often worn or absent. In comparison with Arctic and Longtailed Skuas, is more heavily built and has more white in the wing.
SEXES alike. IMM. more heavily barred on upper- and undertail coverts than imm. Arctic Skua, and is noticeably larger, heavier and has broader-based wings. HABITAT. Open seas, where it harries terns, gulls and other seabirds. STATUS. Regular summer visitor to all coasts. CALL. Usually silent in the region. (Knopstertroofmeeu)

ARCTIC SKUA *Stercorarius parasiticus* (307) 46 cm

Plumage very variable: pale, dark and intermediate colour forms occur. Pomarine Skua is bulkier, broader-winged, larger-billed and the central tail feathers, if present, are spoon-shaped (not pointed). Longtailed Skua is greyer, slimmer, has narrower wings and much longer, pointed central tail feathers (if present).
SEXES alike. IMM. unlikely to be distinguished from imm. Longtailed Skua unless both seen together, when larger size and bulkier build of Arctic Skua are evident. HABITAT. Prefers inshore waters, where it parasitizes terns and gulls. STATUS. Common summer visitor; some overwinter. CALL. Usually silent in the region. (Arktiese Roofmeeu)

LONGTAILED SKUA *Stercorarius longicaudus* (308) 50 cm

Ad. in breeding plumage has elongated central tail feathers. Occurs in both pale and dark forms, the latter extremely rare. Compared to Arctic and Pomarine Skuas, pale form bird has slimmer body, wings and bill, colder grey-brown plumage and the white markings in the upperwings are confined to the outermost primaries.
SEXES alike. IMM. virtually indistinguishable from imm. Arctic Skua except by its smaller size and more tern-like proportions, limited white in the upperwings and paler legs. HABITAT. Offshore waters, where it attends trawlers. More of a scavenger than the other small skuas. STATUS. Regular but uncommon summer visitor to Cape and Namibian waters. CALL. Silent in the region. (Langstertroofmeeu)

GREATER SHEATHBILL *Chionis alba* (912) 40 cm

A plump, pigeon-like white bird with bare pink skin around the eyes and a yellowish base to the bill and sheath.
SEXES similar. IMM. has dark skin around the eyes and lacks the yellow base to the bill. HABITAT. Oceanic islands and Antarctica. STATUS. Vagrant: almost certainly ship-assisted from the Falkland Islands. CALL. Not recorded in the region. (Grootkokerbek)

SUBANTARCTIC SKUA

SOUTH POLAR SKUA

dark form

POMARINE SKUA

imm.

br.

POMARINE SKUA
imm.

imm.

ARCTIC SKUA

br.

ad. dark form

imm. pale form

ad. non-br.

LONGTAILED SKUA

imm.

br.

imm.

GREATER SHEATHBILL

KELP GULL *Larus dominicanus* (312) 60 cm
The largest resident gull of the region. Ad. differs from ad. Lesser Blackbacked Gull in size and by having a larger bill, steeper forehead, and olive (not yellow) legs. Sub-ad. is distinguished by being bigger and more robust than sub-ad. Lesser Blackbacked Gull and by having brownish (not pink) legs. At rest, wings of Lesser Blackbacked Gull project noticeably further beyond the tail.

SEXES alike but FEMALE smaller. IMM. resembles Subantarctic and South Polar Skuas (p. 200) but lacks the white wing patches and has a barred rump. Differs from imm. Herring Gull in being darker and lacking pale windows in the inner primaries. HABITAT. Inshore waters, open coast, estuaries, harbours and dumps. Increasingly using inland habitats. STATUS. Common resident on most coasts, most abundant in the western Cape. CALL. A loud 'ki-ok' and a short, repeated alarm call 'kwok'. A piercing guttural scream in defence of nest and young. (Swartrugmeeu)

LESSER BLACKBACKED GULL *Larus fuscus* (313) 55 cm
At all ages distinguished from Kelp Gull by slightly smaller size, more attenuated appearance with wings projecting well beyond tail at rest, and less robust bill. Compared with Kelp Gull, ad. has rich yellow (not olive) legs.

SEXES alike. IMM. distinguished from Kelp Gull by having flesh-coloured (not brownish) legs and generally by slender proportions and shape. Separated from imm. Herring Gull by lack of pale windows in the inner primaries. HABITAT. Estuaries and inland waterbodies; the only large, dark-backed gull to be found far inland. STATUS. Uncommon summer visitor to the east coast south to Durban; vagrant elsewhere. CALL. A typical, large gull 'kow-kow' and shorter 'kop' call. (Kleinswartrugmeeu)

HERRING GULL *Larus argentatus* (314) 60 cm
A large, pale gull, similar in size and shape to Kelp Gull, larger than Lesser Blackbacked Gull. Very pale grey upperwings with black, white-spotted primary tips make confusion with any local gull unlikely. Even pale races of Lesser Blackbacked Gull have darker upperparts. In flight from below, secondaries of Herring Gull appear all pale; in all races of Lesser Blackbacked Gull, black colour of secondaries shows through on underwing. Leg colour racially variable (pink or yellow).

SEXES alike. IMM. undergoes complex series of plumage changes from brown-mottled juvenile, taking about four years. Generally paler than imm. Lesser Blackbacked Gull and Kelp Gull, with pale window in inner primaries. HABITAT. In Africa, mainly open coast, estuaries and inshore waters. STATUS. Very rare vagrant, recorded once from Natal. CALL. Loud, persistent 'kleeeuw kleeeuw'. (Haringmeeu)

CASPIAN TERN *Hydroprogne caspia* (322) 50 cm
By far the largest tern of the region, with a black (breeding) or streaked (non-breeding) cap and red or orange-red bill, usually black-tipped. Underwing tip is black. Royal Tern (p. 204) has a smaller, more orange bill and a more deeply forked tail.

SEXES alike. IMM. has brown fringes to wing coverts, more grey in the tail and a paler base and more extensive black tip to the bill. HABITAT. Islands, bays, estuaries, lagoons, inshore waters and large rivers. STATUS. Fairly common resident around coast, uncommon and patchy inland. CALL. A harsh, grating 'kraaak'. (Reuse Sterretjie)

AFRICAN SKIMMER *Rhynchops flavirostris* (343) 38 cm
The peculiarly shaped red bill is diagnostic, the lower mandible being longer than the upper. At rest the black upperparts contrast with the white underparts and red legs and bill.

SEXES alike. IMM. resembles ad., but the black upperparts are replaced by pale-fringed brown feathering and the bill is blackish, becoming brighter with age. HABITAT. Large rivers, bays and lakes where there are suitable open stretches of water for feeding and sandbanks for roosting. STATUS. Locally common resident in the far north; vagrant to Natal and the Transvaal. CALL. A harsh 'rak-rak'. (Waterploeër)

KELP GULL

KELP GULL

ad.

imm.

ad.

imm.

imm.

KELP GULL

sub-ad.

ad.

sub-ad.

LESSER BLACKBACKED GULL

ad.

CASPIAN TERN

br.

br.

imm.

ad. non-br.

imm.

HERRING GULL

ad.

imm.

wing pattern in worn plumage

ad.

armenicus

AFRICAN SKIMMER

ad.

ad.

SABINE'S GULL *Larus sabini* (318) 34 cm
A small gull with buoyant, tern-like flight. The boldly tri-coloured upperwing and shallowly forked white tail are diagnostic.
In BREEDING plumage has a dark grey hood and a yellow-tipped, black bill. SEXES alike. IMM. has a brownish back extending on to inner forewing. Superficially resembles imm. Blacklegged Kittiwake but is smaller, has a darker head and upperwing and lacks the blackish hind collar. HABITAT. Generally pelagic, but may frequent inshore waters, including large sheltered bays. STATUS. Common summer visitor. CALL. Silent in the region. (Mikstertmeeu)

BLACKLEGGED KITTIWAKE *Larus tridactyla* (320) 40 cm
May be confused with Sabine's Gull, but is larger and ad. has a diagnostic all-yellow bill, squarish (not forked) tail, and has black only on the tips of the outer primaries.
SEXES alike. IMM. distinguished from ad. Sabine's Gull by its larger size, black bar across the secondary coverts and dark tip to the tail, and from imm. Sabine's Gull by grey back and pale head. Upperwing of imm. has a distinct, black, open 'M' pattern. HABITAT. Inshore and offshore waters. STATUS. Rare summer vagrant to the western Cape. CALL. 'Kitt-e-wake'. (Swartpootbrandervoël)

HARTLAUB'S GULL *Larus hartlaubii* (316) 38 cm
Compared with breeding Greyheaded Gull is slightly smaller, has a thinner, darker bill, only a slight lavender hood, dark (not pale yellow) eyes, and deeper red legs.
In NON-BREEDING plumage has a plain white head. SEXES alike. IMM. compared with imm. Greyheaded Gull has darker legs, lacks the two-tone bill, has less black on the tail and only very faint smudges on the head. HABITAT. Inshore waters, open coast, estuaries, harbours and dumps. STATUS. Very common resident; endemic. CALL. A drawn-out, rattling 'kaaarrh' and 'pok-pok'. (Hartlaubse Meeu)

GREYHEADED GULL *Larus cirrocephalus* (315) 42 cm
Breeding ad. differs from the smaller Hartlaub's Gull in having a more extensive grey hood, a brighter red bill and legs, and pale yellow (not dark) eyes. Both Blackheaded and Franklin's Gulls are smaller, have very different upperwing patterns and lack the dark underwing of Greyheaded Gull.
SEXES alike. IMM. compared with imm. Hartlaub's Gull has more extensive smudges on head, a pinky-orange bill with a dark tip, darker upperwings and more black on the tail. HABITAT. Open coast, coastal and freshwater wetlands. STATUS. Uncommon to abundant resident. CALL. A typical 'karrh' and 'pok-pok'. (Gryskopmeeu)

BLACKHEADED GULL *Larus ridibundus* (319) 40 cm
Breeding ad. is paler grey above than Greyheaded Gull, with a dark hood and partial white eye-ring. Bill is dark red with a black tip (breeding).
In NON-BREEDING plumage is distinguished by a large wedge of white in the outer wing, and the whitish (not grey) underwings. Franklin's Gull is always much darker above. SEXES alike. IMM. has a brown trailing edge to the secondaries and a mottled brown bar across the secondary coverts. HABITAT. Coasts and inland waters. STATUS. Rare summer vagrant. CALL. A typical small gull 'kraah'. (Swartkopmeeu)

FRANKLIN'S GULL *Larus pipixcan* (317) 35 cm
Smaller and darker than Greyheaded and Hartlaub's Gulls. Always has at least a partial black hood and whitish underwings. In breeding plumage has a full black hood, conspicuous white eye-rings and a pinkish breast. Much darker above than Blackheaded Gull. In flight the upperwing pattern is diagnostic: the black subterminal patches on the primaries are separated from the grey inner wing by a white band.
SEXES alike. IMM. has a partial, black-streaked hood and relatively uniform, dark upperwings. HABITAT. Open coast, estuaries and inland waterbodies. STATUS. Vagrant to Namibia and South Africa. CALL. A goose-like 'ha-ha-ha'. (Franklinse Meeu)

ad.

SABINE'S GULL

imm.

BLACKLEGGED KITTIWAKE

ad.
non-br.

imm.

ad. non-br.

imm.

br.

imm.

GREY–
HEADED
GULL

br.

ad.
non-br.

imm.

ad.
non-br.

imm.

GREYHEADED
GULL

HARTLAUB'S GULL

br.

ad. non-br.

BLACKHEADED
GULL

ad.

br.

br.

FRANKLIN'S
GULL

imm.

br.

ad. non-br.

ad.
non-br.

BLACKHEADED GULL

FRANKLIN'S GULL

SWIFT TERN *Sterna bergii* (324) 46 cm

Intermediate in size between Caspian (p. 200) and Sandwich Terns. Has a large yellow or greenish-yellow (not orange) bill, distinguishing it from Lesser Crested Tern which is also smaller and paler above. Royal Tern has much paler upperparts and a rich orange bill. In breeding plumage Swift Tern has a white frons whereas Royal Tern has a black cap reaching the base of the bill.
SEXES alike. IMM. is barred dark blackish brown and has a dusky yellow-olive bill. HABITAT. Inshore waters, islands, large bays and estuaries. STATUS. Common resident and local migrant. Breeds in the Cape and Namibia in late summer (occasionally winter) and then disperses to all coasts. CALL. Ad. call is a harsh 'kree-eck'. Imm. gives a thin, vibrating whistle. (Geelbeksterretjie)

ROYAL TERN *Sterna maxima* (323) 48 cm

A very pale tern with a rich orange bill, differing from the heavy red or black-tipped bill of the larger Caspian Tern (p. 200). In non-breeding plumage has a very extensive white forehead and crown never seen in Caspian Tern. Most resembles Lesser Crested Tern which is much smaller, and has a brighter, more slender orange bill. Paler above than Swift Tern, and has an orange (not yellowish) bill.
SEXES alike. IMM. resembles imm. Swift Tern but shows an orange (not yellow-olive) bill. HABITAT. Coasts, bays and estuaries. STATUS. Rare vagrant to northern Namibia. CALL. A loud, harsh 'ree-ack'. (Koningsterretjie)

LESSER CRESTED TERN *Sterna bengalensis* (325) 38 cm

Smaller and more graceful than Swift Tern from which it also differs in being paler above and in having a more slender and shorter orange (not yellow or greenish-yellow) bill. Royal Tern is much larger, even paler above and has a larger, rich orange bill.
SEXES alike. IMM. like Swift Tern, has blackish brown on the wing coverts and saddle, but it can be distinguished by the orange-yellow bill. HABITAT. Inshore waters, bays and estuaries. STATUS. Common summer visitor to Mozambique and Natal south to Durban; vagrant to the Cape. CALL. A hoarse 'kreck'. (Kuifkopsterretjie)

SANDWICH TERN *Sterna sandvicensis* (326) 40 cm

A very pale tern, similar in size to Lesser Crested Tern. The black, yellow-tipped bill is diagnostic. Could be confused with Gullbilled Tern which has a short, stubby bill, but Sandwich Tern has a white (not grey) rump, and a more forked tail.
In BREEDING plumage has a black cap and the breast may have a faint pinkish hue. SEXES alike. IMM. resembles non-breeding ad., but has mottled upperparts. HABITAT. Inshore waters, estuaries and bays, usually in association with other terns. STATUS. Common summer visitor to all coasts. CALL. 'Kirik'. (Grootsterretjie)

GULLBILLED TERN *Gelochelidon nilotica* (321) 39 cm

A very pale, relatively long-legged tern with a short, stubby black bill resembling a gull's. Similar in size to Sandwich Tern, but heavier-bodied and broader-winged. Seldom seen with the black cap of breeding plumage; instead, has a variable black smudge behind the eye. Sandwich Tern has a longer, yellow-tipped bill and a deeply forked white tail, as opposed to the shallowly forked pale grey tail of Gullbilled Tern.
SEXES alike. IMM. like non-breeding ad. HABITAT. Variable, ranging from fields, marshes and vleis to the coast. STATUS. Rare summer vagrant, recorded in Botswana, Zimbabwe, Mozambique and Natal. CALL. Variations on 'kek-kek'. (Oostelike Sterretjie)

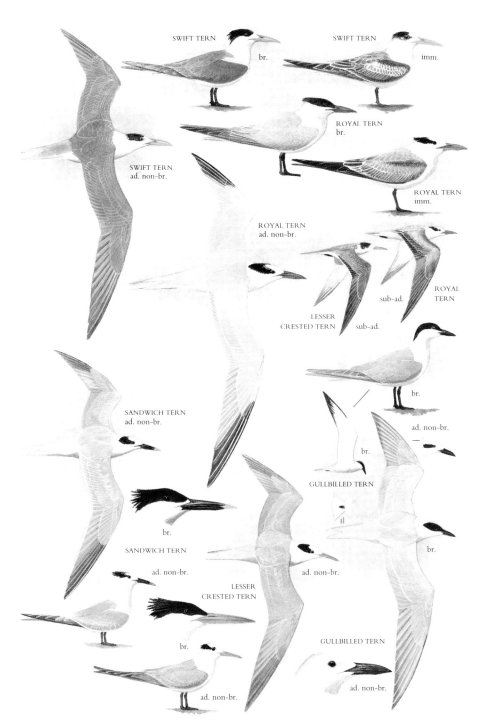

SWIFT TERN
br.

SWIFT TERN
imm.

ROYAL TERN
br.

ROYAL TERN
imm.

SWIFT TERN
ad. non-br.

ROYAL TERN
ad. non-br.

ROYAL
TERN

sub-ad.

LESSER
CRESTED TERN

sub-ad.

SANDWICH TERN
ad. non-br.

br.

br.

GULLBILLED TERN

br.

ad. non-br.

SANDWICH TERN

ad. non-br.

ad. non-br.

LESSER
CRESTED TERN

br.

br.

br.

GULLBILLED TERN

ad. non-br.

COMMON TERN *Sterna hirundo* (327) 33 cm

Differs from Arctic and Antarctic Terns by its noticeably longer bill and legs and, in non-breeding plumage, its greyish (not white) rump and tail. Compared with Whitecheeked Tern has a paler rump and tail which contrast with the back.
In BREEDING plumage differs from Arctic Tern by its darker outer wing and black-tipped, red bill. Roseate Tern has a longer, heavier bill, paler grey upperparts and, early in the breeding season, conspicuously pinkish underparts. SEXES alike. IMM. resembles non-breeding ad., but has dark carpal bars conspicuous at rest and in flight. HABITAT. Open sea and coastal lakes. STATUS. Very common summer visitor to all coasts; regularly overwinters. The most common marine tern. CALL. 'Kik-kik' and 'kee-arh'. (Gewone Sterretjie)

ARCTIC TERN *Sterna paradisaea* (328) 33 cm

Shorter-legged and shorter-billed than Common Tern, Arctic Tern also has a white (not pale grey) rump and tail, and paler wing tips in flight. In breeding plumage bill and legs dark red. In non-breeding plumage most resembles Antarctic Tern but has black (not dark red) bill and legs, is less thickset and has a shorter, more delicate bill. Antarctic Tern attains breeding plumage from October to April and Artic Tern from April to September, so confusion unlikely.
SEXES alike. IMM. distinguished from imm. Common Tern by reduced carpal bar, pale secondaries and marked contrast between grey back and white rump. HABITAT. Pelagic, sometimes roosts ashore, usually with Common Terns. STATUS. Status poorly understood, probably uncommon but regular passage migrant and summer visitor. CALL. A short 'kik-kik' in flight. (Arktiese Sterretjie)

ANTARCTIC TERN *Sterna vittata* (329) 34 cm

More thickset than either Arctic or Common Tern, with a heavier, dusky red or blackish bill.
In BREEDING plumage has full black cap, dusky underparts and white cheek stripe. In NON-BREEDING plumage pale below with conspicuously grizzled crown. White-cheeked Tern has a grey (not white) rump. SEXES alike. IMM. has chequered brown, grey and white upperparts and is confusable only with imm. Roseate and Whiskered Terns (p. 210). Roseate Tern has greyer wings and a much darker cap; Whiskered Tern has a grey (not white) rump. HABITAT. Inshore and offshore waters; roosts ashore in the western and southern Cape, on rocky or sandy shores. STATUS. Fairly common winter visitor to coastal waters of the Cape; vagrant to Natal and Namibia. CALL. A sharp, high-pitched 'kik-kik'. (Grysborssterretjie)

ROSEATE TERN *Sterna dougallii* (330) 36 cm

Distinguished by pale upperparts, long blackish bill with a red base and long white outer tail feathers projecting well beyond the wings at rest. Blacknaped Tern (p. 208) is smaller, lacks black on the crown and has an all-black bill.
In BREEDING plumage, Roseate Tern has very long tail streamers, a pink flush to the breast, a black-tipped, red bill and crimson legs. SEXES alike. IMM. differs from imm. Antarctic Tern by blacker cap, longer bill, greyer wings and more slender body. HABITAT. Coastal waters; breeds on islands in Algoa Bay. STATUS. Endangered resident and local migrant, resident only in the eastern Cape. Uncommon but regular in Natal, vagrant to the western Cape. CALL. A grating 'aarh'. (Rooiborssterretjie)

WHITECHEEKED TERN *Sterna repressa* (336) 32 cm

The uniform colour of the back, rump and tail appears a 'dirtier' grey than that of Common or Arctic Terns, in both of which the tail and rump are paler than the back.
In BREEDING plumage resembles Antarctic Tern, but has a grey (not white) rump, and Whiskered Tern (p. 210), from which it differs by its larger size, deeply forked tail and dusky grey (not white) vent. SEXES alike. IMM. resembles non-breeding ad. HABITAT. Inshore waters and estuaries. STATUS. Rare summer vagrant, recorded in Natal. CALL. A ringing 'kee-leck'. (Witwangsterretjie)

COMMON TERN

ad. non-br.

COMMON TERN
ad. non-br.

COMMON TERN

ARCTIC TERN

COMMON TERN
br.

ARCTIC TERN
br.

ARCTIC TERN
ad. non-br.

imm.

ad. non-br.

ad. non-br.

br.

ANTARCTIC TERN

br.

WHITECHEEKED TERN
ad. non-br.

br.

br.

ROSEATE TERN

imm.

ad. non-br.

br.

br.

BRIDLED TERN *Sterna anaethetus* (333) 35 cm
Could be confused only with Sooty Tern but is smaller with paler, brown-grey upper-parts. The white frons is narrower than in Sooty Tern and extends as an eyebrow stripe slightly behind the eye (Sooty Tern's frons patch ends at the eye). The crown is clearly darker than the back.
SEXES alike. IMM. has wing coverts finely edged buffy-white and underparts white; underparts of imm. Sooty Tern are partially or totally blackish. HABITAT. Pelagic, occasionally roosts ashore. STATUS. Summer vagrant to Mozambique, the Natal coast and the Cape. CALL. 'Wup-wup'. (Brilsterretjie)

SOOTY TERN *Sterna fuscata* (332) 44 cm
Could be confused with Bridled Tern but is larger, the white frons is deeper and extends backwards only as far as the eye and the black crown does not contrast with the blackish back.
SEXES alike. IMM. has largely or partially blackish underparts whereas imm. Bridled Tern is always white below. HABITAT. Pelagic, but blown on to coast during severe storms. STATUS. Common summer visitor to the offshore waters of central and north-ern Mozambique, often foraging in large flocks. A summer vagrant to the Natal and Cape coasts, with inland records from the Transvaal and Zimbabwe during and after cyclones. CALL. Variations on 'wick-a-wick'. (Roetsterretjie)

BLACKNAPED TERN *Sterna sumatrana* (331) 30 cm
Ad. has a black band extending backwards from the eye, broadening on the nape. Crown pure white. Upperparts are pale, recalling Roseate Tern (p. 206), but the latter has black streaking on the crown and is larger. Black marking on wing restricted to the outer primary.
SEXES alike. IMM. has upperparts tipped black and wings with dusky carpal bar; a pink flush on the breast. HABITAT. Coastal waters, sometimes roosting with other terns in estuaries. STATUS. Summer vagrant to Mozambique and Natal. CALL. A clipped, repeated 'ki-ki'. (Swartkroonsterretjie)

LITTLE TERN *Sterna albifrons* (335) 23 cm
Differs from Damara Tern by its shorter, straight bill and white (not grey) tail. Dark outer primaries contrast with remainder of upperwing; more uniform in Damara Tern. Can also be distinguished on call. The legs are brownish yellow and the bill shows varying amounts of yellow at the base, frequently appearing all dark; legs and bill become yellower before northward migration in March.
Sometimes seen in BREEDING plumage, when frons is white (not black as in Damara Tern) and bill is yellow with a black tip. SEXES alike. Does not occur in IMM. plumage in the region. HABITAT. Shallow coastal waters, large bays and estuaries. STATUS. Fairly common summer visitor to the east coast, uncommon and patchily distributed in the west. CALL. A rasping 'kek-kek'. (Kleinsterretjie)

DAMARA TERN *Sterna balaenarum* (334) 23 cm
Differs from Little Tern by longer, slightly decurved bill and more uniform upperparts. Rump and uppertail pale grey (white in Little Tern).
In BREEDING plumage has black bill, yellowish legs (yellow feet) and a complete black cap. SEXES alike. Frons white in NON-BREEDING plumage. IMM. has brown barring on upperparts. HABITAT. Sheltered coastlines, bays and lagoons. STATUS. Locally common resident, breeding summer visitor to southern parts of its range. Breeding endemic. CALL. A high-pitched 'tsit-tsit' and a harsh, rapid 'kid-ick'. (Damarasterretjie)

BRIDLED TERN

ad.

imm.

ad.

SOOTY TERN

ad.

imm.

ad.

ad.

imm.

BLACKNAPED TERN

LITTLE TERN
ad. non-br.

ad. non-br.

ad.

LITTLE TERN
ad. non-br.

DAMARA TERN

DAMARA TERN

br.   ad. non-br.

br.

ad. non-br.

br.

br.

209

COMMON NODDY *Anous stolidus* (340) 42 cm
A brown tern with a wedge-shaped tail, notched only when fanned. Can be confused with Lesser Noddy which is smaller with more uniformly dark upper- and under-wings. The white forehead contrasts sharply with the brown lores. Whitish-grey cap does not extend on to the nape as in Lesser Noddy.
SEXES alike. IMM. as ad., but pale head markings may be confined to the forehead only. HABITAT. Pelagic, but occasionally roosts ashore. STATUS. Rare summer vagrant to the coasts of Mozambique, Natal and the Cape. CALL. A hoarse 'kark'. (Groot-bruinsterretjie)

LESSER NODDY *Anous tenuirostris* (341) 32 cm
Smaller than Common Noddy with a proportionally longer and distinctly thinner bill. The whitish forehead merges with the brown lores and the ashy-grey crown extends further back on to the nape than in Common Noddy. The underwing is dark brown, not pale, rimmed dark as in Common Noddy.
SEXES alike. IMM. closely resembles ad. HABITAT. Pelagic, but occasionally roosts ashore. STATUS. Summer vagrant to Natal and Mozambique following cyclones. CALL. Not recorded in the region. Reported elsewhere as a short, rattling 'churrr'. (Klein-bruinsterretjie)

BLACK TERN *Chlidonias niger* (337) 22 cm
In breeding plumage differs from Whitewinged Tern by whitish (not black) underwing coverts, and upperwings which do not contrast with the back.
In NON-BREEDING plumage superficially resembles Whitewinged Tern, but the dark shoulder smudge is diagnostic (beware of breast smudges on Whitewinged Terns in transitional plumage). Has more black on the head than Whitewinged Tern, and there is no colour contrast between the back, rump and tail. Whiskered Tern is paler, has less black on the head and no shoulder smudge. SEXES alike. IMM. resembles non-breeding ad. HABITAT. Usually forages at sea, often close inshore. Often roosts at coastal wetlands. STATUS. Common summer visitor to the Namibian coast, uncom-mon to rare in the Cape and Natal. Vagrant to Botswana and the Transvaal. CALL. Usually silent in the region; flight call a quiet 'kik-kik'. (Swartsterretjie)

WHITEWINGED TERN *Chlidonias leucopterus* (339) 23 cm
When breeding resembles Black Tern, but has black underwing coverts, predominantly white upperwings and a paler rump and tail.
In NON-BREEDING plumage resembles Whiskered Tern but has a white (not grey) rump and smudged head markings. Non-breeding Black Tern is much darker above, having more black on the head, dark rump and tail similar in colour to back and upperwings, and a diagnostic black smudge on the breast at the base of the forewing. SEXES alike. IMM. similar to non-breeding ad. HABITAT. Open waterbodies, estuaries and marshes; occasionally forages over open veld. Forages at sea in sheltered bays and where large quantities of kelp are washed ashore. STATUS. Common and widespread summer visitor. CALL. A short 'kek-kek'. (Witvlerksterretjie)

WHISKERED TERN *Chlidonias hybridus* (338) 25 cm
In breeding plumage resembles Whitecheeked Tern (p. 206) but is smaller, has a white vent and a less deeply forked tail.
In NON-BREEDING plumage very similar to Whitewinged Tern but has a pale grey rump and a head pattern more closely resembling Antarctic Tern (p. 206). Black Tern is darker with more black on the head and a diagnostic dark shoulder smudge. SEXES alike. IMM. similar to imm. Antarctic Tern, but latter has a white (not grey) uppertail and the two species are most unlikely to be seen in the same habitat. HABITAT. Wide range of open freshwater bodies, from large lakes and river floodplains to small farm dams. STATUS. Fairly common resident and local migrant. CALL. A repeated, hard 'zizz'. (Witbaardsterretjie)

COMMON NODDY

LESSER NODDY

COMMON NODDY

WHISKERED TERN
ad. non-br.

BLACK TERN
ad. non-br.

WHITEWINGED
TERN
ad. non-br.

WHITEWINGED TERN
br.

BLACK TERN
br.

BLACK TERN
ad. non-br.

BLACK TERN
ad. non-br.

WHITEWINGED TERN
ad. non-br.

WHITEWINGED TERN
ad. non-br.

WHISKERED TERN

ad. non-br.

imm.

br.

COMMON TERN
ad. non-br.

ad. non-br.

WHISKERED TERN

br.

211

SANDGROUSE

DOUBLEBANDED SANDGROUSE *Pterocles bicinctus* (347) 25 cm
*Most resembles Namaqua Sandgrouse but male is easily identified by the black and
white markings on the head and by barring on the lower breast and belly. Both male
Doublebanded and Namaqua Sandgrouse have a thin black and white breast band.*
FEMALE and IMM. distinguished from female and imm. Namaqua Sandgrouse by having
a darker streaked crown; barred (not streaked) upper breast, and rounded (not
pointed) tail. HABITAT. Woodland and savanna. Flocks gather at drinking sites at dusk.
STATUS. Scarce to locally common resident. CALL. A whistling 'chwee-chee-chee' and
a soft 'wee-chee-choo-chip-chip' flight call. (Dubbelbandsandpatrys)

YELLOWTHROATED SANDGROUSE *Pterocles gutturalis* (346) 30 cm
*The largest sandgrouse of the region and easily identified in flight by its dark brown
belly and underwings. Male has a creamy yellow throat which is bordered by a thin
black band.*
FEMALE and IMM. also show the very dark belly and underwing, which eliminates
confusion with any other female or imm. sandgrouse. Female lacks the black collar. HABITAT. Open grassland to scrub savanna. Flocks gather at drinking sites during morning. STATUS. Uncommon resident. CALL. In flight, a deep far-carrying
two-syllabled 'aw-aw', the first higher pitched; sometimes preceded by 'ipi'. (Geelkeel-
sandpatrys)

NAMAQUA SANDGROUSE *Pterocles namaqua* (344) 25 cm
*In the region, the only sandgrouse which has a long pointed tail. At rest or when
walking the male most resembles Doublebanded Sandgrouse but lacks the black and
white bands on the head and has a plain (not barred) lower breast and belly.*
FEMALE and IMM. differ from female and imm. Doublebanded Sandgrouse by being
more buffy yellow on throat and breast and by their pointed (not rounded) tails.
HABITAT. Grassland, semi-desert and desert. Avoids mountainous and wet regions.
STATUS. Common resident with local movements; near-endemic. CALL. A nasal
'kalke-ven' in flight. (Kelkiewyn)

BURCHELL'S SANDGROUSE *Pterocles burchelli* (345) 25 cm
*The white-spotted cinnamon breast and belly, combined with the white-spotted back
and wing coverts, render this small sandgrouse unmistakable.*
FEMALE and IMM. resemble male but lack the blue-grey throat and are generally
drabber in coloration. HABITAT. Semi-arid savanna; particularly common on Kalahari
sands. STATUS. Locally common to scarce resident; near-endemic. CALL. A soft,
mellow 'chup-chup, choop-choop' given in flight and around waterholes. (Gevlekte
Sandpatrys)

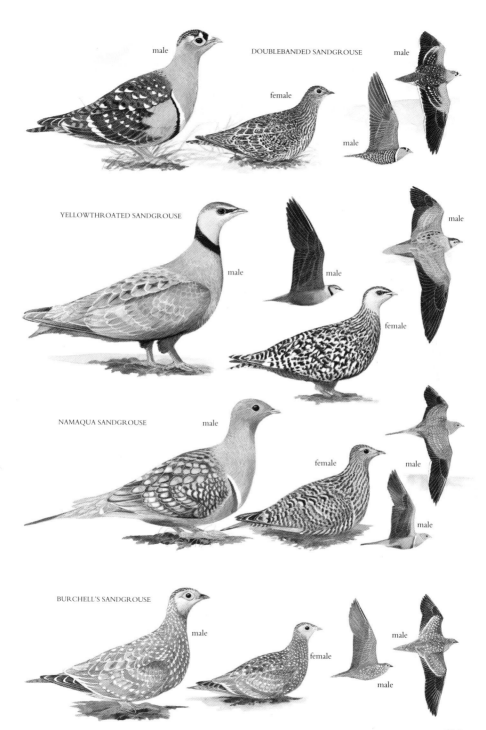

DOUBLEBANDED SANDGROUSE

male

female

male

male

YELLOWTHROATED SANDGROUSE

male

male

male

female

NAMAQUA SANDGROUSE

male

female

male

male

male

BURCHELL'S SANDGROUSE

male

female

male

male

213

ROCK PIGEON *Columba guinea* (349) 33 cm

349

The reddish wings spotted with white, black bill and the bare red patches around the eyes are diagnostic. The only similar pigeon in the region is the Rameron Pigeon which is larger, darker and has bright yellow bare eye patches and legs (legs of Rock Pigeon are red).
SEXES alike. IMM. lacks red on the face. HABITAT. Mountain ranges, rocky terrain, coastal cliffs and cities. STATUS. Common resident. CALL. A deep, booming 'hooo-hooo-hooo' and a softer 'coocoo-coocoo'. (Kransduif)

RAMERON PIGEON *Columba arquatrix* (350) 42 cm

350

The largest pigeon in the region. Easily identified by its dark-coloured purplish plumage, finely speckled with white, the conspicuous yellow patch surrounding the eyes, and the yellow bill, legs and feet. In flight it appears as a large, dark blue or black pigeon.
SEXES alike but female duller. IMM. resembles ad. but has duller coloured eye patches, bill, legs and feet. HABITAT. Evergreen forests and exotic plantations, especially where stands of bugweed *Solanum mauritianum* occur. STATUS. Common resident. CALL. A low but raucous 'coo'. (Geelbekbosduif)

FERAL PIGEON *Columba livia* (348) 33 cm

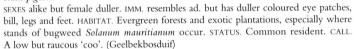

348

Feral pigeons are wild descendants of the domesticated Rock Doves of Europe. Plumage very variable, with black, blue, grey, white and reddish forms occurring. The blue form is identical to the true Rock Dove: bluish grey with black bars on wings and tail, white rump patch, and glossy green and purple on sides of neck.
FEMALE duller than male, with less gloss on neck. IMM. duller than female. HABITAT. Urban areas, also breeds on coastal cliffs in Transkei. STATUS. Abundant resident. CALL. Typical domestic pigeon 'coo-roo-coo'. (Tuinduif)

DELEGORGUE'S PIGEON *Columba delegorguei* (351) 30 cm

351

In the field appears as dark as Rameron Pigeon but is much smaller. The iridescent patches on the sides of the neck are visible only at close range.
MALE has a greyish head and a diagnostic, pale half-moon patch on the hind collar. FEMALE and IMM. lack the pale hind collar and differ from the similar-sized Cinnamon Dove by having much darker upperparts and grey underparts. HABITAT. Lowland forests. Never descends to forest floor as does Cinnamon Dove. STATUS. Uncommon resident. CALL. A frequently repeated hoot, rising and then falling in pitch. (Withalsbosduif)

CINNAMON DOVE *Aplopelia larvata* (360) 26 cm

360

When flushed from the forest floor, it 'explodes' and dashes off swiftly, giving the impression of a small dark dove which lacks the pale, barred rump of the Blue- and Greenspotted Doves (p. 218). When seen at rest on the forest floor, the greyish face and cinnamon underparts are diagnostic.
SEXES alike but female duller. IMM. similar to ad. but drabber and with buff barring on mantle. HABITAT. Undergrowth of evergreen forests; seldom seen in the canopy. STATUS. Common resident. CALL. A deep-based, somewhat raspy 'hooo-oooo' is given from dense thickets. (Kaneelduifie)

ROCK PIGEON

ad.

imm.

ad.

ad.

ad.

RAMERON PIGEON

ad.

ad.

male

DELEGORGUE'S PIGEON

FERAL PIGEON

CINNAMON
DOVE

male

male

female

imm.

female

male

male ad.

215

MOURNING DOVE *Streptopelia decipiens* (353) 30 cm
Distinguished from the similar Cape Turtle Dove by having red skin around yellow eyes and by having a totally grey head. Confusion might arise with Redeyed Dove but that species is much larger, is overall very much darker and has a deep red (not pale-coloured) eye.
SEXES alike. IMM. browner than ad. HABITAT. Thornveld, riverine forests, and cultivated areas and gardens in bushveld. STATUS. Locally common resident. Particularly common at Satara and Letaba Camps in the Kruger National Park. CALL. A soft, dove-like 'coooc-currr'. (Rooioogtortelduif)

REDEYED DOVE *Streptopelia semitorquata* (352) 35 cm
Larger and darker than the similar Cape Turtle Dove, its all-pink head and red eye-ring are diagnostic. In flight, Redeyed Dove shows grey (not white) outer tail feathers. Smaller and paler Mourning Dove differs in having a grey head and a yellow (not red) eye.
SEXES alike. IMM. lacks half-collar and is generally browner than ad. HABITAT. Found in a range of habitats from dry bushveld to coastal forests, and has adapted to city gardens and open parks. STATUS. Common resident. CALL. Alarm call is a 'chwaa'. Other calls are variable but a very dove-like 'coo-coo, kook-co-co' is typical. (Grootringduif)

CAPE TURTLE DOVE *Streptopelia capicola* (354) 28 cm
The white-tipped tail, which is conspicuous in flight, is diagnostic. Much smaller and paler than Redeyed Dove which lacks the white tail tip. Distinguished from Mourning Dove by having a paler grey head, dark eye, and by lacking red skin around the eyes.
SEXES alike. IMM. duller than ad. and lacks half-collar. HABITAT. Found in virtually every habitat in the region but avoids dense coastal forests. STATUS. Abundant resident. CALL. A harsh 'kurrrr' when alarmed, and the well-known dove-call of Africa: 'kuk-cooo-kuk'. (Gewone Tortelduif)

LAUGHING DOVE *Streptopelia senegalensis* (355) 26 cm
Distinguished from the larger Cape Turtle Dove by the lack of black hind collar, by having a diagnostic black-speckled necklace across its cinnamon breast, and by its cinnamon-coloured back. In flight the obvious blue-grey forewings are conspicuous and the white tip and sides of the tail are obvious.
SEXES alike but female smaller and paler. IMM. duller than ad. HABITAT. Found in a wide range of habitats but avoids true desert. STATUS. Abundant resident. The most common and best-known dove in the region, having adapted to gardens and city centres throughout. CALL. Common call is a distinctive rising and falling 'ooo-coooc-coooc-coo-coo'. (Rooiborsduifie)

EUROPEAN TURTLE DOVE *Streptopelia turtur* (919) 27 cm
Similar in size to Laughing Dove but lacks that species' freckled necklace. Has an obvious (diagnostic) oval black and white striped patch on either side of the neck.
SEXES alike. IMM. lacks neck patch and has barred and mottled upperparts, which distinguish it from imm. Laughing Dove. HABITAT. Both South African sightings in thornveld, near water. STATUS. Vagrant to the region, with two records (from the Cape and Transvaal). CALL. Not recorded in the region. (Europese Tortelduif)

MOURNING DOVE

uppertail

undertail

ad.

ad.

REDEYED DOVE

ad.

ad.

uppertail

undertail

ad.

CAPE TURTLE DOVE

ad.

uppertail

ad.

LAUGHING DOVE

ad.

ad.

ad.

EUROPEAN
TURTLE DOVE

ad.

ad.

AFRICAN GREEN PIGEON *Treron calva* (361) 30 cm
When seen clambering about in a tree, the immediate impression is of a green, parrot-like bird. At closer range this species is unmistakable with its green and yellow plumage and chestnut vent. When feeding, it climbs around fruiting trees, sometimes hanging upside-down on branches to obtain fruit.
SEXES alike. IMM. has olive-yellow shoulder patches. HABITAT. Forests, bushveld, savanna: always associated with fruiting trees, especially figs. STATUS. Common resident, subject to local movements. CALL. Unlike any other pigeon in the region: a series of liquid whistles 'thweeeloo, tleeeoo'. (Papegaaiduif)

GREENSPOTTED DOVE *Turtur chalcospilos* (358) 22 cm
At close range the dark bill and green wing spots distinguish this species from Bluespotted Dove. It normally avoids the evergreen forests frequented by Blue-spotted Dove.
SEXES alike. IMM. paler than ad. HABITAT. Woodland and savanna. STATUS. Common resident. CALL. One of the most characteristic calls of the bushveld: a series of low 'du-du-du-du' notes which descends in scale and quickens towards the end. Higher pitched than the calls of Bluespotted and Tambourine Doves. (Groenvlekduifie)

BLUESPOTTED DOVE *Turtur afer* (357) 22 cm
Difficult to differentiate from Greenspotted Dove except at close range when the yellow-tipped red bill and blue wing spots are seen. In flight its back and rump appear more rufous than those of Greenspotted Dove.
SEXES alike. IMM. lacks the bill colouring and blue wing spots of ad. and is overall more rufous than imm. Greenspotted Dove. HABITAT. Moist broadleafed wood-land and along rivercourses in evergreen forests. STATUS. Uncommon resident. CALL. A series of muffled 'du-du-du-du' call notes, like the calls of Greenspotted and Tambourine Doves but more even-toned than the former and shorter than the latter. (Blouvlekduifie)

TAMBOURINE DOVE *Turtur tympanistria* (359) 22 cm
The white face and underparts of the male are diagnostic. In flight the chestnut under-wings contrast strongly with the white belly.
FEMALE and IMM. are slightly darker below but still have paler faces and underparts than all other small doves. HABITAT. Dense evergreen, riverine and coastal forests. Usually flushed before seen; flies fast, straight and low through the forest. STATUS. Common resident. CALL. A series of 'du-du-du' notes similar to that of Greenspotted Dove, but lower pitched, and that of Bluespotted Dove, but more prolonged. (Witborsduifie)

NAMAQUA DOVE *Oena capensis* (356) 28 cm
The smallest-bodied dove of the region and the only one to have a long pointed tail, and a black face and throat (male). In flight the long tail, combined with white under-parts and chestnut flight feathers, render this bird unmistakable.
FEMALE and IMM. lack the black face of the male and have slightly shorter tails. HABITAT. Prefers drier regions such as thornveld, Karoo shrublands and sparse desert grassland. STATUS. Common resident, subject to local movements. CALL. A distinctive, two-syllabled hoot, the first sharp, the second longer. (Namakwaduifie)

AFRICAN GREEN PIGEON

ad.

ad.

ad.

ad.

ad.

GREENSPOTTED DOVE

ad.

undertail

ad.

BLUESPOTTED DOVE

ad.

ad.

ad.

TAMBOURINE DOVE

male

male

male

female

NAMAQUA DOVE

female

male

imm.

male

male

219

CAPE PARROT *Poicephalus robustus* (362) 35 cm
The largest parrot in the region. The combination of its size, red shoulders, forehead and throat is diagnostic.
SEXES alike. IMM. lacks the red shoulders and forehead but its size and massive bill should rule out confusion with other parrots in the region. HABITAT. Evergreen forests and broadleafed woodland. Has adapted to exotic plantations in the east. STATUS. Uncommon resident. CALL. Various loud, harsh screeches and squawks. (Grootpapegaai)

BROWNHEADED PARROT *Poicephalus cryptoxanthus* (363) 24 cm
The greenest parrot in the region, this species has a uniform brown head and bright yellow underwings.
SEXES alike. IMM. resembles ad. but is generally duller with less vivid yellow underwings. HABITAT. Thornveld, riverine forests and open woodland. STATUS. Locally common resident. CALL. A typically parrot-like raucous shriek. (Bruinkoppapegaai)

MEYER'S PARROT *Poicephalus meyeri* (364) 22 cm
May be confused with female Rüppell's Parrot in Namibia, where the ranges overlap. Differs from female Rüppell's Parrot by having a green or turquoise rump and belly, and a brown (not grey) head, which sometimes shows a yellow bar across the crown.
SEXES alike. IMM. resembles ad. but is duller in coloration and lacks the yellow bar across the crown. HABITAT. Broadleafed woodland and savanna. Flocks regularly congregate at waterholes. STATUS. Scarce to locally common. CALL. A loud, piercing 'chee-chee-chee-chee' and various other screeches and squawks. (Bosveldpapegaai)

RÜPPELL'S PARROT *Poicephalus rueppellii* (365) 22 cm
At rest, male best distinguished from Meyer's Parrot by greyish (not brown) throat and head, and by its blue (not green or turquoise) belly. In flight easily differentiated from Meyer's Parrot by brown (not green or turquoise) rump. The yellow bar across the crown of Meyer's Parrot is absent in this species.
FEMALE is brighter than male, with more extensive blue on the vent and with a blue rump. IMM. like ad. but duller. HABITAT. Dry woodland, thornveld and dry rivercourses and, in the north, shows a preference for stands of baobab trees. STATUS. Uncommon resident. CALL. Screeches and squawks similar to those of Meyer's Parrot. (Bloupenspapegaai)

ad.

CAPE PARROT

ad.

imm.

ad.

BROWNHEADED PARROT

ad.

imm.

ad.

imm.

MEYER'S PARROT

ad.

ad.

ad.

imm.

RÜPPELL'S PARROT

female

female

221

ROSERINGED PARAKEET *Psittacula krameri* (366) 40 cm
The only parakeet in the region to have an extremely long, pointed tail. At close range the dark red bill and dark ring around the neck are diagnostic of this bright green species.
FEMALE lacks dark collar and black markings on chin. IMM. like female but has a shorter tail and is brighter green. HABITAT. Urban and suburban parks and gardens. STATUS. Resident. Uncommon and local with small populations established in Durban and Johannesburg. CALL. Various shrieks and screams, being particularly vocal at the roost. (Ringnekpapegaai)

ROSYFACED LOVEBIRD *Agapornis roseicollis* (367) 18 cm
Usually located by its screeching calls and very difficult to detect when it sits motionless in a leafy tree or bush. Flight is rapid, and the blue rump shows up clearly against the green back. There is no range overlap with the similar Lilian's Lovebird which has a green (not blue) rump.
SEXES alike. IMM. paler on face and upper breast. HABITAT. Dry broadleafed woodland, semi-desert and mountainous terrain. STATUS. Common near-endemic. CALL. Typical parrot-like screeches and shrieks. (Rooiwangparkiet)

BLACKCHEEKED LOVEBIRD *Agapornis nigrigenis* (369) 14 cm
The dark brown head contrasting with a bright red bill renders this small lovebird unmistakable. It is often considered a race of Rosyfaced Lovebird.
SEXES alike. IMM. has a dark head like the ad. but its bill is dark grey (not red). HABITAT. Riverine forests and open woodland. STATUS. Resident. Rare and very local in Caprivi and near Victoria Falls. CALL. Shrieking, identical to that of Lilian's Lovebird. (Swartwangparkiet)

LILIAN'S LOVEBIRD *Agapornis lilianae* (368) 14 cm
Slightly smaller than similar Rosyfaced Lovebird, this species differs by having a green (not blue) rump, and a conspicuous white eye-ring. Unlikely to be found with Rosyfaced Lovebird as their ranges do not overlap.
FEMALE has paler pink head than male. IMM. similar to ad. but lacks white eye-ring. HABITAT. Broadleafed woodland. STATUS. Uncommon resident. CALL. A high-pitched, staccato shrieking. (Niassaparkiet)

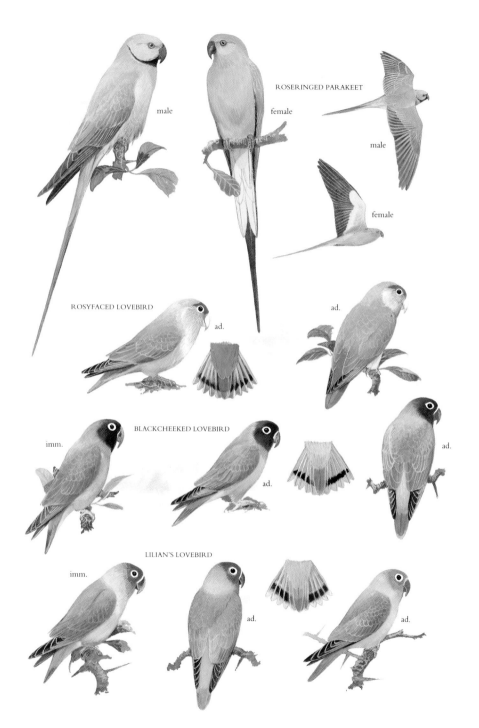

ROSERINGED PARAKEET

male

female

male

female

ROSYFACED LOVEBIRD

ad.

ad.

BLACKCHEEKED LOVEBIRD

imm.

ad.

ad.

LILIAN'S LOVEBIRD

imm.

ad.

ad.

KNYSNA LOURIE *Tauraco corythaix* (370a) 46 cm
The all-green head, white eye-ring and white tips to the crest distinguish this species from Purplecrested Lourie. Livingstone's Lourie differs by having an elongated head crest. In flight shows conspicuous crimson patches on primaries.
SEXES alike. IMM. has a shorter crest which lacks the white tips. HABITAT. Evergreen forests. STATUS. Common resident; endemic. CALL. A hoarse 'kow-kow-kow-kow' and a quieter 'krrr' alarm note. (Knysnaloerie)

LIVINGSTONE'S LOURIE *Tauraco livingstonii* (370b) 46 cm
Differs from Knysna Lourie by having an obvious, very long and pointed crest and a slightly darker back.
SEXES similar. IMM. has a shorter, less developed crest than ad. HABITAT. Riverine, montane and coastal forests. STATUS. Common resident. CALL. Similar to that of Knysna Lourie. (Livingstonese Loerie)

PURPLECRESTED LOURIE *Tauraco porphyreolophus* (371) 46 cm
Darker than the very green-looking Knysna Lourie. Differs from that species mainly by its purple crest, which appears black unless seen in good light, and by the lack of white around the eyes and on the crest. Like Knysna Lourie, it is very furtive and is usually seen only as it leaps from tree to tree, when the red in its wings is conspicuous.
SEXES alike. IMM. like ad. but duller. HABITAT. Coastal and riverine forests and broadleafed woodland. STATUS. Common resident. CALL. A loud 'kok-kok-kok-kok'. (Bloukuifloerie)

ROSS'S LOURIE *Musophaga rossae* (372) 50 cm
The only dark blue lourie of the region and unlikely to be confused with any other. The combination of yellow face and red crest is diagnostic.
SEXES alike. IMM. duller, with a blackish bill. HABITAT. Riverine forests. STATUS. Very rare vagrant to northern Botswana. CALL. Described as a loud cackling. (Rooi-kuifloerie)

GREY LOURIE *Corythaixoides concolor* (373) 48 cm
This ash-grey bird with its long tail and crest is one of the more obvious birds of the bushveld. Vocal and conspicuous, at times appearing like a giant mousebird, it is often seen in small groups perched high in thorn trees.
SEXES alike. IMM. is buffier and has a shorter crest. HABITAT. Thornveld and dry, open woodland. Adapted to wooded suburban gardens in Pretoria and Witwatersrand. STATUS. Common resident. CALL. A harsh, nasal 'waaaay' or 'kay-waaaay', from which it derives its vernacular name of the 'go-away' bird. (Kwêvoël)

KNYSNA LOURIE

KNYSNA LOURIE

LIVINGSTONE'S LOURIE

LIVINGSTONE'S LOURIE

PURPLECRESTED LOURIE

PURPLECRESTED LOURIE

ROSS'S LOURIE

ROSS'S LOURIE

GREY LOURIE

EUROPEAN CUCKOO *Cuculus canorus* (374) 33 cm
In the field virtually indistinguishable from African Cuckoo except on undertail pattern: African Cuckoo has a barred undertail whereas European has a spotted undertail. European Cuckoo is generally less yellow on bill than African, but not consistently so.
SEXES alike. FEMALE may occur in a rare rufous colour form. IMM. may be brown, grey or chestnut; upperparts usually barred, with feathers tipped white; underparts heavily barred. HABITAT. Diverse: woodland, savanna, riverine forests and plantations. STATUS. Scarce to locally common summer visitor. CALL. Silent in the region. (Europese Koekoek)

AFRICAN CUCKOO *Cuculus gularis* (375) 33 cm
The call of this species is its most diagnostic feature. Barred (not spotted) undertail distinguishes it from European Cuckoo.
FEMALE as male but may also occur in a rare rufous form. IMM. as ad. HABITAT. Woodland and savanna. STATUS. Locally common summer visitor. CALL. Similar to Hoopoe's 'hoop-hoop' call but slower. Female utters a fast 'kik-kik-kik'. (Afrikaanse Koekoek)

REDCHESTED CUCKOO *Cuculus solitarius* (377) 30 cm
The characteristic three-note call during summer indicates this cuckoo's presence, otherwise it is usually very difficult to locate as it sits motionless in thick canopy foliage. The chestnut breast is diagnostic.
SEXES alike. IMM. lacks rufous breast and is generally black above with white underparts heavily barred black. HABITAT. Forests, exotic plantations, mature woodland and suburban gardens. STATUS. Common summer visitor. CALL. Male utters a loud, often repeated 'weet-weet-weeoo'; female a shrill 'pipipipipi'. (Piet-my-vrou)

LESSER CUCKOO *Cuculus poliocephalus* (376) 28 cm
Not readily distinguishable from African or European Cuckoo except at close quarters when its smaller size, darker back, nape and crown, and more heavily barred underparts are visible. This species has a rare rufous form, absent in Madagascar Cuckoo. In flight the dark tail and rump contrast with the paler back, a feature not evident in either African or European Cuckoo.
SEXES alike. IMM. resembles ad. HABITAT. Savanna and riparian forests. STATUS. Rare summer vagrant. CALL. Trisyllabic 'kook kook kook'. (Kleinkoekoek)

MADAGASCAR CUCKOO *Cuculus rochii* (925) 28 cm
Virtually indistinguishable in the field from Lesser Cuckoo except on call.
SEXES similar. IMM. mottled rufous on upperparts. HABITAT. Riverine forests and bushveld. STATUS. Rare winter vagrant. CALL. Reminiscent of that of Redchested Cuckoo but deeper in tone and has four, not three notes: 'piet-my-vrou-vrou', the last note being lower. (Malgassiese Koekoek)

EUROPEAN
CUCKOO

EUROPEAN CUCKOO

male ad.

female ad.

EUROPEAN
CUCKOO
sub-ad.

ad.

AFRICAN CUCKOO

imm.

ad.

EUROPEAN   AFRICAN
CUCKOO   CUCKOO

REDCHESTED
CUCKOO
ad.

REDCHESTED
CUCKOO
imm.

LESSER CUCKOO

MADAGASCAR CUCKOO

EUROPEAN
CUCKOO
                    AFRICAN
                    CUCKOO
                                    REDCHESTED
                                    CUCKOO
                                            LESSER CUCKOO   BARRED CUCKOO

BLACK CUCKOO *Cuculus clamosus* (378) 30 cm
The only all-black cuckoo in the region. Similar to dark form Jacobin Cuckoo but lacks the crest and white patches in the wings. At close range, indistinct pale tips to the tail feathers are noticeable.
SEXES alike. IMM. is duller black than ad. and shorter tailed. HABITAT. Woodland, forest, exotic plantations and suburban gardens. STATUS. Common summer visitor. CALL. Male gives a droning three- or four-syllabled 'whoo-wheee-whoo-whoo' ('I'm so sick'); the female gives a fast 'yow-yow-yow-yow'. (Swartkoekoek)

STRIPED CUCKOO *Clamator levaillantii* (381) 38 cm
Unlikely to be confused with any other cuckoo except the pale form Jacobin from which it differs by having diagnostic heavy black striping on the throat and breast.
SEXES alike. IMM. is browner above, very buff below but still shows the diagnostic throat striping. HABITAT. Savanna and woodland. STATUS. Locally common summer visitor. CALL. A loud 'klee-klee-kleeuu' followed by a 'che-che-che-che', descending the scale. (Gestreepte Nuwejaarsvoël)

JACOBIN CUCKOO *Clamator jacobinus* (382) 34 cm
Dark form birds differ from the similar Black Cuckoo by the noticeable crest and white patches on the primaries. Pale form birds resemble Striped Cuckoo but are pure white below, lacking any stripes on throat and breast.
SEXES alike. IMM. browner above; dark form imm. has dull black underparts, pale form imm. has creamy grey underparts. HABITAT. Woodlands, especially thornveld. Dark form is mainly coastal; pale form is found mainly in the interior. STATUS. Common summer visitor. CALL. A shrilly repeated 'klee-klee-kleeuu-kleeuu', indistinguishable from the start of Striped Cuckoo's call. (Bontnuwejaarsvoël)

THICKBILLED CUCKOO *Pachycoccyx audeberti* (383) 34 cm
Resembles Great Spotted Cuckoo but differs by having a uniform dark grey (not white-spotted) back and wing coverts, and by lacking a crest. Has a noticeably thick and heavy bill.
SEXES alike. IMM. is very striking with its white head flecked with black, and white-spotted upperparts: it differs from imm. Great Spotted Cuckoo by lacking the rufous wing patches and the black cap. HABITAT. Riparian forests and woodland. STATUS. Scarce summer visitor, with a few birds wintering on the north-east coast. CALL. A repeated ringing 'wee-yes-yes' and a harsh 'were-wick'. (Dikbekkoekoek)

GREAT SPOTTED CUCKOO *Clamator glandarius* (380) 39 cm
This large cuckoo is unmistakable with its white-spotted dark back, elongated, wedge-shaped tail and long grey crest.
SEXES alike. IMM. is also heavily spotted on the back but has a small black crest, buffish underparts and rufous patches on the primaries. HABITAT. Woodland and savanna. STATUS. Common summer visitor. CALL. A loud, far-carrying 'keeow-keeow-keeow' and a shorter, crow-like 'kark'. (Gevlekte Koekoek)

ad.　imm.　ad.

BLACK CUCKOO

imm.

ad.

imm.

JACOBIN CUCKOO

STRIPED CUCKOO

ad.

ad.

ad.

imm.

ad.

ad. dark form

ad.

THICKBILLED CUCKOO

imm.

imm.

ad.

imm.

ad.

GREAT SPOTTED CUCKOO

imm.

ad.

ad.

imm.

imm.

BARRED CUCKOO *Cercococcyx montanus* (379) 33 cm
Much smaller-bodied than either African or European Cuckoo (p. 226), with an exceptionally long, narrow tail. Often located by its call but, when glimpsed, the brownish, heavily barred upperparts, and the broadly barred underparts, combined with the long tail and slender body, are diagnostic.
SEXES alike. IMM. like ad. but has the underparts more dusky, with some streaking. HABITAT. Lowland forests. STATUS. Uncertain: rare summer visitor. CALL. A long series of 'cheee-phweew's, rising to a crescendo. Also a shorter 'hwee-hooa' or 'hwee-hooo'. (Langstertkoekoek)

DIEDERIK CUCKOO *Chrysococcyx caprius* (386) 18 cm
Male easily distinguished from similar male Klaas's Cuckoo by the broad white eye-stripe, white spots on forewings and by its red (not brown) eyes.
FEMALE differs from female Klaas's Cuckoo by having bolder, but less extensive, barring on the flanks, and by having white spots on the forewings. IMM. resembles female. JUV. differentiated from juv. Klaas's Cuckoo by having a conspicuous red (not black) bill. HABITAT. Woodland, savanna, grassland and suburban gardens. STATUS. Common summer visitor. CALL. A clear, persistent 'dee-dee-deedereek'. (Diederikkie)

KLAAS'S CUCKOO *Chrysococcyx klaas* (385) 18 cm
Male differs from the very similar male Diederik Cuckoo by having only a small amount of white behind the eye, no white markings on the wings, and a brown (not red) eye.
FEMALE differs from female Diederik Cuckoo by having finer, more extensive barring on flanks and breast, and by lacking white wing markings. IMM. resembles female. HABITAT. Forests, woodland, savanna, parks and gardens. STATUS. Common summer visitor; some birds overwinter. CALL. A soft 'huee-jee' repeated five or six times. (Meitjie)

EMERALD CUCKOO *Chrysococcyx cupreus* (384) 20 cm
Male is unmistakable with brilliant emerald green throat, upper breast and upperparts and sulphur-yellow lower breast and belly.
FEMALE differs from female Klaas's and Diederik Cuckoos by lacking white behind the eye and by having a more brownish-bronze cast to upperparts and more heavily barred underparts. IMM. resembles female. HABITAT. Evergreen forests. STATUS. Common summer visitor. CALL. A loud, ringing whistle 'wheet-huiee-wheet', often rendered as 'pretty georg-eee'. (Mooimeisie)

ad.

ad.

BARRED CUCKOO

ad.

ad.

male imm.

imm.

imm.

DIEDERIK CUCKOO

female ad.

male ad.

female ad.

male ad.

female ad.

imm.

KLAAS'S CUCKOO

male ad.

female ad.

male ad.

female ad.

female ad.

male ad.

female imm.

female ad.

EMERALD CUCKOO

female ad.

male ad.

male ad.

male ad.

COPPERYTAILED COUCAL *Centropus cupreicaudus* (389) 48 cm
The largest coucal of the region, this species most closely resembles Burchell's Coucal but it has a longer, broader and floppier tail which, like the head, is black with a coppery sheen.
SEXES alike. IMM. is the same size as ad. (thus ruling out confusion with other imm. coucals), and its long tail is barred black and brown. HABITAT. Marshlands, thick reedbeds and adjoining bush. STATUS. Common resident. CALL. A louder, more resonant bubbling call than that of other coucals. (Grootvleiloerie)

BURCHELL'S COUCAL *Centropus burchelli* (391a) 44 cm
Very similar to the slightly smaller Senegal and Whitebrowed Coucals but has fine rufous barring on the rump and base of tail.
SEXES alike. IMM. indistinguishable in the field from imm. Senegal and Whitebrowed Coucals. HABITAT. Long grass, riverine scrub, reedbeds, woodland and suburban gardens. STATUS. Common resident. CALL. A liquid bubbling 'doo-doo-doo-doo', descending in scale, then rising towards the end of the phrase. (Gewone Vleiloerie)

WHITEBROWED COUCAL *Centropus superciliosus* (391b) 44 cm
Differs from Burchell's Coucal by lacking a glossy black cap and having a clear, creamy eyebrow stripe and white-flecked crown and nape.
SEXES alike. IMM. Doubtful if the imms. of Senegal, Burchell's and Whitebrowed Coucals could be separated in the field. HABITAT. Similar to Burchell's Coucal. STATUS. Common resident. CALL. Bubbling note similar to that of Burchell's Coucal. (Witstreepvleiloerie)

SENEGAL COUCAL *Centropus senegalensis* (390) 40 cm
Where the ranges of this species and Burchell's Coucal overlap, identification difficulties arise. This species differs only by its dark rump, and by having the base of its tail dark, not barred rufous as in Burchell's Coucal. Differs from Copperytailed Coucal by smaller size and brighter chestnut wings and back.
SEXES alike. IMM. of this species and imm. Copperytailed Coucal are indistinguishable in the field except by size. HABITAT. Tangled vegetation and long grass, often near water. STATUS. Uncommon resident. CALL. Bubbling call note, very similar to that of Burchell's Coucal. (Senegalvleiloerie)

BLACK COUCAL *Centropus bengalensis* (388) 35 cm
A small coucal and the only one in the region to have a black head and body contrasting with rich chestnut back and wings.
SEXES alike but female larger. NON-BREEDING AD. and IMM. birds differ from other coucals by their small size, small bill and clear, buff-streaked head and upperparts. HABITAT. Moist grassland with rank vegetation. STATUS. Uncommon summer visitor. CALL. A typical bubbling coucal call and a monotonous, repeated 'poopoop'. (Swartvleiloerie)

GREEN COUCAL *Ceuthmochares aereus* (387) 33 cm
This shy bird is very difficult to see in the thick, tangled undergrowth it frequents and is usually located by its call. When flushed, the dull green upperparts and long tail, combined with the yellow bill, are diagnostic.
SEXES alike. IMM. resembles ad. but has a duller, greenish bill. HABITAT. Thick evergreen, riverine and coastal forests. STATUS. Scarce to locally common resident. CALL. A clicking 'kik-kik-kik', winding up to a loud 'cher-cher-cher-cher'. (Groenvleiloerie)

COPPERYTAILED COUCAL

BURCHELL'S COUCAL

BURCHELL'S COUCAL

WHITEBROWED
COUCAL

SENEGAL
COUCAL

SENEGAL COUCAL

BURCHELL'S COUCAL
imm.

WHITEBROWED
COUCAL

BLACK COUCAL
imm.

BLACK COUCAL

GREEN COUCAL

233

OWLS

GIANT EAGLE OWL *Bubo lacteus* (402) 60-65 cm
The largest owl of the region, its size and pale grey coloration make it easily identifiable. Pink eyelids distinctive. The northern race of the Cape Eagle Owl approaches it in size but that species has rufous coloration and boldly barred underparts.
SEXES alike. IMM. paler grey than ad. and finely barred. HABITAT. Broadleafed woodland, savanna, thornveld and riverine forests. STATUS. Uncommon to locally common resident. CALL. A grunting, pig-like 'unnh-unnh-unnh'. (Reuse Ooruil)

PEL'S FISHING OWL *Scotopelia peli* (403) 63 cm
The large size and ginger coloration render this species unmistakable. When alarmed, the bird fluffs up its head feathers, which gives it a huge, round-headed appearance. At rest, the large, dark eyes dominate the unmarked tawny facial disc. The unfeathered legs and feet are difficult to see in the field.
SEXES alike. IMM. is paler, more buffy coloured, with an almost white head. HABITAT. Large trees around lakes and slow-moving rivers. STATUS. Uncommon resident. CALL. A deep, booming 'hoo-huuuum' and a jackal-like wailing. (Visuil)

CAPE EAGLE OWL *Bubo capensis* (400) 48-54 cm
Not easily distinguished from the more common Spotted Eagle Owl unless heard calling; is larger and has black and chestnut blotching on the breast, and bold (not fine) barring on belly and flanks. It also has much larger feet than Spotted Eagle Owl and orange (not yellow) eyes. Birds in the far north of the region are very much larger.
SEXES alike. IMM. like ad. HABITAT. Rocky and mountainous terrain. STATUS. Scarce, localized resident. CALL. A loud, far-carrying 'hu-hooooo', the first syllable being sharp and penetrating. Also a loud 'wak-wak-wak'. (Kaapse Ooruil)

SPOTTED EAGLE OWL *Bubo africanus* (401) 43-50 cm
Grey and rufous colour forms occur. Grey form is the most common and is distinguished from Cape Eagle Owl by its smaller size, lack of dark breast patches, by the finely barred belly and flanks, yellow (not orange) eyes, and its smaller feet.
SEXES alike. IMM. resembles ad. HABITAT. Diverse, from desert to mature woodland and savanna. STATUS. Resident; the most common eagle owl of the region. CALL. A hooting 'hu-hoo', similar to that of Cape Eagle Owl but softer and less penetrating. (Gevlekte Ooruil)

BARN OWL *Tyto alba* (392) 34 cm
This golden buff and white owl could be confused with Grass Owl but is much paler and has less contrast between the upper- and underparts. The heart-shaped white facial disc highlights the unusually small black eyes.
SEXES alike. IMM. like ad. HABITAT. Diverse; from deserts to moist savanna. Often found near human habitation but also roosts in caves, hollow trees and mine shafts. STATUS. Common resident. CALL. Many and varied calls, the most usual being an eerie 'shreee'. (Nonnetjie-uil)

GRASS OWL *Tyto capensis* (393) 36 cm
Although it could be confused with Barn Owl, this species' much darker upperparts contrast markedly with its whitish underparts. Marsh Owl (p. 236), found in the same habitat, has a dark (not white) face and underparts and noticeably rounded wings with buff patches at the base of the primaries.
SEXES alike. IMM. has rufous facial disc and darker underparts. HABITAT. Marshes and tall grassland; not in reedbeds. STATUS. Uncommon resident. CALL. A soft, cricket-like 'tk-tk-tk-tk...' uttered while on the wing. (Grasuil)

PEL'S FISHING OWL

GIANT EAGLE OWL

CAPE EAGLE OWL

SPOTTED EAGLE OWL

GRASS OWL

BARN OWL

GRASS OWL

BARN OWL

235

WOOD OWL *Strix woodfordii* (394) 35 cm
This medium-sized owl can be identified by its lack of 'ear' tufts, its heavily barred brown underparts and pale, finely barred facial disc with large, dark brown eyes. Plumage coloration is variable, ranging from very dark brown to russet.
SEXES alike. IMM. as ad. HABITAT. Evergreen and riverine forests, mature woodland and exotic plantations. STATUS. Common resident. CALL. Close to the classic owl call 'tuwhit-towhoo' but rendered as 'huoo-hoo-hoo', the female's call being higher-pitched. Also a high-pitched 'weooo'. Pairs regularly duet, the female calling first. (Bosuil)

MARSH OWL *Asio capensis* (395) 36 cm
A plain brown, medium-sized owl with a buff-coloured face, small 'ear' tufts, and dark brown eyes. In flight shows buff 'windows' on the primaries and dark marks on the underwing carpals. When flushed during daytime will circle overhead before alighting.
SEXES alike. IMM. like ad. HABITAT. Marshes and damp grassland; avoids thick reedbeds. Sometimes found in flocks. STATUS. Common resident. CALL. A harsh, rasping 'krikkk-krikkk', likened to the sound of material being torn. (Vlei-uil)

WHITEFACED OWL *Otus leucotis* (397) 28 cm
The only other small owl with 'ear' tufts is African Scops Owl, from which this species differs by having a conspicuous white facial disc edged with black, and by its bright orange (not yellow) eyes. It is also larger, and much paler grey than African Scops Owl.
SEXES alike. IMM. buffier than ad., with greyish face and yellow eyes. HABITAT. Thornveld and dry broadleafed woodland. STATUS. Common resident. CALL. A fast, hooting 'doo-doo-doo-doo-hohoo' call. (Witwanguil)

BARRED OWL *Glaucidium capense* (399) 21 cm
Might be confused with Pearlspotted Owl from which it differs by being larger and having barred upperparts and tail, and conspicuous white edging to the scapulars.
SEXES alike. IMM. less distinctly spotted below than ad. HABITAT. Mature woodland and riparian gallery forests. STATUS. Locally common resident. CALL. A soft, frequently repeated 'kerrr-kerrr-kerrr' and a 'trru-trrre'. (Gebande Uil)

PEARLSPOTTED OWL *Glaucidium perlatum* (398) 18 cm
The smallest owl of the region. The rounded head with no 'ear' tufts and the white spotting on back and tail distinguish this species from African Scops and Whitefaced Owls. Differentiated from Barred Owl by its smaller size and lack of barring on the upperparts. Shows two black 'false eyes' on the nape.
SEXES alike. IMM. as ad. HABITAT. Thornveld and broadleafed woodland. STATUS. Common resident. CALL. A series of 'tu-tu-tuee-tuee' whistles which rises and then descends in pitch. (Witkoluil)

AFRICAN SCOPS OWL *Otus senegalensis* (396) 20 cm
This small owl could be confused with Whitefaced Owl because both have 'ear' tufts, but this species has a grey (not white) face and is considerably smaller and slimmer. A grey and brown form occur. Typically roosts on branches adjacent to tree trunk; very inconspicuous by day.
SEXES alike. IMM. like ad. HABITAT. Bushveld and dry, open woodland. Absent from forested regions. STATUS. Common resident. CALL. A soft, frog-like 'prrrup', repeated at intervals. (Skopsuil)

WOOD OWL
brown form

MARSH OWL

WOOD OWL
rufous form

WHITEFACED OWL

BARRED OWL

AFRICAN SCOPS OWL

PEARLSPOTTED OWL

EUROPEAN NIGHTJAR *Caprimulgus europaeus* (404) 25-28 cm
A large nightjar, it is paler than Freckled Nightjar and shows more white in the wing and tail. Lack of rufous on head and neck separates it from Fierynecked and Rufoucheeked Nightjars. Reduced white on tail differentiates it from Natal and Mozambique Nightjars, and it has much less white in the wing than Pennantwinged.
FEMALE very similar to female Pennantwinged Nightjar but is grey (not brown). IMM. like female. HABITAT. Woodland, savanna, plantations, suburban areas. STATUS. Scarce to common summer visitor. CALL. Silent in Africa. (Europese Naguil)

PENNANTWINGED NIGHTJAR *Macrodipteryx vexillaria* (410) 28 cm
Breeding male is unmistakable: it shows a broad white stripe across the primaries, and white elongated inner primaries which trail well behind the bird.
FEMALE is a nondescript large brown nightjar with no white on wings or tail. IMM. like female. HABITAT. Mature broadleafed woodland. STATUS. Locally common summer visitor. CALL. A continuous, high-pitched twittering note. (Wimpelvlerknaguil)

FRECKLED NIGHTJAR *Caprimulgus tristigma* (408) 28 cm
Differs from both European and Pennantwinged Nightjars by its greyish upperparts, which blend well with the rocky terrain it frequents. In flight distinguished from European Nightjar by having less white on the tips of the outer tail feathers.
FEMALE lacks white tail patches of male. IMM. like female. HABITAT. Rocky outcrops in woodland and hilly terrain. Also found roosting on buildings in towns and cities. STATUS. Locally common resident. CALL. A yapping, double-note 'kow-kow', sometimes extending to 3-4 syllables. (Donkernaguil)

FIERYNECKED NIGHTJAR *Caprimulgus pectoralis* (405) 24 cm
At rest distinguished from Rufoucheeked Nightjar by its rich rufous (not orange-buff) collar. Male in flight distinguished from Rufoucheeked and Mozambique Nightjars by extent of white in outer tail feathers: in Mozambique outer tail feathers wholly white, in Fierynecked lower half white and in Rufoucheeked lower quarter white.
FEMALE and IMM. have white areas in wing and tail replaced by buff. HABITAT. Woodland, savanna and plantations. STATUS. Common resident. CALL. A plaintive, descending 6-syllabled 'good Lord, deliver us'. (Afrikaanse Naguil)

RUFOUSCHEEKED NIGHTJAR *Caprimulgus rufigena* (406) 24 cm
Differs from Fierynecked Nightjar by having an orange-buff (not rufous) collar and by lacking the rufous on its breast.
FEMALE differs from the female Fierynecked by having reduced areas of buff on tail. IMM. as female. HABITAT. Dry thornveld and broadleafed woodland, and scrub desert. STATUS. Locally common summer visitor. CALL. A prolonged churring, usually preceded by a choking 'chukoo, chukoo'. (Rooiwangnaguil)

MOZAMBIQUE NIGHTJAR *Caprimulgus fossii* (409) 24 cm
Resembles Natal Nightjar in having the outer tail feathers white, but differs by being darker brown, less buff above, and by its larger size.
FEMALE distinguished from female Natal Nightjar by having less white on the tail, and by its larger size. IMM. as female. HABITAT. Coastal dune scrub and sandy woodland, often near lakes and rivers. STATUS. Common resident. CALL. A prolonged churring which changes at intervals in pitch ('changing gears'). (Laeveldnaguil)

NATAL NIGHTJAR *Caprimulgus natalensis* (407) 22 cm
Resembles Mozambique Nightjar inasmuch as both have entirely white outer tail feathers, but Natal Nightjar is smaller and paler in colour.
FEMALE lacks white in wings but still shows complete white outer tail feathers. IMM. as female. HABITAT. Palm savanna, and open grassland. STATUS. Rare to locally common resident. CALL. A 'chow-chow-chow' or 'chop-chop-chop' call. (Natalse Naguil)

238

EUROPEAN NIGHTJAR

male

female

PENNANTWINGED
NIGHTJAR

female

female

FRECKLED NIGHTJAR

male

female

male

FIERYNECKED NIGHTJAR

RUFOUSCHEEKED
NIGHTJAR

male

female

male

female

MOZAMBIQUE
NIGHTJAR

NATAL NIGHTJAR

male

female

male

female

male

female

male

239

EUROPEAN NIGHTJAR

One of the three large nightjar species in the region. In flight, the male has white wing and tail panels (one quarter the length of the tail); female shows reduced area of buff in the wing and tail and is greyer than female Pennantwinged Nightjar (which has no white or buff panels in the wing or tail); not as uniformly dark as Freckled Nightjar.

PENNANTWINGED NIGHTJAR

Large. In flight the breeding male is unmistakable; even after dropping its pennants the male is easily identified by the extensive white area in the wings. The female has no white or buff panels in the wing or tail and has ginger-coloured, strongly barred wings. The tail is slightly forked.

FRECKLED NIGHTJAR

Large. In flight this species appears a uniform dark grey; both sexes have white panels in the wing (reduced in the female) but only the male has white panels in the outer tail tips.

FIERYNECKED NIGHTJAR

Medium-sized. In flight this species most easily confused with Rufouscheeked Nightjar; in both species, the male has white panels in the wing and outer tail tips but in Fierynecked Nightjar the tail panel is more extensive, extending half the way up the tail (whereas in Rufouscheeked Nightjar it extends only a quarter of the way up the tail). The female has buffy (not white) panels. In the hand, Fierynecked Nightjar has the white wing panel overlying the notch in the ninth primary.

RUFOUSCHEEKED NIGHTJAR

Medium-sized. In flight the male shows shorter white panels in the tail than the male Fierynecked Nightjar (one quarter the tail length); female lacks any white tail panels and the buff spots in the wing are smaller than in Fierynecked Nightjar.

MOZAMBIQUE NIGHTJAR

Medium-sized. In flight the wholly white outer tail feathers (buff-coloured in the female) distinguish this species from all other nightjars in the region except Natal Nightjar which also has an entirely white outer tail, but additionally has a white tip (buff in female) to the adjacent tail feather.

NATAL NIGHTJAR

Smaller than the other nightjars in the region. In flight likely to be confused only with Mozambique Nightjar, but the broader area of white (or buff in the female) in the outer tail distinguishes it, as does its paler, buffier appearance.

See also pages 238-239

male

EUROPEAN
NIGHTJAR

female

PENNANTWINGED
NIGHTJAR

female   male br.

FRECKLED NIGHTJAR

male

female

female

male

female

male

RUFOUSCHEEKED NIGHTJAR

male

FIERYNECKED NIGHTJAR

male

NATAL NIGHTJAR

male

MOZAMBIQUE NIGHTJAR

female

male

241

ALPINE SWIFT *Apus melba* (418) 22 cm
A very large, fast-flying swift and the only one to show white underparts and a dark breast band. Often seen in mixed flocks with other swift species.
HABITAT. Aerial and wide ranging. Breeds on high inland cliffs with vertical cracks. STATUS. Common resident and summer visitor. CALL. A shrill scream. (Witpenswindswael)

MOTTLED SWIFT *Apus aequatorialis* (419) 20 cm
Much the same size and shape as Alpine Swift but lacks the white underparts of that species. Has scaled and mottled underparts like Bradfield's Swift but is darker and much larger.
HABITAT. Aerial and wide ranging. Breeds in vertical cracks on inland cliffs. Nest site is a vertical crack in a cliff. STATUS. Uncommon resident, found in granite koppie country of Zimbabwe and Mozambique. CALL. A typical swift scream. (Bontwindswael)

BRADFIELD'S SWIFT *Apus bradfieldi* (413) 18 cm
Paler than both European and Black Swifts. At close range and in good light a scaled, mottled effect is discernible on the underparts. In the field unlikely to be distinguished from Pallid Swift unless both are seen together.
HABITAT. Aerial and wide ranging. Breeds in crevices on inland cliffs. STATUS. Locally common resident. CALL. High-pitched screaming at breeding sites. (Muiskleurwindswael)

PALLID SWIFT *Apus pallidus* (414) 17 cm
Very difficult to tell from Black, European and Bradfield's Swifts unless seen together. Differs from Black and European Swifts by being paler with a more extensive white throat patch and paler forehead. Distinguished from Bradfield's Swift by being only slightly paler and lacking the scaled effect on the underparts. Direct field comparison probably required for certain identification. In comparison with all three species, Pallid Swift has a more robust body and a slower flight action.
HABITAT. Aerial. STATUS. A rare summer visitor with one specimen record from the northern Cape. CALL. Silent in Africa. (Bruinwindswael)

BLACK SWIFT *Apus barbatus* (412) 18 cm
Can be distinguished (with difficulty) from European Swift if upperparts are seen clearly. The secondaries, especially the inner secondaries, are paler than the rest of the wing and back and show up as contrasting pale greyish-brown patches.
HABITAT. Aerial. Breeds in crevices on inland cliffs. STATUS. Common resident and partial migrant. CALL. A high-pitched screaming at breeding sites. (Swartwindswael)

EUROPEAN SWIFT *Apus apus* (411) 17 cm
Difficult to distinguish from Pallid and Black Swifts. Differentiated from the former only under optimum viewing conditions when both species are present; European Swift has less white on its throat and has a more slender body. Differs from Black Swift by having secondaries and back uniform in colour.
HABITAT. Aerial and wide-ranging. Sometimes in flocks numbering hundreds. STATUS. Common summer visitor, less common in the south. CALL. Seldom heard in the region; a shrill scream. (Europese Windswael)

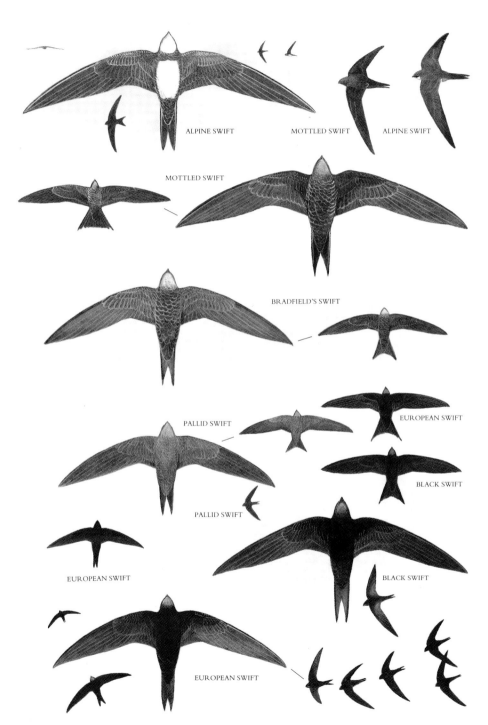

ALPINE SWIFT

MOTTLED SWIFT

ALPINE SWIFT

MOTTLED SWIFT

BRADFIELD'S SWIFT

PALLID SWIFT

EUROPEAN SWIFT

PALLID SWIFT

BLACK SWIFT

EUROPEAN SWIFT

BLACK SWIFT

EUROPEAN SWIFT

LITTLE SWIFT *Apus affinis* (417) 14 cm
The combination of small size, large, square white rump patch which wraps around the flanks, and square tail is diagnostic. In flight seems squat and dumpy, and wing tips appear rounded.
HABITAT. Aerial. The common swift over cities and towns, often seen wheeling in tight flocks during display flights. Usually nests colonially with adjacent nests touching, under eaves of buildings, bridges and rocky overhangs. STATUS. Common resident. CALL. Soft twittering and high-pitched screeching. (Kleinwindswael)

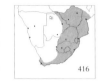

HORUS SWIFT *Apus horus* (416) 16 cm
Most likely to be confused with Little Swift as both show a broad white rump which wraps around the flanks, but this is a larger, more robust bird. It is also distinguished by its forked tail, which sometimes appears square-ended when closed. Differs from Whiterumped Swift by having more white on the rump and a less forked tail.
HABITAT. Aerial, frequently found over mountainous terrain, sandbanks and road cuttings. Breeds in holes in vertical sandbanks. STATUS. Summer visitor but resident in low-lying north-eastern areas. Uncommon and localized. CALL. Normally silent but does scream at breeding sites. (Horuswindswael)

WHITERUMPED SWIFT *Apus caffer* (415) 15 cm
The long, deeply forked tail on this 'white-rumped' swift is diagnostic. The tail is frequently held closed, appearing long and pointed. The thin, white, U-shaped band across the rump is less obvious than in either Little or Horus Swifts.
HABITAT. Aerial, over open country, mountainous terrain and in towns and cities. Usually occupies swallows' nests, sometimes holes in buildings. STATUS. Common summer visitor. CALL. A typical swift scream at breeding sites. (Witkruiswindswael)

SCARCE SWIFT *Schoutedenapus myoptilus* (420) 17 cm
A nondescript, dull grey-brown swift which has the body outline and tail shape of Whiterumped Swift but lacks the white rump of that species. Distinguished from Black and European Swifts (p. 242) by duller brown plumage and longer, more deeply forked tail, and by its smaller size.
HABITAT. Over cliffs and rocky bluffs in forested mountain regions. STATUS. Rare resident in eastern Zimbabwe. CALL. A nasal twittering and trill. (Skaarswindswael)

PALM SWIFT *Cypsiurus parvus* (421) 17 cm
The most slender and streamlined swift in the region. The long, thin wings, the elongated, deeply forked tail, and the grey-brown coloration are diagnostic. Occurs in small groups or in mixed flocks with other swifts.
HABITAT. Usually found in the vicinity of palm trees, including those growing in towns and cities. STATUS. Common resident and local migrant. CALL. A soft, high-pitched scream. (Palmwindswael)

BÖHM'S SPINETAIL *Neafrapus boehmi* (423) 9 cm
The white belly, square white rump and very short tail are diagnostic. Flight action is very fast and erratic, almost bat-like. The smallest swift of the region. Superficially resembles white-bellied form of Brownthroated Martin (p. 286) but differs in flight action and by having a white rump.
HABITAT. Thornveld and open broadleafed woodland; often in the vicinity of baobab trees. Nests inside a hollow baobab. STATUS. Uncommon and localized resident. CALL. Recorded as a high-pitched 'tri-tri-tri-peep'. (Witpensstekelstert)

MOTTLED SPINETAIL *Telacanthura ussheri* (422) 14 cm
Differs from Little Swift in that the white throat extends on to the upper breast where it appears mottled, and by having a small white patch on the undertail coverts.
HABITAT. Along forested rivers, often near baobab trees. STATUS. Uncommon, localized resident. CALL. Recorded as soft twittering. (Gevlekte Stekelstert)

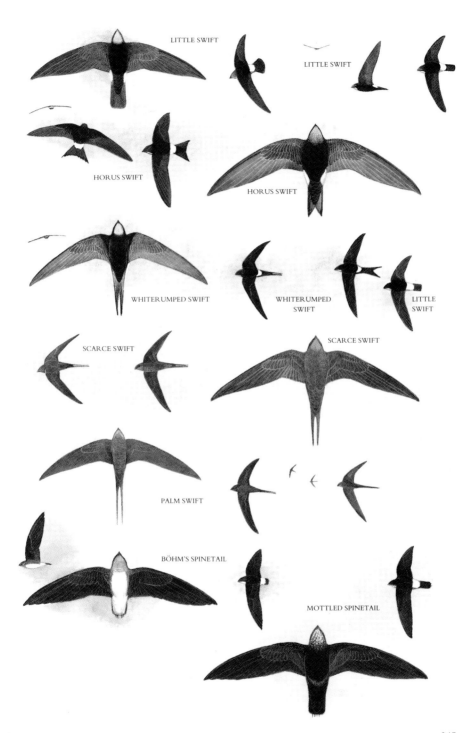

LITTLE SWIFT

LITTLE SWIFT

HORUS SWIFT

HORUS SWIFT

WHITERUMPED SWIFT

WHITERUMPED
SWIFT

LITTLE
SWIFT

SCARCE SWIFT

SCARCE SWIFT

PALM SWIFT

BÖHM'S SPINETAIL

MOTTLED SPINETAIL

245

NARINA TROGON *Apaloderma narina* (427) 34 cm

A furtive species which, although brightly coloured, is difficult to see as it normally sits with its back to the observer, well camouflaged by its leafy green surroundings. The combination of its crimson lower breast and belly and bright emerald green upper breast and back is diagnostic.
FEMALE lacks the green throat of the male and has a duller crimson breast. IMM. resembles female. HABITAT. Riverine and evergreen forests and dense, broadleafed woodland. STATUS. Locally common resident, with local movements. CALL. A soft, hoarse hoot, repeated 6 to 10 times. (Bosloerie)

ANGOLA PITTA *Pitta angolensis* (491) 23 cm

This brilliantly coloured bird is unmistakable but difficult to see in the dark understorey of the forests it frequents. Usually glimpsed as it rises off the forest floor in a bright flash of colour. When disturbed, may remain motionless for long periods.
SEXES alike. IMM. drabber than ad. HABITAT. Thick riverine forests and sandy coastal forests. STATUS. Rare, localized summer visitor; vagrants as far south as Port Elizabeth. CALL. A frog-like 'quoort' in display. (Angolapitta)

AFRICAN BROADBILL *Smithornis capensis* (490) 14 cm

Easily overlooked; usually only detected when displaying. The broad, flattened bill is not easily seen in the field except at close range and at certain angles. Only during the short, circular display flight is the white 'puffball' on the lower back fluffed out and visible.
MALE has a black cap and heavily streaked underparts. FEMALE and IMM. are dowdier and lack an obvious black cap. HABITAT. Coastal forests and thickets, and the understorey of riverine forests. STATUS. Uncommon, localized resident. CALL. At dawn and dusk a frog-like 'prrrrrrruup' is uttered during display flight. (Breëbek)

REDFACED MOUSEBIRD *Colius indicus* (426) 34 cm

Generally paler than Speckled and Whitebacked Mousebirds and, when seen, the red face is diagnostic. In flight the grey rump contrasts slightly with the browner back and tail. The birds usually fly in small parties, and have a fast, powerful and direct flight action, quite unlike the floppy flight of the other two mousebird species.
SEXES alike. IMM. has a yellowish-green face. HABITAT. Thornveld, open broadleafed woodland, and suburban gardens, avoiding forests and extremely dry regions. STATUS. Common resident. CALL. A clear whistle, 'tshivovo', is uttered, the first note being the highest in pitch. (Rooiwangmuisvoël)

SPECKLED MOUSEBIRD *Colius striatus* (424) 35 cm

Distinguished from Whitebacked and Redfaced Mousebirds by drabber brown coloration, black face and black and white bill. Flight action is weaker and floppier than that of the other mousebird species. Often seen in groups dashing from one bush to the next in 'follow-my-leader' fashion.
SEXES alike. IMM. like ad. but lacks black on face. HABITAT. Thick tangled bush, fruiting trees in urban and suburban parks and gardens. STATUS. Common resident. CALL. A harsh 'zhrrik-zhrrik'. (Gevlekte Muisvoël)

WHITEBACKED MOUSEBIRD *Colius colius* (425) 34 cm

In flight the back, with its white stripe bordered by black, is diagnostic. At rest differs from Speckled and Redfaced Mousebirds by whitish bill, grey upperparts and red feet.
SEXES alike. IMM. similar to ad. HABITAT. Thornveld, fynbos scrub, and semi-desert. STATUS. Common resident; endemic. CALL. A whistling 'zwee-wewit'. (Witkruismuisvoël)

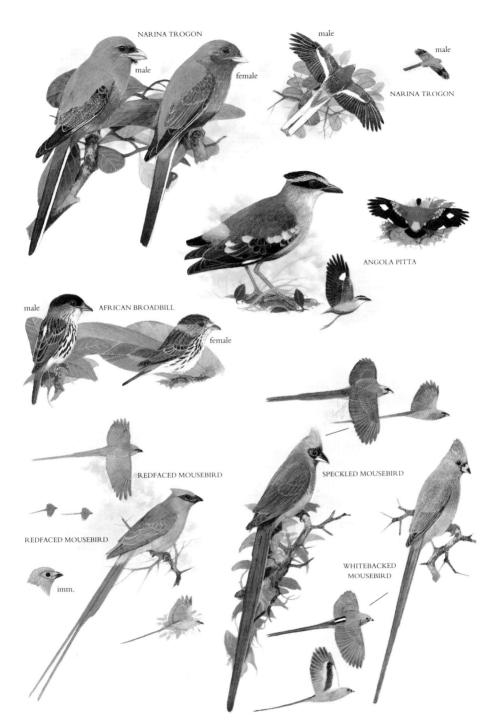

NARINA TROGON

male

female

male

male

NARINA TROGON

ANGOLA PITTA

AFRICAN BROADBILL

male

female

REDFACED MOUSEBIRD

SPECKLED MOUSEBIRD

REDFACED MOUSEBIRD

imm.

WHITEBACKED
MOUSEBIRD

GIANT KINGFISHER *Ceryle maxima* (429) 46 cm

The largest kingfisher in the region, unmistakable with its long, heavy bill, dark, white-spotted back and rufous breast (male) or belly (female). Rarely hovers.
IMM. male has black-speckled chestnut breast, imm. female has white breast. HABITAT. Wooded streams and dams, fast-flowing rivers in mountains, and coastal lagoons. STATUS. Common resident. CALL. A loud, harsh 'kahk-kah-kahk'. (Reuse Visvanger)

PIED KINGFISHER *Ceryle rudis* (428) 28 cm

The only black and white kingfisher in the region. Frequently hovers over water before diving to seize a fish.
MALE has a double breast band. FEMALE has a single, incomplete breast band. IMM. like female. HABITAT. Any open stretch of fresh water, coastal lagoons and tidal rock pools. STATUS. Common resident. CALL. A rattling twitter and a sharp, high-pitched 'chik-chik'. (Bontvisvanger)

HALFCOLLARED KINGFISHER *Alcedo semitorquata* (430) 20 cm

The black bill is diagnostic and is not seen on any other ad. small 'blue' kingfisher in the region. Larger than Malachite Kingfisher, with which it overlaps in distribution, but lacks the turquoise crest and can be differentiated by the black bill. Distinguished from imm. Malachite Kingfisher (which also has a dark bill) by its larger size and the lack of the turquoise crest.
SEXES alike. IMM. has black-tipped breast feathers and appears barred. HABITAT. Wooded streams and, less often, coastal lagoons. STATUS. Uncommon resident. CALL. A high-pitched 'chreep' or softer 'peeek-peek'. (Blouvisvanger)

MALACHITE KINGFISHER *Alcedo cristata* (431) 14 cm

Differs from similar, but smaller, Pygmy Kingfisher by having the turquoise and black barred crown extending below the eye, and by lacking the violet wash on the sides of the head.
SEXES alike. IMM.'s black bill might lead to confusion with Halfcollared Kingfisher, but this species is smaller, has a dark back and reddish-brown underparts. HABITAT. Lakes and dams, and along streams and lagoons. STATUS. Common resident. CALL. A high-pitched 'peep-peep' given in flight. (Kuifkopvisvanger)

PYGMY KINGFISHER *Ispidina picta* (432) 13 cm

The smallest kingfisher in the region. Distinguished from similar Malachite Kingfisher by its smaller size, uniform blue crown which does not extend below the eye, and by a violet wash around the ear coverts.
SEXES alike. IMM. like ad. but with blackish bill. HABITAT. Non-aquatic; frequents woodland, savanna and coastal forests. STATUS. Common summer visitor. CALL. A high-pitched 'chip-chip' flight note. (Dwergvisvanger)

male imm.

GIANT KINGFISHER

male ad.

male ad.

female ad.

PIED KINGFISHER

male

female

ad.

male   female

HALFCOLLARED
KINGFISHER

ad.

MALACHITE KINGFISHER

PYGMY KINGFISHER

ad.

imm.

imm.

249

WOODLAND KINGFISHER *Halcyon senegalensis* (433) 23 cm
Very similar to Mangrove Kingfisher but unlikely to be found in the same habitat. Differs by having a black lower mandible (not an all-red bill) and a much paler head with a black stripe extending from the base of the bill, through and behind the eye. The occasional bird has an all-red bill.
SEXES alike. IMM. has a dusky reddish-brown bill. HABITAT. Non-aquatic; woodland and savanna with tall trees. STATUS. Common summer visitor. CALL. A loud, piercing 'trrp-trrrrrrrrrr', the latter part descending. (Bosveldvisvanger)

MANGROVE KINGFISHER *Halcyon senegaloides* (434) 24 cm
Closely resembles Woodland Kingfisher but is easily identified by its all-red (not red and black) bill, and darker grey head. (Some Woodland Kingfishers have red bills.) Differs from Greyhooded Kingfisher by having a blue back and lacking the chestnut belly, and can be distinguished from Brownhooded Kingfisher as that species has a black back, paler head and rufous patches on the sides of the breast.
SEXES alike. IMM. similar to ad. but with brownish bill and dark scaling on the breast. HABITAT. Mangrove swamps and well-wooded coastal rivers. STATUS. Uncommon resident. CALL. A noisy species in the mangroves, giving a loud ringing 'cheet choo-che che che', the latter part ending in a trill. (Mangliedvisvanger)

BROWNHOODED KINGFISHER *Halcyon albiventris* (435) 24 cm
This species can be distinguished from other similar red-billed kingfishers by its brownish head streaked with black, rufous patches on the sides of the breast and well-streaked flanks. Differs from Striped Kingfisher by all-red (not black and red) bill, and by the lack of a dark cap.
MALE has black back, FEMALE has brown back. IMM. resembles female. HABITAT. Non-aquatic; thornveld, open broadleafed woodland and coastal forests. Has adapted to suburbia and is common in gardens and parks. STATUS. Common resident. CALL. A whistled 'tyi-ti-ti-ti' and a harsher alarm note 'klee-klee-klee'. (Bruinkopvisvanger)

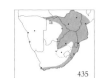

GREYHOODED KINGFISHER *Halcyon leucocephala* (436) 20 cm
The grey head and chestnut belly are diagnostic. Distinguished from Brownhooded Kingfisher by the lack of any streaking on the head and flanks. The Mangrove Kingfisher has a heavier red bill and lacks the chestnut belly.
SEXES alike. IMM. has blackish bill, dark barring on breast and neck. HABITAT. Non-aquatic; broadleafed woodland and savanna. STATUS. Scarce to locally common summer visitor. CALL. A whistled 'cheeo cheeo weecho-trrrrr', similarly pitched but much slower than that of Brownhooded Kingfisher. (Gryskopvisvanger)

STRIPED KINGFISHER *Halcyon chelicuti* (437) 18 cm
The dark cap lightly streaked with grey, the black and red bill and the white collar are diagnostic. Distinguished from Brownhooded Kingfisher, which often occurs in the same habitat, by its smaller size, darker capped appearance and the white collar. The blue rump is evident only in flight.
SEXES differ in underwing pattern: MALE has a black band across the remiges which the female lacks. IMM. has dusky bill and blackish scaled breast and flanks. HABITAT. Thornveld, riverine and coastal forests. STATUS. Common resident. CALL. A high-pitched, piercing 'cheer-cherrrrr', the last notes running together. (Gestreepte Visvanger)

WOODLAND KINGFISHER

ad.

ad.

ad.

ad.

MANGROVE KINGFISHER

ad.

ad.

BROWNHOODED KINGFISHER

male

female

female

male

GREYHOODED KINGFISHER

ad.

ad.

male

female

male

ad.

ad.

STRIPED KINGFISHER

EUROPEAN BEE-EATER *Merops apiaster* (438) 28 cm
In the region, the only bee-eater with a chestnut crown and back.
SEXES alike. IMM. has a green back but its pale blue underparts should eliminate confusion with other bee-eaters in the region. HABITAT. Thornveld, open broadleafed woodland, fynbos and adjacent grassy areas. STATUS. Common summer visitor. CALL. A far-carrying flight call: a frog-like 'prrrup' and 'krroop-krroop'. (Europese Byvreter)

BLUECHEEKED BEE-EATER *Merops persicus* (440) 31 cm
Differs from Olive Bee-eater by having a green (not brown) crown, a blue forehead, eyebrow stripe and cheeks, and a yellow chin.
SEXES alike. IMM. duller than ad. and lacks tail streamers. HABITAT. Floodplains and adjacent broadleafed woodland. STATUS. Localized summer visitor. CALL. A liquid 'prrrup' and 'prrreo', less mellow than that of European Bee-eater. (Blouwangbyvreter)

OLIVE BEE-EATER *Merops superciliosus* (439) 31 cm
Differs from Bluecheeked Bee-eater by its brown (not green) crown, rufous throat and paler green underparts. Vaguely resembles Böhm's Bee-eater (p. 254) but has a dull brown (not chestnut) cap, and is much larger.
SEXES alike. IMM. lacks tail streamers. HABITAT. Open broadleafed woodland near lakes, rivers and swamps. STATUS. Rare summer visitor. CALL. 'Prrrup'. (Olyfbyvreter)

WHITEFRONTED BEE-EATER *Merops bullockoides* (443) 24 cm
The crimson and white throat, white forehead and lack of pointed tail projections are diagnostic.
SEXES alike. IMM. is a duller version of ad. HABITAT. Wide, slow-moving rivers with steep sandbanks, and other freshwater expanses. STATUS. Common resident. CALL. A 'qerrr', like that of Greater Blue-eared Starling, and twittering noises when roosting. (Rooikeelbyvreter)

EUROPEAN BEE-EATER

BLUECHEEKED BEE-EATER

OLIVE BEE-EATER

WHITEFRONTED BEE-EATER

253

CARMINE BEE-EATER *Merops nubicoides* (441) 36 cm
Ad. unmistakable: the only predominantly red bee-eater in the region. Crown dark blue, vent pale blue.
SEXES alike. IMM. lacks the elongated central tail feathers, has a brown (not carmine) back and less brightly coloured underparts. HABITAT. Woodland, savanna, and floodplains. Colonial breeders in river banks. STATUS. Common summer visitor. CALL. A deep 'terk, terk'. (Rooiborsbyvreter)

WHITETHROATED BEE-EATER *Merops albicollis* (917) 30 cm
Unmistakable, with a diagnostic black and white striped head, black breast band and green upperparts.
SEXES alike. IMM. duller green and lightly scalloped above. HABITAT. Forest and woodland margins in equatorial Africa. In South Africa recorded in Kalahari river-bed and south coast thicket. STATUS. Rare vagrant, with two records from the Cape. CALL. Like a high-pitched and more repetitive European Bee-eater. (Witkeelbyvreter)

SWALLOWTAILED BEE-EATER *Merops hirundineus* (445) 22 cm
The only fork-tailed bee-eater in the region. It is most likely to be confused with Little Bee-eater but has a blue (not black) collar, blue-green underparts and a blue, forked tail.
SEXES alike. IMM. shows the diagnostic forked tail, but lacks the yellow throat and blue collar. HABITAT. Diverse: from semi-desert scrub to forest margins. STATUS. Common resident with local movements. CALL. A 'kwit-kwit' or soft twittering. (Swaelstertbyvreter)

BÖHM'S BEE-EATER *Merops boehmi* (442) 21 cm
This species differs from Olive Bee-eater (p. 252) in that it is much smaller, has a chestnut (not dull brown) cap, lacks the pale eyebrow stripe and has a russet throat extending to the breast.
SEXES alike. IMM. duller version of ad. with shorter central tail feathers. HABITAT. Open areas in broadleafed woodland along rivers and streams. STATUS. Rare resident. CALL. A soft 'swee'. (Roeskopbyvreter)

LITTLE BEE-EATER *Merops pusillus* (444) 17 cm
The smallest bee-eater in the region. Easily identified by its combination of small size, yellow throat, black collar, buff-yellow belly and square-ended, dark-tipped tail. In flight shows conspicuous russet underwings.
SEXES alike. IMM. lacks black collar. HABITAT. Savanna, woodland and forest margins. STATUS. Common resident. CALL. A 'zeet-zeet' or 'chip-chip'. (Kleinbyvreter)

CARMINE BEE-EATER

WHITETHROATED BEE-EATER

SWALLOWTAILED BEE-EATER

BÖHM'S BEE-EATER

LITTLE BEE-EATER

LILACBREASTED ROLLER *Coracias caudata* (447) 36 cm

Distinguished from similar Racket-tailed Roller by its obvious lilac (not blue) breast, by being generally paler and by having pointed, elongated outer tail feathers. Ad. loses elongated tail feathers during winter moult.
SEXES alike. IMM. lacks elongated tail feathers but the lilac-coloured breast differentiates it from imm. European and Racket-tailed Rollers. HABITAT. Savanna. Perches conspicuously, often along telephone lines. STATUS. Common resident. CALL. Harsh squawks and screams when displaying. (Gewone Troupant)

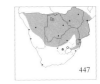

RACKET-TAILED ROLLER *Coracias spatulata* (448) 36 cm

Appears overall more blue than Lilacbreasted Roller, but has less blue in the wings, no lilac on the breast, and has elongated outer tail feathers with spatulate tips. Ad. loses 'rackets' during winter moult.
SEXES alike. IMM. lacks the diagnostic tail and differs from imm. Lilacbreasted Roller by having violet and brown wing coverts, and a blue-green (not lilac-tinged) breast. HABITAT. Tall woodland; doesn't perch openly like Lilacbreasted Roller. STATUS. Uncommon resident. CALL. Similar to that of Lilacbreasted Roller but higher pitched and more cackling. (Knopsterttroupant)

EUROPEAN ROLLER *Coracias garrulus* (446) 31 cm

Differs from Lilacbreasted and Racket-tailed Rollers by having an all-blue head and square-ended tail. Imm. Racket-tailed Roller appears similar when tail streamers are absent but that species has a distinctive white-streaked forehead, and a green (not blue) crown and nape.
SEXES alike. IMM. more olive-green in colour. HABITAT. Savanna. STATUS. Common summer visitor. CALL. Normally silent in the region but when alarmed will give a 'krack-krack' call. (Europese Troupant)

PURPLE ROLLER *Coracias naevia* (449) 38 cm

The largest roller of the region and easily identified by its broad, pale eyebrow stripe and lilac-brown underparts streaked with white.
SEXES alike. IMM. is a duller version of ad. HABITAT. Dry thornveld and open broadleafed woodland. STATUS. Scarce to common resident with local movements. CALL. In display flight utters a harsh, repeated 'karaa-karaa' while flying with an exaggerated, side to side rocking motion. (Groottroupant)

BROADBILLED ROLLER *Eurystomus glaucurus* (450) 27 cm

The smallest roller in the region and the only one that appears dark with a bright yellow bill. In flight shows a blue tail and purple wing coverts.
SEXES alike. IMM. a duller version of ad., has greenish underparts streaked with black but also has the bright yellow bill. HABITAT. Riverine forests and adjacent savanna, with a preference for perching and breeding in dead trees. STATUS. Locally common summer visitor. CALL. Harsh screams and cackles. (Geelbektroupant)

LILACBREASTED ROLLER

ad.

ad.

ad.

RACKET-TAILED ROLLER

ad.

ad.

ad.

ad.

imm.

ad.

EUROPEAN ROLLER

br.

ad.

PURPLE ROLLER

ad.

ad.

BROADBILLED ROLLER

ad.

ad.

ad.

257

SILVERYCHEEKED HORNBILL *Bycanistes brevis* (456) 75 cm
Far larger than Trumpeter Hornbill, with a huge creamy casque on the bill. The black extends well down the belly, giving the impression of a much darker bird than Trumpeter Hornbill. In flight distinguished from Trumpeter Hornbill by the lack of a white trailing edge to the wing and by the whole back being white.
FEMALE and IMM. have much reduced casques. HABITAT. Tall evergreen and riverine forests. STATUS. Uncommon and localized resident, nomadic within its range. CALL. A deep wail, with a harsh 'quark-quark' and nasal calls. (Kuifkopboskraai)

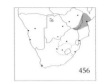

TRUMPETER HORNBILL *Bycanistes bucinator* (455) 58 cm
Similar to Silverycheeked Hornbill but is smaller, has a reduced and less obvious casque on top of its bill (casque and bill both dark), and has a black throat and breast with the lower underparts white. If viewed at close range, it can be seen that the bare skin around the eye is pinkish red, not bluish green as in Silverycheeked. In flight shows white tips to the secondaries and a white rump.
FEMALE'S bill, especially the casque, is much smaller than male's. IMM. shows almost no casque. HABITAT. Lowland, coastal and riverine evergreen forests. STATUS. Common resident, but nomadic within its range. CALL. A wailing, infantile 'waaaaa-weeeee-waaaaa'. (Gewone Boskraai)

BRADFIELD'S HORNBILL *Tockus bradfieldi* (461) 56 cm
Differs from Monteiro's Hornbill by having no white in the wings and by lacking white outer tail feathers. Distinguished from Crowned Hornbill by being paler brown on the head and back, and by having a smaller orange-red bill without a casque.
FEMALE has a smaller bill and has the facial skin turquoise, not black as in male. IMM. similar to ad. HABITAT. Open mopane woodland and mixed thornveld. STATUS. Common resident. CALL. A rapidly repeated whistling 'chleeoo' note, and a calling display in which the bill is raised vertically. (Bradfieldse Neushoringvoël)

MONTEIRO'S HORNBILL *Tockus monteiri* (462) 56 cm
The large expanse of white on the outer tail feathers and the white patches on the secondaries are diagnostic in this large hornbill with its heavy, red bill. The similar Bradfield's Hornbill has no white in the wings and a white-tipped tail.
FEMALE has smaller bill and turquoise (not blackish) facial skin. IMM. has reduced bill. HABITAT. Dry thornveld and broadleafed woodland. STATUS. Common resident, local movements in winter flocks. CALL. A hollow-sounding 'tooaak tooaak'. In display, head is lowered and wings are held closed. (Monteirose Neushoringvoël)

CROWNED HORNBILL *Tockus alboterminatus* (460) 54 cm
Differs from Bradfield's Hornbill in having a shorter, deeper red bill with an obvious casque and by having a darker head, back and tail. Told from Monteiro's Hornbill by the lack of white in the wings and the small amount in the outer tail feathers.
FEMALE lacks obvious casque and has the facial skin turquoise, not black as in male. IMM. lacks casque and has a yellow bill. HABITAT. Inland, coastal and riverine forests. STATUS. Common resident, nomadic during the dry season. Often in flocks. CALL. A whistling 'chleeoo chleeoo'. (Gekroonde Neushoringvoël)

GREY HORNBILL *Tockus nasutus* (457) 46 cm
The male is the only small hornbill in the region which has a dark bill, with a creamy stripe at the base, and a casque. Female has the upper part of the bill pale yellow and the tip maroon, but differs from Southern Yellowbilled Hornbill (p. 260) by having a dark head and breast, and a broad white eyebrow stripe. The white stripe on the back is visible in flight.
IMM. resembles ad. male without casque but with the same bill colour. HABITAT. Thornveld and dry broadleafed woodland. STATUS. Common resident. CALL. A soft, plaintive whistling 'phee pheeoo phee pheeoo'. In calling display, bill is held vertically and the wings are flicked open on each note. (Grysneushoringvoël)

male

SILVERYCHEEKED HORNBILL

female

female

male

TRUMPETER HORNBILL

BRADFIELD'S HORNBILL

MONTEIRO'S HORNBILL

male

female

male

CROWNED HORNBILL

female

male

female

GREY HORNBILL

SOUTHERN YELLOWBILLED HORNBILL *Tockus flavirostris* (459) 55 cm
Very similar to Redbilled Hornbill in plumage coloration but has a diagnostic large yellow bill. Female Grey Hornbill (p. 258) has a shorter, part-yellow bill but has a dark head and throat.
FEMALE and IMM. have the bill and casque notably smaller. HABITAT. Thornveld and dry broadleafed woodland. STATUS. Common resident. CALL. A rapid, hollow-sounding 'tok tok tok tok tok toka toka toka'. In calling display head is lowered and wings are fanned. (Geelbekneushoringvoël)

REDBILLED HORNBILL *Tockus erythrorhynchus* (458) 46 cm
The only small hornbill with an all-red bill. The pale head, broad white eyebrow stripe, and black and white speckled upperparts with a white stripe down the back should obviate confusion with other larger, red-billed hornbills.
MALE has a black patch at the base of the lower mandible. FEMALE has a smaller, all-red bill. IMM. has a less developed bill and buff (not white) spotting on back and wing coverts. HABITAT. Thornveld and savanna. STATUS. Common resident.
CALL. A series of rapid 'wha wha wha' calls followed by a 'kukwe kukwe'. In calling display, head is lowered but wings are held closed. (Rooibekneushoringvoël)

REDBILLED WOODHOOPOE *Phoeniculus purpureus* (452) 36 cm
Larger than Greater Scimitarbill, this species has a long, decurved red bill, red legs, white wing bars and a long, white-tipped tail. In good light, the bottle-green head and back of this species distinguish it from Violet Woodhoopoe.
FEMALE's bill less decurved and shorter than male's. IMM. has a black bill but it is far less decurved than that of Greater Scimitarbill. IMM. male has brown throat patch, imm. female has black throat patch. HABITAT. A wide variety of woodland and thornveld habitats. STATUS. Common resident. CALL. Harsh chattering and cackling calls, usually uttered by groups of birds. (Gewone Kakelaar)

VIOLET WOODHOOPOE *Phoeniculus damarensis* (453) 40 cm
Easily confused with Redbilled Woodhoopoe but, in good light, this species' violet (not bottle-green) head, mantle and back can be seen. Noticeably larger, with a floppier flight action.
FEMALE's bill less decurved and noticeably shorter than male's. IMM. male has brown throat patch, imm. female has black throat patch but this species is very difficult to distinguish from imm. Redbilled Woodhoopoe in the field. HABITAT. Dry thornveld, wooded dry watercourses and mopane woodland. STATUS. Common resident. CALL. Harsh cackling similar to Redbilled Woodhoopoe's, but slower. (Perskakelaar)

GREATER SCIMITARBILL *Rhinopomastus cyanomelas* (454) 26 cm
Smaller and more slender than the Redbilled and Violet Woodhoopoes, this species differs from their imms. (which, like this species, also have black bills) by its long, extremely decurved bill and black (not red) legs and feet. In the field it appears black, except in direct sunlight when a purple sheen is noticeable. White bar on primaries visible in flight.
FEMALE has brownish (not glossy black) head, and a shorter bill. IMM. resembles female. HABITAT. Dry thornveld and open broadleafed woodland. STATUS. Common resident. CALL. High-pitched whistling 'sweep-sweep-sweep' and a harsher chattering. (Swartbekkakelaar)

HOOPOE *Upupa epops* (451) 28 cm
Unmistakable with its long, decurved bill and long, black-tipped crest which is held erect when the bird is alarmed. Its cinnamon-coloured body, and black and white barred wings and tail are conspicuous in flight.
FEMALE duller than male, with less white in wings. IMM. duller than female. HABITAT. Thornveld, open broadleafed woodland, parks and gardens. STATUS. Common resident. CALL. A frequently uttered 'hoop-hoop-hoop'. (Hoephoep)

female

male

SOUTHERN YELLOWBILLED HORNBILL

male

REDBILLED HORNBILL

male

REDBILLED WOODHOOPOE

female

female

GREATER SCIMITARBILL

female

male

VIOLET WOODHOOPOE

male

female

HOOPOE

261

GREATER HONEYGUIDE *Indicator indicator* (474) 20 cm
Male's pink bill, dark crown, black throat and white ear patches are diagnostic.
FEMALE lacks male's facial characteristics and differs from the similar-sized
Scalythroated Honeyguide by having an unmarked throat and breast. IMM. has under-
parts washed yellow and back dark brown. HABITAT. Woodland, savanna, plantations;
avoids forests. STATUS. Scarce to locally common resident. CALL. A ringing 'whit-purr'
or 'vic-tor', repeated at intervals. Call uttered from regularly used site high in tree.
Guiding call a harsh rattling chatter. (Grootheuningwyser)

SCALYTHROATED HONEYGUIDE *Indicator variegatus* (475) 19 cm
The only honeyguide in the region to have the throat and breast mottled and speckled.
When seen in the forest canopy, may be confused with Lesser Honeyguide but note
the lack of moustachial stripes and the scaly, mottled throat.
SEXES alike but MALE larger. IMM. has front washed with green and spotted with black.
HABITAT. Forests. STATUS. Scarce to locally common resident. CALL. An insect-like,
ventriloquistic trill 'trrrrrrr', rising at the end, repeated at 1-2 minute intervals. Same
call-site used for months or years. (Gevlekte Heuningwyser)

LESSER HONEYGUIDE *Indicator minor* (476) 15 cm
Size and jizz of Greyheaded Sparrow (p. 380), from which it is easily distinguished
by white outer tail and streaked olive-coloured wings. Smaller than Greater and
Scalythroated Honeyguides and differently marked and coloured.
SEXES alike. IMM. lacks moustachial stripe of ad. HABITAT. Woodland, forests and
thornveld and has adapted to urban and suburban gardens. STATUS. Common resident.
Usually located from its far-carrying call. CALL. Characteristic 'frip', repeated at short
intervals 15-40 times. Same call-site used for months or years. (Kleinheuningwyser)

EASTERN HONEYGUIDE *Indicator meliphilus* (477) 13 cm
Like Lesser Honeyguide but smaller, greenish on head and nape, and faintly streaked
on throat. The short, thick bill eliminates confusion with Slenderbilled and
Sharpbilled Honeyguides.
SEXES alike. IMM. resembles ad. HABITAT. Lowland riparian forests. STATUS.
Uncommon, localized resident. CALL. A repeated, high-pitched whistle. (Oostelike
Heuningwyser)

SLENDERBILLED HONEYGUIDE *Prodotiscus zambesiae* (479) 12 cm
Distinguished from Sharpbilled Honeyguide by its stockier build, shorter tail and by
having a greenish wash across its back and rump. Similar in shape to the larger
Eastern Honeyguide but differs by having a very small, thin bill and a grey (not
greenish) crown and nape.
SEXES alike. IMM. paler and greyer than ad. HABITAT. Restricted to miombo and
other broadleafed woodland. STATUS. Uncommon to locally common resident.
CALL. A repeated 'skeea' is uttered in display flight. (Dunbekheuningvoël)

SHARPBILLED HONEYGUIDE *Prodotiscus regulus* (478) 13 cm
Like Spotted Flycatcher (p. 342) in appearance and jizz but distinguished by lack of
streaking and the presence of white outer tail feathers. Lack of green wash distin-
guishes it from Slenderbilled Honeyguide and its sharp, thin beak separates it from
Eastern Honeyguide.
SEXES alike. IMM. resembles ad. HABITAT. Woodland, savanna, edges of forests and
plantations. STATUS. Uncommon to locally common resident. CALL. A rapid churring
when perched; utters a metallic 'zwick' during dipping display flight. (Skerpbek-
heuningvoël)

GREATER HONEYGUIDE

imm.

male

female

SCALYTHROATED
HONEYGUIDE

LESSER HONEYGUIDE

EASTERN HONEYGUIDE

SHARPBILLED HONEYGUIDE

SLENDERBILLED HONEYGUIDE

WOODWARDS' BARBET *Cryptolybia woodwardi* (468) 17 cm
A drab, green barbet with a dark crown and pale greenish-yellow ear patches. In flight shows pale green areas at the base of the primaries. Green Tinker Barbet (p. 266) is vaguely similar but confusion is unlikely as their ranges never overlap and Woodwards' Barbet is much larger and lacks a yellow rump.
SEXES alike. IMM. duller than ad. HABITAT. Coastal forests. STATUS. Locally common resident; endemic. Restricted to Ngoye forest, Zululand. CALL. A hollow-sounding 'kwop-kwop-kwop' is repeated many times. (Groenhoutkapper)

WHYTE'S BARBET *Stactolaema whytii* (467) 18 cm
Paler than White-eared Barbet, lacking the white ear patches of that species. The pale yellow forehead, white stripe below the eye and whitish patches on the wings eliminate confusion with any other barbet in the region.
SEXES alike. IMM. has no yellow on forehead and has a paler head and throat than ad. HABITAT. Miombo woodland and riverine forests, showing a preference for fig trees. STATUS. Locally common resident. CALL. A soft 'coo' is repeated several times. (Geelbleshoutkapper)

BLACKCOLLARED BARBET *Lybius torquatus* (464) 20 cm
The bright red face and throat, broadly bordered with black, is diagnostic. Very rare variant has yellow face and throat.
SEXES alike. IMM. has head and throat dark brown, streaked with orange and red. HABITAT. Forests, woodland, savanna and wooded suburbs. STATUS. Common resident. Often found in groups. CALL. Ringing duet starting with a harsh 'krrr krrrr' and exploding into a 'tooo puudly tooo puudly', the 'tooo' being higher pitched. (Rooikophoutkapper)

WHITE-EARED BARBET *Stactolaema leucotis* (466) 17 cm
The white ear-stripes and belly of this species contrast with the dark brown to black head, throat and back.
SEXES alike. IMM. has paler base to bill and slightly paler back and throat. HABITAT. Coastal forests and bush, especially alongside rivers. STATUS. Common resident. Often found in groups. CALL. A loud twittering 'treee treeetee teeetree', and various harsher 'waa waa' notes. (Witoorhoutkapper)

CRESTED BARBET *Trachyphonus vaillantii* (473) 23 cm
The shaggy crest, yellow face speckled with red, and yellow underparts with broad black breast band are diagnostic.
SEXES alike but female usually less vividly coloured. IMM. like ad. HABITAT. Woodland, savanna, riverine forests and suburban gardens. STATUS. Common resident. CALL. Male utters a sustained trilling 'trrrrrrr.....', female responds with a repeated 'puka-puka'. (Kuifkophoutkapper)

WOODWARDS' BARBET

WHYTE'S BARBET

WHITE-EARED BARBET

yellow-headed form

BLACKCOLLARED
BARBET

CRESTED BARBET

265

 BARBETS

ACACIA PIED BARBET *Lybius leucomelas* (465) 18 cm
*Larger size, black throat, and white underparts distinguish it from the similarly pat-
terned, smaller Redfronted Tinker Barbet.*
SEXES alike. IMM. lacks red forehead. HABITAT. Woodland and savanna, especially arid
thornveld, also suburbs, parks and orchards. STATUS. Common resident. CALL. A nasal
'nehh, nehh, nehh' repeated at intervals, and a low-pitched 'poop-oop-oop-oop...'.
(Bonthoutkapper)

GREEN TINKER BARBET *Pogoniulus simplex* (472) 10 cm
*This species is uniformly drab green with a bright yellow rump and pale yellow panel
on the folded wing.*
SEXES alike. IMM. like ad. HABITAT. Canopy of coastal forests. STATUS. Probably rare,
with only one positive record for subregion. CALL. A ringing 'pop-op-op-op-op-op',
not unlike that of other tinker barbets. (Groentinker)

YELLOWFRONTED TINKER BARBET *Pogoniulus chrysoconus* (470) 11 cm
*The yellow forehead colour is the best feature that distinguishes this species from
Redfronted Tinker Barbet. Considerable variation occurs in the forehead coloration: it
ranges from pale yellow to bright orange but never attains the bright red of Redfronted
Tinker Barbet. Overall colour slightly paler than Redfronted Tinker Barbet.*
SEXES alike. IMM. lacks yellow forehead. HABITAT. Woodland and savanna. STATUS.
Common resident. CALL. A continuous 'pop-pop-pop...' or 'tink tink tink...', almost
indistinguishable from that of Redfronted Tinker Barbet, but slightly slower and
lower-pitched. (Geelblestinker)

REDFRONTED TINKER BARBET *Pogoniulus pusillus* (469) 11 cm
*Differs from Yellowfronted Tinker Barbet in having a bright red forehead. It is also
darker overall than Yellowfronted.*
SEXES alike. IMM. lacks red forehead. HABITAT. Coastal and lowland riparian
forests. STATUS. Common resident. CALL. A continuous, monotonous 'pop-pop-
pop...', almost indistinguishable from call of Yellowfronted Tinker Barbet, but
slightly faster and higher pitched. (Rooiblestinker)

GOLDENRUMPED TINKER BARBET *Pogoniulus bilineatus* (471) 10 cm
*Black crown with white stripes on the sides of the head, and black back are diagnostic.
The small yellow rump patch is not easy to see in the field.*
SEXES alike. IMM. has the black upperparts narrowly barred and spotted with yellow.
HABITAT. Coastal and lowland riverine forests. STATUS. Common resident. CALL.
'Doo-doo-doo-doo', a lower pitched, more ringing note than that of Redfronted
Tinker Barbet, repeated in phrases of four to six, not continuously. (Swartblestinker)

ACACIA PIED BARBET

GREEN TINKER BARBET

YELLOWFRONTED TINKER BARBET

orange-fronted form

REDFRONTED TINKER BARBET

GOLDENRUMPED TINKER BARBET

GROUND WOODPECKER *Geocolaptes olivaceus* (480) 25 cm
The only entirely terrestrial woodpecker in the region. Easily identified by its diagnostic pinkish-red belly and rump.
FEMALE and IMM. are very similar to the male but have much reduced and duller pinkish red on belly and rump, and lack the reddish moustachial stripes. Usually in small family parties. HABITAT. Boulder-strewn grassy hill slopes in hills and mountains, to sea level in the south-western Cape. STATUS. Common resident; endemic. CALL. A far-carrying 'pee-aargh', and a ringing 'ree-chick'. (Grondspeg)

REDTHROATED WRYNECK *Jynx ruficollis* (489) 19 cm
The brown barred and mottled plumage should eliminate confusion with any woodpecker. Might be mistaken for Spotted Creeper (p. 294) but is much larger and has a dark chestnut throat and breast. Shows jerky movements, similar to those of woodpeckers. Feeds on the ground.
SEXES alike. IMM. paler than ad. HABITAT. Grassland and open savanna. Has adapted well to suburban gardens and stands of eucalyptus. STATUS. Common resident. CALL. A series of 2-10 squeaky 'kweek' notes; also a repeated, scolding 'peegh'. (Draaihals)

LITTLE SPOTTED WOODPECKER *Campethera cailliautii* (485) 16 cm
Male distinguished from similar-sized male Cardinal Woodpecker by its red forehead and crown, by a yellow-spotted (not barred) back, spotted (not streaked) front, and by the lack of moustachial stripes.
FEMALE differs from female Cardinal Woodpecker by having a red hind crown and by lacking black moustachial stripes. IMM. resembles female but the red on the crown is reduced or absent. HABITAT. Riparian forests and tall broadleafed woodland. STATUS. Uncommon resident. CALL. A high-pitched, whining 'whleeee'. (Gevlekte Speg)

OLIVE WOODPECKER *Mesopicos griseocephalus* (488) 20 cm
The greyish head, unmarked dull green body and red rump are diagnostic.
MALE has a bright red crown and nape. FEMALE has uniformly grey head. IMM. male has reduced red crown, variably mottled black. HABITAT. Montane, coastal and riverine evergreen forests. STATUS. Common resident. CALL. A cheerful, two-syllabled note 'wir-rit', repeated at intervals. (Gryskopspeg)

CARDINAL WOODPECKER *Dendropicos fuscescens* (486) 15 cm
In size could be confused with Little Spotted Woodpecker. Differs in that it has bold black moustachial stripes and appears black and white (not green and white) all over.
MALE can also be distinguished from male Little Spotted Woodpecker by its brown (not red) forehead. FEMALE has black nape. IMM. has red crown and black nape. HABITAT. Frequents a wide range of habitats, from thick forests to dry thornveld. STATUS. Common resident: in general, the most common woodpecker in the subregion. CALL. Makes a soft drumming sound. Call is a high-pitched 'krrrek krrrek krrrek'. (Kardinaalspeg)

REDTHROATED WRYNECK

GROUND WOODPECKER

female

male

LITTLE SPOTTED
WOODPECKER

female

imm.

OLIVE WOODPECKER

imm.

male

CARDINAL WOODPECKER

male

female

imm.

GOLDENTAILED WOODPECKER *Campethera abingoni* (483) 23 cm
Similar to Knysna Woodpecker but is paler below and much less heavily streaked and blotched with brown on breast and belly.
MALE has a black and red forehead, eliminating confusion with male Bennett's Woodpecker. FEMALE lacks red moustachial stripe and has the red restricted to the nape. IMM. as female. HABITAT. Thornveld, dry, open broadleafed woodland and coastal forests. STATUS. Common resident. CALL. A loud, nasal 'wheeeeeaa' shriek. (Goudstertspeg)

BENNETT'S WOODPECKER *Campethera bennettii* (481) 24 cm
Male differs from all other woodpeckers in the region by having an all-red forehead, crown and moustachial stripes.
FEMALE readily identifiable by her brown throat and stripe below the eye. IMM. resembles female. HABITAT. Broadleafed woodland and savanna. Often found feeding on the ground. STATUS. Scarce to common resident. CALL. A high-pitched, chattering 'whirrr-itt-whrrr-itt', often uttered in duet. (Bennettse Speg)

BEARDED WOODPECKER *Thripias namaquus* (487) 25 cm
White face with bold black moustachial stripes and a black stripe through and behind the eye are diagnostic. Both sexes have very dark underparts which are finely barred black and white.
MALE has a red hind crown. FEMALE shows a black hind crown and nape. IMM. has a red crown and nape. HABITAT. Broadleafed woodland, thornveld and riverine forests, especially in areas where there are tall dead trees. STATUS. Common resident. CALL. A loud, rapid 'wik-wik-wik-wik'; drums very loudly. (Baardspeg)

KNYSNA WOODPECKER *Campethera notata* (484) 20 cm
Both male and female are very much darker than Goldentailed Woodpecker and are heavily spotted (not streaked) with dark brown on the underparts.
MALE'S dark red forehead, crown and moustachial stripes are heavily blotched with black and less obvious than those of male Goldentailed Woodpecker. FEMALE has indistinct moustachial stripes. IMM. similar to female. HABITAT. Coastal evergreen forests, euphorbia scrub and mature thicket. STATUS. Locally common resident; endemic. CALL. A higher pitched shriek than that of Goldentailed Woodpecker. (Knysnaspeg)

GOLDENTAILED WOODPECKER

imm.

female

male

male imm.

BEARDED
WOODPECKER

female

male

male

BENNETT'S WOODPECKER

female

imm.

KNYSNA WOODPECKER

female

imm.

male

271

LARKS

DUSKY LARK *Pinarocorys nigricans* (505) 19 cm
This large lark is more likely to be confused with Groundscraper Thrush (p. 302) than with any other lark species. The bold black and white face pattern, heavy spotting on underparts and its habit of perching in trees, all add to its thrush-like appearance. Has shortish, stout bill, pale legs (almost white) and a dark back. Lacks the pale wing panels of Groundscraper Thrush.
SEXES alike. IMM. has heavily mottled underparts. HABITAT. Open grassy areas in thornveld and broadleafed woodland. Frequently found in newly burnt grassland and woodland. STATUS. Uncommon summer visitor. CALL. When flushed it utters a soft 'chrrp, chrrp'. (Donkerlewerik)

FLAPPET LARK *Mirafra rufocinnamomea* (496) 15 cm
Very similar to Clapper Lark but longer tailed, darker plumaged and with darker outer tail feathers. Aerial display also different: flies high, clapping its wings at intervals, but otherwise silent in display.
SEXES alike. IMM. duller than ad. HABITAT. Lowland grassland, open thornveld and broadleafed woodland. STATUS. Common resident. CALL. A short 'tuee' call given when perched. During display flight wings are rattled in a series of short bursts. (Laeveldklappertjie)

CLAPPER LARK *Mirafra apiata* (495) 15 cm
Colour varies regionally: rufous-plumaged birds difficult to distinguish from Flappet Lark unless seen in display flight or heard calling. Shorter tailed than Flappet Lark, with paler outer tail feathers. Display flight comprises a steep climb during which the bird claps its wings. This is followed by a rapid descent, with legs trailing, during which the bird calls. This sequence may begin from the ground, or during high-level flight.
SEXES alike. IMM. paler than ad. HABITAT. Upland grassland, fynbos and open Kalahari scrub. STATUS. Common resident; endemic. CALL. A long drawn-out whistle, 'pooooeeee', preceded by loud wing clapping. (Hoëveldklappertjie)

MONOTONOUS LARK *Mirafra passerina* (493) 14 cm
Shorter tailed and with less distinct facial markings than the similar Melodious Lark. Where the range of this species overlaps with that of Stark's Lark (p. 278), this species can be identified in flight by its chestnut wing patches. Display flight is short, with the bird launching itself from a perch and rising to 15-20 m, calling all the time. It usually sings from a perch on a bush or a tree.
SEXES alike. IMM. more mottled. HABITAT. Thornveld and mopane woodland with sparse grass cover. STATUS. Common resident; near-endemic. Summer visitor to the south of its range, and generally nomadic. CALL. Frequently repeated 'trrp-chup-chip-choop', during day and at night. (Bosveldlewerik)

MELODIOUS LARK *Mirafra cheniana* (492) 12 cm
The white throat contrasts markedly with the lower underparts as the flanks and belly are buffish, not white as in Monotonous Lark. Display flight is characteristic: the bird rises to a great height and circles on whirring wings, singing all the while. Does not overlap in habitat with Monotonous Lark, so confusion unlikely.
SEXES alike. IMM. more mottled above, duller below. HABITAT. Gently sloping areas in upland grassland. STATUS. Common but localized resident; endemic. Nomadic within its range. CALL. Call-note is a 'chuk chuk chuer', with a jumbled melodious song, comprising mimicked notes of other birds. (Spotlewerik)

DUSKY LARK

DUSKY LARK

western form

FLAPPET LARK

eastern form

FLAPPET LARK

eastern form

CLAPPER LARK

western form

CLAPPER LARK

CLAPPER LARK

south-western Cape form

MONOTONOUS LARK

MONOTONOUS LARK

MELODIOUS LARK

MELODIOUS LARK

KAROO LARK *Certhilauda albescens* (502) 17 cm
Variably coloured above (according to region) with a noticeable white eye-stripe, dark ear coverts, and boldly streaked underparts. In flight, shows a very dark-coloured tail. In the north, differs from Red Lark by its shorter, more slender bill and rufous upperparts streaked with dark brown. Distinguished from Dune Lark by having darker rufous-streaked upperparts and darker streaking on underparts.
SEXES alike. IMM. more mottled above. HABITAT. Karoo shrublands, and coastal shrublands on the west coast. STATUS. Common resident; endemic. CALL. Short 'chleeep-chleeep-chrrr-chrrrp' song is given in display flight or from the top of a bush. (Karoolewerik)

RED LARK *Certhilauda burra* (504) 19 cm
Differs from Dune Lark by rich rufous upperparts, and boldly streaked underparts. Similar to red form of Karoo Lark but is larger with a much heavier bill and has plain rufous upperparts. Has a very upright stance. Two distinct colour forms occur: birds on dunes are red above, those on the plains are browner.
SEXES alike. IMM. has slightly mottled upperparts. HABITAT. Scrub-covered red sand dunes and surrounding karroid shrublands. STATUS. Uncommon and highly localized resident; endemic. CALL. When flushed gives a short 'chrrk'. Song described as a short 'toodly-woo tu-wee'. (Rooilewerik)

DUNE LARK *Certhilauda erythrochlamys* (503) 17 cm
Distinguished from Karoo Lark by paler colour, plain or slightly streaked sandy-brown back, and slightly streaked underparts. Differs from Red Lark by longer, more slender bill, less bold spotting on underparts and much paler, sandy-coloured upperparts.
SEXES alike. IMM. shows pale edging to feathers on the back. HABITAT. Scrub growth on gravel plains between sand dunes in the Namib desert. STATUS. Uncommon resident; endemic. CALL. Similar to Karoo Lark's. (Duinlewerik)

LONGBILLED LARK *Certhilauda curvirostris* (500) 20 cm
A large lark with a diagnostic long, decurved bill. Bill of western races particularly long, becoming shorter further east. Very variable in colour (according to region). Distinctive display flight in which the bird rises sharply from the ground and ascends to 10-15 m, closes wings just before top of climb, calls, and drops, opening wings just above ground.
SEXES alike, but female smaller than male and has a shorter bill. IMM. mottled above, speckled below. HABITAT. Grassland with rocky outcrops, coastal fynbos and Karoo shrublands. STATUS. Common resident; near-endemic. CALL. A prolonged 'cheeeee-ooooop' during display flight or from the ground. (Langbeklewerik)

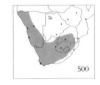

THICKBILLED LARK *Galerida magnirostris* (512) 18 cm
The thick-based, heavy bill, with yellow at the base of the lower mandible, is diagnostic. A robust, heavily built lark with a relatively short dark tail and boldly streaked underparts. Has a noticeable crest which is raised when the bird is alarmed or singing.
SEXES alike. IMM. is spotted white above. HABITAT. Lowland and montane fynbos, montane grassland, Karoo shrublands, and cultivated and fallow fields. STATUS. Common resident; endemic. CALL. A soft but far-carrying 'treeeleeeleee', likened to a rusty gate being opened. Highly vocal. (Dikbeklewerik)

KAROO LARK

Karoo
form

south-western
Cape race

KAROO
LARK

Namaqualand
race

RED LARK

RED LARK

dune form

plains form

DUNE LARK

RED LARK
cavei

DUNE LARK

north-eastern
form

LONGBILLED LARK

LONGBILLED
LARK

south-western
form

central
form

LONGBILLED
LARK

THICKBILLED LARK

THICKBILLED
LARK

north-western
form

SABOTA LARK *Mirafra sabota* (498) 15 cm
Variable in colour (according to region) but consistently boldly marked above and below and lacking rufous in the outer wing. The bill is short and dark (the lower mandible being paler), and a straight white eye-stripe runs from the base of the bill to the nape, giving the head a capped appearance.
SEXES alike. IMM. tawnier than ad., with mottled upperparts. HABITAT. Thornveld. STATUS. Common resident. CALL. A jumbled song of rich, melodious 'chips' and twitterings. Mimics other birds. (Sabotalewerik)

FAWNCOLOURED LARK *Mirafra africanoides* (497) 14 cm
Variably coloured above according to region but white underparts and slightly streaked breast diagnostic.
SEXES alike. IMM. more mottled than ad. HABITAT. Kalahari scrub, broadleafed savanna and thornveld; on sandy soils. STATUS. Common resident. CALL. Sings from tree top or during short aerial flight: a jumble of harsh 'chips' and twitterings, ending in a buzzy slur. (Vaalbruinlewerik)

SHORTCLAWED LARK *Certhilauda chuana* (501) 19 cm
Differs from Rufousnaped Lark by lacking any rufous on the nape or wings but, in flight, it does show a rufous rump. The buff-white eyebrow stripe runs directly from the base of the straight, slender bill to the nape, giving a capped effect.
SEXES alike. IMM. is mottled above and more streaked below. HABITAT. Dry open thornveld and open grassy areas with scattered trees. STATUS. Uncommon resident; endemic. CALL. A short 'chreep-chuu-chree', given when perched in a tree. Display flight similar to Longbilled Lark's. (Kortkloulewerik)

RUFOUSNAPED LARK *Mirafra africana* (494) 18 cm
Variably coloured according to region but the rufous outer wings and nape are consistently present.
SEXES alike. IMM. has blotched breast, not clearly spotted as in ad. HABITAT. Diverse: from open grassland with stunted bushes to thornveld and cultivated areas. STATUS. Common resident. CALL. A frequently repeated, three-syllabled 'tree, treeloo' when perched; wings often flapped during perch song. In display flight, a jumbled mixture of imitated calls. (Rooineklewerik)

REDCAPPED LARK *Calandrella cinerea* (507) 16 cm
Coloration very variable but rufous cap, unmarked white underparts and smudges on sides of breast diagnostic.
MALE redder than female and has a longer crest. IMM. has dark brown upperparts, spotted with white, pale below with heavily spotted breast. HABITAT. Open country with very short grass cover. STATUS. Common resident. In the dry season, often found in flocks. CALL. A sparrow-like 'tchweerp' given in flight. Song is a sustained jumble of melodious phrases given during display flight. (Rooikoplewerik)

SABOTA LARK

SABOTA LARK
small-billed
form

large-billed
form

FAWNCOLOURED LARK

FAWNCOLOURED LARK

pale form

SHORTCLAWED LARK

SHORTCLAWED LARK

western form

RUFOUSNAPED LARK

eastern form

RUFOUSNAPED LARK

REDCAPPED LARK

REDCAPPED LARK
male ad.

RUDD'S LARK *Heteromirafra ruddi* (499) 14 cm

Small, it appears large-headed and long-legged with a very thin tail. If clearly seen, the buff stripe down the centre of the crown is diagnostic. Display flight is high, and long, lasting up to 30 minutes.
SEXES alike. IMM. resembles ad. HABITAT. Short upland grassland, usually near damp depressions. STATUS. Uncommon, localized resident; endemic. CALL. A clear, whistled song, 'pee-witt-weerr', is given in flight. (Drakensberglewerik)

BOTHA'S LARK *Calandrella fringillaris* (509) 12 cm

A small, pink-billed lark with heavily streaked upperparts: distinguished from Pinkbilled Lark by white (not brown) underparts and outer tail feathers.
SEXES alike. IMM. paler than ad. HABITAT. Heavily grazed upland grassland. STATUS. Uncommon, localized resident; endemic. CALL. A cheerful, repeated 'chiree'. In flight utters a 'chuk, chuk'. (Vaalrivierlewerik)

PINKBILLED LARK *Calandrella conirostris* (508) 13 cm

The short, conical, pink bill distinguishes it from most other larks. Differs from Botha's Lark by its dark underparts which contrast boldly with the white throat and unstreaked flanks. Where their ranges overlap, it can be differentiated from Stark's Lark by being less grey, and by lacking any obvious crest.
SEXES alike. IMM. has dark bill and is duller and more speckled than ad. HABITAT. Upland grassland, farmlands and desert scrub. STATUS. A common but nomadic resident; endemic. CALL. When flushed, small flocks utter a soft 'si-si-si'. (Pienkbeklewerik)

SCLATER'S LARK *Calandrella sclateri* (510) 14 cm

When seen at close range, a dark brown teardrop mark below the eye is both obvious and diagnostic. In flight differs from Stark's and Pinkbilled Larks by its bold white outer tail feathers which broaden towards the tail base and which, in profile, suggest a pale rump.
SEXES alike. IMM. paler than ad., with more spotting than streaking above. HABITAT. Stony plains and ridges in arid shrublands. STATUS. Uncommon and nomadic resident; endemic. CALL. Flight call is a repeated 'tchweet-tchweet'. (Namakwalewerik)

STARK'S LARK *Calandrella starki* (511) 14 cm

Much paler than Sclater's and Pinkbilled Larks, this species lacks the teardrop mark of the former and differs from both by having an erectile crest. Sometimes occurs in very large flocks.
SEXES alike. IMM. spotted white on upperparts. HABITAT. Stony desert scrub to gravel plains of the Namib desert; also grassy areas on Namib and Kalahari sands, especially when breeding. STATUS. A common but localized resident; endemic. Nomadic. CALL. Flight call is a short 'chree-chree'. Song given during display flight is a melodious jumble of notes. (Woestynlewerik)

RUDD'S LARK

RUDD'S LARK

BOTHA'S LARK

BOTHA'S LARK

PINKBILLED LARK

PINKBILLED
LARK

SCLATER'S LARK

pale form

dark form   SCLATER'S LARK

STARK'S LARK

dark form

STARK'S
LARK

pale form

279

CHESTNUTBACKED FINCHLARK *Eremopterix leucotis* (515) 12 cm
Differs from Greybacked Finchlark by having a chestnut back and forewings and a black crown.
FEMALE mottled buff and brown above, lower breast and belly black; differs from female Greybacked Finchlark by having chestnut wing coverts. IMM. like female, but paler below. HABITAT. Road verges and cultivated lands, sparsely grassed parts of thornveld, and lightly wooded areas. STATUS. Common but nomadic resident; usually in flocks. CALL. In flight utters a short 'chip-chwep'. (Rooiruglewerik)

GREYBACKED FINCHLARK *Eremopterix verticalis* (516) 13 cm
The greyish back and wings distinguish this species from Chestnutbacked Finchlark.
MALE is further distinguished from male Chestnutbacked by a white patch on the hind crown. FEMALE is very much greyer in appearance than female Chestnutbacked Finchlark. IMM. more mottled than female. HABITAT. Karoo shrublands, desert, grassland and cultivated lands. STATUS. Common but nomadic resident; near-endemic; usually in flocks. CALL. A sharp 'chruk, chruk' flight note. (Grysruglewerik)

BLACKEARED FINCHLARK *Eremopterix australis* (517) 13 cm
The all-black head and underparts are diagnostic in the male. In flight the male appears all black and therefore might be confused with a widowfinch, but the dark chestnut back and relatively broad, all-black underwings are diagnostic.
FEMALE differs from female Chestnutbacked and Greybacked Finchlarks by being dark chestnut above and heavily streaked black below, and by lacking a dark belly patch. IMM. resembles female. HABITAT. Karoo shrublands and grassland, Kalahari sandveld, gravel plains and, occasionally, cultivated lands. STATUS. An uncommon and highly nomadic resident; endemic; usually in flocks. CALL. Flight call is a short 'preep' or 'chip-chip'. (Swartoorlewerik)

GRAY'S LARK *Ammomanes grayi* (514) 14 cm
This small lark is the palest and least marked lark in the region and is unlikely to be confused with any other lark species. The pale desert form of Tractrac Chat (p. 306) is similar in colour but has an obvious white base to its tail, a thin, dark bill and a very upright stance on long legs.
SEXES alike. IMM. more mottled above. HABITAT. Gravel plains along the coastal desert strip of Namibia. STATUS. Resident: uncommon, and nomadic within its range; near-endemic. CALL. Flight call is a short 'tseet' or 'tew-tew'. (Namiblewerik)

SPIKEHEELED LARK *Chersomanes albofasciata* (506) 15 cm
The long, slightly decurved bill, white throat contrasting strongly with the darker breast and belly, and the short, dark tail tipped with white, are diagnostic. Has a very upright stance.
SEXES alike but male larger than female. IMM. mottled with white above and below. HABITAT. Grassland, Karoo shrublands and desert grassland on gravel plains. STATUS. Common resident; usually in small groups. CALL. A trilling 'trrrep, trrrep' flight call. (Vlaktelewerik)

female

CHESTNUTBACKED
FINCHLARK

male

female

female

female

male

GREYBACKED
FINCHLARK

male female

female

female

female

female

male

BLACKEARED
FINCHLARK

female

male

male

GRAY'S LARK

pale form

dark form

south-eastern
form

SPIKEHEELED LARK

central form

north-western
form

REDBREASTED SWALLOW *Hirundo semirufa* (524) 24 cm
This large, very dark swallow can be confused only with Mosque Swallow from which it differs by having a red throat and breast, and dark buffy underwing coverts.
SEXES alike. IMM. has creamy white throat and breast but differs from Mosque Swallow by buffy (not white) underwing coverts. HABITAT. Grassland and savanna. STATUS. Common summer visitor. CALL. A soft warbling song. Twittering notes are uttered in flight. (Rooiborsswael)

MOSQUE SWALLOW *Hirundo senegalensis* (525) 24 cm
Likely to be confused only with Redbreasted Swallow: distinguished by being much paler, having white (not buffy) wing coverts, and a white throat and upper breast. Imm. Redbreasted shows varying degrees of white on throat and breast but always has buffy (not white) wing coverts, and has the blue on its head extending below the eye.
SEXES alike. IMM. is paler below and less glossed above. HABITAT. Open woodland, often near rivers, and especially near baobab trees. STATUS. Uncommon and localized resident. CALL. A nasal 'harrrrp', as well as a guttural chuckling. (Moskeeswael)

GREATER STRIPED SWALLOW *Hirundo cucullata* (526) 20 cm
Larger than Lesser Striped Swallow and appears very much paler, with the striping on buffy underparts discernible only at close range. The orange on the crown is slightly paler and much paler on the rump; there is no rufous on the vent; ear coverts white.
SEXES alike. IMM. has little blue-black gloss above, crown is reddish brown, and the breast has a partial brown band. HABITAT. Grassland and vleis. STATUS. Common summer visitor. CALL. A twittering 'chissick'. (Grootstreepswael)

LESSER STRIPED SWALLOW *Hirundo abyssinica* (527) 16 cm
Smaller and darker than Greater Striped Swallow, with heavy black striping on white (not buffy) underparts. The rufous rump extends on to the vent; ear coverts orange.
FEMALE has shorter outer tail feathers. IMM. has less blue-black gloss above; crown brown (not rufous). HABITAT. Usually near water, frequently perching in trees or on wires. STATUS. Common resident and summer visitor. CALL. A descending series of squeaky, nasal 'zeh-zeh-zeh-zeh' notes. (Kleinstreepswael)

SOUTH AFRICAN CLIFF SWALLOW *Hirundo spilodera* (528) 15 cm
Differs from the striped swallows by having only a slight notch in a square-ended tail and by having a darkly mottled breast. These features, and the pale rump, distinguish it from European Swallow. The crown is dark brown, slightly glossed in front.
SEXES alike. IMM. lacks blue-black gloss above. HABITAT. Upland grassland, usually in the vicinity of road bridges. STATUS. Common summer visitor; breeding endemic. CALL. Twittering 'chooerp-chooerp'. (Familieswael)

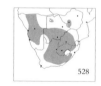

EUROPEAN SWALLOW *Hirundo rustica* (518) 18 cm
The red throat and forehead, blue-black breast band and deeply forked tail are diagnostic. In Angola Swallow, red of throat extends to upper breast and is bordered by an incomplete and narrower breast band.
SEXES alike but MALE has longer tail streamers. IMM. is browner and has shorter outer tail feathers. HABITAT. Cosmopolitan, except closed forest. STATUS. Abundant non-breeding summer visitor. CALL. A soft, high-pitched twittering. (Europese Swael)

ANGOLA SWALLOW *Hirundo angolensis* (519) 15 cm
Less agile in flight than similar European Swallow. It differs further by having the red on the throat extending on to the breast and being bordered by a narrow, incomplete black band. The underparts are pale grey (not white or pinkish). Outer tail streamers are much shorter and the tail is less deeply forked than that of European Swallow.
SEXES alike. IMM. has red replaced by pale rufous and is less glossy above. HABITAT. Rivers and bridges, and in association with man. STATUS. Vagrant. CALL. Weak twittering. (Angolaswael)

REDBREASTED SWALLOW

MOSQUE SWALLOW

REDBREASTED SWALLOW

MOSQUE SWALLOW

GREATER STRIPED SWALLOW

LESSER STRIPED
SWALLOW

GREATER STRIPED
SWALLOW

SOUTH AFRICAN
CLIFF SWALLOW

LESSER STRIPED
SWALLOW

EUROPEAN SWALLOW

ANGOLA
SWALLOW

WIRETAILED SWALLOW *Hirundo smithii* (522) 13 cm
Smaller than Whitethroated Swallow and differs by having an incomplete black breast band, a bright chestnut cap, and a black streak across the vent. Very fast in flight.
SEXES alike. IMM. has chestnut largely replaced by brown and is less glossy blue above. HABITAT. Usually found near water, often breeding under bridges. STATUS. Common resident. CALL. A sharp metallic 'tchik'. (Draadstertswael)

PEARLBREASTED SWALLOW *Hirundo dimidiata* (523) 14 cm
Distinguished from Wiretailed Swallow by lacking both the tail streamers and the breast and vent bands, and by having a blue (not chestnut) cap. When seen from below, differs from Greyrumped Swallow and House Martin (p. 286) by having white (not dark) underwing coverts and, when seen from above, a dark (not pale) rump. It lacks white spots in the tail feathers and the blue gloss is not well developed.
SEXES alike. IMM. less glossy above. HABITAT. Over bushveld, fresh water and in association with man. STATUS. A locally common resident with seasonal movements in parts of its range. CALL. A subdued chipping note uttered in flight. (Pêrelborsswael)

WHITETHROATED SWALLOW *Hirundo albigularis* (520) 17 cm
The white throat and blue-black breast band are diagnostic. Sand and Banded Martins (p. 286) also have white throats and dark breast bands but are brown above.
SEXES alike. IMM. is less glossy than ad. above, with brownish forehead. HABITAT. Closely associated with water: most common in grassland areas. STATUS. Common breeding summer visitor. CALL. Soft warbles and twitters. (Witkeelswael)

WHITEHEADED SAW-WING SWALLOW *Psalidoprocne albiceps* (913) 14 cm
Recognizable by its snowy white head bisected by a black line running through the eye to the nape. The rest of the plumage is black with a slight greenish sheen.
FEMALE and IMM. have the white on the crown partly grizzled. HABITAT. Open forest glades and wooded slopes. STATUS. A very rare vagrant. CALL. Recorded elsewhere as a weak twittering. (Witkopsaagvlerkswael)

EASTERN SAW-WING SWALLOW *Psalidoprocne orientalis* (537) 15 cm
Differs from Black Saw-wing Swallow by having conspicuous white underwing coverts which are easily seen against the black underparts, and by being overall more slender and longer tailed.
SEXES alike. IMM. is very dark brown and lacks gloss. HABITAT. Over evergreen forests, miombo woodland and around rivers in these habitats. STATUS. Locally common resident. CALL. Soft twittering and a short 'chip'. (Tropiese Saagvlerkswael)

BLACK SAW-WING SWALLOW *Psalidoprocne holomelas* (536) 15 cm
An all-black swallow which differs from Blue Swallow by having slightly glossed greenish-black plumage and a less deeply forked tail with shorter tail streamers. Distinguished from Eastern Saw-wing Swallow only by its black (not white) underwing coverts. The smaller size and slow, fluttering flight should eliminate confusion with any of the dark swifts in the region.
SEXES alike. IMM. is very dark brown and lacks gloss. HABITAT. Fringes and clearings in forests and plantations. STATUS. Locally common resident. CALL. A soft 'chrrp' alarm call. (Swartsaagvlerkswael)

BLUE SWALLOW *Hirundo atrocaerulea* (521) 25 cm
The glossy dark blue plumage and long outer tail feathers are diagnostic. Differs from the similar Black Saw-wing Swallow by having blue (not black) plumage, by the long tail streamers (in the male) and by a different flight action.
FEMALE lacks long tail streamers. IMM. has brown throat and generally much less glossy plumage. HABITAT. Upland grassland, often bordering forests. STATUS. Breeding summer visitor. Rare and highly localized: endangered as a result of loss of habitat. CALL. A musical 'bee-bee-bee-bee' uttered in flight. (Blouswael)

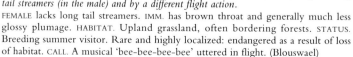

WIRETAILED SWALLOW

PEARLBREASTED SWALLOW

WIRETAILED SWALLOW

PEARLBREASTED SWALLOW

WHITEHEADED
SAW-WING
SWALLOW

WHITETHROATED
SWALLOW

EASTERN
SAW-WING SWALLOW

EASTERN
SAW-WING SWALLOW

female

BLUE SWALLOW

BLACK
SAW-WING SWALLOW

male

BANDED MARTIN *Riparia cincta* (534) 17 cm
Told from Sand Martin by being larger, by having white wing coverts, a small white eyebrow and a square-ended tail. Often has thin brown line across vent.
SEXES alike. IMM. has the upperparts scaled with pale buff, and lacks most of the white eyebrow. HABITAT. Frequents areas of low vegetation or grassland. STATUS. Locally common breeding summer visitor. CALL. Flight call is a 'che-che-che'. Song is a jumble of harsh 'chip-choops'. (Gebande Oewerswael)

SAND MARTIN *Riparia riparia* (532) 12 cm
Distinguished from Brownthroated Martin by having a white throat and brown breast band. Differs from the larger Banded Martin by having all-dark underwings, a forked tail and by lacking the white eyebrow.
SEXES alike. IMM. as ad. HABITAT. Usually over or near fresh water. STATUS. Uncommon summer visitor. CALL. A grating 'chrrr'. (Europese Oewerswael)

BROWNTHROATED MARTIN *Riparia paludicola* (533) 12 cm
Occurs in two colour forms, one dark brown with a small amount of white on the vent, the other having a brown throat and breast with the rest of the underparts white. Told from Sand Martin by its brown throat. Dark form confused with Rock Martin but is smaller, darker brown below and lacks the white tail spots.
SEXES alike. IMM. as ad. but has pale fringes to the secondaries. HABITAT. Over freshwater lakes, streams and rivers, especially near sandbanks. STATUS. Common resident; the brown-bellied form is found chiefly in the south and south-east of its range. CALL. Soft twittering. (Afrikaanse Oewerswael)

MASCARENE MARTIN *Phedina borbonica* (535) 13 cm
In the region, the only martin with heavily striped underparts and a white vent. It might be mistaken for imm. Lesser Striped Swallow (p. 282) but that species has a chestnut crown and rump. At long range resembles the dark form of Brownthroated Martin, but the large amount of white on its vent should eliminate confusion.
SEXES alike. IMM. has pale fringes to the secondaries. HABITAT. Chiefly over dense miombo woodland and forests. STATUS. Rare non-breeding winter visitor. CALL. Usually silent in Africa. (Gestreepte Kransswael)

ROCK MARTIN *Hirundo fuligula* (529) 15 cm
A dark brown martin. Differs from the all-brown form of Brownthroated Martin by being larger, paler on the throat and by having white tail spots visible in the spread tail.
SEXES alike. IMM. as ad. but upper wing coverts and secondaries have pale edges. HABITAT. Cliffs, quarries, rocky terrain and human dwellings. STATUS. Common resident with local movements. CALL. Soft, indistinct twitterings. (Kransswael)

HOUSE MARTIN *Delichon urbica* (530) 14 cm
Swallow-like; the only martin in the region to have pure white underparts and a white rump when adult. In flight from below is easily confused with Greyrumped Swallow but has a less deeply forked tail and broader based, shorter wings.
SEXES alike. IMM. has pale grey rump and less gloss above. HABITAT. Over dry broadleafed woodland and thornveld, and mountainous terrain, and is coastal in the south. STATUS. Common summer visitor; has bred in the southern Cape. CALL. A single 'chirrp'. (Huisswael)

GREYRUMPED SWALLOW *Pseudhirundo griseopyga* (531) 14 cm
The combination of grey crown and rump contrasting slightly with the blue-black upperparts is diagnostic. In flight from below could be confused with House Martin but has a longer, more deeply forked tail.
SEXES alike. IMM. has reddish-brown rump. HABITAT. Over rivers in thornveld, and open grassland adjacent to lakes and vleis. STATUS. Locally common resident; summer visitor to the south. CALL. Flight call note recorded as 'chraa'. (Gryskruisswael)

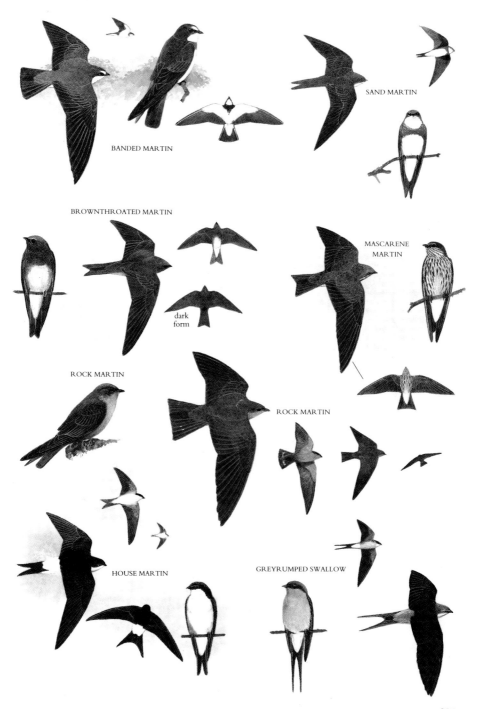

BANDED MARTIN

SAND MARTIN

BROWNTHROATED MARTIN

MASCARENE
MARTIN

dark
form

ROCK MARTIN

ROCK MARTIN

HOUSE MARTIN

GREYRUMPED SWALLOW

FORKTAILED DRONGO *Dicrurus adsimilis* (541) 25 cm
The only all-black perching bird with a deeply forked tail in the region. Squaretailed Drongo and Southern Black Flycatcher (p. 342) are similar but are smaller and have only a slight fork in the tail.
SEXES alike. IMM. has buff-tipped feathers on the underparts and forewing and a yellow gape. HABITAT. Woodland, savanna and exotic plantations. STATUS. Common resident. CALL. A variety of grating or shrill notes; mimics birds of prey, especially Pearlspotted Owl. (Mikstertbyvanger)

SQUARETAILED DRONGO *Dicrurus ludwigii* (542) 19 cm
Smaller than Forktailed Drongo and its tail is only slightly forked. Differs from Southern Black Flycatcher (p. 342) by its smaller, rounder head, and red (not dark brown) eye which can be seen at close range. Distinguished from male Black Cuckooshrike by slightly forked tail and lack of both yellow shoulder and orange-yellow gape.
FEMALE duller black than male. IMM. as female with pale tips to feathers. HABITAT. Evergreen forests. STATUS. Scarce to locally common resident. CALL. Strident 'che-weet-weet-weet' and other phrases. (Kleinbyvanger)

BLACK CUCKOOSHRIKE *Campephaga flava* (538) 22 cm
Male differs from Southern Black Flycatcher (p. 342) and Squaretailed Drongo by having a rounded tail, and by its habit of creeping through the tree canopy and not dashing after insects in flight.
MALE has a yellow shoulder (sometimes absent), but the orange-yellow gape is diagnostic. FEMALE resembles a 'green' cuckoo but is larger, more barred below and has bright yellow outer tail feathers. IMM. as female. HABITAT. Mature woodland and forest margins. STATUS. Locally common resident and summer visitor. CALL. A high-pitched, prolonged 'trrrrrrr'. (Swartkatakoeroe)

GREY CUCKOOSHRIKE *Coracina caesia* (540) 27 cm
The all-grey plumage, white orbital ring, and black patch between the base of the bill and the eye are diagnostic.
FEMALE is paler than male and lacks the black patch at bill base. IMM. has flight and tail feathers tipped with white and a barred black rump. HABITAT. Evergreen forests. STATUS. Uncommon resident. CALL. A soft, thin 'seeeeeeeep'. (Bloukatakoeroe)

WHITEBREASTED CUCKOOSHRIKE *Coracina pectoralis* (539) 27 cm
Differs from Grey Cuckooshrike by having a white breast and belly.
FEMALE is paler than male, sometimes lacking the distinct grey throat and upper breast. IMM. is even paler than either male or female, with spotted underparts, and upperparts barred with white. HABITAT. Tall woodland, especially miombo and riverine forests. STATUS. Uncommon resident. CALL. Male's call is a 'duid-duid' and female's is a 'tchee-ee-ee-ee'. (Witborskatakoeroe)

male FORKTAILED DRONGO

SQUARETAILED DRONGO male

tail during moult

female

female

male

male BLACK CUCKOOSHRIKE

female

male

female

GREY CUCKOOSHRIKE

WHITEBREASTED CUCKOOSHRIKE

ad.

male

male

female

AFRICAN GOLDEN ORIOLE *Oriolus auratus* (544) 24 cm
A brighter yellow bird than European Golden Oriole from which it differs mainly by having yellow wing coverts and a black stripe through and behind the eye.
FEMALE distinguished from female European Golden Oriole by being much yellower and having yellowish-green (not black) wing coverts. IMM. as female. HABITAT. Tall woodland (especially miombo) and riverine forest. STATUS. Uncommon summer visitor. CALL. A liquid whistle 'fee-yoo-fee-yoo'. (Afrikaanse Wielewaal)

EUROPEAN GOLDEN ORIOLE *Oriolus oriolus* (543) 24 cm
Male differs from male African Golden Oriole by having black wings and the black eyestripe extending only marginally behind the eye.
FEMALE is very similar to female African Golden Oriole but is less yellow below, has darker wing coverts and green upperparts. IMM. as female, but more streaked. HABITAT. Tall woodland, savanna and exotic plantations. STATUS. Fairly common non-breeding summer visitor. CALL. A liquid 'chleeooop', seldom heard in southern Africa. (Europese Wielewaal)

BLACKHEADED ORIOLE *Oriolus larvatus* (545) 24 cm
The black head is diagnostic in all plumages. If seen at long range might be confused with the rare Greenheaded Oriole but has a yellow (not green) back.
SEXES alike. IMM. lacks coral red bill of ad. and its head is dark brown, flecked with black. HABITAT. Mature woodland, especially broadleafed, also forest edge, and exotic plantations. STATUS. Common resident. CALL. A clear, liquid whistle 'pooodleeoo' and a harsher 'kweeer' note. (Swartkopwielewaal)

GREENHEADED ORIOLE *Oriolus chlorocephalus* (546) 24 cm
The green head, yellow collar and green back are diagnostic. If seen at long range the head appears black which might lead to confusion with Blackheaded Oriole, but the back also appears black, not yellow as in Blackheaded Oriole.
SEXES alike. IMM. has dull yellow underparts, breast slightly streaked with olive and has a pale olive wash on head and throat. HABITAT. Evergreen montane forest. STATUS. Rare resident. In the region, found only on Mt Gorongoza in Mozambique. CALL. The liquid call typical of orioles. (Groenkopwielewaal)

AFRICAN GOLDEN ORIOLE

male

female

female

male

EUROPEAN GOLDEN ORIOLE

male

female

female

imm.

male

BLACKHEADED ORIOLE

ad.

imm.

ad.

ad.

GREENHEADED ORIOLE

ad.

ad.

ad.

imm.

WHITENECKED RAVEN *Corvus albicollis* (550) 54 cm
The massive black bill with a white tip, and the white crescent on the hind neck are diagnostic. In flight and at long range, distinguished from Black and Pied Crows by its much broader wings, larger, heavier head and short, broad tail.
SEXES alike. IMM. less glossy black than ad. HABITAT. Restricted to mountainous and hilly areas. STATUS. Locally common resident. CALL. A deep, throaty 'kwook'. (Withalskraai)

PIED CROW *Corvus albus* (548) 50 cm
The only white-bellied crow in the region. At long range distinguished from White-necked Raven by longer tail and smaller head.
SEXES alike. IMM. as ad. but black and white plumage less contrasting. HABITAT. Occurs in virtually every habitat. STATUS. Common resident; often in flocks. CALL. A loud 'kwaaa' or 'kwooork' cawing. (Witborskraai)

BLACK CROW *Corvus capensis* (547) 50 cm
Larger than House Crow and differs by being entirely glossy black with a long, slender, slightly decurved bill.
SEXES alike. IMM. duller, lacks the glossy blue-black plumage of ad. HABITAT. Upland grassland, open country, cultivated fields and dry desert regions. STATUS. Common resident; sometimes in flocks. CALL. A crow-like 'kah-kah' (lower pitched than that of Pied Crow) and other deep bubbling notes. (Swartkraai)

HOUSE CROW *Corvus splendens* (549) 42 cm
The only grey-bodied crow in the region. The head, wings and tail are a glossy blue-black.
SEXES alike. IMM. has body colour greyish brown, but in other respects it resembles ad. HABITAT. Not often seen away from human habitation, as it scavenges food scraps from gardens, drive-in cinemas and restaurants. STATUS. Resident. A small population established in Durban since 1972 and on the Cape Flats since the late 1980s. Also in Mozambique. CALL. A higher pitched 'kaah, kaah' than other crows. (Huiskraai)

WHITENECKED RAVEN

PIED CROW

BLACK CROW

HOUSE CROW

ASHY TIT *Parus cinerascens* (552) 13 cm
Differs from Southern Grey Tit by having a blue-grey (not brownish-grey) back, and blue-grey (not buffy) flanks and belly. Darker than Northern Grey Tit, with less white in the wings.
SEXES alike. IMM. duller version of ad. HABITAT. Thornveld and arid savanna. STATUS. Common resident; endemic. CALL. Harsher and more scolding than that of Southern Grey Tit. (Acaciagrysmees)

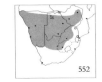

SOUTHERN GREY TIT *Parus afer* (551) 13 cm
Distinguished from Ashy Tit and Northern Grey Tit by having a distinctive brownish-grey (not blue-grey) back, buffy belly and flanks, and a proportionally shorter tail.
SEXES alike. IMM. browner than ad. HABITAT. Fynbos and Karoo scrub. STATUS. Common resident; endemic. CALL. Song is a cheery 'klee-klee-klee-cheree-cheree'. Alarm note is a harsh 'chrrr'. (Piet-tjou-tjougrysmees)

NORTHERN GREY TIT *Parus griseiventris* (553) 13 cm
Distinguished from Southern Grey Tit by having a blue-grey (not brownish-grey) back and pale blue-grey (not buffy) flanks. Thinner-billed and paler in appearance than Ashy Tit with a buffy (not white) cheek stripe and outer tail.
SEXES alike. IMM. duller version of ad. HABITAT. Miombo woodland. STATUS. Common resident. CALL. Scolding 'tjou-tjou-tjou-tjou' notes. (Miombogrysmees)

RUFOUSBELLIED TIT *Parus rufiventris* (556) 15 cm
Unlikely to be confused with any other tit in the region. The dark head and breast, lack of white cheek patches, together with the rufous belly, flanks and vent, are diagnostic. The bright yellow eye is conspicuous at close range. The eastern race (Zimbabwe/Mozambique) has rufous belly replaced with greyish brown.
SEXES alike. IMM. duller, has a brown eye and buffish edges to its wing feathers. HABITAT. Miombo woodland. STATUS. Uncommon resident. CALL. A harsh tit-like 'chrrr chrrr' and a clear 'chick-wee, chick-wee' song. (Swartkopmees)

SOUTHERN BLACK TIT *Parus niger* (554) 16 cm
Male Southern Black Tit has less white in the wings than Carp's Tit and has grey barred undertail coverts.
FEMALE differs from female Carp's Tit by being paler grey below and having less white in the wings. IMM. as female. HABITAT. Forests and broadleafed woodland. STATUS. Common resident. CALL. A harsh, chattering 'chrr-chrr-chrr' and a musical 'phee-cher-phee-cher'. (Gewone Swartmees)

SPOTTED CREEPER *Salpornis spilonotus* (559) 15 cm
Much smaller than any woodpecker in the region. This species' sunbird-like curved bill and brown upperparts, heavily spotted with white, are diagnostic. Creeps jerkily up tree trunks.
SEXES alike. IMM. duller than ad. HABITAT. Confined to miombo woodland. STATUS. Locally common to uncommon resident. CALL. A fast, thin 'sweepy-swip-swip-swip' and a harsher 'keck-keck'. (Boomkruiper)

CARP'S TIT *Parus carpi* (555) 14 cm
Smaller than Southern Black Tit, has a greater expanse of white in the wings, and lacks the grey barred undertail coverts.
FEMALE duller than male, but contrast between sexes not as great as in Southern Black Tit. Female Carp's Tit has more white in the wings than female Southern Black Tit. IMM. as female. HABITAT. Thornveld and arid savanna. STATUS. Common resident; endemic to central and northern Namibia. CALL. Similar to that of Southern Black Tit. (Ovamboswartmees)

ASHY TIT

SOUTHERN GREY TIT

NORTHERN GREY TIT

eastern race

RUFOUSBELLIED TIT

western race

SOUTHERN BLACK TIT

male

female

CARP'S TIT

SPOTTED CREEPER

male

female

N.A.

295

ARROWMARKED BABBLER *Turdoides jardineii* (560) 24 cm
White-streaked ('arrow-marked') breast, red-rimmed yellow eye and uniform brown rump are diagnostic.
SEXES alike. IMM. has brown eye. HABITAT. Woodland and savanna. STATUS. Common resident. Lives in groups of up to 12 birds. CALL. Loud 'chow-chow-chow-chow...' with several birds often calling simultaneously. (Pylvlekkatlagter)

BLACKFACED BABBLER *Turdoides melanops* (561) 28 cm
Differs from Hartlaub's Babbler by having dark remiges and from Arrowmarked Babbler by obvious scalloping (not streaking) on the breast. A small black patch at the base of the bill and the bright yellow eye are diagnostic. It is more furtive than the other babblers.
SEXES alike. IMM. as ad. but with brown eye. HABITAT. Broadleafed woodland. Forages in scattered groups among leaf litter. STATUS. Uncommon resident. CALL. A nasal 'wha-wha-wha' and a harsh, fast 'papapapa'. (Swartwangkatlagter)

HARTLAUB'S BABBLER *Turdoides hartlaubii* (562) 26 cm
Superficially resembles Arrowmarked Babbler but has a diagnostic white rump and vent, and has white scalloping (not streaking) on its head and body.
SEXES alike. IMM. is similar to ad. but is much paler, especially on the throat and breast. HABITAT. Reedbeds and surrounding woodland. STATUS. Common resident. Lives in groups. CALL. Noisy; a loud 'kwekkwekkwek' or 'papapapapapa' with several birds calling simultaneously. (Witkruiskatlagter)

BARECHEEKED BABBLER *Turdoides gymnogenys* (564) 24 cm
Distinguished from Southern Pied Babbler by its dark back and by the lack of white on its wing coverts. Has a small area of bare black skin below and behind the eye.
SEXES alike. IMM. could be confused with imm. Southern Pied Babbler but is generally much darker, especially on the back and nape, and is usually seen in the company of ads. of its own species. HABITAT. Dry broadleafed woodland, frequenting rivercourses and wooded koppies. STATUS. Uncommon resident. Lives in groups. CALL. Typical babbler 'kerrrakerrra-kek-kek-kek'. (Kaalwangkatlagter)

SOUTHERN PIED BABBLER *Turdoides bicolor* (563) 26 cm
The only babbler in the region with an all-white head, back and underparts.
SEXES alike. IMM. initially wholly pale brown but whitens with age. HABITAT. Arid savanna, especially thornveld. STATUS. Common resident; endemic. Lives in groups. CALL. 'Kwee kwee kwee kweer', a higher pitched babbling than the other species. (Witkatlagter)

BOULDER CHAT *Pinarornis plumosus* (610) 25 cm
The brownish-black plumage and the white-tipped outer tail feathers are diagnostic. In flight, a row of small white spots on the edge of the primary and secondary coverts can be seen. Runs and bounds over large boulders, occasionally raising its tail well over its back when landing.
FEMALE duller than male. IMM. like ad. HABITAT. Well-wooded terrain with large granite boulders. STATUS. Locally common resident. CALL. A clear, sharp whistle and softer 'wink, wink' call. (Swartberglyster)

IMM.

ARROWMARKED BABBLER

AD.

BLACKFACED BABBLER

HARTLAUB'S
BABBLER

BARECHEEKED
BABBLER

SOUTHERN
PIED BABBLER

IMM.

AD.

BOULDER CHAT

NA

CAPE BULBUL *Pycnonotus capensis* (566) 21 cm
Overall much darker in appearance than Redeyed and Blackeyed Bulbuls, with the dark brown on the underparts extending on to the lower belly. The white eye-ring is diagnostic.
SEXES alike. IMM. lacks the white eye-ring and is darker below than Blackeyed and Redeyed Bulbuls. HABITAT. Fynbos, coastal scrub, riverine forests, exotic plantations and gardens. STATUS. Common resident; endemic. CALL. A sharp, liquid whistle: 'peet-peet-patata'. (Kaapse Tiptol)

REDEYED BULBUL *Pycnonotus nigricans* (567) 21 cm
The red eye-ring is diagnostic and distinguishes this species from Blackeyed and Cape Bulbuls. Head colour is darker than that of Blackeyed Bulbul and contrasts with the greyish-buff collar and breast.
SEXES alike. IMM. distinguished from imm. Blackeyed Bulbul by its pale pink eye-ring. HABITAT. Thornveld, riverine bush and suburban gardens. STATUS. Common resident; near-endemic. CALL. Liquid whistles similar to those of Blackeyed Bulbul. (Rooioogtiptol)

BLACKEYED BULBUL *Pycnonotus barbatus* (568) 22 cm
Lacks the red eye-ring of Redeyed Bulbul and further differs by having less contrast between dark head and breast.
SEXES alike. IMM. like ad. HABITAT. Frequents a wide variety of habitats, from thornveld to forest edges, parks and gardens. STATUS. Abundant resident. CALL. A harsh, sharp 'kwit, kwit, kwit' given when alarmed or when going to roost. Song is a liquid 'cheloop chreep choop'. (Swartoogtiptol)

TERRESTRIAL BULBUL *Phyllastrephus terrestris* (569) 21 cm
A dull brown bulbul with greyish underparts. The white throat contrasting with the dark brown head is the best field character. In its search for food, it forms small, noisy flocks, the birds scuffling around on the forest floor, scattering earth and leaf litter with their feet and bills.
SEXES alike but male larger. IMM. like ad. HABITAT. Thick thornveld, and evergreen and riverine forests. STATUS. Common resident. CALL. A soft, chattering 'trrup cherrup trrup' given by small foraging groups. (Boskrapper)

BUSH BLACKCAP *Lioptilus nigricapillus* (565) 17 cm
A small, unmistakable bulbul with a black cap and bright coral-pink bill and legs. Shy and unobtrusive, it is usually found in dense foliage.
SEXES alike. IMM. is duller than ad. with dusky pink bill. HABITAT. Montane evergreen forests, mainly in forest margins and in small isolated forest patches. STATUS. Uncommon resident; endemic. Altitudinal migrant, breeding at higher altitudes, wintering at lower. CALL. Not unlike that of Blackeyed Bulbul but more varied and melodious. (Rooibektiptol)

CAPE BULBUL

CAPE BULBUL

REDEYED BULBUL

BLACKEYED BULBUL

TERRESTRIAL BULBUL

BUSH BLACKCAP   ad.

imm.

299

SOMBRE BULBUL *Andropadus importunus* (572) 23 cm
Generally drab olive-green, lacking any diagnostic field characters except the white eye. The north-eastern race hypoxanthus is very yellow below, and could be confused with Yellowbellied Bulbul, except for its white (not red) eye. An inconspicuous, but vocal, canopy-dwelling species.
SEXES alike. IMM. even duller than ad. HABITAT. Evergreen forests, coastal bush and thick thornveld. STATUS. Common resident. CALL. Normal call is a piercing 'weee-wee', followed by a liquid chortle. (Gewone Willie)

SLENDER BULBUL *Phyllastrephus debilis* (571) 14 cm
The smallest green bulbul of the region. Resembles Sombre Bulbul, but is much smaller, paler below, and has a grey crown and cheeks.
SEXES alike. IMM. has greener crown than ad. HABITAT. Lowland forests. STATUS. Common resident. CALL. A shrill 'shriiip' and a bubbling song. (Kleinboskruiper)

STRIPECHEEKED BULBUL *Andropadus milanjensis* (573) 21 cm
Distinguished from the similar Sombre Bulbul by having a grey head, a dark eye with a pale eye-ring, and faint white streaks on the cheeks. A shy forest inhabitant, often difficult to locate in the forest canopy.
SEXES alike. IMM. has greener crown. HABITAT. Montane evergreen forests and forest margins. STATUS. Locally common resident. CALL. A throaty 'chrrup-chip-chrup-chrup'. (Streepwangwillie)

YELLOWSTREAKED BULBUL *Phyllastrephus flavostriatus* (570) 20 cm
Small and slim in build. The back is dull olive, the underparts off-white, with faint yellow streaks only visible at close range in good light. The bill is thin, the eye brown. Best identified by its unusual, woodpecker-like action of creeping about tree trunks, continually flicking open one wing at a time.
SEXES alike but male noticeably larger. IMM. resembles ad. HABITAT. Mid-stratum and canopy of moist evergreen forests. STATUS. Locally common resident. CALL. 'Weet-weet-weet' and a sharp 'kleeet-kleeat'. (Geelstreepboskruiper)

YELLOWBELLIED BULBUL *Chlorocichla flaviventris* (574) 23 cm
Distinguished from Sombre Bulbul by having yellow underparts and a red (not white) eye. The thin white eyebrow is prominent. The race hypoxanthus of Sombre Bulbul also has a very yellow breast and belly but differs by having a greenish (not brown) crown, and a white eye. Bright yellow underwing coverts conspicuous in flight. Not often found in canopy, preferring the thick tangles at a lower level.
SEXES alike. IMM. duller than ad. HABITAT. Evergreen and riverine forests, thornveld and coastal scrub. STATUS. Common resident. CALL. A monotonous, nasal 'neh-neh-neh-neh'. (Geelborswillie)

YELLOWSPOTTED NICATOR *Nicator gularis* (575) 23 cm
The bright yellow spots on the wing coverts are diagnostic of this greenish bird. Could be confused with the female Black Cuckooshrike (p. 288) but that species is heavily barred below. In behaviour acts like a bush shrike, moving slowly through thick tangles, and is very difficult to see. The yellow tips to the tail feathers are obvious when the bird is flying away.
SEXES alike. IMM. duller than ad. HABITAT. Dense riverine and coastal forests and scrub, particularly on sandy soil. STATUS. Common resident. CALL. A short, rich, liquid jumble of notes. (Geelvleknikator)

SOMBRE BULBUL

SLENDER BULBUL

STRIPECHEEKED BULBUL

YELLOWSTREAKED
BULBUL

YELLOWBELLIED
BULBUL

ad.

imm.

YELLOWSPOTTED NICATOR

301

ORANGE GROUND THRUSH *Zoothera gurneyi* (579) 23 cm
Differs from both Southern Olive and Kurrichane Thrushes by the dark bill, bright orange throat and breast, and conspicuous white stripes on the wing coverts.
SEXES alike. IMM. is spotted with buff on the upperparts, and mottled black and orange below, but it still shows the diagnostic white stripes on the wing coverts. HABITAT. Montane evergreen forests. Some altitudinal movement in winter to coastal forests. STATUS. Uncommon resident. CALL. A sibilant 'tseeep'. Melodious song of clear whistled phrases, such as 'chee–cheeleeroo–chruup'. (Oranjelyster)

SOUTHERN OLIVE THRUSH *Turdus olivaceus* (577) 24 cm
Distinguished from Kurrichane Thrush by being darker, having a yellowish (not bright orange) bill, a dark-speckled throat, by lacking the black malar stripes, and by having a black (not yellow) eye-ring. Some birds show bright orange underparts, but they are distinguishable from Orange Ground Thrush by the lack of white spots on the wing coverts.
SEXES alike. IMM. streaked above with buff, wing coverts tipped russet, underparts orange-buff densely mottled with black. HABITAT. Montane forests; also in suburban parks and gardens and plantations. STATUS. Common resident. CALL. A sharp 'chink' or thin 'tseeep'. Song is a fluty 'wheeet-tooo-wheeet'. (Olyflyster)

KURRICHANE THRUSH *Turdus libonyana* (576) 22 cm
The white, faintly speckled throat, broad black malar stripes and bright orange bill and yellow eye-ring are diagnostic. Southern Olive Thrush also has an orange-yellow bill but it has a dark throat and lacks the malar stripes and yellow eye-ring.
SEXES alike. IMM. like imm. Southern Olive Thrush but paler. HABITAT. Thornveld, open woodland, and parks and gardens where it may occur alongside Southern Olive Thrush. STATUS. Common resident. CALL. A loud, whistling 'peet-peeoo'. (Rooibeklyster)

GROUNDSCRAPER THRUSH *Turdus litsitsirupa* (580) 22 cm
Distinguished from Spotted Ground Thrush by lacking white bars on its wing coverts and by having bolder, more contrasting black face markings; habitat also quite different. In flight shows a chestnut panel in the wing. Differs from the much smaller Dusky Lark (p. 272) by having bolder face markings and pale grey upperparts.
SEXES alike. IMM. speckled off-white on underparts with conspicuous white tips to wing coverts; spots on underside smaller than in ad. HABITAT. Dry thornveld, open broadleafed woodland, and parks and gardens. STATUS. Common resident. CALL. This bird's specific name (*litsitsirupa*) is onomatopoeic of its song: a loud, clear, and varied whistling phrase. (Gevlekte Lyster)

SPOTTED GROUND THRUSH *Zoothera guttata* (578) 23 cm
Distinguished from Groundscraper Thrush by having bold white stripes on the wing coverts. This and Groundscraper Thrush superficially resemble Dusky Lark (p. 272) but both are larger, have paler backs and are unlikely to be found in flocks.
SEXES alike. IMM. spotted with buff on upperparts and wing coverts; spotting of underparts finer than in ad. HABITAT. Understorey of coastal evergreen forests. STATUS. Uncommon resident and partial local migrant; predominantly a winter visitor to northern coastal forests. CALL. A quiet 'tseeeep'. A whistled, fluty song of short phrases of four or five notes. (Natallyster)

ORANGE GROUND THRUSH

imm.

SOUTHERN OLIVE
THRUSH

KURRICHANE THRUSH

GROUNDSCRAPER THRUSH

SPOTTED
GROUND THRUSH

303

CAPE ROCK THRUSH *Monticola rupestris* (581) 21 cm
The largest rock thrush in the region. Male differs from the male Sentinel Rock Thrush by having a brown (not blue) back and forewing, and by the blue on its throat not extending on to the breast.
FEMALE has much richer red underparts than other female rock thrushes. IMM. resembles female but has upperparts spotted with buff and feathers of underside edged with black, giving a scaled appearance. HABITAT. Mountainous and rocky terrain, both at the coast and inland. STATUS. Common resident; endemic. CALL. Song is a 'tsee-tsee-tseet-chee-chweeeoo' whistling. Alarm a harsh grating. (Kaapse Kliplyster)

SENTINEL ROCK THRUSH *Monticola explorator* (582) 18 cm
Male distinguished from male Cape Rock Thrush by having a blue (not brown) back and forewing, and by having the blue extending well on to the breast. Could be confused with Short-toed Rock Thrush (although their ranges do not overlap), but Sentinel Rock Thrush lacks the conspicuous pale forehead, crown and nape of Short-toed Rock Thrush.
FEMALE differs from the female Cape Rock Thrush by being smaller, and having a paler, mottled (not uniform red-brown) breast. IMM. like female but upperparts spotted buffy-white; throat, breast and flanks scaled with brown. HABITAT. Mountainous and rocky terrain, often in association with Cape Rock Thrush. STATUS. Locally common resident and partial altitudinal migrant; endemic. CALL. Whistled song similar to that of Cape Rock Thrush but not as loud. (Langtoonkliplyster)

MIOMBO ROCK THRUSH *Monticola angolensis* (584) 18 cm
The blue-grey crown and back of the male are mottled with black, eliminating confusion with any other rock thrush.
FEMALE has distinctly mottled upperparts and bold malar stripes which separate this species from other female rock thrushes. IMM. resembles female but with black and whitish mottling on underparts. HABITAT. Miombo woodland, usually in hilly terrain. STATUS. Locally common resident; unobtrusive. CALL. A two-note whistle; song a high-pitched variety of melodic phrases. (Angolakliplyster)

SHORT-TOED ROCK THRUSH *Monticola brevipes* (583) 18 cm
In the male, the very pale blue forehead, crown and nape are diagnostic: in some birds they are so pale that they appear white. Some individuals show a darker blue head but they usually retain a pale blue eyebrow stripe.
FEMALE has a large white throat patch, streaked brown, and a rufous breast and belly. IMM. spotted with buff on upperparts and with black below. HABITAT. Wooded koppies and rocky slopes. STATUS. Common resident. CALL. A thin 'tseeep'. Song of whistled phrases like other rock thrushes; includes some mimicry of other birds' calls. (Korttoonkliplyster)

CAPE ROCKJUMPER *Chaetops frenatus* (611) 25 cm
Male is similar to Orangebreasted Rockjumper but is slightly larger and has a dark rufous belly and rump.
FEMALE and IMM. are darker buff below than the female Orangebreasted Rockjumper and have a more boldly marked head pattern. HABITAT. Rocky mountain slopes and scree. STATUS. Common but localized resident; endemic. CALL. A loud, clear 'wheeoo' and a range of other loud whistles. (Kaapse Berglyster)

ORANGEBREASTED ROCKJUMPER *Chaetops aurantius* (612) 21 cm
Differs from slightly larger Cape Rockjumper by having an orange-buff belly and rump. Confusion between these species is unlikely as their ranges do not overlap. HABITAT.
FEMALE and IMM. are pale buff below and have less distinctly marked heads. HABITAT. Usually found above an altitude of 2 000 m on rocky mountain slopes and grassy hillsides with scattered boulders. STATUS. Common resident; endemic. CALL. Similar to that of Cape Rockjumper, a rapidly repeated piping whistle. (Oranjeborsberglyster)

CAPE ROCK THRUSH

female

male

female

SENTINEL
ROCK THRUSH

female

male

MIOMBO ROCK THRUSH

male

female

male

SHORT-TOED ROCK THRUSH

CAPE ROCKJUMPER

female

male

ORANGEBREASTED ROCKJUMPER

male

female

305

FAMILIAR CHAT *Cercomela familiaris* (589) 15 cm
Differs from Tractrac and Sicklewinged Chats by being darker grey-brown below, with a richer chestnut rump and outer tail feathers. Like other chats it flicks its wings when at rest, but this species also 'trembles' its tail.
SEXES alike. IMM. spotted with buff above, scaled below. HABITAT. Rocky and mountainous terrain. STATUS. Common resident. CALL. A soft 'shek-shek' alarm call and a warbling trill. (Gewone Spekvreter)

SICKLEWINGED CHAT *Cercomela sinuata* (591) 15 cm
The dark upperparts contrasting with paler underparts distinguish this species from the more uniformly coloured Familiar Chat. It further differs by having the paler chestnut on the rump confined to the tail base, and by its longer legged, more upright stance. In comparison with Familiar Chat, spends more time on the ground and can run more swiftly.
SEXES alike. IMM. has buff-tipped feathers. HABITAT. Short lowland and montane grassland, Karoo scrub vegetation and barren, sandy or stony areas. Agricultural lands on the west coast. STATUS. Common resident; endemic. CALL. A very soft, typically chat-like 'chak-chak', and a warbled song. (Vlaktespekvreter)

TRACTRAC CHAT *Cercomela tractrac* (590) 15 cm
Smaller than Karoo Chat and lacks the all-white outer tail feathers of that species. Paler and greyer than both Familiar and Sicklewinged Chats, it has a white or pale buff rump. The Namib form found on hummock dunes and at the coast is almost white, with darker wings and tail, while the gravel plains bird, found to the south-east, is darker.
SEXES alike. IMM. more mottled. HABITAT. Karoo and desert scrub, hummock dunes and gravel plains. STATUS. Common resident; endemic. CALL. A soft, fast 'tactac'. Song is a quiet musical bubbling; territorial defence call is a loud chattering. (Woestynspekvreter)

KAROO CHAT *Cercomela schlegelii* (592) 18 cm
Paler than the similar grey form female Mountain Chat, it also differs by having a grey (not white) rump, and completely white outer tail feathers. Its larger size and all-white outer tail feathers eliminate confusion with Tractrac and Sicklewinged Chats.
SEXES alike. IMM. buff-spotted above, scaled below. HABITAT. Karoo and desert scrub. STATUS. Common resident; endemic. CALL. A typically chat-like 'chak-chak' or 'trrat-trrat'. (Karoospekvreter)

MOUNTAIN CHAT *Oenanthe monticola* (586) 20 cm
Males show variable plumage coloration, but all have a white rump, white sides to the tail and a white shoulder patch. White cap may or may not be present. Differs from male Arnot's Chat by having a white (not black) rump and white outer tail feathers.
FEMALE is uniform sooty brown except for white rump and outer tail feathers. IMM. resembles female. HABITAT. Mountainous and rocky terrain. STATUS. Common resident; near-endemic. CALL. A clear, thrush-like whistling song, interspersed with harsh chatters. (Bergwagter)

ARNOT'S CHAT *Thamnolaea arnoti* (594) 18 cm
Male distinguished from the similar male Mountain Chat by having an entirely black rump and tail.
FEMALE lacks the white cap but has a conspicuous white throat and upper breast. IMM. has black head and white shoulder patch. HABITAT. Miombo and mopane woodland. STATUS. Common resident. CALL. A quiet, whistled 'fick' or 'feee'. (Bontpiek)

imm.

dark form

pale form
wing-flicking

FAMILIAR CHAT

SICKLEWINGED CHAT

TRACTRAC CHAT
Namib form

dark form

KAROO CHAT

MOUNTAIN CHAT

female

pale form

dark form

male

ARNOT'S CHAT

female

male

PIED WHEATEAR *Oenanthe pleschanka* (907) 15 cm
Male superficially resembles Mountain Chat (p. 306) but is smaller, has a black face and throat, clear white underparts and lacks the white shoulder patches. In transitional plumage, black areas flecked with buff.
FEMALE indistinguishable from female European Wheatear. IMM. similar to female. HABITAT. Usually dry stony regions with scattered scrub. STATUS. Very rare vagrant, with one summer record from Natal. CALL. Not recorded in the region; described elsewhere as a harsh 'zack-zack' . (Bontskaapwagter)

ISABELLINE WHEATEAR *Oenanthe isabellina* (915) 16 cm
Very difficult to distinguish from European Wheatear in non-breeding plumage but is larger, longer legged and the white area on the rump is less extensive. If seen, the darker alula is diagnostic.
SEXES alike. IMM. resembles ad. HABITAT. Bush and scrub. STATUS. Very rare vagrant, with one summer record from Botswana. CALL. Not recorded in the region; described elsewhere as a high-pitched 'wheet-whit' . (Isabellinaskaapwagter)

EUROPEAN WHEATEAR *Oenanthe oenanthe* (585) 15 cm
Breeding male of this species is unmistakable with its blue-grey crown and back, and black ear patches.
FEMALE, NON-BREEDING MALE and IMM. could be confused with imm. Capped Wheatear but show white rumps and have more extensive white on the outer tail feathers, lending a distinct 'T' pattern to the black area of the tail. HABITAT. Dry stony or sandy areas with stunted scrub growth. STATUS. Rare summer visitor. CALL. Harsh 'chak-chak'. Song not recorded in southern Africa. (Europese Skaapwagter)

CAPPED WHEATEAR *Oenanthe pileata* (587) 18 cm
The adult, which has a conspicuous white forehead and eyebrow, and black cap, is unmistakable.
SEXES alike. IMM. is distinguished from the similar European Wheatear by its larger size, by having only a small amount of white at the base of its outer tail feathers, and by buff-tipping to feathers on upperparts. Imm. could also be confused with the female Buffstreaked Chat (p. 310) but has a white (not buff) rump, and is found in quite different habitat. HABITAT. Barren sandy or stony areas and short grassland in flat country. STATUS. Common but thinly distributed resident with local movements. CALL. A 'chik-chik' alarm note. Song is a loud warbling with slurred chattering. (Hoëveldskaapwagter)

WHINCHAT *Saxicola rubetra* (597) 14 cm
Breeding male differentiated from the female Stonechat by having a well-defined white eyebrow stripe, a more extensive white wing bar on its coverts, a white patch at the base of its primaries, and white sides to the base of its tail.
FEMALE, NON-BREEDING MALE and IMM. differ from female Stonechat by having a broad, creamy eyebrow stripe, a white wing bar and diagnostic white bases to the outer tail feathers. HABITAT. Open grassland with patches of stunted scrub. STATUS. Rare summer visitor to the extreme north, with scattered records further south. CALL. Described elsewhere as a scolding 'tick-tick'. (Europese Bontrokkie)

STONECHAT *Saxicola torquata* (596) 14 cm
In all plumages, both sexes of this species are distinguishable from Whinchat, as neither shows a pale eyebrow stripe.
MALE is unmistakable with its black head, white on neck, wings and rump, and rufous breast. FEMALE is duller but retains the white in the wings and shows a buff rump. IMM. mottled with dark buff above and is paler below. HABITAT. Upland grassland and open, treeless areas with short scrub; also wetland areas of Namibia. STATUS. Common resident with local movements. CALL. A 'weet-weet' followed by a harsh 'chak'. (Gewone Bontrokkie)

PIED WHEATEAR

male br.

ISABELLINE WHEATEAR

male ad. non-br.

br.

ad. non-br.

EUROPEAN WHEATEAR
male ad. non-br.

CAPPED WHEATEAR

ad.

imm.

EUROPEAN
WHEATEAR

male br.

STONECHAT

female

male

WHINCHAT

female

male

CHATS

BUFFSTREAKED CHAT *Oenanthe bifasciata* (588) 17 cm
The male's black face, throat and wings and buffy underparts are diagnostic.
FEMALE differs from imm. Capped Wheatear (p. 308) by having a buff (not white)
rump. IMM. is mottled with black and buff on its upper- and underparts and has a
rufous rump. HABITAT. Rock-strewn grassy hill slopes. STATUS. Common but localized resident; endemic. CALL. Loud, rich warbling, including mimicry of other birds'
songs. (Bergklipwagter)

SOUTHERN ANTEATING CHAT *Myrmecocichla formicivora* (595) 18 cm
*In flight, easily distinguished from other chats by the conspicuous white patches on the
primaries. At rest appears very plump and short-tailed, with an upright stance.*
MALE is very dark brown with a white shoulder patch. FEMALE is paler brown than
male. IMM. like female but more mottled. HABITAT. Grassland dotted with termite
mounds, and open, sandy or stony areas. STATUS. Common resident; endemic.
CALL. A short, sharp 'peek' or 'piek'. (Swartpiek)

MOCKING CHAT *Thamnolaea cinnamomeiventris* (593) 23 cm
*The male's black plumage, bright chestnut belly, vent and rump, and the white shoulder
patch are diagnostic.*
FEMALE is dark grey above and chestnut below, lacking any white in plumage. IMM.
resembles female. HABITAT. Bases of cliffs and wooded rocky slopes. STATUS.
Common but localized resident. CALL. Song is a loud, melodious mixture of mimicked bird song. (Dassievoël)

HERERO CHAT *Namibornis herero* (618) 17 cm
*At a glance might be mistaken for a Familiar Chat (p. 306) but has a different head
pattern: the black line which runs through the eye contrasts with the clear white eyebrow stripe. The outer tail feathers and rump are rufous and only at close range can
the faint streaking on the breast be seen.*
SEXES alike. IMM. like female but more mottled. HABITAT. Dry scrub and thornveld at
the base of hills and in boulder-strewn country. STATUS. Uncommon resident; near-
endemic. CALL. Mostly silent except during the breeding season when a melodious,
warbling 'twi-tedeelee-doo' song is uttered. Also soft warbling repertoire. (Herero-
spekvreter)

EUROPEAN REDSTART *Phoenicurus phoenicurus* (916) 14 cm
Breeding male is unmistakable: black throat, white forehead, red breast and tail.
FEMALE and NON-BREEDING MALE might be confused with either a Familiar or
Sicklewinged Chat (p. 306) but can be distinguished from these species by the
brighter rufous tail which is continuously 'trembled' and by the lack of continual
wing-flicking. IMM. as female, but faintly mottled on back and breast. HABITAT.
Wooded areas. STATUS. Very rare vagrant, with one record from the Transvaal. CALL.
Loud 'hooeeet', resembling that of Willow Warbler. (Europese Rooistert)

BUFFSTREAKED CHAT

female

male

male hovering

SOUTHERN ANTEATING CHAT

female

MOCKING CHAT

male

female

male

male

HERERO CHAT

female

EUROPEAN REDSTART

male br.

311

CHORISTER ROBIN *Cossypha dichroa* (598) 20 cm
The dark upperparts, yellow-orange underparts, and lack of white eye-stripe render this large robin distinctive. Superficially resembles Natal Robin but lacks the powder blue forewings and orange face of that species.
SEXES alike. IMM. sooty, mottled tawny-buff above and below, tail red-orange with dark centre. HABITAT. Evergreen forests. STATUS. Common resident with local movements (from interior to coastal forests in winter); endemic. CALL. Contact call a plaintive 'toy-toy, toy-toy'. Song loud and bubbly, including much mimicry of other forest birds. (Lawaaimakerjanfrederik)

NATAL ROBIN *Cossypha natalensis* (600) 18 cm
Distinguished from all other robins by having a powder blue back and wings, russet-brown crown and nape, and bright red-orange face and underparts.
SEXES alike. IMM. sooty, mottled above and below with buff and brown, tail red-orange with black centre as in ad. HABITAT. Dense thickets and tangles in evergreen forests. STATUS. Common resident. CALL. Contact call is a soft 'seee-saw, seee-saw'. Song like that of Chorister Robin but more slurred, a rambling series of melodious phrases, including much mimicry. (Nataljanfrederik)

HEUGLIN'S ROBIN *Cossypha heuglini* (599) 20 cm
Distinguished from the similarly sized and coloured Chorister Robin by having a paler back and a broad, conspicuous white eyebrow stripe.
SEXES alike. IMM. sooty coloured with heavy buff and brown spotting on upper- and underparts; tail red-orange with dark centre as in ad. HABITAT. Dense riverine thickets and tangles, and gardens and parks. STATUS. Common resident. CALL. A characteristic, loud, crescendo song of repeated phrases. (Heuglinse Janfrederik)

CAPE ROBIN *Cossypha caffra* (601) 18 cm
Best distinguished from Heuglin's Robin by its smaller size, shorter white eyebrow stripe, and by having the orange on the underparts confined to the throat and upper breast: the rest of the underparts are grey, except for white belly and undertail coverts.
SEXES alike. IMM. is brownish, heavily mottled with buff and black, and has a red tail with a dark centre. HABITAT. Forest edge, bushveld, scrub and fynbos, gardens and parks (except Natal/Zululand coast where mainly a winter visitor). STATUS. Common resident. CALL. Alarm call is a guttural 'wur-da-durrr'. Song a series of melodious phrases, often starting 'cherooo-weet-weet-weeeet'. (Gewone Janfrederik)

AFRICAN WHITETHROATED ROBIN *Cossypha humeralis* (602) 17 cm
The only robin in the region with a white wingbar and a white throat and breast. The rufous tail with a dark centre also differs from other robins in having black tips to all feathers. Usually seen in dashes for cover, it gives the impression of being a small black and white bird with a red tail.
SEXES alike. IMM. sooty coloured, heavily mottled with buff and brown above and below; no white wingbar, but tail rufous and black as in ad. HABITAT. Dry thornveld, thickets and riverine scrub. STATUS. Common resident; endemic. CALL. Alarm call is a repeated 'seet-cher, seet-cher'. Song an attractive medley of whistled phrases incorporating much mimicry of other birds' calls. (Witkeeljanfrederik)

WHITEBREASTED ALETHE *Alethe fuelleborni* (605) 20 cm
The only robin-like bird in the region to have completely white underparts. The upperparts and the short tail are a rich russet colour. A robust, plump bird which hops about the forest floor.
SEXES alike. IMM. undescribed. HABITAT. The understorey of lowland evergreen forests. STATUS. Rare resident. CALL. A lively, whistling 'fweer-her-hee-her-hee-her'. (Witborsboslyster)

CHORISTER ROBIN

NATAL ROBIN

HEUGLIN'S ROBIN

imm.

CAPE ROBIN

ad.

AFRICAN
WHITETHROATED ROBIN

WHITEBREASTED ALETHE

BROWN ROBIN *Erythropygia signata* (616) 18 cm
Likely to be confused with Eastern Bearded Robin: differs by lacking the buff-coloured flanks of that species, and has less distinct white eyebrow and malar stripes. A shy, skulking bird which enters open forest glades at dawn and dusk.
SEXES alike. IMM. resembles ad. but spotted with buff on upperparts and scaled with sooty black on chest. HABITAT. Thick tangles of coastal and evergreen forests. STATUS. Locally common resident; endemic. CALL. A melodious 'twee-choo-sree-sree' introduces a varied song. Alarm note a sibilant 'zeeeeet'. (Bruinwipstert)

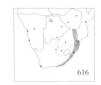

EASTERN BEARDED ROBIN *Erythropygia quadrivirgata* (617) 18 cm
The broad white eyebrow stripe finely edged with black, black malar stripes, and buff to orange flanks and breast combined with rufous rump are diagnostic. This species differs from the duller Brown Robin by having bolder head markings and more brightly coloured flanks.
SEXES alike. IMM. mottled tawny buff above and below; tail as in ad. HABITAT. Prefers drier forest than Brown Robin; also frequents broadleafed woodland and thornveld. STATUS. Common resident; easily overlooked. CALL. Alarm call of one or two sharp notes followed by a 'churr, chek-chek kwezzzzz'. A clear, penetrating song of often-repeated mixed phrases. (Baardwipstert)

WHITEBROWED ROBIN *Erythropygia leucophrys* (613) 15 cm
Resembles Kalahari Robin but differs by having a heavily streaked (not unmarked) breast, and white bars on the wing coverts. The breast streaking eliminates confusion with Brown and Eastern Bearded Robins.
SEXES alike. IMM. speckled with buff and brown above; below whitish, heavily scaled with brown on breast; tail brown with all except central feathers broadly tipped with white, as in ad. HABITAT. Woodland and savanna. STATUS. Common resident. CALL. A harsh 'trrrrrr' alarm note and a fluty but repetitive song; characteristic call at dawn and dusk is a whistled 'seeep po go'. (Gestreepte Wipstert)

KALAHARI ROBIN *Erythropygia paena* (615) 17 cm
Sandy brown, with a pale eyebrow, rufous rump and uppertail; broad black sub-terminal tail bar. Lacks breast streaks and white wingbar of Whitebrowed Robin and in flight shows more rufous on the tail.
SEXES alike. IMM. mottled with sooty black and buff above and below; tail as in ad. HABITAT. Dry thornveld, thicket and tangled growth around waterholes and dry riverbeds. STATUS. Common resident; near-endemic. CALL. Alarm note a harsh 'zzeee'; contact call a whistled 'seeeup'. A musical song of whistles and chirps, more varied than that of Karoo or Whitebrowed Robins. (Kalahariwipstert)

KAROO ROBIN *Erythropygia coryphaeus* (614) 17 cm
Lacks the breast streaking of Whitebrowed Robin, is much darker than Kalahari Robin and lacks rufous in the tail. Distinctive features of this species are the dull grey-brown plumage, white throat patch, small white eyebrow stripe, and white tips to dark tail feathers.
SEXES alike. IMM. sooty brown, mottled with buff; eyebrow indistinct. HABITAT. Karoo scrub and fynbos. STATUS. Common resident; endemic. CALL. A harsh, chittering 'tchik, tchik, tcheet'. Song a mixture of whistles and harsh grating notes. (Slangverklikker)

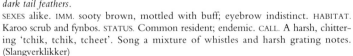

BROWN ROBIN

EASTERN BEARDED ROBIN

WHITEBROWED ROBIN

KALAHARI ROBIN

KAROO ROBIN

315

STARRED ROBIN *Pogonocichla stellata* (606) 16 cm
The ad. of this small, dark blue and yellow robin is unmistakable; the white 'stars' on the throat and forehead are usually concealed, but the bright yellow 'windows' of the tail are conspicuous as the bird flits through the forest undergrowth.
SEXES alike. IMM. Spotted juvenile is sooty coloured, heavily spangled with yellowish buff above and below; sub-ad. is dull olive above and greyish yellow below; the tail of both has same pattern as that of ad. but is dull yellow and dusky. HABITAT. Coastal and inland evergreen forests, winter visitor to coastal Natal and Zululand plain. STATUS. Common, but localized and easily overlooked resident. CALL. A soft 'chuk' or 'zit' note; a whistled 'too-twee' contact call, frequently repeated, and a quiet, warbling song. (Witkoljanfrederik)

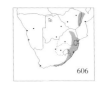

SWYNNERTON'S ROBIN *Swynnertonia swynnertoni* (607) 14 cm
Distinguished from the similar Starred Robin by having an orange (not yellow) breast, and a diagnostic black and white breast band. It also has an all-black (not a yellow and black) tail.
FEMALE has greenish crown and face (not dark grey as in male). IMM. is brown above spotted with buffy yellow; underparts duller than in ad. with throat crescent drab greyish brown; brown and grey mottling on breast and belly. HABITAT. Evergreen montane forests and ravines. STATUS. Uncommon resident. CALL. Song, given by male, is a subdued, three-syllabled 'zitt, zitt, slurr', the last syllable lower pitched. Alarm a monotonous quiet purring. (Bandkeeljanfrederik)

GUNNING'S ROBIN *Sheppardia gunningi* (608) 14 cm
A small, dull forest robin, brown above with orange-yellow throat, olive-yellow flanks and white belly. Diagnostic field characters are difficult to see: powder blue forewings and an indistinct, short white eyebrow stripe. Furtive and infrequently seen.
SEXES alike. IMM. olive brown above spotted with buff; underparts buffy, scaled with russet-brown. HABITAT. Lowland forests. STATUS. Common localized resident. CALL. Alarm is a series of piping 'seeep' notes. A fast, high-pitched but not loud song of several short phrases, frequently repeated. (Gunningse Janfrederik)

THRUSH NIGHTINGALE *Luscinia luscinia* (609) 16 cm
This large, drab warbler is usually located by its song as it is rarely seen, skulking in tangled undergrowth. If seen, the russet tail and slightly mottled breast aid identification.
SEXES alike. IMM. more mottled on head, back and breast than ad. HABITAT. Thickets along rivers and in damp areas. STATUS. Rare (and easily overlooked) summer visitor, found mainly in the north. CALL. A rich, warbling song interspersed with harsh, grating notes. (Lysternagtegaal)

RUFOUSTAILED PALM THRUSH *Cichladusa ruficauda* (604) 18 cm
Similar to Collared Palm Thrush but lacks the black border on the breast and the grey nape and flanks, and has a richer rufous crown and back. It also has a darker eye.
SEXES alike. IMM. as ad. with dark mottling on underparts. HABITAT. Riverine thickets and *Borassus* palm savanna. STATUS. Locally common resident on the Cunene River, west of Ruacana in Namibia. CALL. A melodious whistling including imitations of other birds. (Rooistertmôrelyster)

COLLARED PALM THRUSH *Cichladusa arquata* (603) 19 cm
Buff throat and breast with narrow black collar, and a pale eye are diagnostic. The black line encircling the breast is often incomplete, and the sides of the neck and the flanks are washed with grey.
SEXES alike. IMM. is a mottled buff-brown. HABITAT. *Hyphaene* or *Borassus* palm savanna. STATUS. Scarce to locally common resident. CALL. An explosive whistled song, consisting of 'weet-chuk' or 'cur-lee chuk-chuk' phrases. (Palmmôrelyster)

STARRED ROBIN

ad.　　imm.

imm.

SWYNNERTON'S ROBIN

ad.

GUNNING'S ROBIN

THRUSH NIGHTINGALE

COLLARED PALM THRUSH

RUFOUSTAILED PALM THRUSH

imm.　　ad.

YELLOWTHROATED WARBLER *Seicercus ruficapillus* (644) 11 cm
This small active warbler has a rufous crown and areas of bright yellow on the throat, breast and undertail that contrast with the greyish underparts and olive-grey back. A noticeable yellow eyebrow stripe contrasts with the darker crown.
SEXES alike. IMM. shows a greener wash on the breast. HABITAT. Evergreen forests and wooded gullies. STATUS. Locally common resident. CALL. A 'seee suuu seee suuu' song, with variations in phrasing. (Geelkeelsanger)

WILLOW WARBLER *Phylloscopus trochilus* (643) 11 cm
Most individuals are either olive above and yellow below or brown above and white below, but intermediates also occur. The bill is thin and weak in comparison to that of Icterine Warbler. The distinct yellow on the underparts is restricted to the throat and breast with the belly mainly dull white.
SEXES alike. IMM. has underparts yellow; eyebrow stripe and face much brighter yellow. HABITAT. Wide range of broadleafed woodland and dry thornveld habitats. STATUS. Abundant summer visitor. CALL. A soft 'hoeet hoeet' and a short melodious song, descending in scale. (Hofsanger)

ICTERINE WARBLER *Hippolais icterina* (625) 13 cm
Larger than Willow Warbler, this species is normally a brighter yellow below. Some are whitish below, and greyish brown above. Best distinguished by the large bill and head with a more angular sloping forehead, bluish legs and the pale wing panel. A short yellow eyebrow stripe and a pale eye-ring may be evident.
SEXES alike. IMM. can appear greyer with much paler yellow underparts. HABITAT. Thornveld, dry broadleafed woodland, exotic plantations, gardens and riverine thickets. STATUS. Common summer visitor. CALL. Varied jumbled notes, including a harsh 'tac, tac'. (Spotvoël)

OLIVETREE WARBLER *Hippolais olivetorum* (626) 16 cm
This large grey warbler might be confused with Fantailed Flycatcher (p. 342) but it lacks the conspicuous white outer tail feathers and the tail-spreading action of that species. The bill is long and heavy, and a pale grey panel is noticeable in the wings.
SEXES alike. IMM. as ad. HABITAT. Dense clumps of thicket in thornveld. STATUS. Uncommon summer visitor. CALL. Most easily located by its chattering song, sounding like Great Reed Warbler. (Olyfboomsanger)

GARDEN WARBLER *Sylvia borin* (619) 14 cm
Small greyish or olive brown warbler, paler below but without any marked contrasts or distinctive features. The head is rounded, with an indistinct pale eyebrow stripe.
SEXES alike. IMM. resembles ad. HABITAT. Thick tangles in a range of forest, bush and riverine habitats. STATUS. Common summer visitor. CALL. Often located by its subdued, monotonous song, interspersed with soft grating phrases. (Tuinsanger)

WHITETHROAT *Sylvia communis* (620) 14 cm
The male's grey head contrasts with the silvery white throat and rufous wing panel.
FEMALE has a brown head. IMM. lacks white outer tail feathers. HABITAT. Dry thornveld thickets, often near water. STATUS. Locally common summer visitor. CALL. Soft 'whit' and grating 'tchack' and 'tchurr' alarm calls and a song which is a harsh, snappy mixture of grating and melodious notes. (Witkeelsanger)

EUROPEAN BLACKCAP *Sylvia atricapilla* (911) 14 cm
Male not likely to be confused with Bush Blackcap (p. 298) because of its smaller size and its black (not pink) bill and feet.
FEMALE and IMM. have a brown or blackish-brown cap. HABITAT. Thick bush and forest edge. STATUS. Very rare summer vagrant. CALL. Similar to Garden Warbler's but more varied and less subdued. (Swartkroonsanger)

YELLOWTHROATED WARBLER

WILLOW WARBLER

ICTERINE WARBLER

brown form

yellow form

OLIVETREE WARBLER

GARDEN WARBLER

WHITETHROAT

EUROPEAN BLACKCAP   male

female

BURNTNECKED EREMOMELA *Eremomela usticollis* (656) 10 cm
This small warbler is dark bluish grey above and pale buff below. The main distinguishing marks are around the head and throat where the combination of pale yellow eye, and rufous cheeks and ear coverts are reliable, with the small rusty throat bar often inconspicuous or absent, but diagnostic when seen.
SEXES alike. IMM. lacks rufous patches on face and throat bar. HABITAT. Mainly thornveld but also found in mixed, dry broadleafed woodland and dry rivercourses. Usually in small groups. STATUS. Common resident. CALL. A high-pitched 'chii-cheee-cheee', followed by a sibilant 'trrrrrrrrrr'. (Bruinkeelbossanger)

GREENCAPPED EREMOMELA *Eremomela scotops* (655) 12 cm
The bright yellow underparts, greenish upperparts and greenish-yellow crown are diagnostic and distinguish this species from other eremomelas and similarly coloured warblers. At close range the pale yellow eye is discernible. Resembles a white-eye in jizz and habits.
SEXES alike. IMM. paler and a fresher green above. HABITAT. Open broadleafed woodland and riverine forests. Usually in small groups. STATUS. Uncommon and localized resident. CALL. A repeated 'tweer-tweer-tweer' and a rasping alarm note. (Donkerwangbossanger)

YELLOWBELLIED EREMOMELA *Eremomela icteropygialis* (653) 10 cm
Distinguished from other eremomelas by the combination of olive-grey upperparts and greyish-white throat and breast contrasting with the pale yellow flanks and belly. Intensity and extent of yellow on underparts varies geographically. The dark eye-stripe through the brown eye contrasts with the whitish throat and narrow pale eyebrow stripe. Could be confused with Cape Penduline Tit but is larger and longer billed and lacks the black forehead of that species.
SEXES alike. IMM. has duller yellow underparts. HABITAT. Thornveld, open broadleafed woodland and scrub. Usually solitary or in pairs. STATUS. Common resident. CALL. Song is crombec-like: a high-pitched, frequently repeated 'tchee-tchee-tchuu'. (Geelpensbossanger)

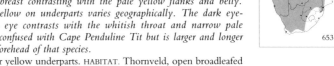

KAROO EREMOMELA *Eremomela gregalis* (654) 12 cm
A long-tailed eremomela distinguished by olive-green upperparts, shading to greyer on face and neck, contrasting with silvery white underparts. The conspicuous pale eye, yellow flanks and undertail coverts distinguish it from the bleating warblers.
SEXES alike. IMM. is browner than ad. HABITAT. Karoo and semi-desert scrub, especially along dry rivercourses. Often in small groups. STATUS. Uncommon, localized resident; endemic. CALL. A wailing 'quee, quee-quee' song. (Groenbossanger)

GREY PENDULINE TIT *Anthoscopus caroli* (558) 8 cm
Lacks the distinctive black forehead, eye-stripe and speckled throat of Cape Penduline Tit and is generally much greyer with buff flanks and belly, whitish on the breast and buff on the face and forehead. Occurs in small groups of three to five.
SEXES alike. IMM. like ad. HABITAT. Broadleafed and miombo woodlands. STATUS. Common resident. CALL. A soft 'chissick' or 'tseeep'. (Gryskapokvoël)

CAPE PENDULINE TIT *Anthoscopus minutus* (557) 8 cm
Distinguished from the eremomelas by its tiny size, short, more conical bill, rotund body and very short tail. Could be confused with Grey Penduline Tit from which it differs by having a black forehead extending as an eye-stripe, yellowish rather than buff belly and flanks and a speckled throat. Black forehead separates it from Yellowbellied Eremomela.
SEXES alike. IMM. has paler yellow underparts. HABITAT. Fynbos, Karoo scrub, semidesert and dry thornveld. STATUS. Common resident; near-endemic. CALL. A soft 'tseep'. (Kaapse Kapokvoël)

BURNTNECKED EREMOMELA

ad.

imm.

GREENCAPPED
EREMOMELA

pale
western
race

YELLOWBELLIED EREMOMELA

KAROO EREMOMELA

GREY PENDULINE TIT

CAPE PENDULINE TIT

321

KNYSNA WARBLER *Bradypterus sylvaticus* (640) 14 cm
This secretive warbler is best located and identified by its song. When seen it is largely olive brown, paler below and smaller than the more widespread Barratt's Warbler, having the spotting restricted to the throat and upper breast. The tail is broad and graduated, but is shorter and squarer than in Barratt's.
SEXES alike. IMM. like ad. HABITAT. Well-wooded gullies, and bracken and briar thickets. STATUS. Uncommon, localized resident; endemic. CALL. A loud, clear song which begins with a 'tseep tseep tseep' and increases to a rattling trill towards the end. (Knysnaruigtesanger)

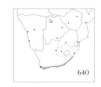

VICTORIN'S WARBLER *Bradypterus victorini* (641) 16 cm
The most colourful of the Bradypterus *warblers, it is distinguished by its reddish-brown cap contrasting with yellow eyes, paler throat and buff-red underparts.*
SEXES alike. IMM. paler below and slightly more rufous above. HABITAT. Short montane fynbos, especially in thicker tangles alongside streams, gullies and damp areas. STATUS. Common, localized resident; endemic. CALL. Diagnostic: a clear, repeated 'weet-weet-weeeo', accelerating towards the end. (Rooiborsruigtesanger)

BARRATT'S WARBLER *Bradypterus barratti* (639) 15 cm
Very similar to African Sedge Warbler in appearance but never frequents reedbeds. Its song, more heavily spotted breast, larger size and longer, heavy, rounded tail distinguish Barratt's Warbler from Knysna Warbler. This secretive species keeps close to, and often feeds and runs on, the ground.
SEXES alike. IMM. has slightly warmer coloration, being more olive above and yellowish below. HABITAT. Thick tangled growth on the edges of evergreen forests and plantations. STATUS. Locally common resident; altitudinal migrant. CALL. A harsh 'chrrrrr' alarm note and an explosive 'seee-pllip-pllip' song. (Ruigtesanger)

BROADTAILED WARBLER *Schoenicola brevirostris* (642) 17 cm
The most conspicuous feature is the long, broad, black tail which is tipped with buff on the underside. This feature is most conspicuous in flight or after heavy rains when the bird is often seen perched on grass stems drying out its tail and wings. The shape of the head is also distinctive with the flattened forehead and culmen forming an almost straight line.
SEXES alike. IMM. has yellowish rather than buffy-white underparts. HABITAT. Long rank grass adjoining rivers, dams and damp areas. STATUS. Resident at lower altitudes, but a summer visitor to higher areas. Locally common but easily overlooked, especially outside the breeding season. CALL. A soft, metallic 'zeenk' repeated at intervals of a few seconds, and a clear, high-pitched 'peee, peee'. (Breëstertsanger)

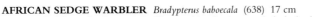

AFRICAN SEDGE WARBLER *Bradypterus baboecala* (638) 17 cm
Distinguished from all other reed-dwelling warblers by its very dark dusky brown coloration, dappled throat and breast and long, rounded tail. Tends to skulk but does a peculiar display flight over reedbeds with rapidly beating wings.
SEXES alike. IMM. like ad. HABITAT. Reed and sedge beds. STATUS. Locally common resident with local movements. CALL. A harsh, ratchet-like 'brrrup...brrrup... trrp...trrp...trrp' song which speeds up towards the end, and a nasal 'nneeeuu'. (Kaapse Vleisanger)

KNYSNA WARBLER

VICTORIN'S WARBLER

BARRATT'S WARBLER

BROADTAILED WARBLER

AFRICAN SEDGE WARBLER

RIVER WARBLER *Locustella fluviatilis* (627) 13 cm
*Distinguished from other 'marsh' warblers by its browner upperparts and its gradu-
ated, rounded tail which is usually a warmer brown than the back. The underparts are
buff with the throat whiter and with dark streaking on the throat and breast. The
sides of the breast and the flanks have a darker wash and the undertail coverts are
brown with broad white tips. Very secretive.*
SEXES alike. IMM. tends to be a warmer rufous above and creamy buff below. HABITAT.
Thickets, often in riverine scrub. STATUS. Rare summer visitor. CALL. Usually only
detected by its buzzy, insect-like 'derr–derr–zerr–zerr' call. (Sprinkaansanger)

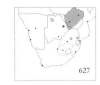

CAPE REED WARBLER *Acrocephalus gracilirostris* (635) 17 cm
*Larger than African Marsh Warbler and appearing much whiter below and around the
face with a distinct white eyebrow stripe. The bill is long and heavy and the legs are
dark brown. This bird is brown above and buffy white below with a distinctive rufous
wash on the flanks. The most easily seen of the reed warblers.*
SEXES alike. IMM. resembles ad. HABITAT. Reedbeds adjoining wetlands. STATUS.
Locally common resident. CALL. A rich, fluty 'cheerup-chee-trrrree' song. (Kaapse
Rietsanger)

AFRICAN MARSH WARBLER *Acrocephalus baeticatus* (631) 13 cm
*Very similar to European Marsh Warbler but smaller, warmer brown above, shorter
winged (folded wing does not extend beyond rump as it does in European Marsh
Warbler), and usually found in different habitat.*
SEXES alike. IMM. resembles ad. HABITAT. Usually found over or close to marshy
ground, in reed or sedge beds, or in willow herb and weeds; non-breeding birds may
range into gardens and bushes. STATUS. Common summer visitor. CALL. A harsher,
more churring and repetitive song than that of European Marsh Warbler including
mimicked phrases of other birds. (Kleinrietsanger)

EUROPEAN REED WARBLER *Acrocephalus scirpaceus* (630) 13 cm
In the field distinguishable from European Marsh Warbler only by song.
SEXES alike. IMM. like ad. HABITAT. Although there is some overlap, this species is
more aquatic in habitat than European Marsh Warbler, frequenting reedbeds and rank
vegetation close to water. STATUS. Rare but possibly regular summer visitor to the
extreme north and north-west; vagrant elsewhere. CALL. Song is a typical *Acrocephalus*
mixture of musical and harsh notes 'tchak, tchak, tchak...churr, churr, churr'.
Callnotes include a low 'churrr'. (Hermanse Rietsanger)

EUROPEAN MARSH WARBLER *Acrocephalus palustris* (633) 13 cm
*Similar to African Marsh Warbler but larger, less rufous and longer winged (folded
wing extends beyond rump). It also frequents different habitats.*
SEXES alike. IMM. like ad. HABITAT. Non-aquatic: bracken and briar on mountain
slopes, forest edges, riverine thickets, thick bush and garden shrubberies. STATUS.
Common summer visitor. CALL. Distinguished from African Marsh Warbler's song by
clear melodious phrases. Often mimics other birds. (Europese Rietsanger)

RIVER WARBLER

CAPE REED WARBLER

Wing formulae to show differences
in primary feather emargination

AFRICAN
MARSH WARBLER

EUROPEAN
REED WARBLER

EUROPEAN
MARSH WARBLER

325

AFRICAN MOUSTACHED WARBLER *Melocichla mentalis* (663) 19 cm
This large warbler might be mistaken for the Grassbird (p. 328) but can be separated by its broad, rounded (not untidy) tail, uniform unstreaked rufous back and crown, pale unstreaked breast and single black malar stripe. Broadtailed Warbler (p. 322) is smaller, lacks the malar stripe and has buff tips to the undertail feathers.
SEXES similar. IMM. lacks chestnut forehead. HABITAT. Long rank grass adjoining forests and in open glades, often near streams or damp areas. STATUS. Rare, localized resident. CALL. A melodious, bubbling 'tip-tiptwiddle-iddle-see'. (Breëstertgrasvoël)

GREATER SWAMP WARBLER *Acrocephalus rufescens* (636) 18 cm
Distinguished from Great Reed Warbler by its smaller size, greyish-brown sides to breast, belly and flanks, and darker brown upperparts. Has no white eyebrow stripe. Differs from Cape Reed Warbler (p. 324) by its larger size, darker appearance and its song.
SEXES alike. IMM. like ad. HABITAT. Papyrus swamps. STATUS. Locally common resident in the Okavango region. CALL. A loud 'churrup, churr-churr' interspersed with harsher notes. (Rooibruinrietsanger)

GREAT REED WARBLER *Acrocephalus arundinaceus* (628) 19 cm
A large and robust reed warbler often located by its harsh guttural song. When seen it resembles a large African Marsh Warbler (p. 324) with a long heavy bill and well-defined pale eyebrow stripe. Larger and darker than Basra Reed Warbler.
SEXES alike. IMM. has warmer coloration, underparts showing a buffy-orange wash. HABITAT. Reedbeds and bush thickets; often in proximity to water. STATUS. Common summer visitor. CALL. A prolonged 'chee-chee-chaak-chaak'. (Grootrietsanger)

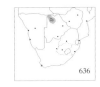

BASRA REED WARBLER *Acrocephalus griseldis* (629) 15 cm
In the field looks like a large, slim 'reed' warbler with a dark tail and a long bill accentuated by the flat forehead. In comparison to Great Reed Warbler the plumage is colder with the upperparts olive-grey and underparts whiter, and build is less robust, closer to smaller 'reed' warblers. Look for the narrow white eyebrow stripe with contrasting dark line through the eye, unstreaked white throat, and greyish legs.
SEXES alike. IMM. like ad. HABITAT. Reedbeds, thickets and rank vegetation, invariably near water. STATUS. Summer vagrant to the east coast. CALL. Not recorded in the region but normally a subdued 'chuc-chuc-churruc-churruc-chuc'. (Basrarietsanger)

YELLOW WARBLER *Chloropeta natalensis* (637) 14 cm
Superficially resembles Icterine Warbler (p. 318) but is distinguished by its darker olive-green upperparts, yellower rump, brighter yellow underparts and dark grey legs. The two species also occupy quite different habitats. Often inconspicuous but sings, and may hawk insects, from an exposed perch.
FEMALE is duller, with less contrast between back and underparts. IMM. like female but with buff wash. HABITAT. Bracken, sedges, rank weeds and tangled vegetation at forest edge. STATUS. Locally common resident with some seasonal altitudinal movements. CALL. A soft 'chip-chip-cheezee-cheeze'. (Geelsanger)

EUROPEAN SEDGE WARBLER *Acrocephalus schoenobaenus* (634) 13 cm
The only 'streaked' Acrocephalus warbler in the region, having an olive-brown back streaked with blackish brown, a short dark brown tail and contrasting unstreaked, more rufous rump. The underparts are creamy white or buff and the head shows a striking broad creamy eyebrow stripe and darker streaked crown. These characters separate it from some of the superficially similar cisticolas which have longer tails with black and white tips.
SEXES alike. IMM. tends to be yellower and more distinctly marked. HABITAT. Reedbeds and rank weedy areas bordering wetlands, and thickets sometimes far from water. STATUS. Common summer visitor. CALL. A harsh churring and chattering interspersed with sharp, melodious phrases and a 'tuk' call. (Europese Vleisanger)

AFRICAN MOUSTACHED WARBLER

GREATER SWAMP WARBLER

BASRA REED WARBLER

GREAT REED WARBLER

YELLOW WARBLER

EUROPEAN SEDGE WARBLER

327

ROCKRUNNER *Achaetops pycnopygius* (662) 17 cm
Spending most of its time on the ground in thick grass or scrambling quickly over rocks, this large warbler can be identified by its heavily streaked dark back, white breast, spotted with black at the sides, and bright rufous belly and undertail.
SEXES alike. IMM. less distinctly marked than ad. HABITAT. Boulder-strewn grassy hillsides and the bases of small hills. STATUS. Fairly common, easily overlooked resident; endemic. CALL. A hollow, melodious warbling 'rooodle-trrooodlee'. (Rotsvoël)

GRASSBIRD *Sphenoeacus afer* (661) 19 cm
The combination of a long, pointed straggly tail, chestnut cap and black malar stripes is diagnostic. The heavily streaked back and the pointed tail eliminate confusion with African Moustached Warbler (p. 326). It is much larger than a cisticola.
SEXES alike. IMM. has streaked cap and is generally duller. HABITAT. Coastal and mountain fynbos, long rank grass on mountain slopes and in river valleys. STATUS. Common resident; endemic. CALL. A nasal 'pheeeoo' and a jangled musical song. (Grasvoël)

CINNAMONBREASTED WARBLER *Euryptila subcinnamomea* (660) 14 cm
Prinia-like, but its generally dark appearance is unlike any other warbler. The rufous breast band, flanks and rump and the frequently cocked black tail are diagnostic.
SEXES alike. IMM. more rufous above. HABITAT. Scrub-covered rocky hillsides, in dry river gullies and gorges. STATUS. Uncommon, localized and easily overlooked resident; endemic. CALL. A shrill, whistled 'peeeee' or 'chreeee'. Song is a short burst of melodious phrases. (Kaneelborssanger)

STIERLING'S BARRED WARBLER *Camaroptera stierlingi* (659) 13 cm
Similar to African Barred Warbler but best distinguished by its white (not buff) underparts more distinctly barred with black, orange-brown (not dark brown) eyes, and flesh-coloured (not brown) legs. Inconspicuous and best located by its call.
SEXES alike. IMM. resembles ad. HABITAT. Mixed thornveld, broadleafed woodland and miombo and mopane woodland. STATUS. Common resident. CALL. A repeated, fast, three-syllable 'plip-lip-lip'. (Stierlingse Sanger)

AFRICAN BARRED WARBLER *Camaroptera fasciolata* (658) 14 cm
A medium-sized warbler with a long tail often held cocked or fanned over its back. The throat and breast are plain brown in the breeding male with the rest of the underparts buff with dusky barring but the undertail coverts are plain, unbarred. Non-breeding males lack the brown throat and breast and are barred from chin to belly. The eyes and legs are brown. Inconspicuous and best located by its call.
FEMALE resembles non-breeding male. IMM. more rufous than adult with a yellowish wash on the breast. HABITAT. Dry thornveld and broadleafed woodland. STATUS. Common resident. CALL. A thin 'trrrreee' and 'pleelip-pleelip'. (Gebande Singer)

GREENBACKED BLEATING WARBLER *Camaroptera brachyura* (657a) 12 cm
Identical to Greybacked Bleating Warbler except that the mantle is green (not grey). Might be confused with Karoo Eremomela (p. 320) which frequents similar habitats but the eremomela has a much longer tail, yellow-washed flanks and a pale (not dark) eye. Has characteristic behaviour of cocking its tail.
SEXES alike. IMM. is slightly streaked below. HABITAT. Moist evergreen forests and scrub. STATUS. Common resident. CALL. A nasal 'neeehhh' and a loud, snapping 'bidup-bidup-bidup'. (Groen Kwê-kwêvoël)

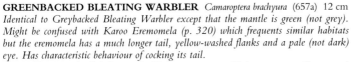

GREYBACKED BLEATING WARBLER *Camaroptera brevicaudata* (657b) 12 cm
A small, rotund warbler with short tail which is often held cocked over its back. Differs from Greenbacked Bleating Warbler by having a grey (not green) mantle when breeding, and an ashy brown mantle when not breeding.
SEXES alike. IMM. is streaked below. HABITAT. Dry woodland and thornveld. STATUS. Common resident. CALL. Like Greenbacked Bleating Warbler's. (Grys Kwê-kwêvoël)

ROCKRUNNER

GRASSBIRD

CINNAMONBREASTED WARBLER

STIERLING'S BARRED WARBLER

AFRICAN BARRED
WARBLER
ad. non-br.

br.

GREENBACKED
BLEATING
WARBLER

GREYBACKED
BLEATING
WARBLER

FAIRY FLYCATCHER *Stenostira scita* (706) 12 cm
Warbler-like in habits; pinkish-grey wash across the breast, a black stripe through the eye topped by a broad white eyebrow stripe, a white stripe in the wing and white outer tail feathers are diagnostic.
SEXES alike. IMM. browner than ad. HABITAT. Karoo scrub and montane fynbos (summer), thornveld (winter). STATUS. Seasonal migrant, breeding in south of range in summer, moving to north of range in winter; endemic. CALL. A repeated, wispy 'tisee-tchee-tchee' and a descending 'cher cher cher'. (Feevlieëvanger)

LAYARD'S TITBABBLER *Parisoma layardi* (622) 15 cm
Paler than Titbabbler. Best distinguishing character is the white (not chestnut) vent. The silvery white eye contrasts with the dark head, and the throat streaking is less pronounced than in Titbabbler. Superficially resembles Fantailed Flycatcher (p. 342) but lacks the tail-spreading action of that species and has streaking on the breast.
SEXES alike. IMM. lacks streaks on throat. HABITAT. Thornveld, coastal fynbos and Karoo scrub, especially in rocky, hilly areas. STATUS. Common resident; endemic. CALL. A clear 'pee-pee-cheeri-cheeri', similar in quality to that of Titbabbler but with different phrasing. (Grysjeriktik)

TITBABBLER *Parisoma subcaeruleum* (621) 15 cm
Darker grey than the very similar Layard's Titbabbler, with chestnut vent, and white on the tail confined to the tip. The streaking on the throat is bolder and more extensive than in Layard's Titbabbler.
SEXES alike. IMM. as ad. but lacks streaks on throat. HABITAT. Thornveld, especially thickets. STATUS. Common resident. CALL. A loud, fluty 'cheruuup-chee-chee', or 'tjerik-tik-tik', hence Afrikaans name. Also imitates calls of other birds. (Bosveldjeriktik)

LONGBILLED CROMBEC *Sylvietta rufescens* (651) 12 cm
Almost tailless; lacks the chestnut breast band and ear patches of Redcapped Crombec and differs from Redfaced Crombec by having a longer bill, brownish (not ashy-grey) upperparts and by lacking the russet tinge to the face.
SEXES alike. IMM. like ad. HABITAT. Woodland, savanna, fynbos and arid scrublands. STATUS. Common resident. CALL. A repeated 'trree-rriit, trree-rriit', and a harsher 'ptttt'. (Bosveldstompstert)

REDFACED CROMBEC *Sylvietta whytii* (650) 11 cm
Appears almost tailless. Distinguished from Longbilled Crombec by having pale ashy-grey upperparts, a noticeably shorter bill, a pale chestnut face and richer, buffier underparts. Differs from Redcapped Crombec by lacking that species' distinctive chestnut ear patches and breast band.
SEXES alike. IMM. brownish grey above. HABITAT. Miombo woodland and riparian forests. STATUS. Locally common resident. CALL. A trilling, repeated 'wit-wit-wit-wit...' and a thin 'si-si-si-see'. (Rooiwangstompstert)

REDCAPPED CROMBEC *Sylvietta ruficapilla* (652) 12 cm
Appears almost tailless. Distinguished from the other two crombec species in the region by its rufous ear patches and breast band. The forehead and crown are a darker chestnut and the back is paler grey than in Redfaced Crombec.
SEXES alike. IMM. buffier above than ad. with buff flecking on wings. HABITAT. Miombo woodland. STATUS. Very rare vagrant. One old specimen record west of Victoria Falls in Zimbabwe. CALL. A ringing, repeated 'richi-chichi-chichir'. (Rooikroonstompstert)

FAIRY FLYCATCHER

LAYARD'S TITBABBLER

TITBABBLER

LONGBILLED CROMBEC

REDCAPPED CROMBEC

REDFACED CROMBEC

BLACKHEADED APALIS *Apalis melanocephala* (647) 14 cm
The only apalis in the region to have black upperparts and white underparts. At close range the white eye, which contrasts strongly with the black cap, is visible.
SEXES alike. IMM. paler than ad.; resembles Chirinda Apalis. HABITAT. Canopy of evergreen, coastal and riverine forests. STATUS. Locally common resident. CALL. A piercing 'wiii-tiiit-wiii-tiiit', repeated many times. (Swartkopkleinjantjie)

CHIRINDA APALIS *Apalis chirindensis* (646) 14 cm
Could be confused with Whitetailed Flycatcher (p. 344) which occurs in the same area but has a slender (not broad, fan-shaped) tail, and completely different habits. A restless bird, it creeps and flits through the canopy when foraging and does not fan its tail or swing from side to side on a perch. No other apalis in the region is uniformly grey in colour.
SEXES alike. IMM. resembles ad., but tinged yellow or green and with a paler bill. HABITAT. Evergreen montane forests. STATUS. Uncommon resident; endemic to the highland forests of Zimbabwe and Mozambique. CALL. A repeated 'chipip chipip'. (Gryskleinjantjie)

YELLOWBREASTED APALIS *Apalis flavida* (648) 13 cm
The combination of grey head, white throat, yellow breast (sometimes with a small black lower bar in males from the south), and white belly, is diagnostic.
SEXES alike but female always lacks black breast bar. IMM. is paler yellow on the breast. HABITAT. Frequents a wide range of woodland habitats but avoids montane evergreen forests. STATUS. Common resident. CALL. A fast, buzzy 'chizzick-chizzick-chizzick', like that of Lesser Honeyguide but more rapid. Pairs often call in duet. (Geelborskleinjantjie)

RUDD'S APALIS *Apalis ruddi* (649) 13 cm
Could be confused with Barthroated Apalis but lacks the white outer tail feathers, has a small white stripe in front of and above the eye, and a dark (not pale) eye. The lime-green back contrasts strongly with the grey head and the bird looks 'neater' than Barthroated Apalis.
SEXES similar but FEMALE has narrower throat band. HABITAT. Thornveld and coastal forests. STATUS. Common resident; endemic. CALL. Male calls a fast 'tuttuttuttut', answered by female with a slower 'clink-clink-clink'. (Ruddse Kleinjantjie)

BARTHROATED APALIS *Apalis thoracica* (645) 13 cm
The only apalis in the region to show both white outer tail feathers and a pale eye. Racially very variable in colour and best distinguished from the similar Rudd's Apalis by the white outer tail feathers and the pale eye, and by the lack of a small white eyebrow stripe.
MALE has broader breast band than female. IMM. resembles ad. HABITAT. Montane forests, wooded kloofs, scrub and fynbos. STATUS. Common resident. CALL. A sharp, rapidly repeated 'pilllip-pilllip-pilllip'; often in duet. (Bandkeelkleinjantjie)

BLACKHEADED APALIS

CHIRINDA APALIS

YELLOWBREASTED APALIS

male
southern race

female

RUDD'S APALIS

male

female

dark form

BARTHROATED APALIS

pale form

333

FANTAILED CISTICOLA *Cisticola juncidis* (664) 10 cm

One of the most abundant and commonly seen of the very small cisticolas. The tail is more boldly marked than in other small cisticolas: black above and below, and broadly tipped with white.
MALE in display flies and calls at a height of 5 to 20 m in undulating flight. It does not snap its wings. FEMALE duller than male. IMM. pale yellow below. HABITAT. Areas of thick grass, especially in damp situations. STATUS. Common resident. CALL. A 'zit', repeated at crest of each undulation during display flight; also a faster 'chit-chit-chit' is given in flight. (Landeryklopkloppie)

DESERT CISTICOLA *Cisticola aridula* (665) 10 cm

Similar to Fantailed Cisticola but is paler and lacks black subterminal bar on tail. Also differs in habitat, display and song.
SEXES alike but female shorter tailed. IMM. paler below. HABITAT. Arid grassland and old fields. STATUS. Common resident. CALL. Song is a fast 'zink zink zink' or 'sii sii sii sii', uttered while making a swooping display flight. When alarmed it utters a 'tuc tuc tuc tuc', and snaps its wings. (Woestynklopkloppie)

CLOUD CISTICOLA *Cisticola textrix* (666) 10 cm

Birds in the southern Cape are easily recognized because of streaking on the breast. Elsewhere, almost indistinguishable from Ayres' and Desert Cisticolas except that this species has a stocky, plump body and unusually long legs and toes.
SEXES alike. IMM. bright yellow below. HABITAT. Grassland. STATUS. Common resident. CALL. A 'see-see-see-see-chick-chick-chick', uttered by displaying male while cruising at great height. Does not snap its wings before landing. (Gevlekte Klopkloppie)

AYRES' CISTICOLA *Cisticola ayresii* (667) 10 cm

Almost indistinguishable from Cloud Cisticola except when heard and seen in display flight. Appears neater and slimmer than Cloud Cisticola, and has shorter legs.
SEXES alike. IMM. paler than ad. HABITAT. Upland grassland and occasionally near the coast. STATUS. Common resident. CALL. Song, a 'soo-see-see-see', is uttered while cruising at a great height. On descending and just before it jinks, loudly snaps its wings many times. (Kleinste Klopkloppie)

PALECROWNED CISTICOLA *Cisticola brunnescens* (668) 10 cm

Male in breeding plumage is easily distinguished from other very small cisticolas as it has black lores contrasting with a pale, buffy crown. In non-breeding plumage it is indistinguishable from Cloud and Ayres' Cisticolas.
FEMALE like non-breeding male. IMM. is yellow below. HABITAT. Frequents damp or marshy areas in upland grassland. STATUS. Uncommon, localized resident. CALL. Display flight is undertaken at both high and low levels. Song is a soft, hardly discernible 'tsee-tsee-tsee-itititititi'. Does not wing snap. (Bleekkopklopkoppie)

SHORTWINGED CISTICOLA *Cisticola brachyptera* (680) 10 cm

Resembles Neddicky but is shorter tailed, has clear buffy underparts, and lacks the rufous crown.
SEXES alike. IMM. has yellowish wash to underparts. HABITAT. Areas of rank grass in miombo woodland. STATUS. Uncommon, localized resident. CALL. A soft, repeated 'see-see-sippi-ippi', uttered from a tree top. (Kortvlerktinktinkie)

NEDDICKY *Cisticola fulvicapilla* (681) 11 cm

The greyish underparts, uniform brownish upperparts and chestnut cap render the southern form one of the easiest cisticolas to identify. The northern form is similar to Shortwinged Cisticola but has buffier underparts, a chestnut cap and a longer tail.
SEXES alike. IMM. yellower than ad. HABITAT. Grassy understorey of woodland, savanna and plantations. STATUS. Common resident. CALL. Song is a monotonous, frequently repeated 'weep' or 'tseep'. Alarm call is a fast 'tictictictic'. (Neddikkie)

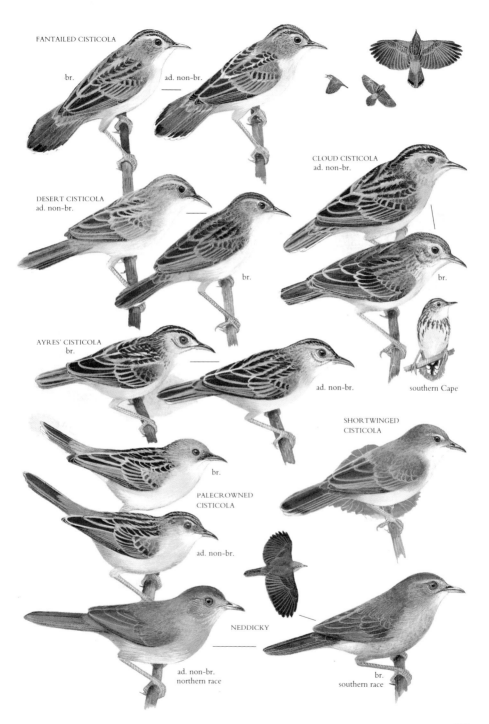

FANTAILED CISTICOLA

br.

ad. non-br.

CLOUD CISTICOLA
ad. non-br.

DESERT CISTICOLA
ad. non-br.

br.

br.

AYRES' CISTICOLA
br.

ad. non-br.

southern Cape

SHORTWINGED
CISTICOLA

br.

PALECROWNED
CISTICOLA

ad. non-br.

NEDDICKY

ad. non-br.
northern race

br.
southern race

GREYBACKED CISTICOLA *Cisticola subruficapilla* (669) 13 cm
The southern form has a diagnostic grey back finely streaked with black, but the northern form is very difficult to distinguish from Wailing Cisticola. The main difference lies in the underpart coloration which, in Greybacked Cisticola, is a cold greyish buff, not the warm buff on the belly and flanks of Wailing Cisticola.
SEXES alike. IMM. duller than ad., with a yellowish face. HABITAT. Fynbos and Karoo scrub. STATUS. Very common resident; near-endemic. CALL. A muffled 'prrrrrrt' and sharp 'hweee phweee' notes. (Grysrugtinktinkie)

WAILING CISTICOLA *Cisticola lais* (670) 13 cm
Distinguished from the northern form of Greybacked Cisticola by having much warmer buff (not cold grey-buff) belly and flanks. The calls and songs of these two species are very similar.
SEXES alike. IMM. washed yellow below. HABITAT. Grassland and bracken on hilly slopes, especially in rocky areas. STATUS. Common resident. CALL. Similar to that of Greybacked Cisticola: a plaintive, drawn-out 'wheee', often accompanied by other shorter notes. (Huiltinktinkie)

TINKLING CISTICOLA *Cisticola rufilata* (671) 14 cm
Long rufous tail, rufous crown and ear patch separated by white eyebrow are diagnostic. Confusion likely only with Rattling Cisticola, which has a duller crown and tail and a different call.
SEXES alike but female has shorter tail. IMM. like ad. HABITAT. Dry broadleafed savanna and scrub. STATUS. Scarce to locally common resident. CALL. A series of tinkling, bell-like notes. (Rooitinktinkie)

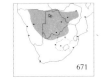

CROAKING CISTICOLA *Cisticola natalensis* (678) 13-17 cm
This large cisticola is unlikely to be confused with any other because of its size, bulky body shape and short tail, and its unusually thick bill. Upperparts are well mottled with dark brown and there is no rufous on the head.
SEXES alike but female is smaller than the male. IMM. warmer brown, with yellowish wash below. HABITAT. Grassland in bush clearings, and grassy hillsides and valleys. STATUS. Common resident. CALL. A deep 'trrrrp' or 'chee-fro' is given during its bounding display flight or from an exposed perch. (Groottinktinkie)

RATTLING CISTICOLA *Cisticola chiniana* (672) 13 cm
Easily confused in plumage coloration with Tinkling Cisticola but has much less red on the head, and the tail is not as brightly rufous.
SEXES alike. IMM. yellower than ad. HABITAT. Woodland, savanna and scrub. STATUS. Common resident. The most obvious and abundant cisticola of the bushveld areas. CALL. Lower pitched rattle at end of short song is diagnostic; may be rendered as 'cher-cher-cher, tooitooitooi'; uttered from top of bush. Alarm a repeated scolding note. (Bosveldtinktinkie)

LAZY CISTICOLA *Cisticola aberrans* (679) 14 cm
In shape and habits, the most prinia-like cisticola of the region (including its habit of jerking the tail) but it differs from any prinia by its rufous crown and warm buffy underparts. Distinguished from Neddicky (p. 334) by its long thin tail which is often held cocked.
SEXES alike. IMM. resembles ad. HABITAT. Grass- and bush-covered hillsides strewn with rocks and boulders. STATUS. Common but localized resident. CALL. Song is a scolding 'tzeeee-tzeeeh-cheee-cheee'. (Luitinktinkie)

northern form

GREYBACKED CISTICOLA

southern form

TINKLING CISTICOLA

ad. non-br.

WAILING CISTICOLA

ad. non-br.

br.

br.

ad. non-br.

tail below

male br.

CROAKING CISTICOLA

male ad. non-br.

male ad. non-br.

female br.

RATTLING CISTICOLA

br.

LAZY CISTICOLA

non-br.

male non br.

br.

BLACKBACKED CISTICOLA *Cisticola galactotes* (675) 13 cm
Most easily confused with Levaillant's Cisticola which also has a black-streaked back. However, this species can be readily distinguished by its call and by its back which is more boldly streaked with black. When breeding it shows a greyish (not red) tail.
SEXES alike. IMM. has a lemon-yellow breast. HABITAT. Reedbeds, long grass and sedges near water. STATUS. Common resident. CALL. A long, harsh 'tzzzzzzrp' and a louder, whistled alarm 'prrrrt'. (Swartrugtinktinkie)

CHIRPING CISTICOLA *Cisticola pipiens* (676) 15 cm
This species could be confused with the similar Blackbacked Cisticola: their distribution ranges overlap and they are often found in association. However, it differs in call, by having its back less boldly streaked with black, and by having a buffish wash on its breast and belly.
SEXES alike. IMM. is white below. HABITAT. Reedbeds and papyrus swamps in the Okavango region. STATUS. Common but localized resident. CALL. A loud 'cheet-cheet-zrrrrr' and 'chwer-chwer-chwer'. (Piepende Tinktinkie)

LEVAILLANT'S CISTICOLA *Cisticola tinniens* (677) 14 cm
Can be confused with Blackbacked Cisticola but normally distinguished by its reddish (not grey) tail and, at close range, it can be seen that the black feathers of its back are edged with brown (not grey). The song and call of this species are different to those of Blackbacked Cisticola.
SEXES alike. IMM. resembles ad. but is yellower below. HABITAT. Reedbeds, sedges and long grass adjacent to rivers and dams. STATUS. Common resident. CALL. A warbling, musical 'chrip-trrrup-trreee' and a wailing 'cheee-weee-weee'. (Vleitinktinkie)

REDFACED CISTICOLA *Cisticola erythrops* (674) 13 cm
Redfaced Cisticola differs from other reed-dwelling cisticolas by having a uniformly coloured (not black-streaked) back. The face, sides of breast and flanks are washed with rufous in non-breeding plumage. Differs from Singing Cisticola by lacking rufous edges to its primaries.
SEXES alike. IMM. resembles ad. but is duller. HABITAT. Reedbeds and rank vegetation bordering streams. STATUS. Common resident. CALL. A series of piercing whistles 'weee, cheee, cheee, cheer, cheer', rising and falling in scale, uttered from a perch. (Rooiwangtinktinkie)

SINGING CISTICOLA *Cisticola cantans* (673) 13 cm
Distinguished from the similar Redfaced Cisticola by having diagnostic rufous edges to the primaries and a rufous cap contrasting with the uniformly grey-brown back. In this species the red on the crown does not envelop the face and ear coverts as it does in Redfaced Cisticola.
SEXES alike. IMM. duller than ad. HABITAT. Long grass in clearings in open woodlands. STATUS. Uncommon localized resident. CALL. A two-syllabled 'jhu-jee' or 'wheecho' uttered from a perch. (Singende Tinktinkie)

REDWINGED WARBLER *Heliolais erythroptera* (682) 13 cm
This long-tailed warbler resembles Tawnyflanked Prinia (p. 340) but is distinguished by its bright rufous wings which contrast with dark brown upperparts. In non-breeding plumage the upperparts assume a rusty colour, blending with the rufous wings.
SEXES alike. IMM. paler than ad. HABITAT. Long grass in woodland clearings and along-side streams. STATUS. Uncommon, localized resident. CALL. A musical 'pseep-pseep-pseep'. (Rooivlerksanger)

INSETS SHOW UNDERTAILS AND OUTER TAIL FEATHERS

br.

BLACKBACKED
CISTICOLA

ad. non-br.

CHIRPING
CISTICOLA
ad. non-br.

br.

ad.
non-br.

LEVAILLANT'S CISTICOLA

ad. non-br.

br.

REDFACED CISTICOLA

centre tail

SINGING CISTICOLA

ad. non-br.

br.

REDWINGED
WARBLER

br.

ad. non-br.

REDWINGED WARBLER

339

NAMAQUA PRINIA *Phragmacia substriata* (687) 14 cm
Likely to be confused only with Spotted Prinia but it differs by having a more russet-coloured back, a longer, wispier tail, and very faint streaking confined to the breast. Unlike Spotted Prinia, it lacks buff tips to its undertail feathers.
SEXES alike. IMM. duller than ad. HABITAT. Thick bush in dry river gullies, and reedbeds adjoining rivers and dams. STATUS. Common resident; endemic to the Karoo. CALL. A high-pitched 'trreep-trreep-trrrrrrrr' song. (Namakwalangstertjie)

RUFOUSEARED WARBLER *Malcorus pectoralis* (688) 15 cm
The reddish ear coverts and narrow black breast band are diagnostic. Prinia-like in appearance and habits, although it forages freely on the ground and often runs swiftly from bush to bush.
SEXES alike but male has broader breast band. IMM. lacks breast band. HABITAT. Arid lowland, fynbos, and Karoo and semi-desert scrub. STATUS. Common resident; endemic. CALL. A scolding 'chweeo, chweeo, chweeo...'. (Rooioorlangstertjie)

DRAKENSBERG PRINIA *Prinia hypoxantha* (686b) 14 cm
Only confusable with Spotted Prinia from which it differs by having a less densely streaked breast, washed with yellow.
SEXES alike. IMM. paler below than ad. HABITAT. Forest edge, wooded gullies and bracken-briar tangles, normally at higher elevations than Spotted Prinia. STATUS. Common resident; endemic. CALL. Similar to Spotted Prinia. (Drakensberglangstertjie)

SPOTTED PRINIA *Prinia maculosa* (686a) 14 cm
Confusable with the closely related Drakensberg Prinia but less yellow below and more heavily streaked on the breast. Distinguished from Namaqua Prinia by having the tail buff-tipped (not plain) and by the more heavily streaked front.
SEXES alike. IMM. yellower below than ad. HABITAT. Fynbos, Karoo scrub and bracken-covered slopes in mountainous terrain. STATUS. Common resident; endemic. CALL. A sharp 'chleet-chleet-chleet' and a faster 'tit-tit-tit-tit'. (Karoolangstertjie)

TAWNYFLANKED PRINIA *Prinia subflava* (683) 11 cm
Distinguished from the non-breeding Blackchested Prinia by having a white (not yellow) throat and breast, warm buff flanks and belly, and russet edges to the wings. Non-breeding Roberts' Prinia is similar but is generally much darker and lacks the russet edges to its wing feathers.
SEXES alike. IMM. as ad. HABITAT. Understorey of broadleafed woodland and thick, rank vegetation adjoining rivers and dams. STATUS. Common resident. CALL. A rapidly repeated 'przzt-przzt-przzt' and a harsh 'chrzzzt'. (Bruinsylangstertjie)

BLACKCHESTED PRINIA *Prinia flavicans* (685) 15 cm
The only prinia in the region with a broad black breast band. This band is usually absent in the non-breeding plumage and the bird might then be mistaken for Tawnyflanked Prinia, but it lacks russet edges to wing feathers and is usually yellow below.
FEMALE has a narrower breast band than the male. IMM. like non-br. ad. but yellower below. HABITAT. Arid scrub, thornveld, exotic plantations and suburban gardens. STATUS. Common resident. CALL. A loud, repetitive 'zzzrt-zzzzrt-zzzrt-zzzrt' note. (Swartbandlangstertjie)

ROBERTS' PRINIA *Prinia robertsi* (684) 14 cm
Unmistakable in breeding plumage when its throat and breast are washed with grey and its upperparts appear very dark. In non-breeding plumage is paler below and could be confused with Tawnyflanked Prinia but has a pale eye and lacks russet edges to the wing feathers.
SEXES alike. IMM. as ad. but with dark eye. HABITAT. Thick bracken and briar adjoining forests. STATUS. Common but highly localized resident; endemic to the highlands of Zimbabwe and Mozambique. CALL. A strident 'cha-cha-cha-cha'. (Woudlangstertjie)

NAMAQUA PRINIA

RUFOUSEARED WARBLER

imm.

ad.

SPOTTED PRINIA

DRAKENSBERG PRINIA

imm.

ad.

TAWNYFLANKED
PRINIA

ROBERTS' PRINIA

buff form
non-br.

br.

br.

BLACKCHESTED PRINIA

non-br.

DUSKY FLYCATCHER *Muscicapa adusta* (690) 12 cm
Smaller and darker than Spotted Flycatcher. At close range, the lack of forehead streaking, which distinguishes these two species, is obvious. The chin is pale and unmarked, the underparts washed grey-brown with ill-defined streaking.
SEXES alike. IMM. spotted with buff above, whitish spotted with brown below. HABITAT. Evergreen forest edges and glades, and riverine forests. STATUS. Common resident. CALL. A soft, high-pitched 'tzzeet' and 'tsirit'. (Donkervlieëvanger)

BLUEGREY FLYCATCHER *Muscicapa caerulescens* (691) 15 cm
In comparison with Fantailed Flycatcher, this species is bluer above, greyer below, and it lacks the white outer tail feathers. Differs in habits from Fantailed Flycatcher by hawking from branches and flying to the ground for food.
SEXES alike. IMM. speckled with buff above and below. HABITAT. Riverine forests and moist, open broadleafed woodland. STATUS. Common resident. CALL. Song is a soft 'sszzit-sszzit-sreee-sreee', descending in scale. (Blougrysvlieëvanger)

SPOTTED FLYCATCHER *Muscicapa striata* (689) 14 cm
Larger than the similar Dusky Flycatcher, this species is also paler below with more definite streaking and blotching on its forehead and underparts. The streaked forehead is diagnostic. Often flicks its wings on alighting.
SEXES alike. IMM. mottled brown and buff, but not likely to be seen in the region. HABITAT. Frequents a wide range of wooded habitats, from the edges of evergreen forests to semi-arid bush. STATUS. Common summer visitor. CALL. A soft 'tzee' and 'zeck, chick-chick'. (Europese Vlieëvanger)

FANTAILED FLYCATCHER *Myioparus plumbeus* (693) 14 cm
White outer tail feathers distinguish it from the otherwise similar Bluegrey Flycatcher. Habits of the two species also differ: Fantailed Flycatcher is found within foliage of trees, frequently fanning its tail as it moves.
SEXES alike. IMM. spotted brown and buff above and below. HABITAT. Riverine forests, mature woodland and savanna. STATUS. Uncommon resident. CALL. A soft, tremulous, whistled 'treee-trooo'. (Waaierstertvlieëvanger)

SOUTHERN BLACK FLYCATCHER *Melaenornis pammelaina* (694) 22 cm
Distinguished from the male Black Cuckooshrike (p. 288) by lacking the yellow gape and by having a square (not rounded) tail. Differs from Squaretailed Drongo (p. 288) by the square (not notched) tail and a brown (not red) eye. Hawks from perches, taking food from the ground.
SEXES alike. IMM. is dull black, scalloped with brown. HABITAT. Woodland, savanna and forest edges. STATUS. Common resident. CALL. Song is a wheezy 'tzzit-terra-loora-loo'. (Swartvlieëvanger)

FISCAL FLYCATCHER *Sigelus silens* (698) 17-20 cm
Often mistaken for Fiscal Shrike (p. 358) but is easily recognized in flight as it has a shorter tail with conspicuous white patches on the sides; its bill is thin and flat (not stubby and hooked), and the white in the wings is confined to the secondaries (not on the shoulders). Larger than male Collared Flycatcher (p. 346) which has a white collar and lacks white tail panels.
FEMALE is brown (not black) above. IMM. is a dull version of female, spotted and scalloped above and below with brown. HABITAT. Bush, scrub, suburban gardens and exotic plantations. STATUS. Common resident; endemic. CALL. A weak, soft, chittering song and a 'tssisk' alarm call. (Fiskaalvlieëvanger)

SPOTTED FLYCATCHER

DUSKY FLYCATCHER

BLUEGREY FLYCATCHER

FANTAILED FLYCATCHER

female

FISCAL
FLYCATCHER

SOUTHERN BLACK
FLYCATCHER

FISCAL SHRIKE

male

(not to scale)

FLYCATCHERS

CHAT FLYCATCHER *Melaenornis infuscatus* (697) 20 cm
A large flycatcher of thrush-like proportions. It is uniform brownish above with paler underparts and a pale brown panel on folded secondaries.
SEXES alike. IMM. is spotted with buff above and below. HABITAT. Dry fynbos, and Karoo and desert scrub. STATUS. Common resident. CALL. Song is a rich, warbled 'cher-cher-cherrip', with squeaky, hissing notes. (Grootvlieëvanger)

MARICO FLYCATCHER *Melaenornis mariquensis* (695) 18 cm
White underparts contrasting with brown upperparts distinguish this species from Mousecoloured Flycatcher. Perches conspicuously along roadsides.
SEXES alike. IMM. is spotted above and streaked below. HABITAT. Thornveld. STATUS. Common resident. CALL. Song is a soft 'tsii-cheruk-tukk'. (Maricovlieëvanger)

MOUSECOLOURED FLYCATCHER *Melaenornis pallidus* (696) 17 cm
The eastern counterpart of Marico Flycatcher, this drab bird differs by having buffish-brown underparts. Smaller than Chat Flycatcher and their ranges do not overlap.
SEXES alike. IMM. paler than ad., mottled with brown and grey. HABITAT. Moist broadleafed woodland. STATUS. Scarce to common resident. CALL. Song is a melodious warbling interspersed with harsh chitters. Alarm call is a soft 'churr'. (Muiskleur-vlieëvanger)

BLUEMANTLED FLYCATCHER *Trochocercus cyanomelas* (708) 18 cm
The glossy black head and shaggy crest render the male unmistakable.
FEMALE could possibly be confused with Whitetailed Flycatcher but is larger, paler grey on the head and throat, has a white wing stripe and lacks white in the tail. IMM. resembles female but is duller buff in colour. HABITAT. Montane, coastal and riverine forests. STATUS. Common resident. CALL. Alarm a harsh 'zweet-zwa' similar to that of Paradise Flycatcher. Song a fluty whistle. (Bloukuifvlieëvanger)

PARADISE FLYCATCHER *Terpsiphone viridis* (710) 23 cm (plus 18 cm tail in male)
The dark head and breast, bright blue bill and eye-ring, and chestnut back and tail render this bird easily identifiable. The male loses its long tail out of the breeding season.
FEMALE has a shorter tail and a duller blue eye-ring and bill. IMM. like female but duller. HABITAT. Evergreen, coastal and riverine forests and bush; also suburban gardens. STATUS. Common summer visitor to most areas, resident in north-east. CALL. Alarm is a harsh 'zweet-zweet-zwayt', similar to Bluemantled Flycatcher. Song is a loud 'twee-tiddly-te-te'. (Paradysvlieëvanger)

VANGA FLYCATCHER *Bias musicus* (699) 16 cm
Male is unmistakable with its diagnostic black crest, black throat and bib, and white wing patch. Male is distinguished from the smaller, female Wattle-eyed Flycatcher (p. 348) by crest and lack of the red wattle over the eye.
FEMALE has a black cap with a slight crest, and a bright chestnut back and tail. IMM. dull version of female, streaked on head. HABITAT. Lowland riverine forests. STATUS. Uncommon resident. CALL. Song is a loud, whistled 'whitu-whitu-whitu' and the alarm note is a sharp 'we-chip'. (Witpensvlieëvanger)

WHITETAILED FLYCATCHER *Trochocercus albonotatus* (709) 15 cm
A small, dark-headed flycatcher easily recognized by its habit of fanning and closing its tail, thereby displaying white outer tail feathers and white spots on the tips of the tail feathers, while moving from side to side on a branch. The female Bluemantled Flycatcher does not display like this and the white in the tail is less conspicuous than in the male.
SEXES alike. IMM. duller than ad. HABITAT. Montane forests. STATUS. Locally common resident. CALL. Song is a fast 'tsee-tsee-teuu-choo' and other jumbled notes, including mimicked calls of other birds. (Witstertvlieëvanger)

CHAT
FLYCATCHER

ad.

imm.

MARICO FLYCATCHER

imm.

ad.

MOUSECOLOURED
FLYCATCHER

male br.

PARADISE
FLYCATCHER

female

female

BLUEMANTLED
FLYCATCHER

male

male

WHITETAILED
FLYCATCHER

female

male

VANGA FLYCATCHER

VANGA FLYCATCHER

male

COLLARED FLYCATCHER *Ficedula albicollis* (692) 12 cm
Male in its pied breeding plumage is unmistakable. It superficially resembles the male Fiscal Flycatcher (p. 343) but that species is much larger and longer tailed, and has no white collar.
FEMALE and NON-BREEDING MALE superficially resemble female Mashona Hyliota but differ by being greyer above and by having a slight grey (not yellow) wash below. Unlike the hyliotas, displays typical flycatcher habits. IMM. resembles female but lacks collar. HABITAT. Miombo and other broadleafed woodland. STATUS. Rare summer visitor. CALL. A 'zip' or soft 'whit-whit-whit'. (Withalsvlieëvanger)

MASHONA HYLIOTA *Hyliota australis* (624) 14 cm
This species is distinguished from the very similar Yellowbreasted Hyliota by having matt blue-black upperparts, a small white panel on the secondary coverts not extending on to the tertials, and pale yellow underparts. Both Hyliota species are distinguished from Collared Flycatcher by having shorter tails and by their habit of foraging in the leafy canopy.
FEMALE has warm brown upperparts, not grey-brown as in the female Yellowbreasted Hyliota. IMM. similar to female but duller. HABITAT. Miombo and other broadleafed woodland. STATUS. Locally common resident. CALL. A high-pitched trilling similar to that of Yellowbreasted Hyliota. (Mashonahyliota)

YELLOWBREASTED HYLIOTA *Hyliota flavigaster* (623) 14 cm
Male distinguished from male Mashona Hyliota by having distinctly glossy blue-black upperparts, more white in the wings and richer yellow underparts.
FEMALE difficult to distinguish from female Mashona Hyliota but has grey-brown (not warm brown) upperparts. IMM. barred with buff above. HABITAT. Miombo and mopane woodland. STATUS. Uncommon resident. CALL. A high-pitched 'trreet trreet'. (Geelborshyliota)

LIVINGSTONE'S FLYCATCHER *Erythrocercus livingstonei* (707) 12 cm
Unmistakable small flycatcher which has a long rufous tail with a black subterminal band (which is not easily seen), sulphur yellow underparts and a blue-grey cap. Continually in motion, flicking and fanning its tail sideways. Usually found in small groups.
SEXES alike. IMM. lacks tail bar. HABITAT. Riverine and coastal forests. STATUS. Locally common resident. CALL. A sharp 'chip-chip' and a clear, warbled song. (Rooistertvlieëvanger)

YELLOW WHITE-EYE *Zosterops senegalensis* (797) 11 cm
The bright sulphur yellow underparts and very pale green, almost yellow upperparts distinguish this species from Cape White-eye. The head is almost completely yellow whereas that of Cape White-eye is green.
SEXES alike. IMM. is a very much paler yellow and green than imm. Cape White-eye. HABITAT. Found in a variety of woodlands, from thornveld to montane forests. STATUS. Common resident. CALL. Similar to that of Cape White-eye. (Geelglasogie)

CAPE WHITE-EYE *Zosterops pallidus* (796) 12 cm
Usually distinguished from Yellow White-eye by its greyish underparts and green (not yellow) upperparts. However, birds in the eastern Transvaal have pale green, almost yellow backs; in which case, only the greyish-green vent and greenish (not yellow) head differentiate this species from Yellow White-eye.
SEXES alike. IMM. duller than ad. HABITAT. Forests, woodland, savanna, exotic plantations, suburban gardens. STATUS. Common resident; endemic. CALL. A soft, sweet 'tweee-tuuu-twee-twee', often repeated. (Kaapse Glasogie)

COLLARED
FLYCATCHER

male br.

female

male
non-br.

MASHONA HYLIOTA

male

male

YELLOWBREASTED
HYLIOTA

LIVINGSTONE'S
FLYCATCHER

female

YELLOW
WHITE-EYE

southern and
western Cape

CAPE WHITE-EYE

CAPE WHITE-EYE

eastern forests

arid west

347

PRIRIT BATIS *Batis pririt* (703) 12 cm
Although the male is very similar to the male Chinspot Batis, their calls differ and their ranges do not overlap.
FEMALE differs from the female Chinspot Batis by having a rufous wash over the throat and breast, not the clearly defined chestnut chin patch. IMM. similar to female. HABITAT. Dry thornveld, broadleafed woodland and dry riverine bush. STATUS. Common resident; near-endemic. CALL. A series of numerous slow 'teuu, teuu, teuu, teuu' notes, descending in scale. (Priritbosbontrokkie)

CAPE BATIS *Batis capensis* (700) 13 cm
Male is the only batis in the region with completely russet-washed wings and flanks.
FEMALE lacks the black breast band of male and has a rufous throat spot. Differs from the smaller female Woodwards' Batis by lacking the complete white eyebrow stripe. IMM. similar to female. HABITAT. Moist evergreen forests and heavily wooded gorges in mountain ranges. STATUS. Common resident; endemic. CALL. A soft 'chewrra-warrra-warrra' and 'foo-foo-foo'. (Kaapse Bosbontrokkie)

WOODWARDS' BATIS *Batis fratrum* (704) 11 cm
Male lacks a black breast band and, although it resembles the female Pririt Batis, their ranges do not overlap.
FEMALE is very similar to the female Chinspot Batis but lacks the obvious chestnut chin patch and has rufous wing panels. IMM. similar to female. HABITAT. Coastal forests and scrub. STATUS. Locally common resident. CALL. A clear, penetrating whistle 'tch-tch-pheeeoooo'. (Woodwardse Bosbontrokkie)

CHINSPOT BATIS *Batis molitor* (701) 13 cm
Male very similar to males of Pririt and Mozambique Batises; latter has narrower breast band and Pririt has indistinct black markings on the flanks, lacking in Chinspot Batis. Calls made by these species are, however, easily distinguishable.
FEMALE has a distinctive, clearly defined rufous spot on the chin, unlike the suffused chestnut on other female batises' throats. IMM. similar to female but has mottled head and breast. HABITAT. Dry broadleafed woodland and dry thornveld. STATUS. Common resident. CALL. A clear descending 'teuu-teuu-teuu' ('three blind mice'), and harsh 'chrr-chrr' notes. (Witliesbosbontrokkie)

MOZAMBIQUE BATIS *Batis soror* (702) 10 cm
The smallest batis in the region. Male is distinguished from the male Chinspot Batis by having a narrower black breast band and a dappled black and white back.
FEMALE is much smaller than the female Chinspot Batis and the chestnut chin patch is ill-defined. IMM. undescribed. HABITAT. Miombo woodland and lowland forests. STATUS. Common resident in northern Mozambique, localized in eastern Zimbabwe. CALL. Soft, frequently repeated 'tcheeo, tcheeo, tcheeo'. (Mosambiekbosbontrokkie)

WATTLE-EYED FLYCATCHER *Platysteira peltata* (705) 18 cm
In the male, the conspicuous, bright red wattle over the eye, the black cap and narrow black breast band are diagnostic.
FEMALE is distinguished from the male Vanga Flycatcher (p. 344) by its much smaller size and by having red eye wattles, a pale rump and by lacking the crest. IMM. resembles female. HABITAT. Coastal and riverine forests and, occasionally, mangrove stands. STATUS. Uncommon and localized resident. CALL. A repeated 'wichee-wichee-wichee-wichee'. (Beloogbosbontrokkie)

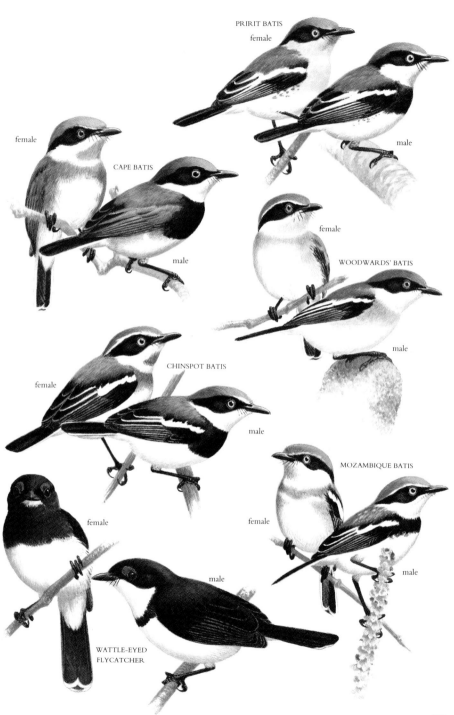

PRIRIT BATIS

female

male

female

CAPE BATIS

male

female

WOODWARDS' BATIS

male

female

CHINSPOT BATIS

male

MOZAMBIQUE BATIS

female

female

male

male

WATTLE-EYED
FLYCATCHER

CAPE WAGTAIL *Motacilla capensis* (713) 18 cm
The unmarked, greyish-brown upperparts, combined with the narrow black breast band, are diagnostic. Distinguished from Longtailed Wagtail by having a shorter tail, buffy (not white) belly and flanks, and by lacking extensive white in the wings.
SEXES alike. IMM. is a duller version of ad. and has a buff-yellow wash over the belly. HABITAT. Usually near fresh water or coastal lagoons but also in city parks and gardens. STATUS. Common resident. CALL. A clear, ringing 'tseee-chee-chee' call and a whistled, trilling song. (Gewone Kwikkie)

AFRICAN PIED WAGTAIL *Motacilla aguimp* (711) 20 cm
Unmistakable large wagtail with black and white pied plumage.
SEXES alike. IMM. might be confused with Cape Wagtail but is distinguished by its white wing coverts. HABITAT. Found along larger rivers and at coastal lagoons. STATUS. Locally common resident. CALL. A loud, shrill 'chee-chee-cheree-cheeroo'. (Bontkwikkie)

GREY WAGTAIL *Motacilla cinerea* (715) 18 cm
This species might be mistaken for Yellow Wagtail but has a blue-grey (not green) back which contrasts with its greenish-yellow rump. The flanks and vent are a bright sulphur yellow. It also has a noticeably longer tail.
BREEDING MALE has a black throat but in non-breeding plumage this is reduced to a speckled area. FEMALE has a white throat. IMM. similar to but duller than female, with a bright yellow vent. HABITAT. Verges of fast-flowing streams and ponds. STATUS. Rare summer vagrant. CALL. A single, sharp 'tit'. (Gryskwikkie)

LONGTAILED WAGTAIL *Motacilla clara* (712) 20 cm
Its unusually long tail, pale grey upperparts and white (not buff) underparts distinguish this species from Cape Wagtail. It also shows more extensive white in the wings and is a more slender bird.
SEXES alike. IMM. browner than ad. HABITAT. Confined to fast-flowing streams in evergreen and coastal forests. STATUS. Locally common resident. CALL. A sharp, high-pitched 'cheeerip' or 'chissik'. (Bergkwikkie)

YELLOW WAGTAIL *Motacilla flava* (714) 16 cm
Confusable only with Grey Wagtail but smaller, has a much shorter tail, and a green (not blue-grey) back. Head colour variable according to race.
FEMALE and NON-BREEDING MALES which are normally seen in the region differ widely in the amount of yellow on the underparts, as a result of racial variation. IMM. yellowish brown above, pale buff below with blackish breast band. HABITAT. Short cropped grassy verges of coastal lagoons, sewage ponds and wetlands. STATUS. Uncommon to locally common summer visitor. Sometimes in flocks. CALL. A weak, thin 'tseeep'. (Geelkwikkie)

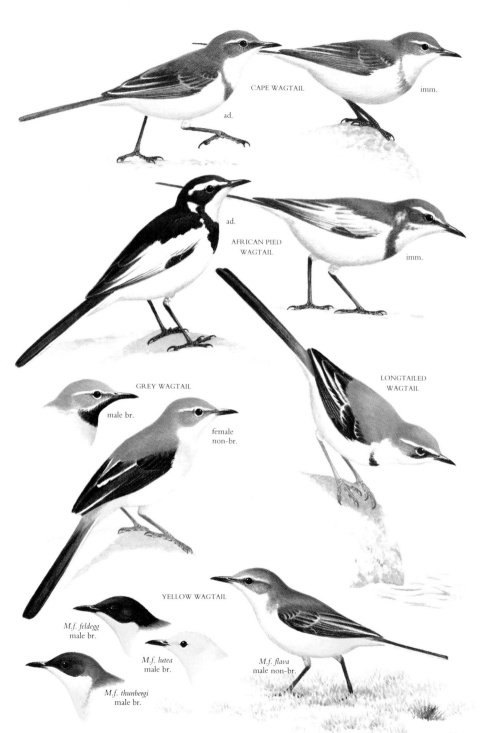

CAPE WAGTAIL

imm.

ad.

ad.

AFRICAN PIED
WAGTAIL

imm.

GREY WAGTAIL

LONGTAILED
WAGTAIL

male br.

female
non-br.

YELLOW WAGTAIL

M.f. feldegg
male br.

M.f. lutea
male br.

M.f. flava
male non-br.

M.f. thunbergi
male br.

 PIPITS

MOUNTAIN PIPIT *Anthus hoeschi* (901) 18 cm
Difficult to distinguish from Grassveld Pipit with which it often associates, but is larger, has bold streaking on the breast, a pink (not yellow) base to the lower mandible and, in flight, shows buff (not white) outer tail feathers. Distinguished from Longbilled and Buffy Pipits by behaviour, display song and heavily marked breast.
SEXES alike. IMM. is more heavily streaked on the underparts than ad. HABITAT. Montane grassland, usually above 2 000 m. STATUS. Common summer visitor; breeding endemic. CALL. Display song, given in flight, closely resembles that of Grassveld Pipit, but slightly deeper in pitch and slower in tempo. (Bergkoester)

GRASSVELD PIPIT *Anthus cinnamomeus* (716) 16 cm
Display flight and song separate it from all species except Mountain Pipit. Differs from Mountain Pipit by its call, the white outer tail feathers and the yellow (not pink) base to its lower mandible. Distinguished from the larger Longbilled Pipit by bolder facial markings and breast streaking, and white (not buff) outer tail feathers.
SEXES alike. IMM. darker above, and has more heavily streaked underparts. HABITAT. Virtually any type of open grassland. STATUS. Common resident. CALL. Song given during display flight is a repeated 3-5 note 'trrit-trrit-trrit', uttered while performing an undulating flight 30-100 m above the ground. (Gewone Koester)

LONGBILLED PIPIT *Anthus similis* (717) 18 cm
Told from Grassveld Pipit by this species' buff (not white) outer tail feathers, less distinct facial markings and streaking on breast, and the song and call. Difficult to distinguish from Mountain Pipit but has a less boldly streaked breast and has a different call and display. Well-marked back separates it from Buffy and Plainbacked Pipits.
SEXES alike. IMM. paler and more heavily spotted than ad. HABITAT. Prefers boulder-strewn hillsides with scant bush cover. STATUS. Locally common resident. CALL. A high-pitched three-note 'tchreep-tritit-churup'. (Nicholsonse Koester)

PLAINBACKED PIPIT *Anthus leucophrys* (718) 17 cm
Differs from Grassveld and Longbilled Pipits by having a uniform, unstreaked back, by lacking distinct breast markings and by its narrow, buff outer tail feathers. Very difficult to distinguish from Buffy Pipit; Plainbacked has yellowish (not pink) base to lower mandible, darker upperparts with contrast between the buffy flanks and belly and stronger breast markings, although this character varies in both species.
SEXES alike. IMM. heavily mottled above. HABITAT. Hillsides covered with short grass and, when not breeding, forms flocks in stubble grain fields. STATUS. Locally common resident, subject to local movements. CALL. A loud, clear 'chrrrup-chereeoo'. Also gives single calls, often in flight, but does not have a display flight. (Donkerkoester)

WOOD PIPIT *Anthus nyassae* (909) 18 cm
Closely resembles Longbilled Pipit, but occurs in woodland rather than open grassland. It has a shorter tail and bill than Longbilled Pipit, and has more extensive pale areas in the base of the outer tail feathers.
SEXES alike. IMM. spotted above and more heavily streaked below. HABITAT. Confined to miombo woodland where it forages in rocky clearings on the ground. STATUS. Locally common resident. CALL. Song similar to that of Longbilled Pipit, but more variable and slightly higher pitched. (Boskoester)

BUFFY PIPIT *Anthus vaalensis* (719) 18 cm
Difficult to distinguish from Plainbacked Pipit but breast markings are often faint, with a rich, buffy belly and flanks. Base of the bill is pink (not yellow). On the ground it behaves more like a wagtail: stops often, and moves its tail up and down.
SEXES alike. IMM. resembles ad. but is mottled above. HABITAT. Similar to that frequented by Plainbacked Pipit (hillsides covered with short grass) but usually at lower altitudes. STATUS. Uncommon resident. CALL. A repeated two-note song, 'tchreep-churup'. When flushed gives a short 'sshik'. (Vaalkoester)

352

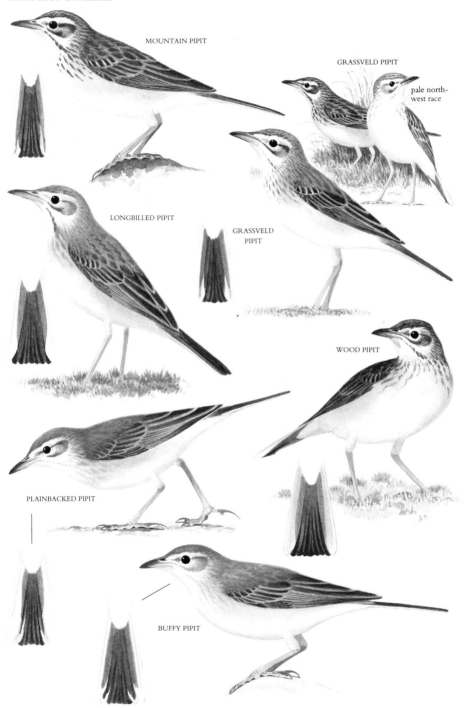

INSETS SHOW UNDERTAILS

MOUNTAIN PIPIT

GRASSVELD PIPIT

pale north-west race

LONGBILLED PIPIT

GRASSVELD PIPIT

WOOD PIPIT

PLAINBACKED PIPIT

BUFFY PIPIT

353

BUSHVELD PIPIT *Anthus caffer* (723) 14 cm

Distinguished from Tree Pipit by being smaller, having a shorter tail, paler plumage, and suffused, less distinct streaking on its breast. Throat is washed brown, with faint streaking, not almost white as in Tree Pipit. In comparison with Short-tailed Pipit, it is larger, has a longer, broader tail and is less heavily streaked below.
SEXES alike. IMM. paler than ad., speckled above. HABITAT. Thornveld and open broadleafed woodland. STATUS. Fairly common but localized resident. CALL. A characteristic 'zeet' as it flies from the ground to a tree; song a treble note: 'zrrrt-zrree-chreee', uttered from a perch in a tree. (Bosveldkoester)

SHORT-TAILED PIPIT *Anthus brachyurus* (724) 12 cm

A small, squat pipit, very much darker and more heavily streaked above and below than either Tree or Bushveld Pipit. In flight, shows a noticeably shorter, thinner tail than other small pipits. When flushed flies off speedily, resembling a large cisticola, with the white outer tail feathers showing clearly.
SEXES alike. IMM. resembles ad. HABITAT. Grassy hillsides, scantily covered with protea scrub, and grassy glades in miombo woodland. Natal population winters on Zululand coastal plain. STATUS. Resident and local migrant. CALL. Calls from perches or during circling display flights. Similar to Bushveld Pipit, a buzzy, bubbling 'chrrrrt-zhrrrreet-zzeeep'. (Kortstertkoester)

REDTHROATED PIPIT *Anthus cervinus* (903) 15 cm

Most likely to be confused with Tree Pipit but is darker, has clear white underparts heavily streaked with black, and a streaked (not uniformly coloured) rump. In breeding plumage, the dull red throat and breast are diagnostic.
SEXES alike. IMM. does not occur in the region. HABITAT. Damp grassland, usually near water. STATUS. Very rare vagrant, with one record from Natal. CALL. A clear, penetrating 'chup', and a buzzy 'skeeeaz'. (Rooikeelkoester)

TREE PIPIT *Anthus trivialis* (722) 15 cm

Longer tailed and larger than either Bushveld or Short-tailed Pipit and has a short bill. Shows much more contrast between the pale throat and dark upperparts than the other two species. Differentiated with difficulty from Redthroated Pipit, but has less clearly streaked underparts and lacks dark brown streaking on rump.
SEXES alike. IMM. buffier than ad. HABITAT. Grassy areas in open broadleafed woodland. STATUS. Scarce summer visitor. CALL. A soft, nasal 'teeez' given in flight or when flushed. Song is melodic and canary-like. (Boomkoester)

ROCK PIPIT *Anthus crenatus* (721) 17 cm

A drab, uniformly coloured pipit with a stout, heavy bill. At a distance, the pale eye-stripe is the only plumage feature evident. Only at close range can the very faint, narrow streaking on the breast and the greenish edges to the secondary coverts be seen. Usually located by its distinctive song; fairly secretive when not calling.
SEXES alike. IMM. similar to ad., but mottled above. HABITAT. Boulder-strewn, steep, grassy hillsides, and Karoo koppies. STATUS. Locally common resident; endemic. CALL. A carrying 'tseeet-tserrroooo', the second note descending. Calls with typical erect stance, bill pointed upwards, from a low perch. (Klipkoester)

STRIPED PIPIT *Anthus lineiventris* (720) 18 cm

A fairly plump, heavily built pipit which differs from all others by its boldly striped underparts, the dark stripes extending on to the belly. The dark upperparts have variably yellow-edged wing feathers, and the tail is very dark with conspicuous white outer tail feathers.
SEXES alike. IMM. paler than ad., speckled above. HABITAT. Thickly wooded, boulder-strewn hillslopes. STATUS. Locally common resident. CALL. A loud, penetrating thrush-like song, uttered from a rock or tree perch. (Gestreepte Koester)

BUSHVELD PIPIT

SHORT-TAILED PIPIT

TREE PIPIT

br.

REDTHROATED PIPIT

ad. non-br.

STRIPED PIPIT

ROCK PIPIT

YELLOWBREASTED PIPIT *Anthus chloris* (725) 17 cm

The only pipit in the region to show an all-yellow throat and breast. The upperparts are heavily streaked and blotched, giving a scaled appearance, and are similar to those of a longclaw. In flight, the yellow underparts and underwing coverts are diagnostic. In non-breeding plumage it lacks the yellow underparts and is identified by its boldly scaled upperparts and plain buffy underparts.
SEXES alike. IMM. buff below, paler than ad. above. HABITAT. Short dense grassland at altitudes above 1 500 m. STATUS. Uncommon resident; endemic. CALL. A rapid, repeated 'chip, chip, chip', like the call of a displaying male Longtailed Widow; also a subdued 'suwiep'. (Geelborskoester)

GOLDEN PIPIT *Tmetothylacus tenellus* (726) 15 cm

Although it resembles a diminutive bright golden Yellowthroated Longclaw, the predominantly bright yellow upper- and underwings render this bird unmistakable.
FEMALE and IMM. duller than the male on the breast and lack the black breast band. HABITAT. Open dry broadleafed woodland and thornveld. STATUS. A rare summer vagrant, with records from Zimbabwe and the Transvaal. CALL. A short burst of scratchy notes. (Goudkoester)

YELLOWTHROATED LONGCLAW *Macronyx croceus* (728) 20 cm

Could be confused with Golden Pipit (which is smaller, much brighter and more extensively yellow) and with imm. Orangethroated Longclaw (which has a browner, more uniform back and a greatly reduced collar).
SEXES alike but female duller. IMM. differentiated from imm. Orangethroated Longclaw by being buff-yellow below and by having bright yellow edging to its wing feathers. HABITAT. Grassland adjoining freshwater areas, coastal estuaries and lagoons. Also in well-grassed savanna woodland away from water. STATUS. Common resident. CALL. A loud, whistled 'phooooeeet' or series of loud whistles, frequently uttered from a perch on top of a bush or small tree. Also calls in flight. (Geelkeelkalkoentjie)

ORANGETHROATED LONGCLAW *Macronyx capensis* (727) 20 cm

Could be confused with Yellowthroated Longclaw but has deeper yellow underparts and a diagnostic orange throat encircled with black. Unlike Yellowthroated Longclaw, seldom lands in trees when disturbed.
FEMALE duller than male. IMM. has a yellow throat with a vestigial collar; differs from imm. Yellowthroated Longclaw by having buffish to orange underparts, and wing feathers edged with buff (not yellow). HABITAT. Wide range of coastal and upland grassland. STATUS. Common resident and the most widespread longclaw; endemic. CALL. A fairly melodious song, 'cheewit-cheewit', often given in flight. Also a cat-like mewing alarm call and a loud, high-pitched 'tsweet' contact call. (Oranjekeel-kalkoentjie)

PINKTHROATED LONGCLAW *Macronyx ameliae* (730) 20 cm

Much more pipit-like in shape than either Yellow- or Orangethroated Longclaw, being slender and long tailed. The pink throat and breast are diagnostic. White outer tail feathers, extending right up to the base of the tail, show clearly in flight.
FEMALE and IMM. lack the black breast band and are less pink but still show a rosy hue over the belly and flanks. HABITAT. Moist grassland surrounding open areas of fresh water. STATUS. Uncommon and patchily distributed resident. CALL. A sharp, pipit-like 'chiteeet'. (Rooskeelkalkoentjie)

male
non-br.

YELLOWBREASTED PIPIT

imm.

male br.

female

GOLDEN PIPIT

male

YELLOWTHROATED
LONGCLAW

ORANGETHROATED
LONGCLAW

imm.

male

PINKTHROATED LONGCLAW

male

CRIMSONBREASTED SHRIKE *Laniarius atrococcineus* (739) 23 cm
Striking combination of bright crimson underparts and black upperparts renders it unmistakable. A rare form occurs in which the crimson is replaced with yellow.
SEXES alike. IMM. is barred greyish brown with varying amounts of crimson below; above, finely barred black with buff edges to the feathers. HABITAT. Thornveld, dry rivercourses, and semi-arid scrub. STATUS. Common resident; near-endemic. CALL. A harsh 'trrrrr' and a whistled 'qwip-qwip' duet. (Rooiborslaksman)

LONGTAILED SHRIKE *Corvinella melanoleuca* (735) 40-50 cm
The combination of the black and white plumage and long, wispy tail is diagnostic. Gregarious, often in groups of 4-8 birds.
FEMALE has a slightly shorter tail and whiter flanks than male. IMM. is shorter tailed than ad. and dull black with fine barring. HABITAT. Thornveld. STATUS. Common resident. CALL. A liquid, whistled 'peeleeo'. (Langstertlaksman)

SOUSA'S SHRIKE *Lanius souzae* (734) 17 cm
Resembles a very pale female Redbacked Shrike but is easily distinguished by its white shoulder patches and very pale grey head. Distinguished from imm. Fiscal Shrike by its smaller size and by the lack of crescentic barring below.
FEMALE similar to male but with pale rufous flanks. IMM. lacks grey on head and is barred below. HABITAT. Miombo and mopane woodlands. STATUS. Vagrant to the extreme north-central region. CALL. Soft grating sounds. (Souzase Laksman)

REDBACKED SHRIKE *Lanius collurio* (733) 17 cm
In the region, the only shrike with a chestnut-coloured back and grey crown.
MALE'S blue-grey head and rump and the light underparts contrast with the chestnut back and are diagnostic. FEMALE and IMM. are duller reddish brown above and have greyish-brown crescentic barring below. HABITAT. Thornveld and savanna. STATUS. Common summer visitor. CALL. A harsh 'chak, chak' and a soft, warbler-like song. (Rooiruglaksman)

LESSER GREY SHRIKE *Lanius minor* (731) 21 cm
In comparison with Redbacked Shrike, this species is larger, has a more extensive black mask which encompasses the forehead, and a grey (not chestnut) back.
FEMALE duller, often with less black on forehead. IMM. differs from the imm. and female Redbacked Shrikes by its much larger size and buffier, less barred underparts. HABITAT. Mixed dry thornveld and semi-desert scrub. STATUS. Common summer visitor. CALL. A soft 'chuk'. Warbled song heard before migration. (Gryslaksman)

FISCAL SHRIKE *Lanius collaris* (732) 23 cm
One of the most common shrikes of the region, hunting from exposed perches along roadsides and in suburbia. The Puffback (p. 364) and boubou shrikes (p. 360) are also black and white but are shy, skulking birds. Fiscal Flycatcher (p. 342) male similar but lacks the white shoulder patches and white outer tail feathers. Races in the arid west and north-west have a conspicuous white eyebrow stripe.
MALE is black above, white below with prominent white shoulder patches. FEMALE like male but shows a rufous patch on the flanks. IMM. is greyish brown with grey crescentic barring below. HABITAT. Found in virtually every habitat except dense forest. STATUS. Common resident. CALL. Harsh grating, a melodious whistled song jumbled with harsher notes, and mimicry of other bird calls. (Fiskaallaksman)

CRIMSONBREASTED SHRIKE

yellow form

imm.

ad.

male

LONGTAILED
SHRIKE

imm.

SOUSA'S
SHRIKE

female

male

REDBACKED
SHRIKE

FISCAL SHRIKE

imm.

male

LESSER
GREY
SHRIKE

arid
west

SOUTHERN BOUBOU *Laniarius ferrugineus* (736) 23 cm
Similar to Fiscal Shrike (p. 358) but has a shorter tail, has the white in the wing extending on to the secondaries, and is retiring in its habits. Distinguished from Tropical and Swamp Boubous by having rufous flanks, undertail and belly.
FEMALE slightly greyer above with rufous wash on breast. IMM. is mottled buff-brown above, barred below. HABITAT. Thickets in riverine and evergreen forests. STATUS. Common resident; endemic. CALL. A variable duet with basic notes of 'boo-boo' followed by a whistled 'whee-ooo'. (Suidelike Waterfiskaal)

TROPICAL BOUBOU *Laniarius aethiopicus* (737) 23 cm
Easily confused with Southern Boubou but is paler below, showing a more marked contrast between its black upperparts and pinkish-white underparts. The pink-tinged underparts distinguish this species from Swamp Boubou which is pure white below.
SEXES alike. IMM. duller than ad. and spotted buffy above and below. HABITAT. Thickets, riverine and evergreen forests, and gardens. STATUS. Common resident. CALL. Duet call, distinctive and different from that of Southern Boubou. Whistles, croaking 'haw' and tearing 'weer-weer' calls. (Tropiese Waterfiskaal)

SWAMP BOUBOU *Laniarius bicolor* (738) 23 cm
Distinguished from both Southern and Tropical Boubous by having pure white underparts with no trace of rufous or pink coloration.
SEXES alike. IMM. spotted buff above, barred below. HABITAT. Thickets alongside rivers, and papyrus swamps. STATUS. Common resident. CALL. Duets consist of whistled 'hoouu' and harsh rattling sounds. (Moeraswaterfiskaal)

BLACKCROWNED TCHAGRA *Tchagra senegala* (744) 23 cm
The black forehead and crown, and paler underparts distinguish this species from other tchagras. It is also larger, bolder and more conspicuous in its behaviour.
SEXES alike. IMM. has mottled crown and a horn-coloured bill. HABITAT. Mixed thornveld and riverine scrub. STATUS. Common resident. CALL. Song is a loud, whistled 'whee-cheree, cherooo, cheree-cherooo' on a descending scale, slurring towards the end. (Swartkroontjagra)

MARSH TCHAGRA *Tchagra minuta* (745) 18 cm
This marsh-dwelling shrike is easily identified by its black cap, russet upperparts and creamy to buff underparts.
FEMALE has a broad white eyebrow stripe. IMM. is similar to female but has an off-white crown. HABITAT. Rank bracken and sedges growing in damp hollows, and marshy areas with long grass. STATUS. Uncommon localized resident. CALL. A shrill, trilling song is given in display flight. (Vleitjagra)

THREESTREAKED TCHAGRA *Tchagra australis* (743) 19 cm
Very similar in appearance to Southern Tchagra, this species has a paler crown and forehead, and its broad white eyebrow stripe is bordered by black stripes. It is also smaller and paler, and has a less massive bill.
SEXES alike. IMM. duller than ad. HABITAT. Thick tangles and undergrowth in thornveld. STATUS. Common resident. CALL. Aerial display flight and song are very similar to those of Southern Tchagra. (Rooivlerktjagra)

SOUTHERN TCHAGRA *Tchagra tchagra* (742) 21 cm
Differs from the similar Threestreaked Tchagra by having a longer, heavier bill and by lacking conspicuous black stripes bordering its buff eyebrow stripe. It is also slightly larger and darker in appearance.
SEXES alike. IMM. duller than ad. HABITAT. Coastal scrub, forest edges and thickets. STATUS. Common resident; endemic. CALL. Song given in aerial display is a 'wee-chee-chee-cheee', descending in pitch. (Grysborstjagra)

SOUTHERN BOUBOU

SWAMP BOUBOU

TROPICAL BOUBOU

MARSH TCHAGRA

female

male

BLACKCROWNED TCHAGRA

THREESTREAKED TCHAGRA

SOUTHERN TCHAGRA

361

GREYHEADED BUSH SHRIKE *Malaconotus blanchoti* (751) 26 cm
Its large size and heavy, hooked bill eliminate confusion with Orangebreasted and Blackfronted Bush Shrikes. The bright yellow underparts sometimes have a faint orange wash across the breast.
SEXES alike. IMM. has greyish, barred head, and is pale yellow below. HABITAT. Thornveld and mixed broadleafed woodland. STATUS. Common resident. CALL. A drawn-out 'oooooop' (hence colloquial name of Ghostbird) and a 'tic-tic-oooop'. (Spookvoël)

BOKMAKIERIE *Telophorus zeylonus* (746) 23 cm
The bright lemon yellow underparts and broad black breast band are diagnostic. The vivid yellow tip to the dark tail is conspicuous in flight.
SEXES alike. IMM. lacks breast band and is greyish green below. HABITAT. Fynbos, Karoo scrub and suburban gardens. STATUS. Common resident; endemic. CALL. Very varied, but is usually a 'bok-bok-kik'. (Bokmakierie)

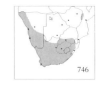

GORGEOUS BUSH SHRIKE *Telophorus quadricolor* (747) 19 cm
More often heard than seen, but the bright red throat, black breast band and yellow-orange belly are diagnostic.
FEMALE duller than male. IMM. has a yellow throat, lacks the black breast band, and is distinguished from imm. Orangebreasted and Blackfronted Bush Shrikes by having green (not grey) upperparts. HABITAT. Dense tangled thickets. STATUS. Common resident. CALL. An often-repeated 'kong-kong-kooit' and variations of this call. (Konkoit)

BLACKFRONTED BUSH SHRIKE *Telophorus nigrifrons* (749) 19 cm
Confusable with Orangebreasted Bush Shrike (which lacks the broad black face mask and forehead and has a yellow eyebrow), and the olive form of Olive Bush Shrike (which has a green, not black forehead).
FEMALE has reduced black on forehead and is duller than male. IMM. has buff-yellow, barred underparts. HABITAT. A less skulking species than other bush shrikes, it frequents the canopy of evergreen forests. STATUS. Uncommon, localized resident. CALL. A harsh 'tic-chrrrrr' and a ringing 'oo-pooo' call. (Swartoogboslaksman)

OLIVE BUSH SHRIKE *Telophorus olivaceus* (750) 18 cm
Occurs in two colour forms. The ruddy form has a blue-grey head and, unlike any other bush shrike, has a white eyebrow stripe. The olive form is duller: the bird has a green (not blue-grey) head and lacks the white eyebrow stripe.
FEMALE of both forms lacks black on cheeks. IMM. of both forms lacks ad. head markings and is faintly barred below. HABITAT. Evergreen and riverine forests. STATUS. Common resident; endemic. CALL. Varied, includes a whistled 'cheeoo-cheeoo-cheeoo-cheeoo' and a call similar to Orangebreasted Bush Shrike's 'poo-poo-poo-poooo'. (Olyfboslaksman)

ORANGEBREASTED BUSH SHRIKE *Telophorus sulfureopectus* (748) 19 cm
Differs from all other similar bush shrikes by having a conspicuous yellow forehead and eyebrow stripe. Superficially resembles a diminutive Greyheaded Bush Shrike.
FEMALE is duller than the male. IMM. is distinguished from imm. Blackfronted Bush Shrike by being paler grey on the head and paler yellow below. Resembles imm. Olive Bush Shrike (ruddy phase). HABITAT. Thornveld and riverine forests. STATUS. Common resident. CALL. Frequently repeated 'poo-poo-poo-pooooo' and a 'titit-eeezz'. (Oranjeborsboslaksman)

imm.

GREYHEADED
BUSH SHRIKE

imm.

ad.

BOKMAKIERIE

imm.

GORGEOUS BUSH SHRIKE

ad.

ad.

imm.

BLACKFRONTED
BUSH SHRIKE

female

male

female

OLIVE
BUSH SHRIKE

imm.

olive form

ruddy form

ad.

ORANGEBREASTED
BUSH SHRIKE

imm.

CHESTNUTFRONTED HELMETSHRIKE *Prionops scopifrons* (755) 18 cm
*The chestnut-coloured forehead distinguishes this species from Redbilled Helmetshrike.
It also differs by having a dark grey (not jet black) body. Gregarious.*
SEXES alike. IMM. uniform grey, lacks bristly chestnut forehead. HABITAT. Lowland
forests. STATUS. Uncommon and localized resident. CALL. A repeated 'churee', with
bill-snapping and other notes. (Stekelkophelmlaksman)

REDBILLED HELMETSHRIKE *Prionops retzii* (754) 22 cm
*Differs from Chestnutfronted Helmetshrike by being larger, lacking the chestnut forehead,
by having a red eye-ring, and by its jet black (not dark grey) plumage. Gregarious.*
SEXES alike. IMM. paler than ad. with brown eye-ring, bill and legs. HABITAT. Mostly
mopane and miombo woodlands. STATUS. Common resident. CALL. Harsh grating
calls, much like those of White Helmetshrike. (Swarthelmlaksman)

WHITE HELMETSHRIKE *Prionops plumatus* (753) 20 cm
*The grey crown, white collar, white flashes in the wings and the white outer tail
feathers are diagnostic. Gregarious.*
SEXES alike. IMM. duller than ad. with brown eye and lacks yellow eye-ring and black
ear coverts. HABITAT. Mixed woodland and thornveld. STATUS. Common resident
with local movements and occasional 'invasions' beyond its normal range. CALL. A
repeated 'cherow', often taken up by the group in chorus. (Withelmlaksman)

WHITETAILED SHRIKE *Lanioturdus torquatus* (752) 15 cm
*The striking black, white and grey plumage, long legs and very short, white tail are
diagnostic. Often seen on the ground or hopping over rocks and, with its very upright
posture, it appears almost tailless.*
SEXES alike. IMM. similar to ad. but with mottled crown. HABITAT. Dry thornveld and
scrub desert. STATUS. Common resident; near-endemic. CALL. Clear, drawn-out
whistles and harsh cackling. (Kortstertlaksman)

PUFFBACK *Dryoscopus cubla* (740) 18 cm
*The only shrike in the region to have a large white rump which is conspicuous (in
male) when it is spread and puffed up during display. At other times, the bird
resembles a small boubou but is shorter tailed, has white wing coverts and a bright
red eye.*
MALE glossy black above. FEMALE duller than male, has a white eyebrow. IMM. similar
to female, but has a brown eye. HABITAT. A wide variety of woodland and forests.
STATUS. Common resident. CALL. A sharp, repeated 'chick, weeo'. (Sneeubal)

SOUTHERN WHITECROWNED SHRIKE *Eurocephalus anguitimens* (756) 24 cm
*This large, robust bird is the only shrike in the region to have a white crown and fore-
head. The throat and breast are also white, while the belly and flanks are washed
with buff. Gregarious, usually in groups of 5-6 birds.*
SEXES alike. IMM. paler than ad., mottled crown. HABITAT. Mixed, dry woodland and
thornveld. STATUS. Common resident. CALL. A shrill, whistling 'kree, kree, kree',
bleating and harsh chattering. (Kremetartlaksman)

BRUBRU *Nilaus afer* (741) 15 cm
*Could be mistaken for a large batis but its size and thick bill should obviate confu-
sion. The black and white chequered back, broad white eyebrow stripe and russet flank
stripe are diagnostic.*
FEMALE duller than male. IMM. mottled buff and brown above and below. HABITAT.
Dry thornveld and open broadleafed woodland. STATUS. Common resident. CALL. A
soft, trilling 'prrrrr' by male, often answered by 'eeeu' from female. (Bontroklaksman)

CHESTNUTFRONTED
HELMETSHRIKE

REDBILLED
HELMETSHRIKE

WHITE HELMETSHRIKE

WHITETAILED SHRIKE

female

PUFFBACK

male

PUFFBACK

female

BRUBRU

male

male display

SOUTHERN
WHITECROWNED
SHRIKE

GREATER BLUE-EARED STARLING *Lamprotornis chalybaeus* (765) 23 cm
*Distinguished from Glossy Starling by having a broad dark blue (not green) ear patch,
and blue (not green) belly and flanks. Larger than Lesser Blue-eared Starling, it also
has a broader ear patch, and blue (not magenta) belly and flanks.*
SEXES alike. IMM. less glossy than ad. HABITAT. Thornveld and mopane woodland.
STATUS. Common resident. CALL. A distinctive nasal 'squee-aar' (unlike any call of
Glossy Starling) and a warbled song. (Groot-blouoorglansspreeu)

LESSER BLUE-EARED STARLING *Lamprotornis chloropterus* (766) 20 cm
*Although it could be confused with Greater Blue-eared Starling, this is a smaller bird
with a more compact head and a finer bill. The dark blue ear patch is less extensive
and appears as a black line through and behind the eye. The belly and flanks are
magenta (not blue).*
SEXES alike. IMM. has distinctive chestnut underparts or mottled blue and brown
plumage. HABITAT. Confined to miombo woodland. STATUS. Common but localized
resident. CALL. Higher pitched than that of Greater Blue-eared Starling, and with a
'wirri-girri' flight call. (Klein-blouoorglansspreeu)

GLOSSY STARLING *Lamprotornis nitens* (764) 25 cm
*The short-tailed 'glossy' starlings are difficult to distinguish in the field unless seen at
close range. This species differs from Greater and Lesser Blue-eared Starlings by having uniform glossy green ear patches and head, and glossy green belly and flanks.
Distinguished from the smaller Blackbellied Starling by its generally brighter, shinier
plumage and by lacking the dull black belly.*
SEXES alike. IMM. duller than ad., with dull straw-yellow (not bright orange-yellow)
eyes. HABITAT. Thornveld, mixed woodland and suburbia. STATUS. Common and
widespread resident. CALL. Song is a slurred 'trrr-chree-chrrrr'. (Kleinglansspreeu)

PLUMCOLOURED STARLING *Cinnyricinclus leucogaster* (761) 19 cm
*Male's upperparts and throat are an unusual glossy amethyst colour; out of breeding
season becomes dull purplish brown.*
FEMALE is mottled and streaked dark brown above, and the white underparts are heavily streaked with brown. IMM. resembles female, with dark eyes. HABITAT. Found in
most woodland but avoids thick, evergreen forests. STATUS. Common summer visitor.
CALL. A soft, but sharp 'tip, tip'. Song is a short series of buzzy whistles. (Witbors-
spreeu)

BLACKBELLIED STARLING *Lamprotornis corruscus* (768) 21 cm
*The smallest and least glossy of all the starlings in this group, having a black belly
and flanks.*
MALE has bronze gloss on belly which is visible at close range. FEMALE and IMM. are
duller than the male and appear black in the field. HABITAT. Coastal and riverine
forests. STATUS. Locally common resident; irregular visitor in the extreme south of its
range. CALL. Harsh, chippering notes interspersed with shrill whistles. (Swartpens-
glansspreeu)

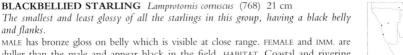

GREATER BLUE-EARED STARLING

LESSER BLUE-EARED STARLING

ad.

imm.

GLOSSY STARLING

BLACKBELLIED STARLING

male non-br.

PLUMCOLOURED
STARLING

female

male br.

367

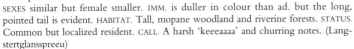

BURCHELL'S STARLING *Lamprotornis australis* (762) 34 cm
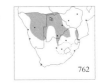
A large, glossy starling which is more heavily built and larger than Longtailed Starling. This species has broader, more rounded wings and a shorter, broader tail.
SEXES alike. IMM. duller than ad. HABITAT. Thornveld and dry, broadleafed woodland. STATUS. Common resident. CALL. Song is a jumble of throaty chortles and chuckles. (Grootglansspreeu)

LONGTAILED STARLING *Lamprotornis mevesii* (763) 34 cm

The long, pointed tail is diagnostic. Although similar, this species is a smaller, more compact bird than Burchell's Starling. These are the only two glossy starlings with dark eyes when adult.
SEXES similar but female smaller. IMM. is duller in colour than ad. but the long, pointed tail is evident. HABITAT. Tall, mopane woodland and riverine forests. STATUS. Common but localized resident. CALL. A harsh 'keeeaaaa' and churring notes. (Langstertglansspreeu)

SHARPTAILED STARLING *Lamprotornis acuticaudus* (767) 26 cm

Difficult to distinguish from the other short-tailed glossy starlings unless the diagnostic wedge-shaped tail is seen. In flight, the underside of the primaries appears pale (not black as in similar starlings).
SEXES differ in eye colour: red in the male, orange in female. IMM. duller than ad., greyish below, with buff-edged feathers. HABITAT. Dry, broadleafed woodland and dry rivercourses. STATUS. Uncommon resident. CALL. A reedy 'chwee-chwee-chwee' when in a flock. (Spitsstertglansspreeu)

PALEWINGED STARLING *Onychognathus nabouroup* (770) 26 cm

Could be confused with Redwinged Starling but has a white (not chestnut) patch in the primaries, visible only in flight. Shows a bright orange (not dark) eye.
SEXES alike. IMM. duller than ad. HABITAT. Rocky ravines and cliffs in dry and desert regions. STATUS. Common resident; near-endemic. CALL. In flight, ringing 'preeoo'; warbling calls like those of Glossy Starling, quite unlike the whistles of Redwinged Starling. (Bleekvlerkspreeu)

REDWINGED STARLING *Onychognathus morio* (769) 27 cm

Bright chestnut flight feathers and dark (not orange) eyes distinguish this species from Palewinged Starling.
FEMALE has an ash grey head and upper breast. IMM. resembles the male, with a dark head. HABITAT. Rocky ravines, cliffs and suburbia. STATUS. Common resident. CALL. A clear, whistled 'cherleeeeoo' and a variety of other musical whistles. (Rooivlerkspreeu)

BURCHELL'S STARLING

LONGTAILED STARLING

SHARPTAILED
STARLING

imm.

ad.

PALEWINGED
STARLING

female

REDWINGED STARLING

male

INDIAN MYNA *Acridotheres tristis* (758) 25 cm
The only myna of the region and unlikely to be confused with any starling because of its white wing patches, white tips to tail feathers and bare yellow skin around the eyes. Moulting adults sometimes lose most of their head feathers and the head then appears yellow.
SEXES alike. IMM. paler than ad. HABITAT. Urban and suburban regions. STATUS. Locally abundant resident. CALL. Jumbled titters and chattering. (Indiese Spreeu)

EUROPEAN STARLING *Sturnus vulgaris* (757) 21 cm
Male is easily identified by its yellow beak and glossy black plumage which is speckled with white.
FEMALE has paler abdomen and is more speckled. IMM. similar to the female Wattled Starling but is uniform grey, lacks the pale rump, and has a dark bill. HABITAT. Frequents a wide range of habitats, from cities to open farmland, but always close to human habitation. STATUS. Common to abundant resident. CALL. Song includes mimicry, whistles and chattering. (Europese Spreeu)

WATTLED STARLING *Creatophora cinerea* (760) 21 cm
Short-tailed and pointed-winged like European Starling, but always shows greyish-white rump in flight.
BREEDING MALE is distinctive with its pale grey body, black and yellow head and black wattles; all ad. males have black wings and tail. FEMALE is grey with a whitish rump. IMM. resembles female but is browner. HABITAT. Grassland and open broadleafed woodland. Often in large flocks. STATUS. Common resident, subject to local movements. CALL. Various hisses and cackles, and a 'ssreeeeo' note. (Lelspreeu)

PIED STARLING *Spreo bicolor* (759) 27 cm
This large, dark brown starling is distinguished by its conspicuous white vent and undertail coverts. At close range the diagnostic yellow base to the lower mandible and the bright creamy-white eyes can be seen.
SEXES alike. IMM. is matt black, with a dark eye and paler base to the bill. HABITAT. Grassland and Karoo scrub, often around farmyards and stock. Usually in flocks. STATUS. Common resident; endemic. CALL. A loud 'skeer-kerrra-kerrra'; also a warbling song. (Witgatspreeu)

REDBILLED OXPECKER *Buphagus erythrorhynchus* (772) 22 cm
Distinguished from Yellowbilled Oxpecker by having an all-red bill, bare yellow skin around its eyes and a dark (not pale) rump.
SEXES alike. IMM. has a yellow base to a black bill and is darker than imm. Yellowbilled Oxpecker, showing a dark (not pale) rump. HABITAT. Savanna, in association with game and cattle. Usually in flocks. STATUS. Common resident in game reserves; scarce elsewhere. Formerly more widespread. CALL. A scolding 'churrrr' and a hissing 'zzzzzzist'. (Rooibekrenostervoël)

YELLOWBILLED OXPECKER *Buphagus africanus* (771) 22 cm
Paler than Redbilled Oxpecker and easily identified by its bright yellow bill with a red tip, and pale lower back and rump.
SEXES alike. IMM. has a brown (not black) bill and is paler than imm. Redbilled Oxpecker. HABITAT. Thornveld and broadleafed woodland, often near water. Frequently found in association with buffalo, rhino and hippo. Usually in flocks. STATUS. Locally common resident, formerly more widespread. CALL. A short, hissing 'kriss, kriss'. (Geelbekrenostervoël)

INDIAN MYNA

imm.

EUROPEAN STARLING

ad. non-br.

ad. br.

WATTLED STARLING

male br.

ad. non-br.

PIED STARLING

YELLOWBILLED OXPECKER

REDBILLED OXPECKER

ad.

ad.

imm.

imm.

371

CAPE SUGARBIRD *Promerops cafer* (773) m=34-44 cm; f=25-29 cm
Confusion between this species and Gurney's Sugarbird should not occur except in the narrow area where their ranges overlap. The Cape Sugarbird is easily recognized by its exceptionally long, wispy tail; lacks the russet breast and crown of Gurney's Sugarbird and has distinct malar stripes.
MALE. Tail constitutes 65% or more of total body length. FEMALE. Tail constitutes only 50% of total body length. IMM. tail relatively short, and lacks yellow undertail. HABITAT. Stands of flowering proteas on mountain slopes, and in commercial protea nurseries. STATUS. Common resident; endemic. CALL. A complex song, including starling-like chirps and whistles, and harsh grating noises. (Kaapse Suikervoël)

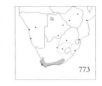

GURNEY'S SUGARBIRD *Promerops gurneyi* (774) m=29 cm; f=23 cm
Unlikely to be confused with Cape Sugarbird because of its smaller size, shorter tail, and conspicuous russet breast and crown.
SEXES often indistinguishable; males usually have marginally longer tails. IMM. (resembles female). HABITAT. Stands of flowering proteas and aloes in mountainous regions. STATUS. Common but localized resident; some movement to lower altitudes in winter. Endemic. CALL. A higher pitched, more melodious rattling song than that of Cape Sugarbird. (Rooiborssuikervoël)

MALACHITE SUNBIRD *Nectarinia famosa* (775) m=25 cm; f=15 cm
Breeding male has a metallic green plumage with yellow pectoral tufts and elongated central tail feathers. Bronze Sunbird also has tail projections but that species appears black in the field.
MALE in eclipse plumage resembles female, sometimes has a few metallic green feathers. FEMALE is very similar to the female Bronze Sunbird with its brown back but is larger, paler yellow below and lacks distinct streaking. IMM. similar to female. HABITAT. Fynbos, protea- and aloe-covered hills, and mountain scrub. STATUS. Common resident. In winter there is some movement to lower altitudes. CALL. A loud 'tseep-tseep'. Song is a series of twittering notes. (Jangroentjie)

BRONZE SUNBIRD *Nectarinia kilimensis* (776) m=21 cm; f=14 cm
Slightly smaller than the similarly shaped Malachite Sunbird.
MALE'S metallic bronze plumage appears black unless seen in good light. No eclipse plumage in male. FEMALE is similar to the female Malachite Sunbird but is smaller, has a shorter, more decurved bill, and has brighter yellow underparts which are distinctly streaked with brown. Has slightly elongated central tail feathers. IMM. resembles female. HABITAT. Evergreen forest edges, bracken and adjoining grassland. STATUS. Common but localized resident. CALL. A loud, piercing 'chee-wit', repeated at half-second intervals. Also high-pitched twittering. (Bronssuikerbekkie)

ORANGEBREASTED SUNBIRD *Nectarinia violacea* (777) m=15 cm; f=12 cm
The dark head, orange-yellow breast and belly, and elongated central tail feathers of the male are diagnostic.
FEMALE is larger than the female Lesser Doublecollared Sunbird (p. 378) and is a more uniform olive green above and below. IMM. resembles female. HABITAT. Fynbos, and flowering montane protea and aloe stands. STATUS. Common resident; endemic. CALL. A metallic twanging; rapid 'ticks' in pursuit flight. (Oranjeborssuikerbekkie)

CAPE SUGARBIRD

male

female

GURNEY'S SUGARBIRD

female

male

(smaller scale)

male br.

MALACHITE SUNBIRD

female

male eclipse plumage

male

female

BRONZE SUNBIRD

male

female

ORANGEBREASTED SUNBIRD

male sub-ad.

SCARLETCHESTED SUNBIRD *Nectarinia senegalensis* (791) 15 cm
The male's black body and scarlet chest are diagnostic. No eclipse plumage.
FEMALE is greyish olive above and distinguished from the female Black Sunbird by the very heavily mottled underparts. IMM. resembles female. HABITAT. Woodland, savanna and suburban gardens. STATUS. Common and widespread resident. CALL. A loud, whistled 'cheeup, chup, toop, toop, toop' song. (Rooikeelsuikerbekkie)

BLACK SUNBIRD *Nectarinia amethystina* (792) 15 cm
At a distance the male appears all black, but at close range a greenish iridescence can be seen on the forehead, and the throat is metallic purple. No eclipse plumage.
FEMALE could be confused with the female Scarletchested Sunbird but has paler underparts, which are streaked rather than mottled. IMM. resembles female. HABITAT. Forest edge, woodland, savanna and suburban gardens. STATUS. Common resident. CALL. A fast, twittering song. (Swartsuikerbekkie)

COPPERY SUNBIRD *Nectarinia cuprea* (778) 12 cm
Male resembles a small Bronze Sunbird (p. 372) but lacks the elongated central tail feathers of that species.
FEMALE is smaller than the female Malachite and Bronze Sunbirds (p. 372), and is brighter yellow below, with faint speckling on the throat and breast. IMM. resembles ad. female, but imm. male shows a dark throat. HABITAT. Diverse: usually found in woodland, forest edges and clearings, and riverine forests. STATUS. Uncommon, localized breeding summer visitor. CALL. A harsh 'chit-chat', and a soft warbling song. (Kopersuikerbekkie)

SHELLEY'S SUNBIRD *Nectarinia shelleyi* (781) 12 cm
Occurs in association with the similar Miombo Doublecollared Sunbird (p. 378), but the male can be distinguished by its black (not pale olive) belly, and green (not blue) rump. This species is similar to Neergaard's Sunbird (p. 378) but their distribution ranges do not overlap.
FEMALE differs from the female Miombo Doublecollared Sunbird by having the yellow underparts lightly streaked with brown. IMM. resembles female. HABITAT. Miombo and riverine scrub. STATUS. Uncertain: recently reported from south bank of the Zambezi River, east of Lake Kariba. CALL. Described as a 'didi-didi', and a nasal 'chibbee-cheeu-cheeu' song. (Swartpenssuikerbekkie)

GREY SUNBIRD *Nectarinia veroxii* (789) 14 cm
A dully-coloured sunbird which has uniformly grey underparts and darker grey upperparts. It differs from Olive Sunbird in its call, by its grey (not olive) coloration and, when seen, by its red (not yellow) pectoral tufts. At close range a subtle green wash can be seen on the forehead and wrist.
SEXES alike. IMM. resembles ad. but more olive below. HABITAT. Coastal and riverine forests. STATUS. Common but localized resident. CALL. A harsh, grating 'tzzik, tzzik' and a short 'chrep, chreep, peepy' song. (Gryssuikerbekkie)

OLIVE SUNBIRD *Nectarinia olivacea* (790) 14 cm
Generally dull olive, darker above, paler below. The yellow pectoral tufts are often concealed when the bird is perched. Likely to be confused only with Grey Sunbird which occurs in the same habitat.
SEXES alike. IMM. paler on throat. HABITAT. Coastal, riverine and mistbelt forests and moist, broadleafed woodland. STATUS. Common resident. CALL. A sharp 'tuk, tuk, tuk' and an accelerating, descending piping song. (Olyfsuikerbekkie)

374

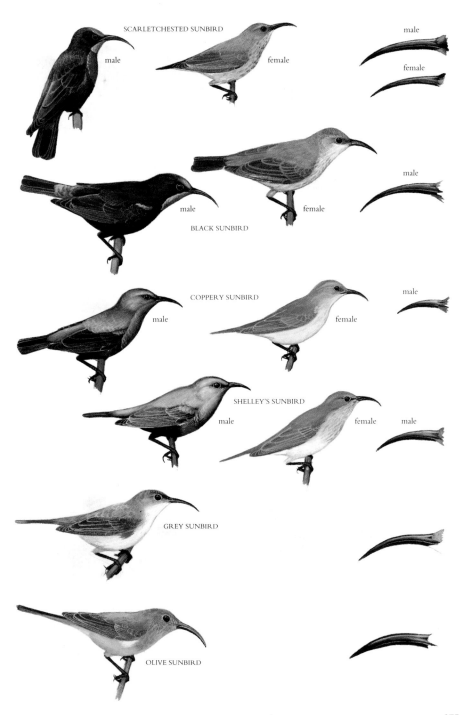

SCARLETCHESTED SUNBIRD

male

female

male

female

BLACK SUNBIRD

male

female

male

COPPERY SUNBIRD

male

female

male

SHELLEY'S SUNBIRD

male

female

male

GREY SUNBIRD

OLIVE SUNBIRD

COLLARED SUNBIRD *Anthreptes collaris* (793) 10 cm
Smaller than the similarly coloured Yellowbellied Sunbird, with a much shorter bill and a green (not blue) throat extending only to the upper breast.
FEMALE is metallic green above, uniformly yellow below and resembles a small warbler. IMM. resembles female. HABITAT. Mistbelt, coastal and riverine forests, and dense woodland. STATUS. Common resident. CALL. A soft 'tswee' and a harsh, chirpy song. (Kortbeksuikerbekkie)

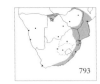

BLUETHROATED SUNBIRD *Anthreptes reichenowi* (794) 10 cm
Size of Collared Sunbird, but slimmer bodied, and bright yellow below with dull, brownish-green upperparts. The short, almost straight, black bill imparts a warbler-like appearance.
MALE shows a blue-black throat patch and forehead. Confusion possible with imm. male Yellowbellied and Whitebellied Sunbirds moulting into full ad. plumage. FEMALE'S dull green upperparts distinguish her from the female Collared Sunbird. IMM. resembles female. HABITAT. Mixed moist woodland and coastal forests. STATUS. Uncommon to locally common resident. CALL. A sharp 'tik-tik'. (Bloukeelsuikerbekkie)

YELLOWBELLIED SUNBIRD *Nectarinia venusta* (786) 11 cm
The male superficially resembles Collared Sunbird but has a much longer bill, is more blue than green on the back and head, and has a broad purple breast band.
FEMALE resembles the female Whitebellied Sunbird but differs by having a pale yellow belly and flanks. IMM. resembles female. Imm. male can resemble ad. male Bluethroated Sunbird, but has a small metallic green wrist patch and lacks the blue forehead. HABITAT. Miombo and broadleafed riverine woodland. STATUS. Locally common resident in Zimbabwe and Mozambique, with vagrants further south. CALL. A 'tsui-tse-tse' and a trilling song. (Geelpenssuikerbekkie)

WHITEBELLIED SUNBIRD *Nectarinia talatala* (787) 11 cm
The male is the only sunbird in the region to have a bottle-green head and breast, and a white belly.
FEMALE is very similar to the females of several other species: uniform dull brown above, off-white below with a few indistinct streaks. IMM. resembles female. Imm. male can resemble ad. male Bluethroated Sunbird, but has a small metallic green wrist patch and lacks the blue forehead. HABITAT. Drier woodland and savanna; parks and gardens. STATUS. Common and widespread resident. CALL. A loud 'pichee, pichee', followed by a rapid tinkle of notes. (Witpenssuikerbekkie)

VIOLETBACKED SUNBIRD *Anthreptes longuemarei* (795) 13 cm
The male's violet head, back and tail are diagnostic and are conspicuous in sunlight.
FEMALE is brown above and white below, with a violet-coloured tail, and a conspicuous white eyebrow stripe. IMM. lacks the violet on the tail and resembles an imm. Whitebellied or Yellowbellied Sunbird but has a very much shorter bill. HABITAT. Miombo woodland. STATUS. Uncommon localized resident. CALL. A sharp 'chit-chit' or 'skee'. (Blousuikerbekkie)

DUSKY SUNBIRD *Nectarinia fusca* (788) 10 cm
The slightly metallic black head, throat and back, and contrasting white belly are diagnostic in the male. However, male plumage is variable and sometimes has only a black line running from the throat on to the breast. The pectoral tufts are orange.
FEMALE is light grey-brown above, off-white below. Resembles the female Lesser Doublecollared (p. 378) and Whitebellied Sunbirds but is paler and more uniformly coloured below. IMM. resembles female but has blackish throat. HABITAT. Dry thornveld, dry, wooded rocky valleys and scrub desert. STATUS. Common resident; near-endemic. CALL. A 'chrrrr-chrrrr' and a short warbling song. (Namakwasuikerbekkie)

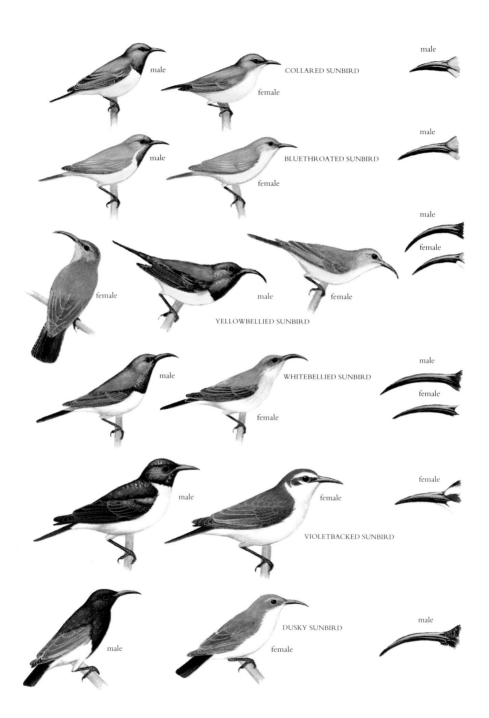

male

female

COLLARED SUNBIRD

male

male

male

BLUETHROATED SUNBIRD

male

female

male

female

female

male

female

YELLOWBELLIED SUNBIRD

male

WHITEBELLIED SUNBIRD

male

female

female

female

male

female

VIOLETBACKED SUNBIRD

male

female

DUSKY SUNBIRD

male

male

female

377

GREATER DOUBLECOLLARED SUNBIRD *Nectarinia afra* (785) 14 cm
Larger than Lesser Doublecollared Sunbird, and has a longer, heavier bill and a much broader red breast band.
FEMALE has upperparts grey-brown, underparts yellow-grey. Differs from female Lesser Doublecollared Sunbird by its longer, heavier bill, and larger size. IMM. resembles female. HABITAT. Fynbos, evergreen scrub, mountainous terrain, and suburbia. STATUS. Common resident; endemic. CALL. A harsh, frequently repeated 'tchut-tchut-tchut' and a fast twittering song. (Grootrooiborssuikerbekkie)

LESSER DOUBLECOLLARED SUNBIRD *Nectarinia chalybea* (783) 12 cm
Male is very similar to but smaller than Greater Doublecollared Sunbird, and distinguished from that species by having a shorter bill and a narrower red breast band.
FEMALE. Of the species with which it co-exists, it is most similar to the female Orangebreasted Sunbird (p. 372), but is greyer below. IMM. resembles female. HABITAT. Coastal scrub, fynbos and forests. STATUS. Common resident; endemic. CALL. A harsh 'chee-chee' and a fast, variable, rising and falling song. (Klein-rooiborssuikerbekkie)

MIOMBO DOUBLECOLLARED SUNBIRD *Nectarinia manoensis* (784) 13 cm
Occurring in the same habitats as the very similar Shelley's Sunbird (p. 374), this species is differentiated by its pale olive (not black) belly. In the field, the male of this species, apart from its grey upper rump, is virtually indistinguishable from Lesser Doublecollared Sunbird. However, their ranges do not overlap.
FEMALE is buffy green above, pale yellowish grey below. IMM. resembles female. HABITAT. Miombo woodland and the edges of montane forest. STATUS. Common resident. CALL. Similar to that of Lesser Doublecollared Sunbird. (Miombo-rooiborssuikerbekkie)

MARICO SUNBIRD *Nectarinia mariquensis* (779) 14 cm
Distinguished from the very similar Purplebanded Sunbird by its larger size and longer, thicker bill, and broader purple breast band. Differs from the doublecollared sunbirds by its black (not grey) belly and from Shelley's (p. 374) and Neergaard's Sunbirds by its purple (not red) breast band.
FEMALE has upperparts grey-brown, underparts pale yellow, streaked dusky. Distinguished from female Purplebanded by being larger and having a longer, thicker bill. IMM. resembles female. HABITAT. Thornveld and dry broadleafed woodland. STATUS. Common resident. CALL. A long series of closely spaced 'tsip's and a fast, warbling song. (Maricosuikerbekkie)

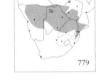

NEERGAARD'S SUNBIRD *Nectarinia neergaardi* (782) 10 cm
Within its restricted range, the male of this green and black sunbird cannot be confused with any other sunbird. It is small, with a thin, short, decurved bill, a black belly and a red breast band.
FEMALE has upperparts greyish brown, underparts pale dull yellow. Differs from the female Purplebanded Sunbird (with which it co-exists) by its paler, unstreaked underparts. IMM. resembles female. HABITAT. Thornveld and sand forests. STATUS. A common but very localized resident; endemic. CALL. A thin, wispy 'weesi-weesi-weesi' and a short, chippy song. (Bloukruissuikerbekkie)

PURPLEBANDED SUNBIRD *Nectarinia bifasciata* (780) 12 cm
Smaller than Marico Sunbird, and has a thinner, shorter and less decurved bill.
MALE differs from the male Neergaard's Sunbird by having a purple (not red) breast band. FEMALE is less yellow below and has a shorter bill than the female Marico Sunbird. IMM. resembles female but has a dark throat. HABITAT. Thornveld, moist broadleafed woodland and coastal scrub. STATUS. Common resident. CALL. A high-pitched 'teeet-teeet-tit-tit' song, accelerating at the end, never sustained as is the call of Marico Sunbird. (Purperbandsuikerbekkie)

male

female

GREATER
DOUBLECOLLARED SUNBIRD

male

male

LESSER
DOUBLECOLLARED SUNBIRD

female

male

female

MIOMBO
DOUBLECOLLARED SUNBIRD

male

female

male

female

MARICO SUNBIRD

male

female

male

female

NEERGAARD'S SUNBIRD

male

female

male

female

PURPLEBANDED SUNBIRD

GREAT SPARROW *Passer motitensis* (802) 15 cm
Differs from House Sparrow by its larger size, bright chestnut back and sides of head, and chestnut (not grey) rump.
FEMALE is larger and much redder on the back and shoulders than the female House Sparrow. IMM. resembles female. HABITAT. Dry thornveld; not usually associated with human habitation. STATUS. Locally common resident. CALL. A 'cheereep, cheereeu', very similar to that of House Sparrow. (Grootmossie)

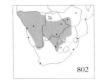

HOUSE SPARROW *Passer domesticus* (801) 14 cm
The male is easily recognized by its grey crown and rump, reddish-brown back, black throat and white cheeks. Distinguished from Great Sparrow by lacking the bright chestnut rump.
FEMALE and IMM. are a dull grey-brown and show a narrow off-white eye-stripe which differentiates them from Yellowthroated Sparrow. HABITAT. Towns, cities and gardens; rarely away from human habitation. STATUS. Common to abundant resident. CALL. Various chirps, chips and a 'chissick'. (Huismossie)

CAPE SPARROW *Passer melanurus* (803) 15 cm
Male is unmistakable: it is the only sparrow in the region to have a pied head.
FEMALE is distinguished from the female House and Great Sparrows by having a grey head with faint shadow markings of the male's pied head pattern, and a chestnut back. IMM. resembles female. HABITAT. Grassland, grain fields, and human habitation. STATUS. Common resident; near-endemic. CALL. A series of musical cheeps. (Gewone Mossie)

GREYHEADED SPARROW *Passer griseus* (804) 15 cm
The chestnut rump, back and wings, combined with the unmarked grey head, should preclude confusion with any other sparrow. Female House, Great and Cape Sparrows superficially resemble this species but all have white or buff head markings. Bill black in breeding season, dull yellow in winter.
SEXES alike. IMM. duller than ad. HABITAT. Mixed woodlands and, in some regions, suburbia. STATUS. Common resident. CALL. Various chirping notes. (Gryskopmossie)

YELLOWTHROATED SPARROW *Petronia superciliaris* (805) 15 cm
The dark head with its broad, creamy white eyebrow stripe is the best field character. The yellow throat spot is not often seen except at close range. Distinguished from the much larger Whitebrowed Sparrow-weaver (p. 382) by its lack of a white rump.
SEXES alike. IMM. lacks yellow on throat. HABITAT. Thornveld, broadleafed woodland, and riverine bush. STATUS. Locally common resident. CALL. A loud, sparrow-like chipping. (Geelvlekmossie)

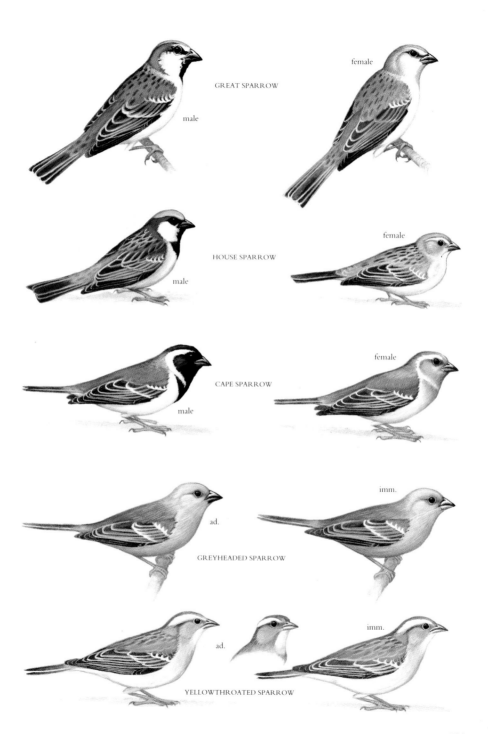

GREAT SPARROW

female

male

HOUSE SPARROW

male

female

CAPE SPARROW

male

female

GREYHEADED SPARROW

ad.

imm.

YELLOWTHROATED SPARROW

ad.

imm.

REDBILLED BUFFALO WEAVER *Bubalornis niger* (798) 24 cm
The robust red bill, black plumage and white wing patches are diagnostic in this large weaver. In flight, might be mistaken for a Palewinged Starling (p. 368) but the chunky bill should eliminate confusion.
FEMALE and IMM. are brown versions of the male. HABITAT. Dry thornveld and broadleafed woodland. Breeds communally, making untidy masses of sticks in large trees or electricity pylons. STATUS. Nomadic resident. CALL. Song is a 'chip-chip-doodley-doodley-dooo'. (Buffelwewer)

WHITEBROWED SPARROW-WEAVER *Plocepasser mahali* (799) 19 cm
This large, plump, short-tailed weaver is distinctive with its broad white eyebrow stripe and conspicuous white rump. The smaller Yellowthroated Sparrow (p. 380) has a buff (not white) eyebrow stripe and lacks the white rump. Birds in the north show faint speckling across the breast.
MALE has a black bill, FEMALE has horn-coloured bill. IMM. similar to ad. but has pinkish-brown bill. HABITAT. Thornveld and dry, scrubby rivercourses. Makes an untidy nest of dry grass in the outside branches of a tree. STATUS. Common resident. CALL. A harsh 'chik-chik' and a loud, liquid 'cheeoop-preeoo-chop' whistle. (Koringvoël)

THICKBILLED WEAVER *Amblyospiza albifrons* (807) 18 cm
The only dark weaver to have a massive, thick bill, white wing patches and a white forehead.
FEMALE and IMM. are heavily streaked below but still show the diagnostic heavy bill. HABITAT. Reedbeds, and coastal and evergreen forests. STATUS. Common resident. CALL. A 'tweek, tweek' flight call, and chattering when breeding. (Dikbekwewer)

FOREST WEAVER *Ploceus bicolor* (808) 16 cm
In the region, the only weaver with black upperparts and bright yellow underparts.
SEXES alike. IMM. has dark brown upperparts, grizzled forehead and throat, and yellow underparts. HABITAT. Evergreen, riverine and coastal forests. STATUS. Locally common resident. CALL. Song is a 'cooee-cooee-squizzzz', and variations of this. (Bosmusikant)

SOCIABLE WEAVER *Philetairus socius* (800) 14 cm
The black chin, black barred flanks and scaly-patterned back render this species unmistakable. Gregarious, they build huge communal nests which appear to 'thatch' the trees in which they are built.
SEXES alike. IMM. lacks black face mask. HABITAT. Dry thornveld and broadleafed woodland. STATUS. Common resident; endemic. CALL. A chattering 'chicker-chicker' flight call. (Versamelvoël)

REDBILLED BUFFALO WEAVER

male

female

WHITEBROWED
SPARROW-WEAVER

male

THICKBILLED
WEAVER

male

female

FOREST WEAVER

FOREST WEAVER

ad.

imm.

SOCIABLE WEAVER

ad.

imm.

SPOTTEDBACKED WEAVER *Ploceus cucullatus* (811) 17 cm
Larger than Southern Masked and Lesser Masked Weavers; breeding male has mottled black and yellow back and the mask does not extend above the bill. (The race in northern Zimbabwe has a wholly black head.)
NON-BREEDING MALE resembles female. FEMALE has a yellow throat which contrasts with a whitish breast and belly. Eye may be red. IMM. resembles female. HABITAT. Savanna. Colonial nester in reedbeds, trees overhanging water and, in thornveld, sometimes away from water. Forms large flocks and frequents grassland when not breeding. STATUS. Common resident. CALL. A throaty 'chuck-chuk' and buzzy, swizzling notes. (Bontrugwewer)

SOUTHERN MASKED WEAVER *Ploceus velatus* (814) 15 cm
Breeding male is distinguished from Lesser Masked Weaver by its brown legs, red (not white) eyes, and by the black mask, which does not extend behind the eye on top of the head, and forms a point on the throat. Differs from the larger Spottedbacked Weaver by having a uniform green (not yellow-spotted) back.
NON-BREEDING MALE resembles female but has red eyes. FEMALE has a greenish back with some streaking, is buffy on breast and belly. Eye colour brown. IMM. resembles female. HABITAT. Savanna and grassland. Breeds colonially in trees overhanging water; sometimes nests far from water in thornveld and suburbia. STATUS. Common resident. CALL. A sharp 'zik, zik' and the usual swizzling weaver notes. (Swartkeelgeelvink)

LESSER MASKED WEAVER *Ploceus intermedius* (815) 15 cm
In breeding plumage, the shape of the black mask distinguishes the male from the similar Southern Masked Weaver: the mask extends well on to the crown and comes to a rounded (not pointed) end on the throat. This species also has a white (not red) eye and has blue (not brown) legs.
FEMALE and NON-BREEDING MALE lack the mask, and are yellower below than Southern Masked Weaver. The female has a dark eye. IMM. is similar to female. HABITAT. Savanna. Breeds colonially in trees overhanging rivers and dams, and in reeds. STATUS. Locally common resident. CALL. The typical swizzling sounds of weavers. (Kleingeelvink)

SPECTACLED WEAVER *Ploceus ocularis* (810) 15 cm
Diagnostic features of both sexes are the sharp, pointed bill, the black line through the very pale yellow eye, and the chestnut-brown wash over the head.
MALE has a black bib. FEMALE resembles male but lacks the black bib; shows a yellow eye and black bill throughout the year. IMM. resembles the female, but shows the black line through the eye and has a brown bill. HABITAT. Coastal, evergreen and riverine forests, and moister areas in thornveld. A shy, skulking weaver which is more often heard than seen. STATUS. Common resident. CALL. Call is a descending 'dee-dee-dee-dee-dee'; also a swizzling song. (Brilwewer)

REDHEADED WEAVER *Anaplectes rubriceps* (819) 15 cm
The breeding male's scarlet head, breast and mantle are diagnostic.
FEMALE and NON-BREEDING MALE have lemon-yellow heads, show diagnostic orange-red bills, and have clear white bellies and flanks. IMM. resembles female. HABITAT. Thornveld, and mopane and miombo woodland. STATUS. Locally common resident. CALL. 'Cherrra-cherrra' and a high-pitched swizzling. (Rooikopwewer)

CHESTNUT WEAVER *Ploceus rubiginosus* (812) 15 cm
The black head, chestnut back and underparts render the breeding male unmistakable.
FEMALE and NON-BREEDING MALE are drab, sparrow-like birds with grey-brown, rather than greenish coloration, and a well-defined yellowish throat which ends in a brownish breast band. IMM. as female but with streaking on the breast. HABITAT. Thornveld and dry, broadleafed woodland. STATUS. Locally common in Namibia. CALL. Usual 'chuk, chuk' and swizzling weaver-type notes. (Bruinwewer)

male br.

SPOTTEDBACKED WEAVER

female

SOUTHERN MASKED WEAVER

male br.

female

LESSER
MASKED WEAVER

male br.

female

SPECTACLED WEAVER

male

female

REDHEADED WEAVER

male br.

female

CHESTNUT
WEAVER

male br.

female

CAPE WEAVER *Ploceus capensis* (813) 17 cm
Breeding male distinguished from the smaller Yellow Weaver by its heavier bill, less brilliant yellow plumage, white eye and by the brown or orange wash over its face. Differs from both Southern Brownthroated and Golden Weavers by being greener on the back, and by the orange wash over the face and forehead. It lacks the well-defined chestnut bib of Southern Brownthroated Weaver from which it further differs by its pale (not dark) eye.
FEMALE and NON-BREEDING MALE are olive brown above. The large size and long, pointed bill help distinguish them from other species. IMM. similar to female. HABITAT. Grassland and fynbos, often along rivers. Nests communally in reedbeds and trees. STATUS. Common resident; endemic. CALL. A harsh 'azwit, azwit' and swizzling noises. (Kaapse Wewer)

SOUTHERN BROWNTHROATED WEAVER *Ploceus xanthopterus* (818) 15 cm
The breeding male is the brightest of all the 'yellow' weavers and, with its chestnut bib, is unmistakable. Distinguished from Cape Weaver by being a more brilliant yellow, by lacking the orange wash over the face and crown, and by having a brown (not pale) eye.
BREEDING FEMALE has yellow underparts and brown eyes. NON-BREEDING MALE and FEMALE have bill and legs horn-coloured, head and nape olive-green, mantle brown, throat, breast and flanks buff, remainder of underparts white. IMM. as non-breeding male. HABITAT. Forest and scrub. Breeds over water in reedbeds. STATUS. Uncommon and localized resident. CALL. A soft 'zweek, zweek' and swizzling notes. (Bruinkeelwewer)

GOLDEN WEAVER *Ploceus xanthops* (816) 18 cm
Distinguished from the smaller Yellow Weaver by its large, heavy, black bill and yellow (not red) eye in both sexes.
MALE is brightest yellow in the non-breeding season and has a green back in the breeding season. FEMALE is a duller version of the breeding male. IMM. resembles female, but is greener. HABITAT. Woodland and savanna. Breeds in reedbeds and trees. STATUS. Uncommon resident in the south-east, becoming locally more common in the extreme north and east. CALL. A typical weaver-like 'chuk' and swizzling calls. (Goudwewer)

YELLOW WEAVER *Ploceus subaureus* (817) 15 cm
Smaller and a brighter yellow than Golden Weaver, this species has a smaller, shorter bill and a red (not yellow) eye. It is distinguished from the larger, pale-eyed Cape Weaver by having more vivid yellow plumage with little or no brown on the face.
FEMALE and NON-BREEDING MALE have greenish backs with some streaking, and are yellowish below. IMM. resembles female. HABITAT. Breeds in reedbeds, and trees near water, mostly in savannas during winter. STATUS. Locally common resident. CALL. Softer 'chuks' and swizzling than other, larger weavers. (Geelwewer)

OLIVEHEADED WEAVER *Ploceus olivaceiceps* (809) 14 cm
The golden crown, olive cheeks and orange breast of the male are diagnostic.
FEMALE has an olive head and back, and bright yellow underparts. IMM. similar to female but paler, especially above. HABITAT. Miombo woodland. STATUS. Locally common resident in Mozambique. CALL. A loud chattering. (Olyfkopwewer)

CAPE WEAVER

male br.

female

SOUTHERN BROWNTHROATED
WEAVER

male br.

female

GOLDEN WEAVER

male br.

female

YELLOW WEAVER

male br.

female

OLIVEHEADED WEAVER

male

female

REDBILLED QUELEA *Quelea quelea* (821) 13 cm
Breeding male is unmistakable with a black mask, ringed with pink, and bright red bill and legs.
NON-BREEDING MALE and FEMALE are drab, sparrow-like birds, which also show red bills and legs. BREEDING FEMALE has a yellowish bill. IMM. similar to female; has a yellowish-pink bill. HABITAT. Savanna, especially thornveld; and croplands. STATUS. Nomadic; at times abundant, in flocks numbering millions. CALL. Flocks make a chittering noise. Song is a jumble of harsh and melodious notes. (Rooibekkwelea)

REDHEADED QUELEA *Quelea erythrops* (822) 12 cm
Breeding male differs from male Redbilled Quelea by having a red head, lacking the black mask, and by having a black (not red) bill.
FEMALE and NON-BREEDING MALE have a much more yellow wash across the face and breast than Redbilled Quelea; brown bill and legs. BREEDING FEMALE has face, throat and breast pale pinkish orange. IMM. similar to non-breeding female. HABITAT. Damp grassland and adjoining woodland. STATUS. Locally common and nomadic migrant. May flock with Red Bishop. CALL. Described as a soft twittering. (Rooikopkwelea)

CARDINAL QUELEA *Quelea cardinalis* (823) 11 cm
Breeding male likely to be confused only with Redheaded Quelea, but red coloration of head extends on to upper breast and bill is black (not brown).
NON-BREEDING MALE has head narrowly streaked tawny and black, usually with some red markings, and a buff supercilium; throat and breast yellowish, bill horn-coloured. FEMALE resembles non-breeding male but lacks any red facial markings. IMM. buffier below than female, with dusky streaking on breast. HABITAT. Grassland and cultivated areas. STATUS. Uncertain; probably vagrant to extreme north-central regions. CALL. Described as a sizzling chatter. (Kardinaalkwelea)

RED BISHOP *Euplectes orix* (824) 14 cm
Breeding male similar to Firecrowned Bishop but differs by having a black forehead and crown, and by having brown (not black) primaries.
FEMALE, NON-BREEDING MALE and IMM. are difficult to distinguish from similar plumage stages of Golden Bishop but this species has darker, more heavily streaked underparts. HABITAT. Grassland and savanna, usually associated with water. Breeds in reedbeds, sometimes in crops. STATUS. Common and widespread resident. Highly gregarious. CALL. In display, males give a buzzing, chirping song. Normal flight call is a 'cheet-cheet'. (Rooivink)

FIRECROWNED BISHOP *Euplectes hordeaceus* (825) 14 cm
Distinguished from Red Bishop in breeding plumage by having a darker mantle, black primaries and a red (not black) forehead and crown.
FEMALE and NON-BREEDING MALE closely resemble those plumage stages of Red Bishop but have a heavier bill, and the male retains black primaries. IMM. resembles female. HABITAT. Damp grassy areas and reedbeds in miombo woodland. STATUS. Uncommon and localized resident. CALL. A buzzing chatter, similar to that of Red Bishop. (Vuurkopvink)

GOLDEN BISHOP *Euplectes afer* (826) 12 cm
Breeding male is distinctive with its black and yellow plumage. Difficult to distinguish from Red Bishop when not breeding, but is smaller, paler below with faint streaking confined to the sides of the breast and flanks, and has a prominent yellow eye-stripe.
FEMALE and IMM. resemble non-breeding male. HABITAT. Grassland and vleis. Breeds in wet areas, often low down in grass or reeds. STATUS. Locally common resident. Highly gregarious. CALL. Buzzing and chirping notes. (Goudgeelvink)

REDBILLED QUELEA

male br.

male br.

male non-br.

male transitional

REDBILLED QUELEA

male br.

male br.

female br.

REDHEADED QUELEA

female br.

female

male transitional

CARDINAL QUELEA

RED BISHOP

female

male transitional

male

male br.

male transitional

male br.

male non-br.

GOLDEN BISHOP

female

female

male br.

male non-br.

FIRECROWNED BISHOP

LONGTAILED WIDOW *Euplectes progne* (832) m=19 cm (plus 40 cm tail); f=16 cm
The largest widow of the region. Breeding male is unmistakable with its extra-long tail, and bright red shoulder bordered by a whitish or buffy stripe.
NON-BREEDING MALE has black wing feathers and is distinguished from non-breeding male Redshouldered Widow by its larger size, broad, rounded wings and buff stripe below the red shoulder. FEMALE and subadult male are far larger than all other similarly coloured widows. HABITAT. Open grassland, especially in valleys and damp areas. STATUS. Common resident. CALL. The male's call is a 'cheet, cheet' and a harsher 'zzit, zzit'. (Langstertflap)

REDCOLLARED WIDOW *Euplectes ardens* (831) 15 cm (plus 25 cm tail in br. male)
Breeding male is unmistakable with its long wispy tail and its black plumage offset by a red throat collar.
FEMALE, NON-BREEDING MALE and IMM. show a bold black- and buff-striped head pattern, have unstreaked buffy underparts, and the male retains black primaries. HABITAT. Grassy and bracken-covered mountain slopes and, frequently, in sugarcane in Natal. STATUS. Locally common resident. CALL. A fast, high-pitched 'tee-tee-tee-tee-tee' is given by displaying males. (Rooikeelflap)

WHITEWINGED WIDOW *Euplectes albonotatus* (829) 15-19 cm
The only widow in the region in which the male has white on the primary coverts.
BREEDING MALE distinguished from Yellowbacked Widow by having a shorter tail, no yellow on its back and by having white in the wings. In non-breeding plumage shows yellow shoulders and white patch at the base of the primaries. FEMALE is very pale below, and is less streaked than the other widows. IMM. resembles female. HABITAT. Rank grass in savanna. STATUS. Common resident. Gregarious. CALL. A nasal 'zeh-zeh-zeh' and a repetitive 'witz-witz-witz'. (Witvlerkflap)

REDSHOULDERED WIDOW *Euplectes axillaris* (828) 19 cm
Breeding male is the only small, short-tailed widow with a red shoulder. Told from non-breeding Longtailed Widow by its smaller size and lack of buff stripe below the red shoulder.
FEMALE and NON-BREEDING MALE are heavily streaked above, often with a chestnut brown wash below. The male retains black primaries and the red epaulettes in non-breeding plumage. IMM. resembles female. HABITAT. Reedbeds, damp grassland and stands of sugarcane. STATUS. Common resident. CALL. Various twittering and chirping sounds are given by the male during display. (Kortstertflap)

YELLOWRUMPED WIDOW *Euplectes capensis* (827) 15 cm
In comparison with Yellowbacked Widow, the breeding male has a much shorter tail, and a yellow rump and lower back (not a yellow mantle).
NON-BREEDING MALE is streaked greyish brown above, pale below with breast and flanks heavily streaked brown, but retains a bright yellow rump and shoulder. FEMALE differs from female Yellowbacked Widow by being far more heavily streaked below, and by having a dull yellow rump. IMM. resembles female. HABITAT. Damp grassy areas, bracken-covered mountain valleys, and fynbos. STATUS. Common resident. CALL. Male gives a 'zeet, zeet, zeet' and a harsh 'zzzzzzzzt' in flight. (Kaapse Flap)

YELLOWBACKED WIDOW *Euplectes macrourus* (830) 15-22 cm
Breeding male is the only widow with a long black tail and a yellow mantle. Told from Yellowrumped Widow by its longer tail and lack of yellow on the lower back and rump, and from Whitewinged Widow by the lack of white in the wings.
FEMALE and NON-BREEDING MALE are less heavily streaked on the breast and lack the dull yellow rump of the female Yellowrumped Widow. Female lacks any yellow in the wings; male has black wings with small yellow epaulettes. IMM. resembles female. HABITAT. Damp grassland and marshy areas. STATUS. Locally common resident. CALL. A buzzing twitter. (Geelrugflap)

LONGTAILED WIDOW

male non-br.

female

male non-br.

female

REDCOLLARED WIDOW

male br.

female

female

male non-br.

female

WHITEWINGED WIDOW

male br.

RED-SHOULDERED WIDOW

male br.

male non-br.

male non-br.

male br.

YELLOW-BACKED WIDOW

male non-br.

male br.

male br.

YELLOW-RUMPED WIDOW

female

PINTAILED WHYDAH *Vidua macroura* (860) 12 cm, plus 22 cm tail in br. male
*Breeding male is unmistakable, being black above, with white nape and underparts, a
red bill and long 'pintails'. Differs from breeding male Shaft-tailed Whydah by being
white (not buff) below and by lacking spatulate ends to the tail.*
FEMALE and NON-BREEDING MALE are buff above, pale below and have a boldly striped
black and buff head. The bill is red in the male, brownish in the female. IMM. is plain
brown. Parasitizes mainly waxbills, also cisticolas, mannikins, and prinias. HABITAT.
Savanna, grassland, scrub, parks and gardens. STATUS. Common resident. CALL.
Displaying males give 'tseet-tseet-tseet' calls. (Koningrooibekkie)

SHAFT-TAILED WHYDAH *Vidua regia* (861) 12 cm, plus 22 cm tail in br. male
*Breeding male has buff and black plumage (not black and white as in breeding male
Pintailed Whydah) and has diagnostic spatulate tips to its elongate tail feathers.*
FEMALE and NON-BREEDING MALE have streaked head markings, not the bold black
stripes of the similarly plumaged Pintailed Whydah. IMM. dull brown with dark
streaking on the back. Parasitizes Violeteared Waxbill. HABITAT. Grassy areas in thorn-
veld. STATUS. Common resident. CALL. Similar to but harsher than that of Pintailed
Whydah. (Pylstertrooibekkie)

PARADISE WHYDAH *Vidua paradisaea* (862) 15 cm, plus 23 cm tail in br. male
*Breeding male has black upperparts and head, with a yellow hind collar and belly,
and a chestnut breast. The elongate tail feathers of the breeding male are stiff, downward curving and taper to a point.*
FEMALE, NON-BREEDING MALE and IMM. are grey-brown above, with an off-white
head striped black. Bill is black. Virtually indistinguishable from the similarly
plumaged Broadtailed Paradise Whydah. Parasitizes Melba Finch. HABITAT. Mixed
woodland, especially thornveld. STATUS. Common resident with local movements.
CALL. A sharp 'chip-chip' and a short 'cheroop-cherrup' song. (Gewone Paradysvink)

BROADTAILED PARADISE WHYDAH *Vidua obtusa* (863) 15 cm, plus 15 cm
tail in br. male
*Breeding male virtually identical in coloration to the breeding male Paradise Whydah,
but has a shorter tail, which is broad and rounded at the tip, and the nape is orange
(not yellow).*
FEMALE, NON-BREEDING MALE and IMM. are virtually indistinguishable from the similarly plumaged Paradise Whydah in the field. Parasitizes Goldenbacked Pytilia.
HABITAT. Miombo and other broadleafed woodland. STATUS. Uncommon resident.
CALL. Similar to that of Paradise Whydah. (Breëstertparadysvink)

PINTAILED WHYDAH

male
display flight

imm.

male
whydah x
widowfinch hybrid

PINTAILED WHYDAH

female

male br.

male transitional

SHAFT-TAILED
WHYDAH

imm.

PARADISE
WHYDAH

female

male
br.

female

male br.

BROADTAILED
PARADISE
WHYDAH

male
display flight

male br.

female

393

BLACK WIDOWFINCH *Vidua funerea* (864) 11 cm
Breeding male is jet black, with a white bill and red or orange-red legs and feet.
FEMALE, NON-BREEDING MALE and IMM. are mottled black and buff above, with an off-white head striped black. Bill off-white, legs red. Parasitizes Bluebilled Firefinch. HABITAT. Forest edge, thornveld, riverine scrub, and suburbia. STATUS. Common resident. CALL. A short, canary-like jingle, and a scolding 'chit-chit-chit'. (Gewone Blouvinkie)

PURPLE WIDOWFINCH *Vidua purpurascens* (865) 11 cm
In breeding plumage the combination of white or pale pink bill, and whitish or pale pink legs and feet distinguish both male and female from other widowfinches.
Indistinguishable from other widowfinches when in non-breeding and imm. plumages. Parasitizes Jameson's Firefinch. HABITAT. Savanna, especially thornveld. STATUS. Locally common resident in the south of its range, becoming more common in the north-east. CALL. A rapid chattering which includes mimicked calls and song of Jameson's Firefinch. (Witpootblouvinkie)

STEELBLUE WIDOWFINCH *Vidua chalybeata* (867) 11 cm
Breeding male is jet black, and, over most of its range, the combination of red bill, legs and feet distinguish both male and female from other widowfinches. West of Victoria Falls, the bill is white. White-billed form does not occur with Black Widowfinch so confusion unlikely.
FEMALE, NON-BREEDING MALE and IMM. resemble other widowfinches except for their red bills and legs. Parasitizes Redbilled Firefinch. HABITAT. Woodland, tall grassveld, old cultivated lands. STATUS. Common resident. CALL. A canary-like song which includes clear, whistled 'wheeet-wheeet-wheeetoo' notes, and mimicked notes of its host, Redbilled Firefinch. (Staalblouvinkie)

VIOLET WIDOWFINCH *Vidua incognita* (866) Not illustrated
The taxonomic status of Violet Widowfinch is uncertain; it may be a subspecies of Wilson's Widowfinch (V. wilsoni). Its potential occurrence in the region is based on the occurrence of its putative host, Brown Firefinch. It has been removed from the regional list pending taxonomic and distributional clarification. (Persblouvinkie)

CUCKOO FINCH *Anomalospiza imberbis* (820) 13 cm
Similar to a small female 'yellow' weaver but its yellow colouring is brighter, especially below, and it has a diagnostic short, conical black bill.
FEMALE is a streaky brown, resembling a female bishop, but the heavy bill is characteristic. IMM. resembles female. HABITAT. Open grassland, especially near damp areas. STATUS. Uncommon local migrant. CALL. A swizzling noise is uttered during display. (Koekoekvink)

BLACK WIDOWFINCH
female

BLACK WIDOWFINCH
male non-br.

BLACK WIDOWFINCH
male

PURPLE
WIDOWFINCH

female

male

male
transitional

female

STEELBLUE WIDOWFINCH
male

female

CUCKOO FINCH

male

BLUEBILLED FIREFINCH *Lagonosticta rubricata* (840) 10 cm
The distinct grey (not pink) crown and nape differentiate this species from the very similar Jameson's Firefinch. In the northern race, the whole head is washed pinkish and the Bluebilled is then distinguished from Jameson's Firefinch by showing no trace of pink on its darker back and wings.
MALE has face and underparts deep red, shading to black on the belly and undertail. FEMALE is pinkish brown below. Both sexes have white spots on the flanks. IMM. like female but overall less pink, more brown. HABITAT. Thickets in thornveld, riverine scrub, forest edges and suburbia. STATUS. Common resident. CALL. A fast, clicking 'trrt-trrt-trrt-trrt', like a fishing reel as the line is played out, and a 'wink-wink-wink'. (Kaapse Robbin)

JAMESON'S FIREFINCH *Lagonosticta rhodopareia* (841) 10 cm
The crown, nape, back and wing coverts are suffused with pink. Back and wings of Bluebilled Firefinch are dark grey-brown in all races.
MALE is pink below with black undertail. FEMALE has pinkish-buff underparts. Both sexes have white spots on flanks. IMM. resembles female but is duller. HABITAT. Thickets and grassy tangles in thornveld. STATUS. Common resident. CALL. A tinkling trill similar to that of Bluebilled Firefinch, but higher pitched and interspersed with a sharp 'vit-vit-vit'. (Jamesonse Robbin)

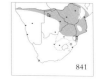

REDBILLED FIREFINCH *Lagonosticta senegala* (842) 10 cm
Pink bill and bright yellow eye-ring diagnostic in both sexes.
MALE is the reddest of the firefinches. FEMALE is much duller, with only rump and upper tail pink, otherwise sandy brown. IMM. similar to female, but lacks yellow eye-ring and white spots. HABITAT. Mixed woodland, especially near water, and throughout suburbia in Zimbabwe. STATUS. Common resident. CALL. A sharp, fast 'vut-vut-vut-chit-chit' and a 'sweeep'. (Rooibekrobbin)

BROWN FIREFINCH *Lagonosticta nitidula* (843) 10 cm
Easily distinguished from the Redbilled and other firefinches by its diagnostic grey (not red) rump.
MALE is brown above, with face and throat pale red. The breast is densely speckled with white. FEMALE has a duller red face and throat. IMM. lacks red in plumage and has dark bill. HABITAT. Found in thick scrub and reeds close to water. STATUS. Locally common resident. CALL. Described as a guttural trill, and a 'tsiep, tsiep' flight call. (Bruinrobbin)

SWEE WAXBILL *Estrilda melanotis* (850) 10 cm
The grey head, black face and red rump are diagnostic of the male. Upper mandible black, lower mandible red.
FEMALE lacks the black face and is indistinguishable in the field from East African Swee. However, the ranges of the two species do not overlap. IMM. similar to female but has all-black bill. HABITAT. Long grass and scrub at forest edges, usually in mountainous areas. STATUS. Common but localized resident; endemic. Gregarious. CALL. A soft 'swee-swee' call is uttered in flight. (Suidelike Swie)

EAST AFRICAN SWEE *Estrilda quartinia* (851) 10 cm
Lacks the black face of the male Swee Waxbill and is indistinguishable from the female of that species; however, their ranges do not overlap. Superficially resembles Orangebreasted Waxbill (p. 402) but lacks the bright yellow-orange belly and the barred flanks of that species.
SEXES alike. IMM. resembles ad. but has all-black bill. HABITAT. Forest edges in mountainous terrain. STATUS. Locally common resident. CALL. The same as that of Swee Waxbill. (Tropiese Swie)

396

female

BLUEBILLED FIREFINCH

male

JAMESON'S
FIREFINCH

male

female

REDBILLED FIREFINCH

female

male

BROWN FIREFINCH

female

male

male

imm.

SWEE WAXBILL

EAST AFRICAN SWEE

male

male

female

BRONZE MANNIKIN *Spermestes cucullatus* (857) 9 cm
Distinguished from Redbacked Mannikin by having less black on the head and by having a brown (not chestnut) back. Differs from Pied Mannikin by its smaller size and less massive, bi-coloured bill.
SEXES alike. IMM. is a uniform dun brown, unlike the imm. Redbacked Mannikin which has a reddish-brown back and paler underparts. HABITAT. A wide variety of grassy areas in woodland, forest edges, damp regions and suburbia. STATUS. Very common resident. Gregarious. CALL. A soft, buzzy 'chizza, chizza'. (Gewone Fret)

REDBACKED MANNIKIN *Spermestes bicolor* (858) 9 cm
The conspicuous chestnut back, black and white spangles on the wings and flanks, and the pale grey bill distinguish this species from Bronze and Pied Mannikins.
SEXES alike. IMM. differs from imm. Bronze Mannikin by its chestnut-tinged back and paler underparts. HABITAT. Moist, broadleafed woodland and forests. STATUS. Common resident. Gregarious. CALL. A thin, soft 'seeet-seeet', uttered when flushed from grass. (Rooirugfret)

PIED MANNIKIN *Spermestes fringilloides* (859) 13 cm
The largest mannikin of the region, it is easily distinguished from Bronze and Redbacked Mannikins by its markedly black and white appearance, its large, heavy bill, and the dark bars on its flanks.
SEXES alike. IMM. is grey-brown above, off-white below. HABITAT. Bamboo stands, and riverine and coastal forests. STATUS. Uncommon and localized resident. CALL. A chirruping 'peeoo-peeoo'. (Dikbekfret)

CUT-THROAT FINCH *Amadina fasciata* (855) 12 cm
The pinkish-red band across the throat is diagnostic in the male. Plumage is generally brown, heavily barred and mottled black and white.
FEMALE is smaller than the female Redheaded Finch, is boldly barred on the head, and has the back distinctly streaked and mottled. IMM. similar to female, but male imm. shows pale throat band. HABITAT. Dry thornveld. STATUS. Locally common resident. CALL. An 'eee-eee-eee' flight call. (Bandkeelvink)

REDHEADED FINCH *Amadina erythrocephala* (856) 13 cm
Upperparts generally brown, underparts pale and heavily scalloped.
MALE has a bright red head. Redheaded Quelea (p. 388) is similar but has plain underparts. FEMALE differs from the smaller female Cut-throat Finch by having the head uniformly brown, and the under- and upperparts less heavily barred and streaked. IMM. duller than ad. HABITAT. Dry grassland, thornveld and broadleafed woodland. STATUS. Common resident; near-endemic. CALL. A soft 'chuk-chuk', and a 'zree, zree' flight call. (Rooikopvink)

SCALYFEATHERED FINCH *Sporopipes squamifrons* (806) 10 cm
An unmistakable small finch with a black and white freckled forehead, black malar stripes, and white-fringed wing and tail feathers.
SEXES alike. IMM. like ad. but lacks the freckling on the forehead and the black malar stripes. HABITAT. Dry thornveld, bushy desert watercourses, cattle kraals and around farm buildings. STATUS. Common resident; near-endemic. Gregarious. CALL. A soft 'chizz, chizz, chizz', given by small groups when in flight. (Baardmannetjie)

BRONZE MANNIKIN

ad.

imm.

imm.

REDBACKED
MANNIKIN

imm.

ad.

ad.

CUT-THROAT FINCH

PIED MANNIKIN

female

REDHEADED FINCH

male

female

male

SCALYFEATHERED FINCH

399

VIOLETEARED WAXBILL *Uraeginthus granatinus* (845) 15 cm
The red bill, violet cheeks, brilliant blue rump and black tail are diagnostic.
MALE has head and body plumage chestnut, chin black. FEMALE has head and body
biscuit-coloured with less extensive violet cheeks than male. IMM. resembles female
but lacks violet on face. HABITAT. Woodland and savanna, especially thornveld.
STATUS. Common resident. CALL. A soft, whistled 'tiu-woowee'. (Koningblousysie)

BLACKCHEEKED WAXBILL *Estrilda erythronotos* (847) 13 cm
*The greyish-brown body and head, conspicuous black face patch, and dark red rump
and flanks render this species unmistakable.*
FEMALE and IMM. are duller versions of the male. HABITAT. Grassy areas and thick
tangles in dry thornveld. STATUS. Common resident. Gregarious. CALL. A high-
pitched 'chuloweee'. (Swartwangsysie)

GREY WAXBILL *Estrilda perreini* (848) 11 cm
*Could be confused with Cinderella Waxbill but their distributions do not overlap.
This species differs by having the red confined to the rump and uppertail coverts. The
East African Swee and Swee Waxbill (p. 396) are similar and also show the red
rump, but they lack the grey on the body and have green backs.*
SEXES alike. IMM. is duller and lacks black eye-stripe. HABITAT. Edges of evergreen
forests, and in thick coastal and riverine forests. STATUS. Locally common resident.
CALL. A soft, whistled 'pseeu, pseeu'. (Gryssysie)

COMMON WAXBILL *Estrilda astrild* (846) 13 cm
*This small, brownish, long-tailed finch is best distinguished by its red bill and eye-
stripe, and by the small reddish patch on the belly.*
SEXES alike. IMM. is a dull version of ad. with black bill. HABITAT. Long grass in damp
areas, alongside rivers and in reedbeds. STATUS. Common resident. Gregarious. CALL.
A nasal 'cher-cher-cher' and a 'ping, ping' flight note. (Rooibeksysie)

CINDERELLA WAXBILL *Estrilda thomensis* (849) 11 cm
*The western counterpart of Grey Waxbill. It is distinguished by being generally paler
grey, with the base of the bill red, and by the red on the rump extending to the lower
belly and flanks.*
SEXES alike. IMM. lacks red on flanks. HABITAT. Riverine scrub and forests. STATUS.
Uncommon resident, restricted to the Cunene River west of Ruacana. CALL. A
thin, reedy 'sweee-sweee-sweeeooo-swoooo' and a short, repeated 'trrt-tsoo'.
(Swartoogsysie)

BLUE WAXBILL *Uraeginthus angolensis* (844) 13 cm
Its powder blue face, breast and tail render this species unmistakable.
FEMALE has a reduced area of blue on the front. IMM. similar to female but paler.
HABITAT. The drier areas of mixed woodland, and suburbia in some regions. STATUS.
Common resident. CALL. A soft 'kway-kway-sree-seee-seee-seee'. (Gewone Blousysie)

VIOLETEARED WAXBILL

female

male

BLACKCHEEKED WAXBILL

imm.

GREY
WAXBILL

ad.

COMMON WAXBILL

CINDERELLA WAXBILL

BLUE WAXBILL

female

male

MELBA FINCH *Pytilia melba* (834) 12 cm

Could be confused with Goldenbacked Pytilia but is much more brightly coloured, the male showing a crimson face, bill and throat, blue-grey nape, boldly barred belly and flanks. It lacks the orange wing panel.
FEMALE has an all-grey head and breast; differs from female Goldenbacked Pytilia by being brighter, more boldly marked below and by lacking the orange wing panels. IMM. like female but is more olive above, plain greyish below. HABITAT. Thornveld and dry, broadleafed woodland. STATUS. Common resident. CALL. Utters a pretty, trilling song that rises and falls in pitch; also a short 'wick'. (Gewone Melba)

GOLDENBACKED PYTILIA *Pytilia afra* (833) 11 cm

The male could be confused with the male Melba Finch, but has an all-red face, is less distinctly barred on belly and flanks, and shows an orange wing panel.
FEMALE is distinguished from the female Melba Finch by being drabber, less distinctly barred below and by showing the orange wing panel. IMM. similar to female, but is more orange on the rump. HABITAT. Thick, tangled scrub, usually near water and often in miombo woodland. STATUS. Uncommon and localized resident. CALL. Described as a 'seee', and a piping whistle of two, widely spaced notes. (Geelrugmelba)

QUAIL FINCH *Ortygospiza atricollis* (852) 9 cm

Rarely seen on the ground but, when flushed from the grass, it has a diagnostic jerky flight and a distinctive call. The black and white face pattern, barred black and white breast and flanks, and the lack of red on the rump, distinguish it from Orangebreasted Waxbill.
SEXES similar, but forehead, cheeks and throat black in male, grey in female. IMM. plain buff below. HABITAT. Open grassland. STATUS. Common resident. CALL. In flight, gives a continual, tinny 'skreaky-skreak' call. (Gewone Kwartelvinkie)

LOCUST FINCH *Ortygospiza locustella* (853) 9 cm

Although similar to Quail Finch in habits, their calls are very different.
MALE is easily told by its red face, throat and breast, rufous wings, black back spotted with white, and black belly. FEMALE is distinguished from the female Quail Finch by rufous wings and lack of white facial markings. IMM. streaked black and brown above; browner than female below. HABITAT. Grassland, especially in damper areas. STATUS. Uncommon and localized resident. CALL. A fast 'tinka-tinka-tinka' given in flight. (Rooivlerkkwartelvinkie)

ORANGEBREASTED WAXBILL *Sporaeginthus subflavus* (854) 10 cm

Superficially resembles the swees (p. 396) but it lacks the grey on the head and has a bright yellow-orange belly and barred flanks. Distinguished from Quail Finch by having a red (not dark) rump, and by its call.
FEMALE has a yellow belly and lacks the red eyebrow. IMM. similar to female but plain buff below. HABITAT. Grassland and weedy areas, especially near water. STATUS. Common resident, sometimes found in large flocks. CALL. A soft, clinking 'zink zink zink' flight call; rapid 'trip-trip' on take-off. (Rooiassie)

MELBA FINCH

female

male

GOLDENBACKED PYTILIA

female

male

QUAIL FINCH

female

male

LOCUST FINCH

female

male

ORANGEBREASTED WAXBILL

male

female

PINKTHROATED TWINSPOT *Hypargos margaritatus* (838) 12 cm
Male is much paler than the male Redthroated Twinspot and has a pinkish face, throat and breast.
FEMALE has a light grey-brown throat, breast and belly; differs from female Redthroated Twinspot by having no trace of red or pink on the throat and breast. IMM. resembles female, but is plain buff below. HABITAT. Thicker tangles of thornveld and coastal scrub. STATUS. Locally common resident; endemic. CALL. A soft, reedy trill. (Rooskeelrobbin)

REDTHROATED TWINSPOT *Hypargos niveoguttatus* (839) 12 cm
Male distinguished from Pinkthroated Twinspot by its grey crown and deep red (not pink) face, throat and breast.
FEMALE differs from female Pinkthroated Twinspot by its grey crown and pinkish-red wash across the breast. IMM. resembles female but is duller above. HABITAT. Prefers more moist situations than Pinkthroated Twinspot, and the edges of evergreen forests. STATUS. Locally common resident. CALL. A trill similar to that of Pinkthroated Twinspot. (Rooikeelrobbin)

GREEN TWINSPOT *Mandingoa nitidula* (835) 10 cm
The combination of a red face, predominantly dull green upperparts and black belly and flanks boldly spotted with white is diagnostic.
FEMALE has buff face. IMM. duller than female, lacking black and white belly flanks. HABITAT. Mistbelt, coastal and riverine forests, usually adjacent to small clearings. STATUS. Locally common resident: easily overlooked because of its secretive habits. CALL. A soft, rolling, insect-like 'zrrreet'. (Groenrobbin)

REDFACED CRIMSONWING *Cryptospiza reichenovii* (836) 12 cm
Superficially resembles Nyasa Seedcracker but has a black (not red) tail, a dull red (not dark brown) back and wings and, on the head, the red is confined to eye patches.
FEMALE lacks the male's red eye patches and differs from the female Nyasa Seedcracker by having red in the wings. IMM. has less red on the upperparts. HABITAT. The understorey and thick tangles of evergreen forests. STATUS. Uncommon and localized resident. CALL. A soft, repeated 'zeet'. (Rooirugrobbin)

NYASA SEEDCRACKER *Pyrenestes minor* (837) 13 cm
Differs from Redfaced Crimsonwing by having a bright red face and throat, a red (not black) tail, and by lacking any red in the wings.
FEMALE closely resembles the male but has a reduced red face patch. IMM. lacks red on the head. HABITAT. Thickets along small streams, and near water in forest clearings and miombo woodland. STATUS. Uncommon to locally common resident. CALL. A 'tzeet' and a sharp, clipped 'quap'. (Rooistertrobbin)

PINKTHROATED TWINSPOT

male

female

REDTHROATED TWINSPOT

male

female

GREEN TWINSPOT

male

female

REDFACED CRIMSONWING

female

male

NYASA SEEDCRACKER

female

male

405

YELLOW CANARY *Serinus flaviventris* (878) 13 cm
Males grade in colour from being uniform bright yellow in the north-west to streaked, olive-backed birds in the south-east. The bill is always slighter than that of Bully Canary and the head less marked than that of Yelloweyed Canary.
FEMALE is drab grey-brown above, paler below, and streaked darker brown on both upper- and underparts. IMM. like female, but more heavily streaked. HABITAT. Karoo and coastal scrub, and scrubby mountain valleys. STATUS. Common resident; near-endemic. CALL. A fast, jumbled series of 'chissick' and 'cheree' notes. (Geelkanarie)

BULLY CANARY *Serinus sulphuratus* (877) 15 cm
Has a more massive bill than any other yellow canary. The birds found in the southern and eastern Cape are greener than other forms.
FEMALE duller than male. IMM. greyer than ad. HABITAT. A wide range of scrub, woodland and grassland, but prefers coastal scrub. STATUS. Common resident. CALL. Lower pitched and slower than other canaries. (Dikbekkanarie)

LEMONBREASTED CANARY *Serinus citrinipectus* (871) 11 cm
Resembles but is smaller than Yelloweyed Canary with which it sometimes flocks.
MALE has a pale lemon throat and breast, well demarcated from the remainder of its pale buff underparts. It lacks the bold head markings of Yelloweyed Canary and has a small white ear patch. FEMALE resembles Blackthroated Canary but is buff below and lacks the black-speckled throat. IMM. resembles female. HABITAT. Palm savanna and adjoining thornveld, and open grassland. STATUS. A locally common resident; near-endemic. CALL. Similar to that of Blackthroated Canary, but higher pitched and shorter. (Geelborskanarie)

YELLOWEYED CANARY *Serinus mozambicus* (869) 12 cm
Varies regionally in colour saturation (eastern birds being brightest yellow). Facial pattern is diagnostic. Distinguished from Bully Canary by its smaller size, less robust bill, and bright yellow rump and white tail tips.
SEXES alike. IMM. has buffy yellow, lightly streaked underparts. HABITAT. Thornveld, and mixed woodland and savanna. STATUS. Common to abundant resident. Gregarious. CALL. A 'zeee-zereee-chereeo'. (Geeloogkanarie)

BLACKTHROATED CANARY *Serinus atrogularis* (870) 11 cm
A small, pale grey canary, heavily streaked dark brown on the upperparts, with a diagnostic bright lemon-yellow rump and white tail tips which contrast with the otherwise drab plumage. The black throat is most obvious in the breeding season.
FEMALE has less black on the throat. IMM. is spotted on the throat. HABITAT. Thornveld, dry broadleafed woodland, and near waterholes in dry regions. STATUS. Common resident, subject to local movements. Gregarious. CALL. A prolonged series of wheezy whistles and chirrups. (Bergkanarie)

FOREST CANARY *Serinus scotops* (873) 13 cm
A very dark, heavily streaked canary which has a small black chin, greyish cheeks and a yellow eye-stripe. The pale base to the bill contrasts with the dark face.
FEMALE and IMM. have a less prominent black bib. HABITAT. Evergreen forests, edges and clearings. STATUS. Common but localized resident; endemic. CALL. A single, high-pitched 'tseeek' contact call, and a quiet, jumbled song. (Gestreepte Kanarie)

CAPE CANARY *Serinus canicollis* (872) 13 cm
Told from Yelloweyed Canary by lack of bold facial markings, by the yellow forehead and crown, and by the greater amount of grey on the nape.
FEMALE has less grey on the nape. IMM. has greenish-yellow underparts overlaid with heavy brown streaking. HABITAT. Fynbos, grassland, suburban gardens; prefers mountainous terrain. STATUS. Common resident. Gregarious. CALL. Utters a typical canary song from a high perch, but also occasionally during display flight. (Kaapse Kanarie)

406

YELLOW CANARY
female

male

imm.

BULLY CANARY

ad.

ad.
yellow
form

YELLOWEYED
CANARY

ad.

LEMONBREASTED CANARY
female

male

CAPE CANARY

FOREST CANARY

female

female

male

male

male

BLACKTHROATED
CANARY

407

WHITETHROATED CANARY *Serinus albogularis* (879) 15 cm
Differentiated from other drab-coloured canaries by the combination of its small white throat patch and greenish-yellow rump. In similar habitat, distinguishable from female Yellow Canary (p. 406) by the massive bill, and the absence of breast streaking.
SEXES alike. IMM. like ad. HABITAT. Fynbos, Karoo scrub and scrub-filled mountain valleys. STATUS. Common resident; near-endemic. CALL. A mixture of canary- and sparrow-like notes, given from a perch. (Witkeelkanarie)

PROTEA CANARY *Serinus leucopterus* (880) 15 cm
A dark canary distinguishable from Whitethroated Canary by lacking the greenish-yellow rump and by its small black chin. The large, deep, pale bill contrasts with the dark face. The narrow white edgings to its secondary coverts are diagnostic.
SEXES alike. IMM. resembles ad. HABITAT. Thick, tangled valley scrub and dense stands of proteas on hillsides. STATUS. Locally common resident; endemic. CALL. Contact call is a 'tree-lee-loo'. Song is loud and varied. (Witvlerkkanarie)

STREAKYHEADED CANARY *Serinus gularis* (881) 15 cm
The broad, whitish eyebrow stripe is the most distinctive feature. Distinguished from Whitethroated Canary by having a finely streaked grey and white crown, bordered by the white eyebrow stripe, and by having a streaked brown (not plain) greenish-yellow rump. Differs from Blackeared Canary in lacking the streaked breast and distinct black ear patches.
SEXES alike. IMM. resembles ad. but is heavily streaked with brown below. HABITAT. Mixed woodland and scrub. STATUS. Common resident. CALL. A soft, weak 'trrreet', and a short song. (Streepkopkanarie)

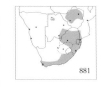

BLACKEARED CANARY *Serinus mennelli* (882) 14 cm
Told from Streakyheaded Canary by the distinct black cheeks and streaked breast.
FEMALE and IMM. have dark grey cheeks, but still show a streaked breast. HABITAT. Miombo and mopane woodland. STATUS. Uncommon and localized resident. CALL. A twittering whistle 'teeu-twee-teeu, twiddy-twee-twee'. (Swartoorkanarie)

BLACKHEADED CANARY *Serinus alario* (876) 12 cm
The male has a chestnut back and tail, and black stripes down the sides of the breast. The amount of black on the head is variable: the race south of the Orange River comprises black-headed birds whereas those birds to the north have largely white heads.
FEMALE lacks the black markings but does show the diagnostic chestnut back and tail. IMM. as female, but is more streaked above and below. HABITAT. Karoo scrub and adjacent mountainous terrain, preferring bushy vegetation; cultivated lands. STATUS. Locally common resident; endemic. CALL. A soft 'sweea' or 'tweet'. (Swartkopkanarie)

DRAKENSBERG SISKIN *Serinus symonsi* (875) 13 cm
Resembles only Cape Siskin, and their ranges never overlap. Lacks the white-tipped secondary and tail feathers of Cape Siskin, but has diagnostic white outer tail feathers.
FEMALE lacks any yellow in its plumage. IMM. is heavily streaked on the head and breast. HABITAT. Montane scrub and grassland. STATUS. Locally common resident; endemic. CALL. Similar to that of Cape Siskin. (Bergpietjiekanarie)

CAPE SISKIN *Serinus tottus* (874) 12 cm
Resembles Drakensberg Siskin but has white tips to its secondary and tail feathers (not white outer tail feathers). Also, the ranges of these two species do not overlap.
FEMALE is less richly coloured than male, and has less extensive white tips to the secondaries (often not visible in the field). IMM. is heavily streaked on the head and breast. HABITAT. Montane fynbos, forest margins, and sometimes along the coast. Also frequents exotic pine plantations. STATUS. Common but localized resident; endemic. CALL. Diagnostic contact call 'voyp-veeyr' is often given in flight. Also has a typical canary-like song. (Kaapse Pietjiekanarie)

WHITETHROATED
CANARY

PROTEA
CANARY

dark-cheeked
race

STREAKYHEADED CANARY

BLACKEARED
CANARY

BLACKHEADED CANARY

male

male
white-headed
race

female

male

male

CAPE SISKIN

female

male

DRAKENSBERG SISKIN

male

female

male

female

male

CHAFFINCH *Fringilla coelebs* (868) 16 cm
Male is the only finch of the region to have a pinkish face and breast, a blue-grey head, and conspicuous white wing bars.
FEMALE is a dowdy grey-brown, sparrow-like bird but still shows clear white wing bars. IMM. similar to female. HABITAT. Exotic pine and oak plantations, and well-wooded gardens. STATUS. Introduced from Europe. Uncommon and localized resident on the eastern slopes of the Cape Peninsula. CALL. A clear 'pink, pink, pink' and a short, rattling song, typically uttered from high in a tree. (Gryskoppie)

CABANIS'S BUNTING *Emberiza cabanisi* (883) 16 cm
Distinguished from Goldenbreasted Bunting by having a greyish (not chestnut) mantle, and black cheeks without a white stripe below the eye.
FEMALE and IMM. are duller versions of the male. HABITAT. Miombo woodland. STATUS. Uncommon and localized resident. CALL. A clear 'tsseeoo' contact note. Song described as a 'wee-chidder-chidder-wee'. (Geelstreepkoppie)

ROCK BUNTING *Emberiza tahapisi* (886) 14 cm
In comparison with Cape Bunting, this species has cinnamon (not grey) underparts, a black (not white) throat, and it lacks the chestnut wing coverts.
FEMALE and IMM. have less bold black and white head markings but still show the diagnostic cinnamon underparts. HABITAT. Rocky slopes in mountainous terrain, and mixed woodland in the north. STATUS. Common resident; nomadic when not breeding. CALL. A grating, rattling song and a soft 'pee-pee-wee'. (Klipstreepkoppie)

GOLDENBREASTED BUNTING *Emberiza flaviventris* (884) 16 cm
Although very similar to Cabanis's Bunting, this species differs by having a white stripe below the eye, a chestnut (not greyish) mantle, and a richer yellow breast, washed with orange. The white wing bars are conspicuous in flight.
FEMALE and IMM. are duller versions of the male. HABITAT. Thornveld, broadleafed woodland and exotic plantations. STATUS. Common resident. CALL. A nasal, buzzy 'zzhrrrr'. Song is a varied 'weechee, weechee, weechee'. (Rooirugstreepkoppie)

LARKLIKE BUNTING *Emberiza impetuani* (887) 14 cm
A dowdy, nondescript bird which looks like a lark but behaves in typical bunting fashion, hopping over stones and grubbing for seeds on bare ground. Lacks any diagnostic field characters apart from the pale cinnamon wash over the breast and rufous edging to wing feathers.
FEMALE and IMM. are paler than male. HABITAT. Dry rocky valleys and open plains, thornveld and dry broadleafed woodland. Gathers in large numbers at waterholes to drink. STATUS. Common resident, subject to local movements; near-endemic. CALL. A soft, nasal 'tuc-tuc' and a short, rapid song, consisting of a series of alternating high and low notes. (Vaalstreepkoppie)

CAPE BUNTING *Emberiza capensis* (885) 16 cm
The greyish breast, chestnut wing coverts, and lack of black on the throat distinguish this species from Rock Bunting.
SEXES alike. IMM. has less definite head markings and duller chestnut wings. HABITAT. Sandy coastal scrub in the south, and mountainous terrain further north. STATUS. Common resident. CALL. A nasal, ascending 3-4 note 'zzoo-zeh-zee-zee', and a loud chirping song. (Rooivlerkstreepkoppie)

CHAFFINCH

male

female

male

CABANIS'S BUNTING

female

male

ROCK BUNTING

female

male

GOLDENBREASTED BUNTING

female

male

CAPE BUNTING

LARKLIKE BUNTING

Further reading

Brown, L.H., Urban, E.K. & Newman, K.B. (eds). 1982. *The Birds of Africa*, Vol. 1. Academic Press, London.

Chittenden, H. (ed) 1992. *Top Birding Spots in Southern Africa*. Southern Book Publishers, Johannesburg.

Clancey, P.A. 1967. *Gamebirds of Southern Africa*. Purnell, Cape Town.

Clancey, P.A. 1971. *A Handlist of the Birds of Southern Moçambique*. Instituto de Investigaçao Científica de Moçambique, Lourenço Marques (Maputo).

Clancey, P.A. (ed) 1980. *SAOS Checklist of Southern African Birds*. Southern African Ornithological Society, Johannesburg.

Clancey, P.A. 1985. *The Rare Birds of Southern Africa*. Winchester Press, Johannesburg.

Clinning, C. & Butchart, D. 1989. *Southern African Bird Names Explained*. Southern African Ornithological Society, Johannesburg.

Colston, P. & Burton, P. 1988. *A Field Guide to the Waders of Britain and Europe*. Hodder & Stoughton, Sydney.

Cyrus, D. & Robson, N. 1980. *Bird Atlas of Natal*. University of Natal Press, Pietermaritzburg.

Earlé, R. & Grobler, N. 1987. *First Atlas of Bird Distribution in the Orange Free State*. National Museum, Bloemfontein.

Fry, C.H., Fry, K. & Harris, A. 1992. *Kingfishers, Bee-eaters and Rollers: a Handbook*. Christopher Helm, London.

Fry, C.H., Keith, S. & Urban, E.K. (eds) 1988. *The Birds of Africa*, Vol. 3. Academic Press, London.

Ginn, P.J., McIlleron, W.G. & Milstein, P. le S. 1989. *The Complete Book of Southern African Birds*. Struik Winchester, Cape Town.

Harrison, P. 1983. *Seabirds: an Identification Guide*. Croom Helm, London.

Harrison, P. 1987. *Seabirds of the World: a Photographic Guide*. Christopher Helm, London.

Hayman, P., Marchant, J. & Prater, T. 1986. *Shorebirds: an Identification Guide to the Waders of the World*. Croom Helm, London.

Hockey, P.A.R., Underhill, L.G., Neatherway, M. & Ryan, P.G. 1989. *Atlas of the Birds of the Southwestern Cape*. Cape Bird Club, Cape Town.

Irwin, M.P.S. 1981. *The Birds of Zimbabwe*. Quest Publishing, Salisbury (Harare).

Maclean, G.L. 1984. *Roberts' Birds of Southern Africa*. John Voelcker Bird Book Fund, Cape Town.

Madge, S. & Burn, H. 1988. *Wildfowl: an Identification Guide to the Ducks, Geese and Swans of the World*. Christopher Helm, London.

Newman, K.B. 1983. *Birds of Southern Africa*. Southern Book Publishers, Johannesburg.

Newman, K.B. 1987. *Birds of the Kruger National Park*. Southern Book Publishers, Johannesburg.

Quickelberge, C.D. 1989. *Birds of the Transkei*. Durban Natural History Museum, Durban.

Rowan, M.K. 1983. *The Doves, Parrots, Louries and Cuckoos of Southern Africa*. David Philip, Cape Town.

Sibley, C.G. & Ahlquist, E. 1990. *Phylogeny and Classification of Birds.* Yale University Press, New Haven.

Sibley, C.G. & Monroe, B.L. jr. 1990. *Distribution and Taxonomy of Birds of the World*. Yale University Press, New Haven.

Sinclair, J.C. 1987. *Field Guide to the Birds of Southern Africa*. Struik, Cape Town.

Skead, C.J. 1967. *The Sunbirds of Southern Africa; also Sugarbirds, White-eyes and Spotted Creeper*. A.A. Balkema, Cape Town.

Solomon, D. & Williams, J. 1992. *Birds of a Feather*. Birdwatch Zimbabwe, Harare.

Steyn, P. 1982. *Birds of Prey of Southern Africa*. David Philip, Cape Town.

Tarboton, W.R., Kemp, M.I. & Kemp, A.C. 1987. *Birds of the Transvaal*. Transvaal Museum, Pretoria.

Turner, A. & Rose, C. 1989. *A Handbook to the Swallows and Martins of the World*. Christopher Helm, London.

Urban, E.K., Fry, C.H. & Keith, S. 1986. *The Birds of Africa*, Vol. 2. Academic Press, London.

Index to Scientific Names

The numbers refer to the page on which the species' account appears.

415

Turnix sylvatica 140
Turtur afer 218
T. chalcospilos 218
T. tympanistria 218
Tyto alba 234
T. capensis 234

Upupa epops 260
Uraeginthus angolensis 400

Uraeginthus granatinus 400

Vanellus albiceps 166
V. armatus 166
V. coronatus 164
V. crassirostris 166
V. lugubris 164
V. melanopterus 164
V. senegallus 166

Vidua chalybeata 394
V. funerea 394
V. incognita 394
V. macroura 392
V. obtusa 392
V. paradisaea 392
V. purpurascens 394
V. regia 392

Xenus cinereus 176

Zoothera gurneyi 302
Z. guttata 302
Zosterops pallidus 346
Z. senegalensis 346

INDEX TO AFRIKAANS NAMES

Gans
Dwerg- 74
Kol 72
Glasogie
Geel- 346
Kaapse 346
Grasvoël 328
Breëstert- 326
Griet
Amerikaanse 180
Bandstert- 180
Swartstert- 180
Grootkokerbek 198
Gryskoppie 410

Hadeda 70
Hamerkop 68
Heuningvoël
Dunbek- 262
Skerpbek- 262
Heuningwyser
Gevlekte 262
Groot- 262
Klein- 262
Oostelike 262
Hoender
Bles- 142
Grootwater- 142
Kleinwater- 142
Hoephoep 260
Houtkapper
Bont- 266
Geelbles- 264
Groen- 264
Kuifkop- 264
Rooikop- 264
Witoor- 264
Hyliota
Geelbors- 346
Mashona- 346

Ibis
Glans- 70
Kalkoen 70

Jakkalsvoël
Berg- 102
Bruin- 102
Langbeen- 100
Rooibors- 100
Witbors- 100
Janfrederik
Bandkeel- 316
Gewone 312
Gunningse 316
Heuglinse 312
Lawaaimaker- 312

Janfrederik
Natal- 312
Witkeel- 312
Witkol- 316
Jangroentjie 372

Kakelaar
Gewone 260
Pers- 260
Swartbek- 260
Kalkoentjie
Geelkeel- 356
Oranjekeel- 356
Rooskeel- 356
Kanarie
Berg- 406
Bergpietjie- 408
Dikbek- 406
Geel- 406
Geelbors- 406
Geeloog- 406
Gestreepte 406
Kaapse 406
Pietjie-, Kaapse 408
Streepkop- 408
Swartkop- 408
Swartoor- 408
Witkeel- 408
Witvlerk- 408
Kapokvoël
Grys- 320
Kaapse 320
Katakoeroe
Blou- 288
Swart- 288
Witbors- 288
Katlagter
Kaalwang- 296
Pylvlek- 296
Swartwang- 296
Wit- 296
Witkruis- 296
Kelkiewyn 212
Kemphaan 172
Kiewiet
Bont- 166
Grootswartvlerk- 164
Kleinswartvlerk- 164
Kroon- 164
Lel- 166
Witkop- 166
Witvlerk- 166
Klappertjie
Hoëveld- 272
Laeveld- 272
Kleinjantjie
Bandkeel- 332

Kleinjantjie
Geelbors- 332
Grys- 332
Ruddse 332
Swartkop- 332
Klopkloppie
Bleekkop- 334
Gevlekte 334
Kleinste 334
Landery- 334
Woestyn- 334
Knoet 168
Koekoek
Afrikaanse 226
Dikbek- 228
Europese 226
Gevlekte 228
Klein- 226
Langstert- 230
Malgassiese 226
Swart- 228
Koester
Berg- 352
Boom- 354
Bos- 352
Bosveld- 354
Donker- 352
Geelbors- 356
Gestreepte 354
Gewone 352
Goud- 356
Klip- 354
Kortstert- 354
Nicholsonse 352
Rooikeel- 354
Vaal- 352
Konkoit 362
Korhaan
Blou- 154
Bos- 156
Langbeen- 156
Swart- 156
Vaal- 154
Witpens- 154
Witvlerkswart- 156
Woestyn- 154
Koringvoël 382
Kraai
Huis- 292
Swart- 292
Witbors- 292
Withals- 292
Kraanvoël
Lel- 150
Blou- 150
Krapvreter 158

Kwartel
Afrikaanse 140
Blou- 140
Bont- 140
Kwartelkoning 146
Kwarteltjie
Bosveld- 140
Kaapse 140
Kwartelvinkie
Gewone 402
Rooivlerk- 402

Kwê-kwêvoël
Groen 328
Grys 328
Kwelea
Kardinaal- 388
Rooibek- 388
Rooikop- 388
Kwêvoël 224
Kwikkie
Berg- 350
Bont- 350
Geel- 350
Gewone 350
Grys- 350

Laksman
Bontrok- 364
Fiskaal- 358
Grys- 358
Kortstert- 364
Kremetart- 364
Langstert- 358
Olyfbos- 362
Oranjeborsbos- 362
Rooibors- 358
Rooirug- 358
Souzase 358
Stekelkophelm- 364
Swarthelm- 364
Swartoogbos- 362
Withelm- 364
Langstertjie
Bruinsy- 340
Drakensberg- 340
Karoo- 340
Namakwa- 340
Rooioor- 340
Swartband- 340
Woud- 340
Langtoon
Dwerg- 144
Groot- 144
Lepelaar 68
Lewerik
Bosveld- 272

419

Suikervoël, Kaapse 372
Rooibors- 372
Swael, Angola- 282
Blou- 284
Draadstert- 284
Europese 282
Familie- 282
Grootstreep- 282
Gryskruis- 286
Huis- 286
Kleinstreep- 282
Krans- 286
Krans-, Gestreepte 286
Moskee- 282
Pêrelbors- 284
Rooibors- 282
Saagvlerk-, Tropiese 284
Swartsaagvlerk- 284
Witkeel- 284
Witkopsaagvlerk- 284
Swartpootbrandervoël 202
Swempie 136
Swie, Suidelike 396
Tropiese 396
Sysie
Blou-, Gewone 400
Grys- 400
Koningblou- 400
Rooibek- 400
Swartoog- 400
Swartwang- 400

Tarentaal
Gewone 138
Kuifkop- 138
Tinker
Geelbles- 266
Groen- 266
Rooibles- 266
Swartbles- 266
Tinktinkie
Bosveld- 336
Groot- 336
Grysrug- 336
Huil- 336
Kortvlerk- 334
Lui- 336
Piepende 338
Rooi- 336
Rooiwang- 338
Singende 338
Swartrug- 338
Vlei- 338
Tiptol, Kaapse 298
Rooibek- 298
Rooioog- 298
Swartoog- 298

Tjagra
Grysbors- 360
Rooivlerk- 360
Swartkroon- 360
Vlei- 360
Tjeriktik
Bosveld- 330
Grys- 330
Tobie
Bont- 158
Swart- 158
Troupant
Europese 256
Geelbek- 256
Gewone 256
Groot- 256
Knopstert- 256

Uil, Bos- 236
Gebande 236
Gras- 234
Nonnetjie- 234
Oor-, Gevlekte 234
Oor-, Kaapse 234
Oor-, Reuse- 234
Skops- 236
Vis- 234
Vlei- 236
Witkol- 236
Witwang- 236

Valk, Akkedis- 110
Bleeksing- 108
Blou- 108
Boom-, Afrikaanse 118
Boom-, Europese 118
Dickinsonse 120
Donkergrys- 120
Donkersing- 108
Dwerg- 110
Edel- 116
Eleonora- 118
Grootrooi- 122
Kaalwang- 102
Kleinrooi- 122
Kleinsing- 112
Koekoek- 110
Krans- 122
Roet- 120
Rooinek- 116
Rooipoot-, Oostelike 122
Rooipoot-, Westelike 122
Swerf- 116
Teita- 116
Vis- 88
Vlermuis- 118
Versamelvoël 382

Vink, Bandkeel- 398
Breëstertparadys- 392
Goudgeel- 388
Klein- 384
Koekoek- 394
Paradys-, Gewone 392
Rooi- 388
Rooikop- 398
Swartkeelgeel- 384
Vuurkop- 388
Visvanger
Blou- 248
Bont- 248
Bosveld- 250
Bruinkop- 250
Dwerg- 248
Gestreepte 250
Gryskop- 250
Kuifkop- 248
Manglied- 250
Reuse- 248
Vleikuiken
Gestreepte 148
Gevlekte 148
Rooibors- 148
Streepbors- 148
Witvlerk- 148
Vleiloerie
Gewone 232
Groen- 232
Groot- 232
Senegal- 232
Swart- 232
Witstreep- 232
Vlieëvanger
Blougrys- 342
Bloukuif- 344
Donker- 342
Europese 342
Fee- 330
Fiskaal- 342
Groot- 344
Marico- 344
Muiskleur- 344
Paradys- 344
Rooistert- 346
Swart- 342
Waaierstert- 342
Withals- 346
Witpens- 344
Witstert- 344
Volstruis 138

Wagter
Bergklip- 310
Walvisvoël
Breëbek- 44

Walvisvoël
Dunbek- 44
Swartstert- 44
Waterfiskaal
Moeras- 360
Suidelike 360
Tropiese 360
Waterploeër 200
Watertrapper 142
Wespedief 100
Wewer
Bontrug- 384
Bril- 384
Bruin- 384
Bruinkeel- 386
Buffel- 382
Dikbek- 382
Geel- 386
Goud- 386
Kaapse 386
Olyfkop- 386
Rooikop- 384
Wielewaal
Afrikaanse 290
Europese 290
Groenkop- 290
Swartkop- 290
Wildemakou 72
Willie
Geelbors- 300
Gewone 300
Streepwang- 300
Windswael
Bont- 242
Bruin- 242
Europese 242
Horus- 244
Klein- 244
Muiskleur- 242
Palm- 244
Skaars- 244
Swart- 242
Witpens- 242
Witkruis- 244
Wipstert
Baard- 314
Bruin- 314
Gestreepte 314
Kalahari- 314
Wou
Geelbek- 108
Swart- 108
Woudapie 62
Wulp
Groot- 180
Klein- 180

421

INDEX TO COMMON NAMES

THE NUMBERS REFER TO THE PAGE ON WHICH THE SPECIES' ACCOUNT APPEARS.